NATIONALITY AND PLANNING

IN SCOTLAND AND WALES

Nationality and Planning in Scotland and Wales

edited by

RODERICK MACDONALD and HUW THOMAS

*Published on behalf of
the Board of Celtic Studies
of the University of Wales*

UNIVERSITY OF WALES PRESS
CARDIFF
1997

© The Contributors, 1997

British Library Cataloguing-in-Publication Data
A catalogue record for this book is available from the British Library.

ISBN 0-7083-1398-1

All rights reserved. No part of this book may be reproduced, stored in a retrieval system, or transmitted, in any form or by any means, electronic, mechanical, photocopying, recording or otherwise, without clearance from the University of Wales Press, 6 Gwennyth Street, Cardiff, CF2 4YD.

Typeset at the University of Wales Press
Printed in Great Britain by Bookcraft Ltd., Midsomer Norton, Avon

In memory of

Jane Melvin

Contents

List of Figures		ix
Acknowledgements		x
List of Contributors		xi
Map of old administrative boundaries in Scotland		xii
Map of new administrative boundaries in Scotland		xiii
Map of old administrative boundaries in Wales		xiv
Map of new administrative boundaries in Wales		xv
1	Nationality and Planning RODERICK MACDONALD AND HUW THOMAS	1
2	Scotland and Wales in Europe MIKE DANSON	14
3	The Organization and Effectiveness of the Scottish Planning System JEREMY ROWAN-ROBINSON	32
4	Land-Use Planning in Wales: The Conflict between State Centrality and Territorial Nationalism MARK TEWDWR-JONES	54
5	The Fallible Servant: Evaluating the Welsh Development Agency KEVIN MORGAN AND DYLAN HENDERSON	77
6	The Politics of Regional Development Strategy: The Programme for the Valleys GARETH REES	98

7	Structure and Culture: Regional Planning and Institutional Innovation in Scotland M. G. Lloyd	113
8	Planning Capital Cities: Edinburgh and Cardiff Compared Cliff Hague and Huw Thomas	133
9	Urban Growth Management: Distinctive Solutions in the Celtic Countries? Martin J. Elson and Roderick Macdonald	159
10	Contrasting Approaches to Rural Economic Development Christopher L. W. Minay	181
11	The Designation of Valued Landscapes in Scotland John Moir	203
12	The Challenge of Convergence: Countryside Conservation and Enjoyment in Scotland and Wales Kevin Bishop	243
13	Language and Planning in Scotland and Wales Clive James and Colin H. Williams	264
Index		303

Figures

5.1	The changing structure of the Welsh Development Agency	79
5.2	Receipts and payments for the Welsh Development Agency, 1994/5	81
5.3	The Welsh Medical Technology Forum	87
9.1	Green Belts in Scotland	160
9.2	The Glasgow Green Belt	163
9.3	The Edinburgh Green Belt	166
11.1	National Scenic Areas in Scotland	208
11.2	Conservation designations in the Cairngorms	212
11.3a	Nature conservation designations in Loch Lomond and the Trossachs	214
11.3b	Landscape and heritage designations in Loch Lomond and the Trossachs	215
13.1	Local planning areas and language strength before 1996: Scotland	267
13.2	Local planning areas and language strength before 1996: Wales	270

Acknowledgements

This project has taken some time to come to fruition, and some of our contributors were exceptionally patient as they kept to deadlines which others did not meet. Ned Thomas, Sandra McAllister and (especially) Ceinwen Jones of the University of Wales Press have been supportive throughout. We are extremely grateful to the Board of Celtic Studies of the University of Wales, which has made publication possible with a grant. It is a moot point whether new technology has made the preparation of manuscripts any easier, and we are grateful to Jane Melvin in Cardiff and Maureen Pether in Oxford who worked hard to produce a single manuscript from disks in every format imaginable. Maps have been prepared by Janice Cole (Cardiff), Rob Woodward (Oxford), the School of Town and Regional Planning, University of Dundee and Gwynedd County Council. Jane Melvin died in the summer of 1996, and this volume is dedicated to her memory, as a young, able and much-loved colleague.

List of Contributors

Kevin Bishop, Department of City and Regional Planning, University of Wales, Cardiff

Mike Danson, Department of Economics, University of Paisley

Martin Elson, School of Planning, Oxford Brookes University

Cliff Hague, School of Planning and Housing, Heriot-Watt University

Dylan Henderson, Department of City and Regional Planning, University of Wales, Cardiff

Clive James, Gwynedd Council

M. G. Lloyd, School of Town and Regional Planning, University of Dundee

Roderick Macdonald, School of Planning, Oxford Brookes University

Christopher L. W. Minay, School of Planning, Oxford Brookes University

Kevin Morgan, Department of City and Regional Planning, University of Wales, Cardiff

John Moir, School of Town and Regional Planning, University of Dundee

Gareth Rees, School of Education, University of Wales, Cardiff

Jeremy Rowan-Robinson, Department of Land Economy, University of Aberdeen

Mark Tewdwr-Jones, Department of City and Regional Planning, University of Wales, Cardiff

Huw Thomas, Department of City and Regional Planning, University of Wales, Cardiff

Colin H. Williams, Department of Welsh, University of Wales, Cardiff

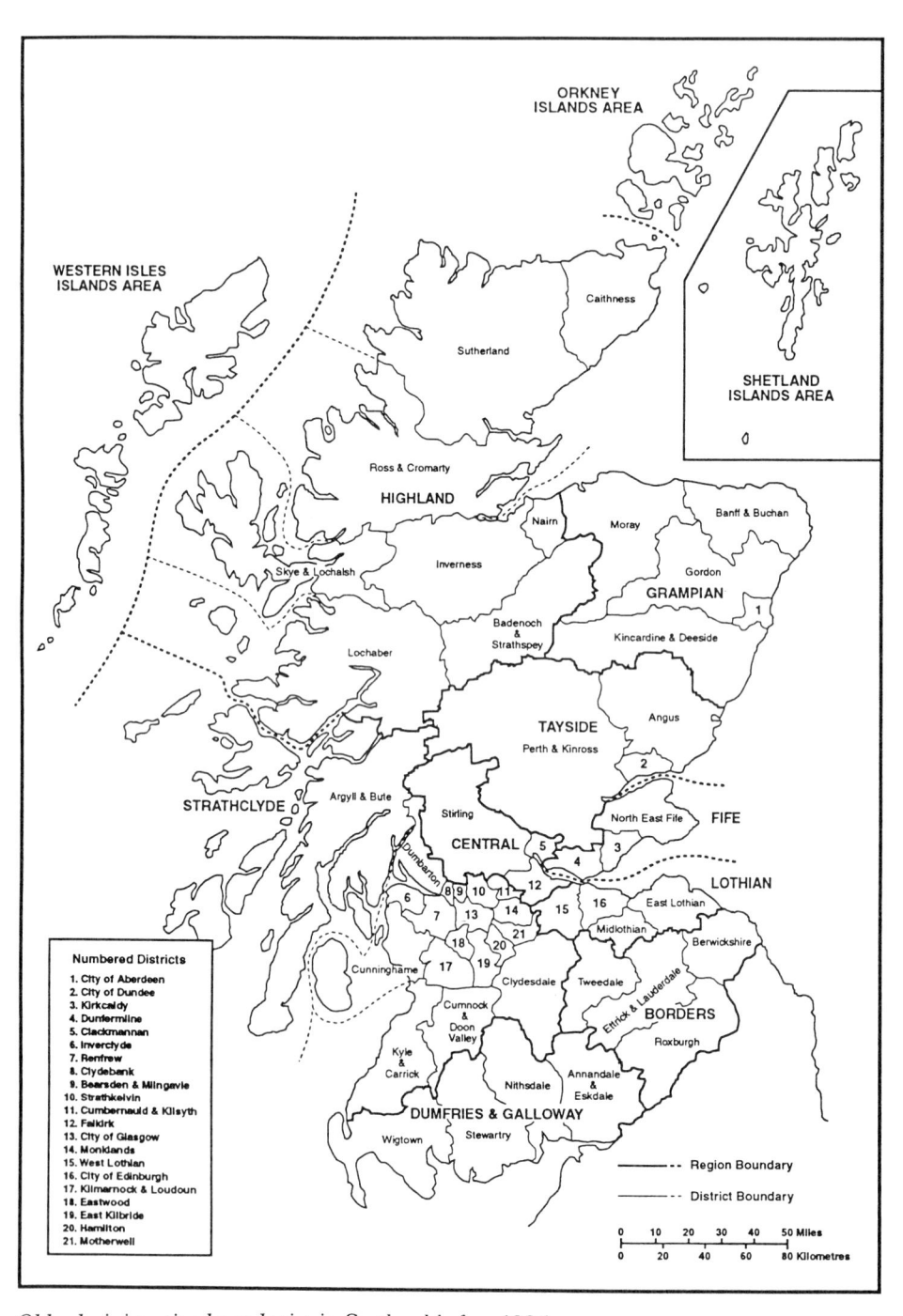

Old administrative boundaries in Scotland before 1996

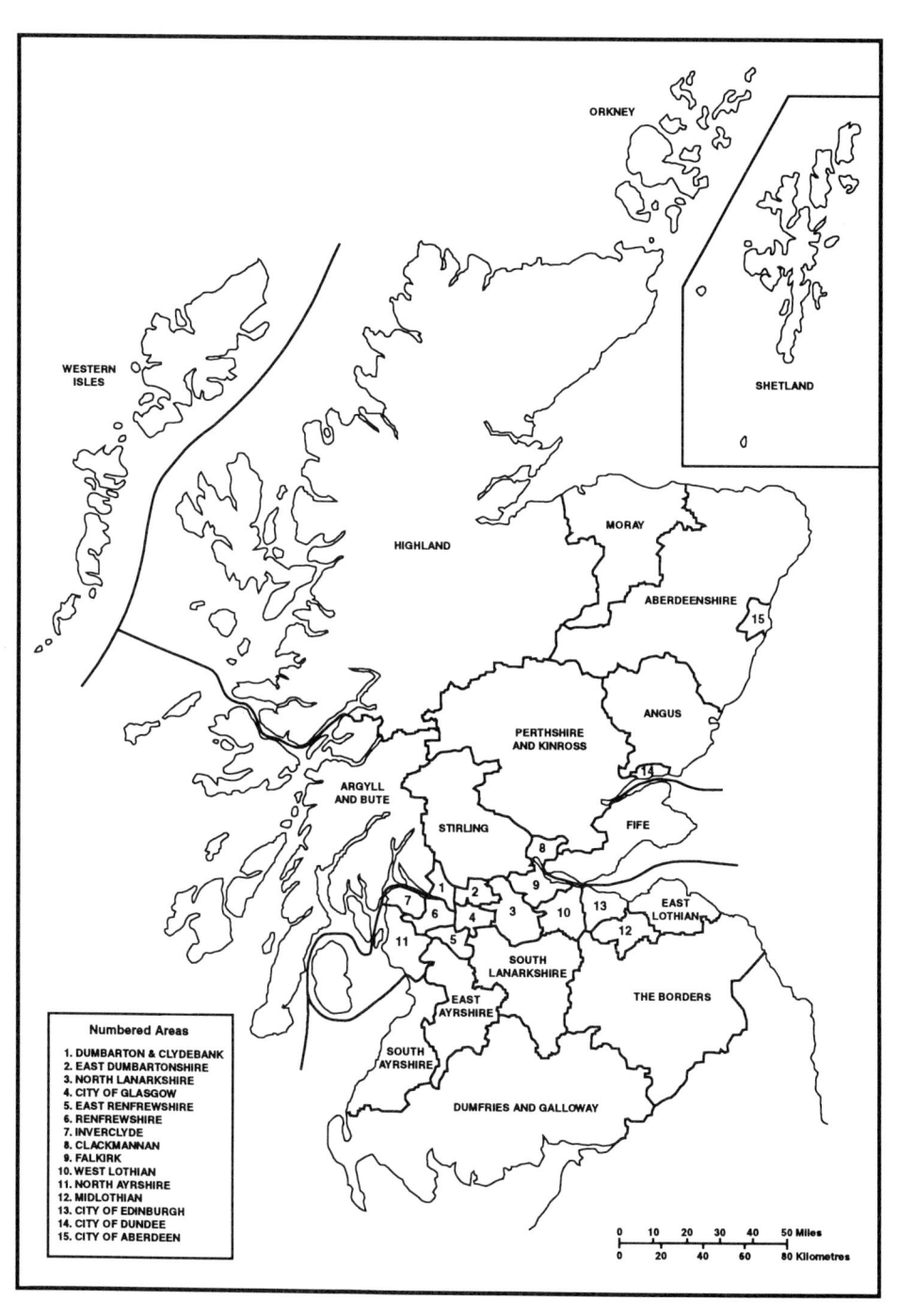

New administrative boundaries in Scotland operative from 1996

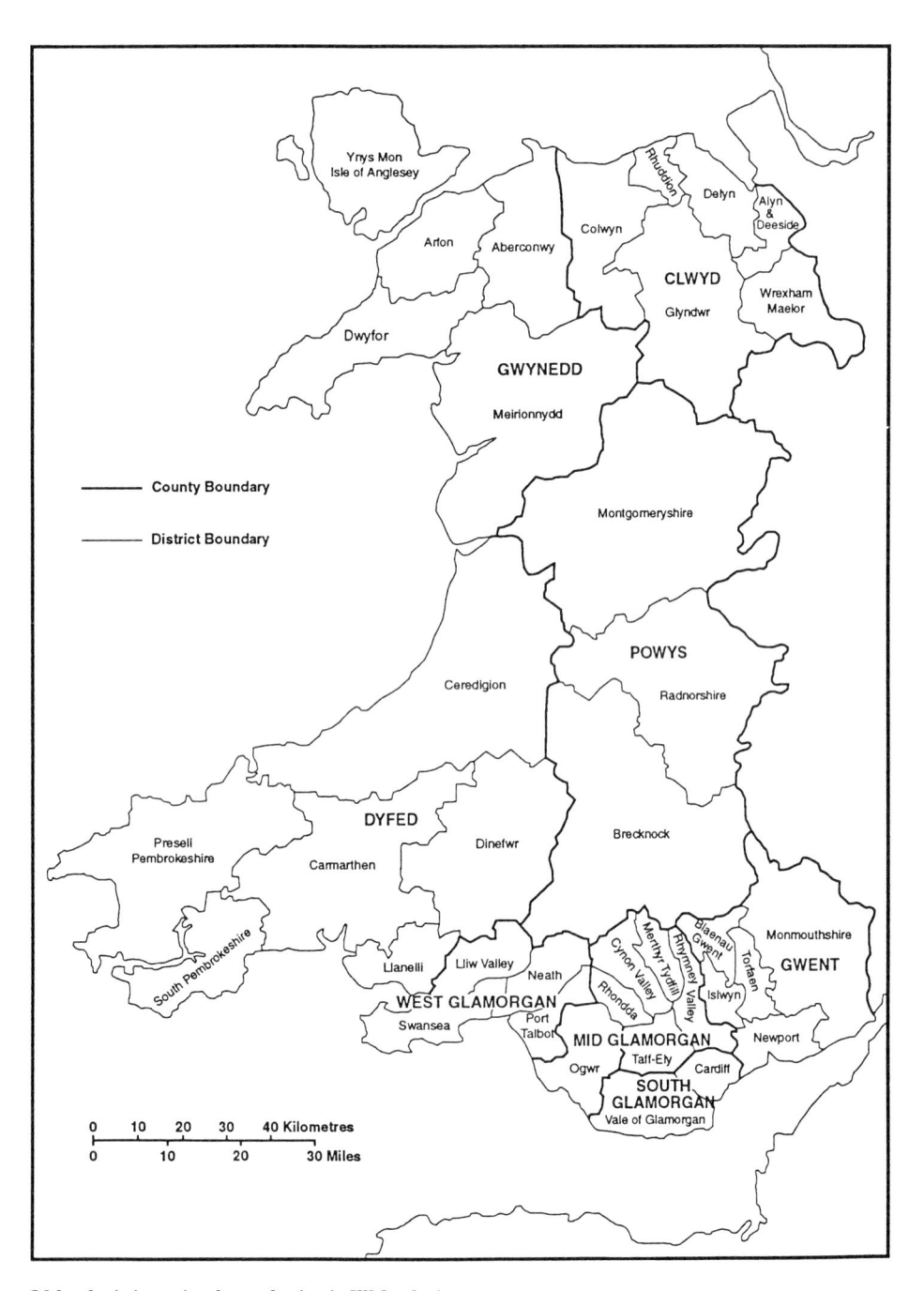

Old administrative boundaries in Wales before 1996

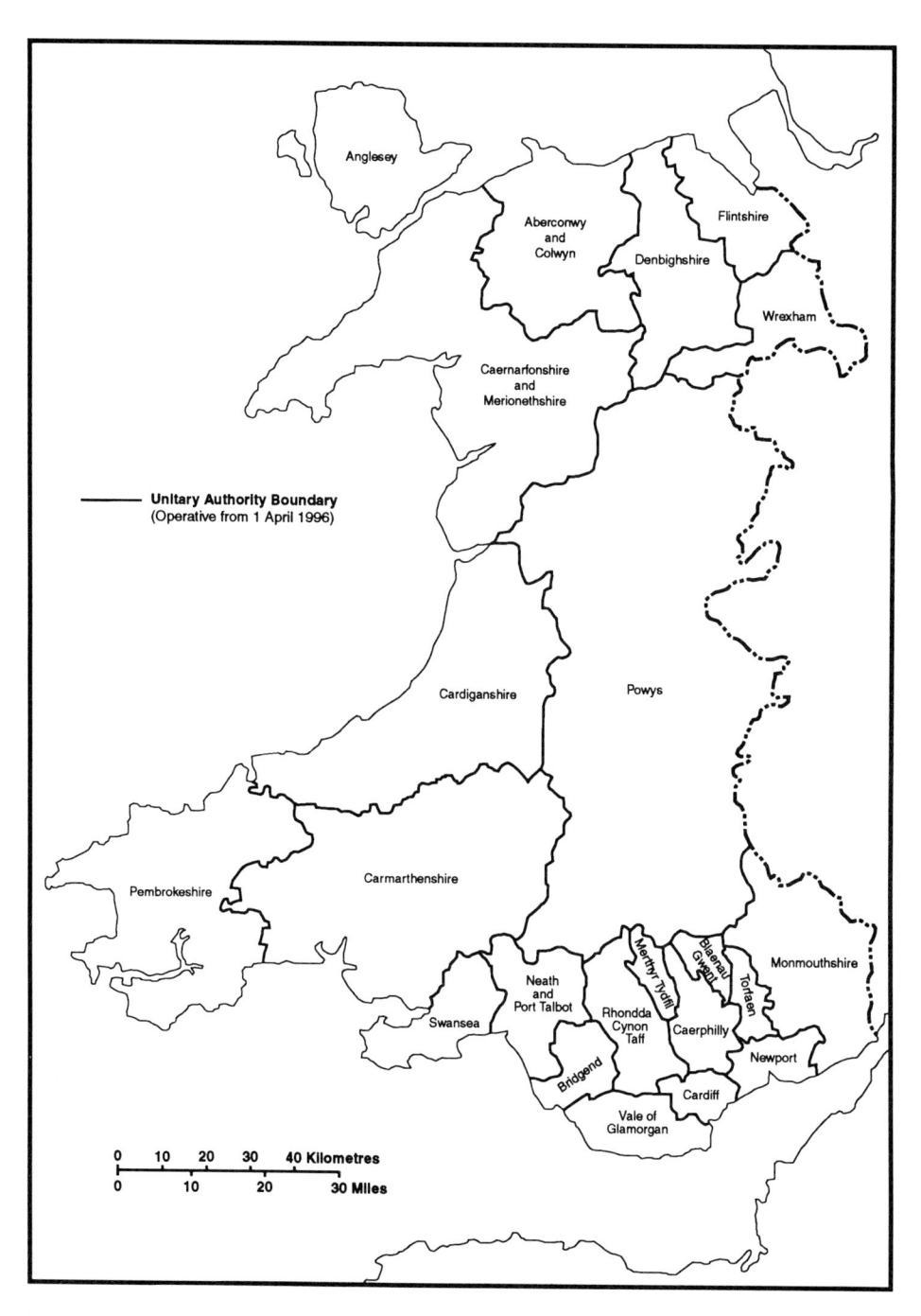

New administrative boundaries in Wales operative from 1996

1

Nationality and Planning

RODERICK MACDONALD and HUW THOMAS

Our original reason for wanting to produce this book was a concern, almost amounting to an irritation, that accounts of British town and country planning – whether the latter term was broadly or narrowly construed – concentrated almost exclusively on English planning, on English urban (and rural) policy. From time to time there have been academic and policy audiences for analyses of Welsh or Scottish initiatives – the attention devoted to Glasgow's Eastern Area Renewal (GEAR) project is one celebrated example (Donnison and Middleton, 1987), and more recently there have been comparisons of the effects of local government reorganization – further advanced in Scotland and Wales than in England – on planning (Clotworthy and Harris, 1996; Figs 1, 2). But, even in such cases, the attention has tended to focus on the lessons which policy-makers outside Scotland (or Wales) can learn; and often the conclusions drawn have not been based on an understanding of the episodes as Scottish or Welsh phenomena, rooting them in their national context. The purpose of this book is to assist the understanding of key aspects of planning by setting them in such contexts, a task which we would argue is an essential prerequisite to fruitful discussions of policy transfer, even within the boundaries of a unitary state like Britain.

If these were the personal motivations for putting the book together, then the intellectual roots were the arguments, by now well rehearsed in the academic and policy literature, that the uneven spatial development of capitalism has created distinctive *places*, localized 'structured coherences' (Harvey, 1989) – villages, towns, cities, regions with their particular mix of economic activity, social mores and political concerns, with these facets interrelated and interdependent, of course, but also building upon (or reacting to) the varied histories of their inhabitants (many of whom, in some places, will be immigrants). The distinctiveness of places has assumed increasing economic and political importance in recent decades. Global economic ferment has involved mobile capital seeking out profitable locations for investment, encouraging a bidding process as places 'sell' their attractiveness to potential investors (Cooke, 1990). Significantly, this activity has involved concerted action and political brokering (of varying success) at spatial levels both above and below the nation-state (Marquand, 1988). Of course, securing (national) state support, for, and investment in, particular localities remains a major task for spatial coalitions engaged in place marketing but, increasingly, supra-national agencies, notably the European Union, are targets of lobbying by cities and regions.

Yet, the European Union (EU) is not a passive target of lobbying by coalitions. As Davies *et al.* (1993) have documented in relation to land-use planning, there are a variety of ways in which the EU has affected, and will continue to affect, the balance of power between the nation-state and sub-national political activity (both *ad hoc* activity and that contained within more permanent institutional forms such as local councils). The working out in practice of the implications of the notion of subsidiarity, for example, will be of great significance in this respect. In addition, EU involvement in certain policy areas – notably, regional development, environmental issues and, increasingly, urban policy – will continue to provide reasons for concerted political action at sub-national levels. Such action can be facilitated by the existence in a particular place of a widely shared feeling of common identity, a sentiment which can have the function of obscuring, or rendering irrelevant, questions of the distribution of benefits from promoting the 'interests' of that place and can assist in mobilizing support for place promotion across social cleavages such as class. In this context, the potential to use a sense of national identity can be a significant resource.

Some have suggested that a return to 'roots', a reawakening of local (including 'national') identities is also a reaction to increasing global economic integration and an attendant trend of cultural homogenization. There is much that is questionable in this thesis (Hall, 1992a), but for our purposes it is sufficient to point out that Harvie (1994) has demonstrated that the 'aggressive regionalism' (p.4) so characteristic of 'The Rise of Regional Europe' has involved the creation of some *new* regional identities, rather than simply a reawakening of old ones. Regionalism, it is clear, is a political project, the first step in which is creating a hegemonic narrative which validates the very existence of the region. Creating, and sustaining, a coalition of interests which will promote a particular place (whether a region or not) requires political skills, and, even then, success is not guaranteed (Harvey, 1989; Stoker and Mossberger, 1994). Among the resources which can help bind coalitions are ideologies which emphasize a sense of belonging, of shared histories, culture and, perhaps, destiny. For what Hague and Thomas (Chapter 8) refer to as the stateless nations of Europe, nationalist sentiments can be very useful in mobilizing coalitions of interests within their boundaries.

The book has two complementary strands which derive from the mixed motivation for putting it together. The first is the straightforward provision of an opportunity to consider at reasonable length key aspects of modern planning in the two countries – hence part of the value of chapters on the institutional and legal framework for planning and on various dimensions of urban and rural economic development and rural policy (for example). The second strand is an examination of the extent to which various aspects of planning in Scotland and Wales can be, or need to be, understood as shaped by a distinctive national politics. A particularly important element in this second strand is the significance for planning of the claims typically involved in discussions of national identity, the latter being a durable component of political life in the two countries for over a century (Evans, 1989).

Kofman and Williams (1989, p.2) have argued that 'self-determination is the *sine qua non* of the modern nationalist movement', but as Harvie (1977, p.275) has pointed out in relation to Scottish politics in the mid-1970s, a 'rediscovery' or creation of a sense of national identity does not entail advocating separatism. In the politics of both Scotland and Wales, this distinction has been a crucial one. In Wales, for example, there have been prominent Labour politicians, such as Aneurin Bevan and Neil Kinnock, who have been extremely suspicious of, and antipathetical toward, separatist sentiments. Yet it is the case that nationality has been a key element in the hegemonic modernizing ideology which has shaped the politics of the country since at least the First World War (Rees and Lambert, 1981), a period of overwhelming electoral supremacy for the Labour Party, especially in south Wales (Davies, 1993). National identity has been an idea, and a sentiment, which has shaped the views and responses of Welsh people of all party political affiliations, of all social classes. In Scotland advocacy of separation is represented by the Scottish National Party (SNP), which has had mixed electoral fortunes over the past two decades. It was particularly successful in some areas in the 1980s, when Thatcherism was seen as a direct attack on distinctive interests which Scottish people shared (McCrone, 1992). But, as Agnew (1989) and McCrone (1992) demonstrate, there is no neat correspondence between voting SNP and wanting self-determination; the meaning of nationalism can vary over time and place. Yet a sense of national identity is undoubtedly a potent force in current Scottish politics, underpinning a widely held view that 'government by Westminster' is unacceptable and that some form of devolution in terms of an elected, accountable Scottish Assembly with resources is required (Midwinter *et al.*, 1991). This now appears to be higher on the political agenda than for many years.

McCrone (1992) also argues that, in reality, Scotland has few linguistic or religious justifications for separation. However, such a line of argument, with its implication that nationalism 'naturally' follows in certain circumstances ignores the ways in which national identity and nationalist sentiments are socially constructed. There has been considerable discussion and theorization of national identity, and related ideas; it is not the aim of this book to contribute to these debates, but it is important that it (or, more properly, our views as editors) are located in relation to them. Our position is influenced by the arguments of G. Williams (1991) and C. H. Williams (1994) that the social construction of identity is bound up with struggle and resistance. National identity is a construction negotiated in the process of political mobilization as a component of resistance (typically, to the authority of the state). It follows that, firstly, specific claims made about, and experiences of, the nature of national identity, and its territorial scope, are historically contingent; not simply in the sense that they are created for particular reasons at certain times, but – more significantly – that the claims, and the experience of national identification, are not manifestations of an essential characteristic or quality which lies dormant until roused by some trauma.[1]

A second aspect of our view of national identity, which is an implication of this point, is that the experience of feeling part of a particular nation is inherently mediated by other bases of social identity, such as gender and class. It is not that these social cleavages cut across national identification, but rather that what national identity *means* is likely to vary with gender, ethnicity and other factors (Beddoe, 1986) (and to have its influence in turn, on those). As Hall (1992b, p.256) has put it in relation to the combating of racism 'a great deal of black politics . . . has been predicated on the assumption that the categories of gender and sexuality would stay the same and remain fixed and secured'. The assumption of an 'additive model' (Rattansi, 1992) of social identity is as mistaken in relation to individuals as it is in relation to society as a whole. The conceptions of national identity which figure in the analyses of this volume will, generally, revolve around the experiences and interests of political élites in Scotland and Wales, but we are conscious that these views may neither be universal in the two countries, nor uncontested.

Constructions of national identity invariably involve references, explicit or implicit, to space, to geography. As Smith (1991) notes, not all claims to nationhood involve reference to occupation of a particular territory, but even those constructed on the basis of ethnicity – of a supposed common culture and history – will typically involve, albeit indirectly, references to place (for example, via the importance of historically significant places, or symbolically significant landscapes). Gruffydd (1994) has argued that different conceptions of Welshness are associated with commonly held 'imagined landscapes', so that 'Y Fro Gymraeg', for example, the bastion of Welsh speaking, is imagined as a place of rural villages, agricultural activity, and so on. State activity which regulates land use (that is, town and country planning) will therefore attract the attention of all those interested in promoting (or undermining) particular conceptions of national identity. If the boundaries of 'planning' are drawn wider (as they are in this book) to encompass economic development, then the significance of the activity for conceptions of nationhood is even greater. This book will discuss the more important instances of this in Scotland and Wales.

It will also examine ways in which the state (or supra-national agencies) may, unwittingly, promote the construction of national identity. Pickvance (1985) has argued that spatial policies – that is, policies (such as regional policy) which are targeted spatially – encourage the creation of broad-based territorial coalitions aimed at securing for *their* area the benefits of policies. This phenomenon extends beyond economic development. Bishop's chapter in this book documents the way in which the creation of a Welsh countryside agency has stimulated the development of a network of national voluntary organizations and pressure groups. As was mentioned above, putting together, and then sustaining, spatial coalitions is not easy, and there is no guarantee of success; it can be very useful to promote an appropriate ideology, a set of beliefs which obscures real power relations and conflicts of interests between coalition 'partners' by suggesting the existence of shared interests and destiny. A national identity, with its myths of community and origins (Appiah, 1995), can fit this bill very well. Creating the identity is not a straightforward task. An extended quotation from Osmond (1992, p.5) summarizes some of the significant demographic obstacles to the task in Wales:

> The lack of cohesion is further emphasized by the instability of the Welsh population. During the 1980s an estimated 40,000 to 50,000 people moved into Wales every year with a similar number moving out. This means that before the end of the century perhaps as much as a third of Wales's 3 million population will have moved within a twenty-year period.
>
> This is a major demographic shift whose impact affects different communities disproportionately. Many rural villages in north and west Wales are seeing native young people displaced by a combination of older, retired people, and sometimes younger people moving in because they can more easily afford the housing. In the Valleys of south Wales the trend is for people to move or at least commute to the coast and further afield to find work.
>
> Again, it is often asserted that Wales is split into at least three regions – north, middle, and south – with each having more in common with adjacent parts of England than with each other.

Smith (1991) argues that, historically, there have been two broad models for national identity – the civic and the ethnic. We would interpret his analysis as being about the kinds of *claims* which are made in relation to national identity. On that basis, we wanted this book to address the various ways in which such claims or sentiments touched upon the planning system.

The civic claim or model Smith (1991, p.9) suggests, is 'a predominantly spatial or territorial conception', one which emphasizes the significance of a 'homeland', and venerates its particular physical attributes. Other elements of the model are the idea that the nation is a community of laws and institutions 'with a single political will' (p.10), that citizenship carries with it some sense of equality (as a member of the nation) and that there is a common civic culture and ideology. We need hardly elaborate how a state activity concerned with regulating the use of land, with promoting its development (or conservation), will find itself a subject of interest to those for whom the civic claim to national identity has any force. By way of contrast, the ethnic claim (or model), places 'its emphasis on a community of birth or native culture' (p.11). Descent, rather than territory, is the key notion in this model, and vernacular culture (including languages) are important elements in it. But, as we have pointed out, even this kind of model will make implicit claims about space.

Smith acknowledges that the kinds of nationalist arguments used at various times in various places can shift from one 'model' to another and in both Wales and Scotland there have, historically, been a variety of views about what underpins national distinctiveness (G. A. Williams, 1985). In recent decades, however, it would be fair to say that nationalist consciousness in both countries has a vital territorial underpinning (often associated with or triggered by resentments about exploitation of resources by 'outsiders') (Agnew, 1989). In Wales there is an absence of distinctive legal or institutional structures of any antiquity though, as Osmond (1992) demonstrates, there is by now quite a complex of more recent national institutions. Wales was incorporated into rather than united with England, and it has been ruled by English governments for 700 years; more recently, the forerunner of the Welsh Office was created in 1951; the Welsh Office itself in 1964 (Davies, 1993). This has led some to emphasize the importance of the Welsh language as a signifier of nationhood, a claim resisted by others (Osmond, 1989). For the individuals involved in these debates, the concern is, generally, far from simply academic. As Delamont (1995, p.193) puts it, 'The tongues we use are part of our identity our . . . sense of self and our gender, our class, our age and our ambitions are embodied and made public in our speech and our writing'. State support for Welsh – as, for example, through the creation of a (largely) Welsh-medium television channel – can be interpreted, then, as threatening by those whose identity as Welsh people is not bound up with speaking Welsh and who fear that some kind of implicit 'language test' of Welshness is gaining ground. G. A. Williams (1985, p.294) is not alone in sometimes feeling that 'whom the Gods wish to destroy they first afflict with a language problem'. In Scotland, on the other hand, there is an infrastructure of venerable national institutions, including ones in key areas of the law and education. However, such institutions do not exist, or persist, without sustained political support. Scottish society is as riven by major cleavages such as those of class as England or Wales (for example, see references in Moir's chapter in this volume on the political mobilization by landowners in some parts of Scotland), but it also appears that a conception of national identity can, at times, transcend these by building on perceptions of shared interests.

National identity, then, is created and contested, and particular constructions are not natural features of the world, awaiting discovery. Nationalist sentiments must be fostered and focused if they are to be politically salient, and we have touched upon some of the ways in which use of territory, and land-use planning may play a part in that process. The contributions to this book examine this process, but they also remind us that the national identity of Scotland and Wales can be exploited by politicians operating on a British platform. A number of contributors highlight the ambiguous position of the Scottish and Welsh Offices – on the one hand departments of the British state, but on the other, of necessity, sensitive to the national peculiarities and needs of the two countries for which they are responsible. While it is important to emphasize the way in which national sentiment 'from the grassroots' can influence policy, it should also be noted that Welsh and Scottish Office policy can sometimes reflect the political ambitions and concerns of secretaries of state who have no sympathy with nationalism, but for whom having distinctive Scottish or Welsh policies is expedient. John Redwood's shake-up of Welsh planning, economic development and countryside policy in the 1990s comes into this category (see chapters by Tewdwr-Jones, Morgan and Henderson, Rees and Bishop in this volume) as does the reconfiguration of countryside agencies in Scotland (see Bishop in this volume).

The book

No account of planning in Scotland and Wales can ignore the economic fortunes of the two countries. In Chapter 2, Mike Danson sets out the European context. He paints a picture of economic weakness being compounded (historically) by political and institutional peripherality within the United Kingdom, a situation which is getting worse as the European Union assumes greater influence over economic policy. He acknowledges (but is sceptical of) the positive interpretations which have been given to recent economic changes; his analysis would support the view that political debate in the two countries will continue to be shaped by a need to promote (and be seen to be promoting) economic development in circumstances where options are severely limited. The kinds of planning and economic development agencies, initiatives and rhetoric analysed in this book, therefore, are likely to continue to be significant through the 1990s.

Chapters 3 and 4 discuss the lineaments of the land-use planning systems in Wales and Scotland. Both clarify the legal and institutional differences between Scotland, Wales and England, but while Rowan-Robinson (Chapter 3) can identify some significant examples in Scotland, there are considerably fewer in Wales. Jeremy Rowan-Robinson concentrates more on the legal and administrative framework within which the planning process operates in Scotland and then investigates the significant differences which exist from the English system. National planning guidance, regional reports, development plans and development control are investigated and some important differences from English practice are highlighted. It is, however, concluded that the two systems are converging; national planning guidance in the two countries is becoming similar and regional reports have disappeared in Scotland. However, Scotland's different legal system will ensure differences remain in development control. It is noted that the replacement of the regional councils by unitary authorities will lessen opportunities for effective strategic planning. The importance of liaison between the much smaller planning community in Scotland will however remain. The author notes that for the most part the differences identified reflect Scottish solutions to problems which are common to both systems. It is concluded that the disappearance of some of the differences will be missed in the Scottish planning system but that the autonomy of the Scottish Office will remain. Furthermore, it is hoped that from time to time Scottish solutions to planning problems may be developed from which both systems may learn. Unlike Scotland, Wales does not have a legal system which is different from England's. However, Tewdwr-Jones (Chapter 4) argues that it is the manner in which planning operates (in at least some parts of Wales) which is truly distinctive, rather than the legal or administrative apparatus. He suggests that major influences on the system's operation are the local attempts to counter what are perceived as social and economic problems (notably, lack of housing and work for locally born people). He concedes that these problems (and reactions) can be found in rural areas throughout the UK, but, he argues, their being interpreted within nationalist terms of reference is distinctively Welsh.

In Chapter 5, Kevin Morgan and Dylan Henderson analyse the working of the Welsh Development Agency, an institution which has aroused considerable interest elsewhere in Britain. The authors provide an authoritative account of the Agency's current trajectory. They make it clear that this cannot be understood as a simple response to the economic problems facing the country, but must also be related to the complex and shifting way in which Welsh political aspirations and agendas interact with the disposition of political forces, and fortunes, in the UK (and, more particularly, within the Conservative government). Like Tewdwr-Jones, in Chapter 4, they recognize the tension inherent in the Welsh Office's position as a regional arm of central government which, nevertheless, can be – on occasion – an important orchestrator of a regional political consensus. This tension, in turn, can have a direct effect on both the work of particular agencies (such as the WDA) and the development of urban policy initiatives. Gareth Rees's dissection of the 'Programme for the Valleys' in Chapter 6 shows how politically potent images of the south Wales Valleys have been both constraints upon, and a resource for, policy-makers concerned about the modernization of the Welsh economy. Yet these images have not *determined* policy; successive Conservative secretaries of state for Wales have brought their own concerns (generated outside Wales) to their task of addressing the country's problems: policy outcomes, and policy reviews, are complex products of the interactions of these influences.

In Chapter 7, Greg Lloyd argues that Scotland's history, culture and socio-economic structure has shaped the development of a distinctive approach to regional planning which has corporatist values and practices at its heart. The legal and institutional infrastructure represented by bodies such as the Scottish Office underpins this distinctiveness. However, in his account of institutional innovation in Scottish regional planning in the 1980s he makes it clear that while distinctiveness remains, Scotland has been affected by a UK-wide Conservative agenda (an agenda which has very little support in Scotland itself). Regional planning in the Scotland of the 1990s, therefore, appears to be a fascinating mixture of rhetoric which owes its provenance south of the border and practices whose lineage can be traced to an indigenous corporatist tradition.

The discussions of land-use planning and of economic development/urban policy initiatives in Wales highlight a tension between a rhetoric of (and desire for) distinctively Welsh approaches, and a reality where these are circumscribed by the political dynamics of a centralized state. The planning of the capital cities – Cardiff and Edinburgh – does not exhibit this tension, however. Hague and Thomas (Chapter 8) suggest that the planning of the two cities can best be understood as an outcome of a different tension – between political mobilization around domestic issues in the cities and the aspirations of (at least some) of their economic and political élites that the cities play a role on a national (and, latterly, European) stage. The authors discuss these similarities, but also highlight differences between the planning of the two cities which arise from their very different histories and roles as capital cities in Scotland and Wales.

Martin Elson and Roderick Macdonald (Chapter 9) examine urban growth management policies and ask whether distinctive solutions have emerged in the Celtic countries. They start by noting a fundamental difference between Scotland and Wales in terms of growth management policies; the existence of Green Belts in Scotland but not in Wales. Closer examination of practice in Wales, however, indicates that Green Belt policies exist under different names in parts of Wales, such as Green Barrier policies in Clwyd. By examining urban growth management practice in Strathclyde, Lothian, South Glamorgan, Gwent and Clwyd they conclude that Green Belt policies in Scotland and similar policies in Wales share the key characteristics of Green Belts in England in terms of controlling and managing urban form. They note that the policy approach taken in both the Celtic countries is more positive; advocating environmental improvements, leisure and recreation uses, and the use of Green Belt and other greenfield sites for economic development purposes, particularly as part of regeneration strategies such as in Strathclyde. A deeper look at the English system suggests that this approach is also advocated in the

North-East of England and parts of the Midlands, although rarely in the South. The authors conclude that Green Belt and urban growth management policies will continue to be key parts of the planning strategies for both Celtic offices, but point to a number of future changes and concerns, particularly the decline of strategic planning through local government reorganization.

Contrasting approaches to rural economic development are explored by Chris Minay in Chapter 10. The chapter assesses the extent to which approaches to rural development in Scotland and Wales are different to those in England and attempts to assess whether these differences are related to geographical, economic or cultural distinctiveness. The chapter undertakes this by examining the context for rural development in the two countries, and the institutions of rural development and policies and practice in the two countries. The author notes that more conformity than cultural distinctiveness exists, particularly as a result of increasing globalization. It is suggested that policies for rural development tend to concentrate on relative remoteness rather than cultural or institutional distinctiveness. The chapter concludes by highlighting limitations to such a policy approach particularly when the ideology of government has little support in the Celtic countries. Finally, the importance of achieving rural development in some areas through more locally-based economic development is highlighted, particularly if such development is more clearly accountable to the entire community than present externally-appointed agencies.

Chapter 11, by John Moir, examines the designation of valued landscapes in Scotland. Noting that little Scottish literature exists on the subject, the author seeks to highlight the distinctiveness of the approaches adopted in Scotland to landscape conservation and designation and goes on to explain some of the reasons behind this distinctiveness and explore some of the issues and conflicts within the Scottish approach to landscape conservation. The author notes a fundamental difference between Scotland and England in that there are no National Parks in Scotland but then goes on to chart three main attempts to set up Scottish National Parks. Despite this lack of National Parks, Scotland is seen to have a variety of distinctive designations such as National Scenic Areas and Regional Parks. The author suggests the distinctive approach taken in Scotland is as a result of physical factors such as geology and climate; historical and cultural factors; and, most importantly, political factors. It is concluded that although there are valuable lessons to be learnt from the Scottish system of designation, there are limitations to the system such as the lack of positive management powers and an overlap between different designations.

In Chapter 12, Kevin Bishop provides a fascinating account of the interplay of nationalist, or at least devolutionist, politics with concerns about the coherence of public policy formulation and delivery in relation to countryside conservation. Whatever the motives for setting up integrated agencies in Wales and Scotland responsible for nature conservation and the enjoyment and protection of landscapes, the opportunity is being taken to address long-standing difficulties in policy-making in these areas. Bishop provides a timely review of the progress and pitfalls to date which will be of interest well beyond the borders of the two countries.

Even those who resist bestowing upon the Welsh or Gaelic languages a special status in discussions of nationality generally acknowledge the value of sustaining it. In an age when ethnicity and difference is chic, and indigenous cultures are fêted by Western intelligentsia, it is a little difficult to justify indifference to the fate of an indigenous language on one's doorstep. As James and Williams point out in Chapter 13, there is a long-standing orthodoxy in language planning that the future of Welsh and Gaelic are tied to the fates of (rural) communities in which they remain the media of everyday life. These fates, in turn, are determined by the degree to which they can continue to manage the massive social and economic changes which have affected them for two centuries through *emigration*, but are now more threatening, because they involve *immigration* (of a largely non-Welsh (or Gaelic) speaking population) (Giggs and Pattie, 1992; Griffiths, 1992). The planning system cannot (and should not) avoid being involved in public debates about these issues – witness the recent furore in the professional and news media about Ceredigion District Council's draft proposals to try to limit the provision of new homes to local people ('Anti-incomer row goes on', *Carmarthen Journal*, 24 May 1995; *Planning Week*, 25 May 1995). James and Williams document a growing awareness in the planning system (in Wales, especially) of its linguistic context and some halting, but encouraging, steps towards a more supportive approach to securing the future of the two languages.

Notes

[1] An implication of this view is that distinctions such as those drawn by Smith (1991, ch.4) between territorial and ethnic bases of national identity are seen as useful categorizations of mechanisms deployed in the social construction of identity, rather than guides to timeless driving forces which periodically erupt into social or political life. This is not to say that the particular conception of 'ethnicity' Smith employs is not itself open to question (see Hall, 1992b).

[2] Evans (1989, p. 70) points out that as early as 1938 the distinguished intellectual Iorwerth Peate was opposing proposals for a trunk road linking north and south Wales on the grounds that it would open up rural areas and destroy the Welsh language.

References

Agnew, J. 1989. 'Nationalism: autonomous force or practical politics? Place and nationalism in Scotland', in C. H. Williams and E. Kofman (eds.), *Community Conflict, Partition and Nationalism* (London, Routledge).

Appiah, K. A. 1995. 'African Identities', in L. Nicholson and S. Seidman (eds.), *Social Postmodernism* (Cambridge, Cambridge University Press).

Beddoe, D. 1986. 'Images of Welsh women', in T. Curtis (ed.), *Wales: The Imagined Nation* (Bridgend, Poetry Wales Press).

Clotworthy, J. and N. Harris 1996. 'Planning policy implications of local government reorganization', in M. Tewdwr-Jones (ed.), *British Planning Policy in Transition* (London, UCL Press).

Cooke, P. 1990. 'Manufacturing miracles: the changing nature of the local economy', in M. Campbell (ed.), *Local Economic Policy* (London, Cassell Educational).

Davies, H. W. E., J. A. Gosling with M. T. Hsia 1993. *The Impact of the European Community on Land Use Planning in the United Kingdom*, 2 vols. (London, RTPI).

Davies, J. 1993. *A History of Wales* (London, Allen Lane. The Penguin Press) (first published in Welsh as *Hanes Cymru*, 1990).

Delamont, S. 1995. *Appetites and Identities* (London, Routledge).

Dickson, T. 1989. 'Scotland is different, OK', in D. McCrone, S. Kendrick and P. Straw (eds.), *The Making of Scotland – Nation, Culture and Social Change* (Edinburgh, Edinburgh University Press), pp.53–69.

Donnison, D. and A. Middleton (eds.) 1987. *Regenerating the Inner City: Glasgow's Experience* (London, Routledge & Kegan Paul).

Evans, N. 1989. 'Gogs, Cardis and Hwntws: Region, nation and state in Wales, 1840–1940', in N. Evans (ed.), *National Identity in the British Isles* (Harlech, Coleg Harlech).

Giggs, J. and C. Pattie 1992. 'Wales as a plural society', *Contemporary Wales*, Vol.5, pp.25–63.

Griffiths, D. 1992. 'The political consequences of migration into Wales', *Contemporary Wales*, Vol. 5, pp.65–80.

Gruffydd, P. 1994. 'Tradition, modernity and the countryside: the imaginary geography of rural Wales', *Contemporary Wales*, Vol.6, pp.33–47.

Hall, S. 1992a. 'The question of cultural identity', in S. Hall *et al.* (eds.), *Modernity and its Futures* (London, Sage).

Hall, S. 1992b. 'New ethnicities', in J. Donald and A. Rattansi (eds.), *'Race', Culture and Difference* (London, Sage).

Harvey, D. 1989. 'From managerialism to entrepreneurialism: the transformation in urban governance in late capitalism', *Geografiska Annaler*, Vol.71B, pp.3–17.

Harvie, C. 1977. *Scotland and Nationalism* (London, George Allen and Unwin).

Harvie, C. 1994. *The Rise of Regional Europe* (London, Routledge).

Kofman, E. and C. H. Williams 1989. 'Culture, community and conflict', in C. H. Williams and E. Kofman (eds.), *Community Conflict, Partition and Nationalism* (London, Routledge).

Marquand, D. 1988. *The Unprincipled Society: New Demons and Old Politics* (London, Fontana).

McCrone, D. 1992. *Understanding Scotland – The Sociology of a Stateless Nation* (London, Routledge).

Midwinter, A., M. Keating and J. Mitchell 1991. *Politics and Public Policy in Scotland* (Edinburgh, Mainstream).

Osmond, J. 1989. 'The modernisation of Wales', in N. Evans (ed.), *National Identity in the British Isles* (Harlech, Coleg Harlech).

Osmond, J. 1992. *The Democratic Challenge* (Llandysul, Gomer).

Pickvance, C. 1985. 'Spatial policy as territorial politics', in G. Rees *et al.* (eds.), *Political Action and Social Identity* (London, Macmillan).

Rattansi, A. 1992. 'Changing the subject?', in J. Donald and A. Rattansi (eds.), *'Race', Culture and Difference* (London, Sage).

Rees, G. and J. Lambert 1981. 'Nationalism as legitimation?', in M. Harloe (ed.), *New Perspectives in Urban Changes and Conflict* (London, Heinemann Education).

Smith, A. D. 1991. *National Identity* (Harmondsworth, Penguin).

Stoker, G. and K. Mossberger 1994. 'Urban regime theory in comparative perspective', *Environment and Planning C. Government and Policy*, Vol.12, pp.195–212.

Williams, C. H. 1994. *Called Unto Liberty!* (Clevedon, England, Multilingual Matters).

Williams, G. 1991. *The Welsh in Patagonia: The State and the Ethnic Community* (Cardiff, University of Wales Press).

Williams, G. A. 1985. *When Was Wales?* (Harmondsworth, Penguin).

2

Scotland and Wales in Europe

MIKE DANSON

Introduction

Although the means of promoting social and economic cohesion in the European Union – the Structural Funds – have been applied for twenty years, the threats and challenges presented to the community's peripheral and lagging regions have been intensified since the mid-1980s. The completion of the Single European Market in 1992, the Single European Act, the Maastricht Treaty, moves to greater integration and enlargements, economic and monetary union and the introduction of a Committee of the Regions – all have raised the importance of uneven development across regions and member-states. Related to this are the external pressures created by the globalization of production, increased competition for mobile investments from the transformed economies of Eastern Europe, and the enhanced market performance of the corporations and countries of the Pacific.

This chapter introduces the European dimension to the theme of planning in Scotland and Wales. Rather than discussing the detail of Structural Fund legislation and short-term forecasts of their impacts, it attempts to bed the analysis in a long-term framework, mapping the continuing legacy of the particular industrial evolutions of Scotland and Wales onto the extensive list of characteristics, as outlined below, which define their present economic structures and performances. Speculation on the future development of these two Celtic nations of Britain is introduced to provide the contexts within which planning and strategic intervention will be undertaken over the next few decades. The pessimistic conclusion is that the logic of the European Union is for a continuation of uneven development, with but weak forces for convergence assisted by the Structural Funds. If the problems raised by the economic and time-geographic distance of the periphery from the continent's powerful core are to be tackled effectively, then massive shifts in resources will be required in the form of more significant transfer payments than have been suggested up until now.

To the extent that regional and social policies continue to be subordinated to the needs of capital and so to competition and industrial objectives, the European Union will fail to reduce regional disparities across the continent and may exacerbate patterns of uneven development. Given the enduring after-effects of the respective imperial pasts of the member-states and an immediate future of further periods of difficult transformation, Wales may at best slowly gain a foothold on the edge of the golden triangle/banana, but more probably it will remain with Scotland languishing in a declining periphery. These are the environmental constraints at the European level on the future of planning in the two nations. A more political economic analysis would suggest additional factors will need to be brought to bear if substantial development is to be promoted.

The European Union

While many now forget the idealism of the founders of the European Union or only choose certain dishes from the menu of treaties, agreements and directives, the logic of the creation of the European Community went far beyond a Customs Union. For political and economic reasons, the Europeanization of industrial, social, regional and other policies has become increasingly significant and dominant over national programmes throughout the European Union (EU). As Keating (1995), *inter alia*, argues, however, there have been seemingly contradictory forces for greater regional autonomy in many of the nation-states of this community. The extension of sub-national development policies and strategies across the continent and, later, down from Brussels has been but one feature of the pressures from below that have re-awakened notions of the city-region, the semi-autonomous region and of nationalism in absorbed states.

Creating a single European market, and so realizing economies of scale across the industries and corporations of the EU, has been an objective throughout the history of the European Economic Community. In order to compete with the United States, Japan and more recently the so-called 'Tiger Economies' of the Pacific Rim, the EU has considered a customs union with an industrial and competition policy framework that would sponsor the growth of world-class companies. Both the threats of global competition and the globalization of the world economy and multinational enterprises led to the perceived need to create the conditions for genuine Europe-wide corporations which could meet these challenges. From the early days of the Community, but increasingly as the original member-states were joined by new partners and as the continent and the national economies appeared to stagnate relative to North America and Pacific competitors, the impetus for growth has dominated the development of the European Union. Industrial and competition policy are promoted, therefore, with other areas of intervention secondary to these.

Over time, the EU has organized the rationales and strategies for the regional and social dimensions of Europe according to this prime objective. Their introduction, establishment, encouragement and fulfilment are within the context of the growth directive. So, the creation of the Single European Market has intensified the forces of uneven development inherent within the EU, as expected by most analysts (such as Myrdal, 1957; Holland, 1976), with spatial and distributional effects unfortunate by-products of corporate restructuring.

The growing influence of the EU in regional and social policies up to 1992 was explained in terms of the need to manage such trends of divergence and convergence across the Community. Critically, Cecchini (1988) was clear about the new tensions which would be realized by moves to complete the single market. As '1992' would bring about mass redundancies, restructuring and dislocation in all member-states, there would be a real threat that the resources released early in this process would not be reabsorbed efficiently; and without redeployment the benefits of 1992 would not be realized. A return to non-trade barriers, national restrictions and protectionism would more than nullify the positive potential of factory and office closures, the withdrawal of excess capacity from production and the amalgamation and merger of companies across the Union. A strong range of policies which would allow the EU to intervene to ameliorate the effects of these necessary stages in completing the Single Market was seen as essential if the process was to be taken to fruition. The Structural Funds have been strengthened and expanded to go some way towards squaring the virtuous circle identified by Cecchini (1988). The Maastricht Treaty and Edinburgh Summit formed the debating chambers for these discussions. In many ways, though, this new phase in the development of the Structural Funds – the European Regional Development Fund (ERDF), the European Social Fund (ESF), and the European Agricultural Guidance and Guarantee Fund – represents a continuation of past policy frameworks and strategies.

Most importantly, the maturing of the European Union has been at the expense of the nation-state, with regional and industrial policies, especially, subordinated to the higher level. Over time, while there has been a decline in the coverage and size of the regional aid budget in the UK, this has been accompanied, and has been obscured to an extent, by the expansion of the European funds. Although the net budgetary shortfall has been less than clear, however, two further elements have emerged to define the environment in which regions develop. Firstly, within the UK, for much of the period up to the mid-1970s there was a strong tendency for industrial policy to benefit the peripheral regions, with support for nationalized industries providing jobs, incomes and investment in Scotland, Wales and the North of England. The fundamental change in macro-economic policies from 1977 reversed this. So, the move to monetarism, laissez-faire economics, privatization and deregulation of markets tended to produce strong regional effects (Townroe and Martin, 1992). In particular, the massive declines in the coal, steel, shipbuilding and engineering industries have had catastrophic effects on the economies of Scotland and Wales. Secondly, and not totally independently, the European Commission has increasingly scrutinized national policies to ensure they are not anti-competitive, that is they do not provide subsidies to member-states' companies which damage the position of other players in the market. Though little used outwith the publicly-owned sector, such direct support to industry could have been applied formerly to benefit certain regions. In reality, national and EU regional policy in the 1970s and 1980s was dominated by infrastructure investments.

Thus the loss of locally-owned corporations and the nationalized industries has removed the traditional modes of expanding effective demand and promoting restructuring in Scotland and Wales. Concomitantly, the form of intervention has come to be dependent on physical developments – roads, water and sewerage, factory and industrial estates, and more recently on business development activities – training, advice and grants to small and medium enterprises. In essence, the restructuring of the Scottish and Welsh economies was first assisted by Europe, then made essential by the moves to a more integrated Single Market. At the same time, the traditional instruments of intervening to benefit the regions have either come into disrespect – according to the new economic orthodoxy and the needs of the wider European good – or become redundant as the traditional industries have closed.

From the early 1970s it has been clear that the original Community of six would become progressively larger over time, as well as deepening through integration. Questions over the speed of these respective processes and over which should dominate have been paramount in many of the debates of the last two decades. As this is being written (late 1995), there is no clear conclusion that either tendency will predominate. However, the forces which favour enlargement seem to have fewer obstacles than those behind the proposals for closer economic and monetary union. To an extent this may be a moot point. The transformation of Eastern Europe and the former Soviet Union and the global mobility of capital, especially finance capital, mean that the competition for EU markets and for foreign direct investment has intensified further. Whether Poland, the Czech Republic, Hungary and other aspiring members were to join the European Union may matter less for the Celtic nations of the west than their simple ability to compete for mobile jobs and investment.

While a 'Europe of the Regions' may have been promoted by the prescriptions of the Commission, the terms of the Single European Act and the commitment to subsidiarity, many would argue otherwise, with some force. These same processes, it is proposed, do not address the continuing democratic deficit, remove many key issues from political control, and further strengthen the power of capital over labour (see Keating (1995), Bachtler

(1995) and Mackay (1992) for a discussion of such debates). In many ways, the ability of the local authorities, and the government in Scotland, Wales and the UK to influence and direct the economy have become more difficult because of the EU's regulation of industrial, competition and trading policies. The Union now controls many of the instruments of economic policy, demand management, subsidies, regional policy, public contracts, etc. As many of the infrastructural, business development and training schemes are now also funded by Europe through Community Support Frameworks for ERDF and ESF, so the EU sets the agenda for the paths of development of the Scottish and Welsh economies. Without coverage of much of the Social Chapter of the Maastricht Treaty, it seems fair to argue that deindustrialization and restructuring have left these communities with 'less control over their own economies and lives than at any time in the last two centuries' (Danson, 1995b).

Scotland and Wales: on the periphery of Europe

It was stressed above that the pre-conditions for Scotland and Wales becoming dependent on external agencies and forces, and on the EU especially, were laid by the failure of the two economies since the 1970s. If an environment of strong inherent growth had been established and flourished within the two economies, based on successful indigenous capital, then discussions of European contexts, limitations and assistance would have been largely redundant. Compared to some equally peripheral neighbours, the Nordic countries for instance, the relatively subordinated economic and political positions of Scotland and Wales have been significant in determining their continuing regional problems and passages of development.

In the terminology of the European Union, Wales and Scotland are within the 'Atlantic Arc', one of eight geographical areas outlined in the 'Europe 2000' document (CEC, 1991). Although criticized for the underlying quality of definition and cohesion (see Gripaios and Mangles, 1993, for instance), these trans-regional study areas and the research on them are instructive for the insights they allow into the European Commission's view of the periphery. What is demonstrated is the low population density, the geographical peripherality, the underdeveloped nature of much of the rural economy and the fragility of the few industrial complexes. For Scotland and Wales, the consequences of the UK joining the European Community in 1973 are seen as deleterious. They were 'weakened by an increasingly ageing industrial base and by the redirection of commercial activities towards Europe at the expense of the Commonwealth' (CEC, 1994, p.42).

However, while the period since 1973 may have refocused the trade, industry and so regions of the British Isles, in many ways this was merely exacerbating a much longer decline of the north and west of these islands. As argued previously with regard to Scotland, but applying with equal force to Wales, over 'most of this century Scotland has been declining relative to the rest of the United Kingdom and, by extension, the rest of Europe' (Danson, 1991, p.89). Both nations are essentially rural with a concentration of population in an industrialized core. These urban agglomerations, with old coal and steel communities in their hinterlands, were two of the original industrialized areas of the continent. Each, however, has experienced both an early period of growth and a long history of stagnation. Behind the development of both economies – and Clydeside and south Wales, in particular – were factors associated with the British Empire. Britain's role as an imperial power, based on naval supremacy, prompted the establishment of the coal and steel industries of central Scotland and south Wales. These two regional economies, and through linkages and migration the rest of their nations, became inextricably dependent on the trading and military position of the UK as a whole. Both experienced very significant growth in industry and population in the years up to 1914 – with Glasgow suffering the worst urban slums in the history of the planet (Damer, 1990) and south Wales only being beaten by America in the rate of immigration (Smith, 1980). Records on shipbuilding tonnage (Slaven, 1975) and coal mined (Cooke, 1987) confirm that these areas were at the heart of the Empire in terms of industrial output and importance. The First World War was perhaps the watershed; although the seeds of external destruction may have been made inherent before then, the decline of British power and controlled imperial markets exposed a rapid and deep structural imbalance in the Scottish and Welsh economies. Massive unemployment, poverty, deprivation and emigration marked the period up to the next world war. Since 1930 this industrial legacy has ensured that Scotland and Wales have been subject to a broad set of economic policies targeted at relieving the worst effects of the rundown and closure of the staple industries – steel, coal, shipbuilding, heavy engineering and textiles.

It seems relevant to seat the consideration of the present position of Wales and Scotland, and to speculate on their futures in the European Union, in the contexts of their pasts. There has been a tendency in recent collections to divorce the period since the mid-1970s from the processes of economic history up to that time (see for instance the anthologies by Day and Rees, 1991; Damesick and Wood, 1987; Townroe and Martin, 1992, which, although containing excellent summaries of current and future prospects, lack a historical perspective. This is in marked contrast to the treatments by Lovering (1996) and Lee (1995)) .

Having struggled to maintain former glories in output and trade terms through most of the century, the periphery of Britain has been in almost constant benefit of various forms of regional development aid. While comprehensive analyses of the role and successes of different phases of regional and industrial policies have been undertaken since the 1960s, it will be sufficient here to catalogue the positions of Scotland and Wales across a number of indicators. The Standing Commission on the Scottish Economy (1989), and several publications from the University of Wales Press, especially the interdisciplinary yearbook *Contemporary Wales*, have captured much of the accessible writing on the major economic issues facing the Celtic nations. Periodicals such as the *Fraser of Allander Institute Quarterly Economic Commentary* (University of Strathclyde) and the *Welsh Economic Review* (Cardiff Business School) have not only supplemented such texts but also identified common and contrasting themes between the two. The importance of their common economic histories and current policy environments are clear in the discussion of inward investment to Scotland and Wales (Hill and Munday, 1994), with only comparisons with Ireland rating as much attention in the Scottish academic and popular media.

Over most of the twentieth century, Scotland and Wales have lagged behind the UK as a whole in economic terms. Unemployment has remained higher and incomes and expenditure improved more slowly than in the south. Behind such headlines, the degree of external control and ownership of the industries of Scotland and Wales have continued to increase, at times through merger and takeover, through nationalization and privatization, at others through differential rates of decline and growth of native and foreign companies. Research suggests that such changes, in complex ways, put a relative brake on the rates of new firm formation and indigenous development (Ashcroft, Love and Schouller, 1987). Concomitantly, output, trade and investment have become more narrowly dependent on a few key sectors in both countries. In Scotland, electronics (especially computers) and whisky have accounted for over half of non-oil manufacturing exports, and about 50 per cent of all manufacturing investment in recent years. Both these sectors are dominated by overseas companies, with over 90 per cent of output by non-Scottish firms. For Wales, the metal manufacture (steel), electrical and electronic engineering, food and drink sectors contribute over a third of all value added in industry, while up to 60 per cent of investment is made by the top three or four sectors each year. Over a third of employment in manufacturing in Wales is in overseas-owned plants, over a quarter in Scotland. Much of the rest is controlled by UK corporations with their headquarters in the South East.

This degree of domination is often blamed, in a simple way, for the massive restructuring of the Scottish and Welsh economies since 1979. However, the role of inward investment in the dynamic processes of growth and decline has not been straightforward. Indeed, although both have suffered from a 'Celtic divide' (McKendrick, 1995), with higher rates of poverty and deprivation, there is a need to review and evaluate the performance of the two economies in terms of wider indicators than unemployment and redundancies, placing such analysis in a European context.

At the beginning of the twentieth century, output per head (GDP) in Wales and Scotland was more than 50 per cent higher than in Norway or Denmark (Boyle et al., 1989); by the early 1990s, it had fallen to less than 90 per cent of Denmark's and 75 per cent of Norway's. As noted above, such long-run and apparently endemic relative decline has extended across output, population and incomes so that much of their territory is now eligible for EU Structural Fund support: most of rural Wales and Scotland because of problems of agricultural decline and depopulation, the Highlands and Islands because of low living standards, and the old industrial heartlands of the central belt of Scotland and south Wales because of depressed economies and deindustrialization.

In the developed world (OECD), even by 1987 Scotland was 15 per cent below average for GDP per head, with Wales a further 10 per cent poorer. Within 'Western' Europe, only Greece, Ireland, Spain and Portugal were worse off. Since then, the position of the UK has not improved, perhaps the converse, although Scotland may have recovered some of the losses of the 1980s as the recession hit the south. In the environment of the late 1990s, it is significant that these Celtic nations lie within a declining UK, and so offer less protection and rights for women, young people, trades unionists, the low paid, and other disadvantaged groups compared with the rest of the European Union, outwith some parts of the Mediterranean.

The 1970s and 1980s saw massive restructuring, with 40 per cent of all Scottish and of all Welsh manufacturing jobs lost since 1980. In key traditional sectors such as coal, steel and engineering, the decline in employment was heavier though, in both cases, some replacement jobs in engineering (electronic: Scotland; motor vehicles: Wales) allowed a better net picture to emerge. In many sectors – agriculture, fishing, energy and water, manufacturing and construction – employment is historically at its lowest levels in both Scotland and Wales, with jobs for both men and women disappearing. Only services are showing any growth over time, and then only in part-time work.

A measure of the decline in the standing of the two countries in European terms can be gauged from rates of participation in the labour market. A strong geographical divide is apparent, with the prosperous south experiencing record activity rates of over 90 per cent for men, and 73 per cent for women after the long growth period of the 1980s; in Wales, the figures were below 84 per cent and 67 per cent respectively, in Scotland, 86 per cent and 69 per cent. Such have been the degrees of decline that some have re-estimated true unemployment as being double the official claimant count in mining valleys and other communities devastated by the recessions of the 1980s and 1990s (Beatty and Fothergill, 1994).

Against this background of despair and deepened depression, other statistics claim that Scotland and Wales are leaner, fitter and performing better than the prosperous South East. So, Scottish GDP per head has improved five percentage points in the five years up to 1993, reaching 98.4 per cent of the UK average. Gross value added per employee is above the UK average, and the unemployment rate below – probably for the first time this century. In the business cycles of the past (that is up to the late 1980s), when the UK economy slowed Wales and Scotland descended rapidly into recession, recovering only slowly and after the south had turned. The statistics now appear to show only a shallow reduction in output in Wales over the latest depression, while Scotland maintained production levels throughout the period, escaping the devastation of the recession. On the back of inward investment, the Celtic nations have been displaying stability and steady growth since the mid 1980s (Scotland), and leading the UK recovery out of recession fed by strong manufacturing growth (Wales) (*Welsh Economic Review*, 1995, 8:1). At the UK level, there is much more evidence of a 'boom-and-bust' cyclical pattern, exactly as experienced by the peripheral regions for the rest of the century. Perhaps, then, the structural changes of the last twenty years have created long-term benefits for the Welsh and Scottish economies?

Given the lags in publication of government statistics, never mind the questions over the quality, comprehensiveness and continuity of many statistical series, short-term analysis of recent regional economic development frequently leans heavily on surveys and econometric modelling of past trends. The main forecasting bodies – BSL (Business Strategies Ltd), Cambridge Econometrics and Oxford Economic Forecasting/Northern Ireland Economic Research Centre (OEF/NIERC) – suggest that 1994 and 1995 have witnessed export-led economic growth to the benefit of manufacturing. Although Wales still lacks a significant business services sector, this is believed to have promoted the economy close to the top of the growth league, easily outstripping the UK recovery. However, Scotland's recently gained stability also suggests that it has performed marginally more poorly than average over this two-year period. Discussion over whether a north–south divide may reappear is continued below, but for now what is relevant are the lessons that these recent developments disclose.

The statistics underlying these forecasts and the apparent improvement in Scotland's fortunes disclose the domination of the economy and of the recovery by a few sectors. Whereas the UK recovery is widespread with all manufacturing and construction sectors growing over 1994–5 and in the longer term, in the case of Scotland most sectors are declining. Even where Scottish industrial output is expanding, at best it is only regaining the levels of past years: in the significant oil and gas sector, output has increased by 25 per cent since 1993, reaching the levels of 1986, but at the expense of falling employment – and for those who remain, work is becoming more unstable and insecure; in whisky, production is now back up to 1990 output levels; most markedly, electronics/electrical engineering has doubled output since 1990 (Scottish Office Education and Industry Department, 1995).

To reconcile the growth in these leading sectors with the overall pattern, it is necessary to recognize the dominance of the electronics industry. All the increase in Scottish GDP in recent years has derived from electronics and whisky, with the former alone in Scottish productive sectors expanding in real terms over the long run. Over half of non-oil manufacturing exports, investment, and dynamism in the Scottish economy can be explained by these two sectors: both are owned, controlled and dependent upon multinational corporations headquartered far from this country.

Services, with over two-thirds of jobs, may be seen as the saviour of the economy but as a sector it is dependent on disposable incomes and benefits of people working in other sectors. A particular dynamic is expected from tourism, yet this industry is highly cyclical – falling by over 10 per cent in some years, yet increasing in value by 16 per cent in 1995; such fluctuations have major consequences for local economies.

Considering exports, the Scottish economy is highly dependent on trade in electronics, whisky, chemicals and oil, of course, to maintain its prosperity. However, removing electronics from the output statistics reveals an economy in decline. The picture is much closer to the UK cycle, but shows a slower rate of recovery in the upturn.

For Wales, recovery appears to have been more broadly based with production almost 5 per cent higher in 1994 than in 1990, consumer goods leading the improvement (Welsh Office, 1995). As with Scotland and indeed most of Europe, electronics continued to expand output, over a third higher than even four years earlier. Other major sectors such as food and drink, paper and paper products, steel, engineering and motor vehicles had all grown by about 10 per cent over the period since the depths of the recession. Nevertheless, the long retreat from coalmining and quarrying, volatility in wood and wood products, coke and refined petroleum products, and the stagnation in textiles, chemicals and other manufacturing sectors, suggest caution is necessary when considering the overall improvement. In fact, some degree of internal counter-cyclical patterns of development are apparent, with late catching up by the utilities and mining, paralleling downturns in manufacturing.

If Scotland is an export-oriented economy, now relatively protected from UK business cycles, Wales is open to new sensitivities – locked into the supply needs of multinational oligopolies in the steel, car and electronics sectors. For each it is clear that their futures rely on the European markets, and also, consequently, on attracting foreign direct investment from North America and the Pacific Rim as locations for entry into the EU. Although not available for Wales, exports surveys for Scotland show the degree to which the historical patterns of trade have been transformed. According to a well-established survey (Scottish Council Development and Industry, 1995), two-thirds of Scottish exports go to western Europe. Electronics account for 49 per cent of all sales overseas, most going to Europe and to a lesser extent the Middle East and Africa. Given the structure of the Welsh industry, the patterns of exports and the dependence on the French and German economies must be similar. Globalization of production in essence means multinational enterprises arranging a configuration of plants across the world which meets their needs to supply in and into a number of trading blocs. The deepening reliance of Scotland and Wales on the attraction of such titans means competing for highly mobile investment, with this very competition between regions and states threatening to heighten the propensity of such capital to be mobile. Without a counteracting, long-term sustainable development of indigenous companies, such peripheral economies will progressively lose further control over their own destinies: the development of underdevelopment.

Within Scotland and Wales, the processes described above promote uneven development. Some areas and sectors have benefited from the restructuring of the last twenty years. Dominated by targeted foreign, sector-specific capital investment, certain groups in the labour market have experienced improving living standards since 1977 – in finance and business services especially. However, sector growth does not automatically lead to higher wages – value added may be captured in increased profits, with capital re-exported. For many others within the local labour market, high unemployment and underemployment, low wages, a dependency on benefits, and falling participation rates have been the legacy of the restructuring. Ironically, these deeper divides in the economy and society *do not* make for a more efficient labour market; the opposite may indeed be the case with the creation of obstacles to worker mobility, skill acquisition, and so forth (Mackay, 1995).

Within urban areas and conurbations, the development of such divisions into a dual economy have been mapped over the decades. Between regions, commuting and migration have restricted destructive segmentations within Wales and Scotland. However, Grampian, Skye and the Edinburgh financial sector and the commuting belts of north-east Wales and south Glamorgan, for example, have prospered in the recent past, apparently developing in superior ways relative to the average trends. Nevertheless, most such communities are highly dependent for their (relatively) high living standards on a narrow sectoral base with a comparative advantage over the rest of Scotland and Wales, the EU and the world which is fragile. The ability of these pools of prosperity to retain their positions is highly dependent on retaining oil, tourism, financial and business services, and central government administration.

Changing contexts

The contradictory pictures outlined above, of past-dependent economies attracting non-EU mobile capital anxious to surmount customs barriers, presents the rationale for UK and European intervention to overcome continuing market failures and historical obstacles to redevelopment. While the 1970s and 1980s were dominated by regional development measures aimed at improving physical infrastructures, the future is being reoriented to favour investments in human capital, business development activities and other forms of strategic renewal. Compared with former times, not only will the intervening authorities be different under (European) Community Support Frameworks – now including the European Commission, local enterprise companies (LECs) or training and enterprise councils (TECs) – but also powers will be restricted, and many of the key employers will be outwith the public sector in the form of privatized utilities and former state corporations following new and different agendas.

Local economic development therefore reduces to following other agents' agendas, rather than establishing alternative strategies and modes to introduce them. Given this restrictive environment, although policy initiatives can take two forms: supply side and demand side, in reality, the former has dominated local economic development strategies for most of this century. The main aim of supply-side interventions has been to improve the attractiveness of localities, and primarily therefore to change the decisions of mobile inward investment. It is thus an element in a zero-sum game. Any net benefits to the region or state would come only from lower costs faced by companies arising from investment induced efficiencies, economies of scale and scope, release of redundant and idle resources, etc.

Most expenditure on supply-side policies in recent times has been undertaken by the European Union (with more than two-thirds of EU spending in Wales and Scotland being accounted for by infrastructure investment). Central government, quangos (LECs and TECs especially), employers, and local authorities have been joined by the EU in supporting training investment. Never high anyway, and now more limited than formerly, direct capital investment in companies is encouraged with grants and loans from central government, regional development agencies (the Scottish Enterprise network, Highlands and Islands Enterprise, the Welsh Development Agency, and the Development Board for Rural Wales) and the EU. Traditionally, land and property have been popular forms of supply-side policy, with the WDA and SDA in the past treating factory building and industrial site provision as major areas of intervention. As a prerequisite for the *Locate In Scotland* or *Team Wales* promotion of a location, regional development agencies and local authorities arrange for property investment as a priority, improving the image of the area in the process. Technology transfer, IT and telecommunications are further areas favoured for investment where local, UK and EU investments are becoming more common and important.

Critically, however, all such interventions in land, labour and capital markets present limited opportunities to overcome market forces. Most have as a prime focus changing external perceptions of the locality, with the objective of diverting mobile investment from elsewhere – usually from competing areas in the UK, although increasingly competition is coming from Eastern Europe, etc.

Briefly, demand-side policy interventions tend to be limited, and in many ways restricted to Keynesian automatic stabilizers. It can be argued that, although any increase in incomes will tend to lead to improvements locally, a unit increase in benefits will have a greater impact than a comparable decrease in taxes – the multiplier effect is higher because the poor purchase more locally. Transferring income from the rich to the poor will have a real positive effect on the local economy, other things being equal; GDP can be increased, therefore, although production industries may not benefit greatly in terms of greater capacity. Nevertheless, apart from such fiscal transfers, most demand for an area is determined at the national level. However, local purchasing plans and strategies have been seen as able to improve local GDP significantly, often through import substitution, although many such contract compliance policies now fall foul of EU public procurement regulations.

If automatic stabilizers and small-scale local interventions have a limited, though significant, impact then, at all levels, but especially with regard to European Community Support Frameworks, partnerships are being promoted as the way forward in local economic development. While there may be benefits in rearranging agendas and prioritizing initiative areas, two decades and more of Enterprise Zones, Area Initiatives and European Partnerships suggest limited success, little new investment, and few catalytic effects. (The lack of major change is shown by the ranking of regions in the EU in 1981 and 1991 in terms of GDP per capita: Wales 85 and 83, Scotland 93 and 94, compared with EU averages of 100 and an improving UK position.)

However, it would be churlish not to recognize what has been achieved. As Alden (1995) argues, the Welsh economy has been transformed in the 1990s and 'has made considerable progress in achieving greater convergence with national performance' across a series of indicators. However, he continues, 'a prosperity gap remains' and is reflected in incomes. For Scotland, scepticism has been expressed on the sustainability of many developments initiated since the mid-1970s (Boyle *et al.*, 1989; Danson, 1991).

In a past-dominated, narrow economy, new firm formation and small and medium enterprises have become the panaceas in the mission statements of many agencies, and of the EU in particular. The business birth rate has increased, undoubtedly, since 1980 but questions should be raised over the ability of companies dependent on the local market to reverse decline. Limited success in replacing traditional major manufacturing employers has been achieved. More prosperous areas of the UK tend to have higher rates of new firm formation (and closure), suggesting that greater levels of incomes and wealth create the conditions for enterprise development rather than the converse. There is some evidence that a reliance on economic management through new firm birth and growth – nurtured by tax cuts, privatization giveaways and other monetary and fiscal policies – may promote instability in the local economy with surplus resources flowing into new ventures during the upturn, and out as readily in the recession (Danson, 1995a and 1996).

Building a new industrial structure based on small service sector companies and niche suppliers to multinational branch-plants may not lead to instant turnaround, therefore; indeed new problems may be generated. Research from across the developed world seems to confirm the economic programmes of the GLC (Greater London Council), many US states, Germany and the Alternative Economic Strategy (AES) had a critical theme in common: supporting indigenous, medium-sized enterprises arguably presents the best opportunity for long-run stable and sustainable development.

For the next few years, the prospects for Scotland and Wales, according to the regional forecasting organizations in the UK and Europe, are related to a gentle reaffirmation of the relevance of the north–south divide. Although predictions vary as to where this division will settle and when, long-established peripheral status appears to be promised to become apparent again in the two countries. The longer-term effects of the developments being introduced since the early 1970s by the UK's entry to the European Economic Community, the reorientation of Britain's trade towards the Continent, the completion of the Single Market, moves towards European Monetary Union are being consolidated, therefore; and these must be seen as of greater significance than the impact of the Structural Funds and other countervailing powers. As Mackay (1995) strongly argues, the European Union is failing to introduce sufficient and effective regional transfers to compensate for loss of independence and the centripetal forces of integration. Further, there is a clear suspicion in the work by Ramsden (1995) for the European Commission and by Morgan (1995), *inter alia*, that attempts 'to bridge the technology gap between European regions' will be as unsuccessful as strategies within the UK to reduce regional technology disparities (Danson, Lloyd and Newlands, 1991).

The other major planks of national and European regional development regeneration programmes – new firm formation and small and medium enterprises (SMEs) – seem equally open to scrutiny. Malecki and Nijkamp (1988) suggest uneven development is endemic, with no possibilities to overcome metropolitan core bias by compensating the periphery, although Vaessen and Keeble (1995) appear to see enough examples of the counterfactual, successful SME in the periphery to argue that divergence need not be inevitable.

Within the UK and across the EU, identification of the factors behind differential regional company birth rates continues to be problematic (Reynolds, Storey and Westhead, 1994). However, as with many other dimensions of relative economic performance, the ranking within countries appears fairly stable over time. So, even with major initiatives, a lack of alternative employment and an expanding economy, Scotland's proportion of self-employed was the lowest of any 'standard region' in Britain in 1994, with one of the lowest growth rates. By way of contrast, Wales performed well on this indicator both in historical and developmental terms (*Welsh Economic Review*, 1995).

Studies of the success of support for SMEs by the EU and national agencies are similarly unconvincing. Any strategic intervention by such actors in the regional economies of Scotland and Wales cannot be expected to reverse the long run declines described above. However, official evaluations for the Scottish Office (Turok *et al.*, 1994), the Strathclyde Integrated Development Operation (PIEDA, 1993) and for the European Commission do raise doubts over the sustainability of many regeneration efforts and over the effectiveness of the favoured market-oriented approach. While thousands of jobs are credited to business development activities under such programmes in Strathclyde and eastern Scotland over a decade, critically for the future there is no evidence of a 'real relative shift in the [region's] economic position', with no expansion of growth industries and no consistent pattern of change.

If the strategies drawn up for the qualifying areas of Wales and Scotland under various Community Support Frameworks are to succeed, then either these evaluations will have to be overturned retrospectively as overly pessimistic, or the deepening of a reliance on inward investment must be realized. In this regard, the failure of the UK government to sign the Social Chapter of the Maastricht Treaty so protecting the flexible and competitive labour markets here, the continuing perceived attractiveness of Scotland and Wales to mobile capital, and the low relative costs identified by the Northern Ireland Economic Research Centre should consolidate the ability to induce US and Japanese capital to locate in these parts of the periphery. Counter to such hopes, Bryan and Hill (1995) introduce additional factors to such analysis of location, beginning to unpick the importance of very high levels of capital investment and individual plants in improving Welsh, and by extension Scottish, industrial productivity improvements.

The message which comes through from these disparate studies is that relative regional economic performances are intrinsically stable over fairly long periods of time. The Commission's study of the future prospects for Scotland and Wales (CEC, 1994) suggests that major interventions – that is, interventions beyond current planned CSFs and other EU co-ordinated initiatives – would at best 'give more stability to Scotland and facilitate the process of industrial redeployment while maintaining minimum subsistence in rural zones'. This would require overcoming most of the entrenched and traditional tendencies described above, and imply a degree of intervention that is not currently being proposed by a UK party. For Wales, major changes would be necessary to diversify the economy sufficiently to overcome equally enduring obstacles to real, sustainable improvements.

Conclusion

In summary, the European Union and government agencies such as Scottish Enterprise and the Welsh Development Agency to a large extent have promoted and continue to promote the philosophy of regeneration through supply-side intervention. Policies and programmes are designed to be enabling and facilitating – laying the pre-conditions for enterprise. However, this is insufficient, with the market only able to create jobs through underemployment (graduates not using the full range of their skills and expertise, the unemployed being offered short-term contracts and 'training' periods between periods of idleness), while forcing activity rates lower (with the participation of many prime age males curtailed prematurely – activity rates fell in old industrial areas 1981 onwards to historically low levels, and increased in prosperous regions to record heights). On the demand side, progressive cuts in direct taxes and benefits deepen divides and exaggerate forces of uneven development, while the forces unleashed by 1992 and the completion of the Single European Market unfettered by a Social Chapter have done little to close the 'prosperity gap'. It is not at all apparent that, in the long run, the best efforts of the EU and EC, even with a more interventionist UK government, will reverse the well-established cycles of decline endemic in the parts of peripheral Europe. Maintaining sufficient cohesion between regions, states and communities to allow the benefits of 'Europe' to be realized remains the prime objective of structural interventions. However, until these challenge the dominant centripetal forces of the common market economy, the peripheralization of the Celtic nations will continue unabated. It is within this environment, and according to largely EU-determined policy frameworks, that planners must seek to promote sustainable economic development in Scotland and Wales. Constraints, limitations and threats describe their operating environment. Yet, while challenges and opportunities are market determined for regions, for nation-states the story is different.

References

Alden, J. 1995. *Transfer from Problem to Powerful Region: The Experience of Wales* (Cardiff, University of Wales).
Ashcroft, B., J. Love and J. Schouller 1987. *The Economic Effects of Inward Acquisition of Scottish Manufacturing Companies 1965–1980* (Edinburgh, Industry Department for Scotland, ESU Research Paper no.11).
Bachtler, J. 1995. 'Policy agenda for the decade', in S. Hardy, M. Hart, L. Albrechts and A. Katos (eds.), *An Enlarged Europe: Regions in Competition?* (London, Jessica Kingsley Publishers).
Beatty, C. and S. Fothergill 1994. 'Registered and hidden unemployment in areas of chronic industrial decline: the case of the UK coalfields', in S. Hardy, G. Lloyd and I.

Cundell (eds.), *Tackling Unemployment and Social Exclusion* (London, Regional Studies Association).

Boyle, S., M. Burns, M. Danson, J. Foster, D. Harrison and C. Woolfson 1989. *Scotland's Economy: Claiming the Future* (London, Verso).

Bryan, J. and S. Hill 1995. 'Made in Wales III: the European context', *Welsh Economic Review*, Vol.8, pp.56–64.

CEC (Commission of the European Communities) 1991. *Europe 2000* (Brussels, CEC).

CEC (Commission of the European Communities) 1994. *Study of Prospects in the Atlantic Regions* (Brussels, CEC).

Cecchini, P. 1988. *The European Challenge: 1992 The Benefits of a Single Market* (London, Wildwood House).

Cooke, P. 1987. 'Wales', in P. Damesick and P. Wood (eds.), *Regional Problems, Problem Regions, and Public Policy in the United Kingdom* (Oxford, Oxford University Press).

CSE London Working Group 1980. *The Alternative Economic Strategy: A Labour Movement Response to the Economic Crisis* (London, CSE Books).

Damer, S. 1990. *Glasgow: Going for a Song* (London, Lawrence and Wishart).

Damesick, P. and P. Wood (eds.) 1987. *Regional Problems, Problem Regions, and Public Policy in the United Kingdom* (Oxford, Oxford University Press).

Danson, M. 1991. 'The Scottish economy: the development of underdevelopment?', *Planning Outlook*, Vol.34, pp.89–95.

Danson, M. 1995a. 'New firm formation and regional economic development: an introduction and review of the Scottish experience', *Small Business Economics*, Vol.7, pp.81–7.

Danson, M. 1995b. 'Spatial impact of the social chapter', in S. Hardy, M. Hart, L. Albrechts and A. Katos (eds.), *An Enlarged Europe: Regions in Competition?* (London, Jessica Kingsley Publishers).

Danson, M. (ed.) 1996. *Small Firm Formation and Regional Economic Development* (London, Routledge).

Danson, M., G. Lloyd and D. Newlands 1991. 'The Scottish Development Agency, economic development and technology policy', in H. ter Heide (ed.), *Technological Change and Spatial Policy, Nederlande Geografische Studies* 112, pp.179–90.

Day, G. and G. Rees (eds.) 1991. *Regions, Nations and European Integration: Remaking the Celtic Periphery* (Cardiff, University of Wales Press).

Greater London Council 1985. *London Industrial Strategy* (London, GLC).

Gripaios, P. and T. Mangles 1993. 'An analysis of European super regions', *Regional Studies*, Vol.27, pp.745–50.

Hill, S. and M. Munday 1994. *The Regional Distribution of Foreign Manufacturing Investment in the UK* (London, Macmillan Press).

Holland, S. 1976. *Capital Versus the Regions* (London, Macmillan).

Keating, M. 1995. 'Europeanism and regionalism', in B. Jones and M. Keating (eds.), *The European Union and the Regions* (Oxford, Clarendon Press).

Lee, C. 1995. *Scotland and the United Kingdom: The Economy and the Union in the Twentieth Century* (Manchester, Manchester University Press).

Lovering, J. 1996. 'New myths of the Welsh economy', *Planet*, 116, pp.6–16.

Mackay, R. 1992. '1992 and relations with the EEC', in P. Townroe and R. Martin (eds.), *Regional Development in the 1990s: The British Isles in Transition* (London, Jessica Kingsley Publishers).

Mackay, R. 1995. 'European integration and public finance: the political economy of regional support', in S. Hardy, M. Hart, L. Albrechts and A. Katos (eds.), *An Enlarged Europe: Regions in Competition?* (London, Jessica Kingsley Publishers).

Malecki, E. and P. Nijkamp 1988. 'Technology and regional development: some thoughts on policy', *Environment and Planning C*, Vol.6, pp.383–99.

McKendrick, J. 1995. 'Poverty in the United Kingdom: the Celtic divide', in C. Philo (ed.), *Off the Map: The Social Geography of Poverty in the UK* (London, Child Poverty Action Group).

Morgan, K. 1995. *Institutions, Innovation and Regional Renewal: The Development Agency as Animateur* (Cardiff, Department of City and Regional Planning, University of Wales, Cardiff).

Myrdal, G. 1957. *Economic Theory and Underdeveloped Regions* (London, Duckworth).

PIEDA 1993. *Strathclyde IDO: Interim Evaluation* (Edinburgh, The Scottish Office Industry Department).

Ramsden, P. 1995. *The Right Kind of R&D?: Research and Technological Development in the New Objective 1 Programmes*, 1994–9 (Brussels, CEC).

Reynolds, P., D. Storey and P. Westhead 1994. 'Cross-national comparisons of the variation in new firm formation rates: an editorial overview', *Regional Studies*, Vol.29, pp.343–6.

Scottish Council Development and Industry 1995. *Exports Survey* (Edinburgh, SCDI).

Scottish Office Education and Industry Department 1995. *Index of Industrial Production*, Statistical Bulletin (Edinburgh, SOEID).

Slaven, A. 1975. *The Development of the West of Scotland: 1750–1960* (London, Routledge & Kegan Paul).

Smith, D. (ed.) 1980. *A People and a Proletariat: Essays in Welsh History 1880–1980* (London, Pluto Press).

Standing Commission on the Scottish Economy 1989. *Final Report* (STUC).

Townroe. P. and R. Martin (eds.) 1992. *Regional Development in the 1990s: The British Isles in Transition* (London, Jessica Kingsley Publishers).

Turok, I., J. Gray, K. Hayton, P. Raines, K. Clement and G. McBride 1994. *ERDF Business Development Evaluation* (Glasgow, University of Strathclyde).

Vaessen, P. and D. Keeble 1995. 'Growth-oriented SMEs in unfavourable regional environments', *Regional Studies*, Vol.29, pp.489–506.

Welsh Economic Review 1995. Vol.8 (Cardiff, University of Wales).

Welsh Office 1995. *Welsh Economic Trends, No. 16* (Cardiff, Welsh Office).

3

The Organization and Effectiveness of the Scottish Planning System

JEREMY ROWAN-ROBINSON

Introduction

The purpose of this chapter is to describe the legal and administrative framework within which the planning process in Scotland operates. A practitioner from England and Wales would find much that is familiar in this framework. None the less, there are some important differences – differences that go far beyond the addition of the word 'Scotland' to the principal planning Act. Indeed, in 1980 Derek Lyddon, then chief planner with the Scottish Development Department, stated that colleagues from the Department of the Environment had noted that Scottish planning '. . . is no longer an adaptation of English practice but a significantly different system . . .' (Lyddon, 1980, 66). Why this should have been so then, and how far this may be true today, are questions which this chapter will address.

The most obvious difference is in the administrative structure of the system and that is the starting-point for this chapter. However, the differences go much further than that and subsequent sections in the chapter consider national planning policy, regional reports, development plans and development control. It is not possible to draw attention to every difference; indeed, many of them are very minor. This chapter focuses on the most significant. The differences between the two systems are now considered in turn.

The administrative structure of the planning system

First of all, the administrative structure of the planning system in Scotland differs in important respects from that south of the border. Overall responsibility for planning in Scotland rests with the secretary of state for Scotland. The secretary of state operates through the Scottish Office. The Scottish Office is unusual in that it is central government organized on a territorial rather than a functional basis. Within its territory, it is in some ways a microcosm of Whitehall in that its separate functions are discharged through five departments. Planning functions are exercised on a day-to-day basis through the Scottish Office Development Department (SODevD), formerly the Scottish Development Department (SDD) and then the Scottish Office Environment Department. Although the Scottish Office operates within the economic and political mould set by the United Kingdom context (Begg and Pollock, 1991), it has some autonomy in policy-making, particularly where policy has no direct cross-border spill-overs (Midwinter *et al.*, 1991). Planning is one such policy area. It was this autonomy which allowed planning in Scotland to diverge significantly from that in England and Wales during the 1970s.

The most obvious manifestation of this divergence was the Local Government (Scotland) Act 1973. This introduced a regional structure of local government into Scotland. However, the structure ushered in by the 1973 Act did not spring up overnight. It developed from 'a long period of germination' (Mackenzie, 1989, 9). The period began in the 1960s and the early 1970s when regional planning was first undertaken in Scotland in an extensive way. The interest in regional planning was not new. Patrick Geddes had done much to develop the concept in the early part of the century. The first attempt at regional planning in Scotland was the Clyde Valley Regional Plan published in 1946. It was an advisory plan. Its objective was to guide local authorities in the Clyde Valley in tackling the problems of industrial growth and urban expansion arising from the industrial revolution. Regrettably, there was no provision for continuity and the plan was able to make no more than a one-off contribution.

The revival of interest in regional planning in the 1960s owed much to the perceived need to integrate physical and economic planning. The revival was given a considerable boost by the two white papers: *Central Scotland: a Programme for Development and Growth* (HMSO, 1963) and *The Scottish Economy 1965–1970: a Plan for Expansion* (HMSO, 1966). What was then the Development Department in the Scottish Office reflected this revival by containing divisions dealing with planning and with regional development. A series of eight regional plans were prepared in conjunction with the local authorities, addressing the twin themes of encouraging industrial expansion and accommodating population growth. Mackenzie observes that the plans:

> ... covered a large part of the country but were essentially advisory documents since no single local authority was capable of ensuring their implementation. They were in effect to suffer the same fate as their illustrious predecessor the Clyde Valley Regional Plan. (Mackenzie, 1989, p.9)

In other words, the plans were inevitably one-offs; there was no regional administration to oversee their implementation or to ensure monitoring and updating. The exercise none the less persuaded SDD officials of the benefits of a regional approach to policy implementation.

In 1966 the Royal Commission on Local Government in Scotland was set up to review the structure of local government and to make recommendations for reform. Midwinter *et al.* (1991) state that the reorganization was part of a wider movement towards modernizing municipal structures and creating larger units based on the needs of physical, social and economic planning. The Royal Commission concluded that, for the most part, existing local authorities were too small, the boundaries were out of date, the services were wrongly distributed and the financial resources were inadequate. It proposed in their place a two-tier structure of regions and districts which would combine power and effectiveness with local democracy and local accountability (HMSO, 1969a). South of the border, the Royal Commission on Local Government in England was recommending a new structure comprising fifty-eight unitary authorities and three areas of two-tier authorities (HMSO, 1969b). In England, the radical reform proposals were largely frustrated. In Scotland, however, they survived largely intact. Midwinter *et al.* suggest this was because of the strong role played by the civil servants and the weak input from politicians.

So far as the planning system is concerned, the Local Government (Scotland) Act 1973 introduced a two-tier structure of regional and district planning authorities for much of Scotland. In Strathclyde, Lothian, Fife, Central, Tayside and Grampian the regional planning authorities were given responsibility for the preparation of the structure plan. They were also given reserve powers to intervene in local plan preparation and in development control to safeguard the structure plan. The district planning authorities were to be responsible for local plan preparation and for day-to-day development control, although in both cases they had to have regard to the appropriate structure plan. In the three rural regions of Scotland (Highlands, Borders and Dumfries and Galloway) and the three islands areas (Orkney, Shetland and Western Isles), the regional councils, because of their small, dispersed populations, were constituted as unitary or all-purpose planning authorities.

The structure of the planning system in Scotland prior to the further reorganization in April 1996 (below) was, therefore, significantly different from that existing in England and Wales. The secretary of state for Scotland combines within the Scottish Office a number of portfolios which in England are held by separate ministers. As a result, the secretary of state and the civil servants are able to bring a more co-ordinated or integrated approach to planning at the national level. The creation of regional councils represented the outcome of Mackenzie's 'long period of germination'. The councils combined strategic planning with responsibility for key infrastructure provision such as roads, water supply, sewage disposal and education. Not only did they separate matters of strategy from detailed local planning; they were also able to bring a more integrated approach to the formulation and implementation of policy and proposals. 'The introduction of regional authorities . . .', observed the report of the Select Committee on Land Resource in Scotland,

... will have the effect of bringing into the ambit of one planning authority a number of areas at present each governed by its own authority, thus enabling planning to be approached on a wider and more comprehensive scale without the need for constant liaison between a number of different authorities with its attendant difficulties. (HMSO, 1972, para.54)

The 1973 Act would seem to be an illustration of the autonomy in policy – making referred to earlier, the structure of local government being a policy area with no serious cross-border spill-overs. The structure had implications for the distribution of planning functions and these are considered in more detail below. The structure did not, however, met with universal acclaim. It was criticized as remote, bureaucratic and inefficient. In 1988, the Scottish Conservative Party at its annual conference approved a motion calling for fundamental reform. The motion reflected dislike of Labour dominance of the regional councils; it may also have reflected a swing back towards small-scale local government in terms of areas and functions (Midwinter *et al.*, 1991). The outcome was the Local Government etc. (Scotland) Act 1994. This abolished the regional structure of local government as from 1 April 1996 and replaced it with a one-tier system of local authorities comprising twenty-nine unitary councils. The three all-purpose islands areas continue as before. At the same time, responsibility for water-supply and sewerage services has been removed from local authority control altogether and given to three new water authorities. The implications of this for planning are considered later in this chapter but the advantage of combining strategic planning with key infrastructure provision has been lost. After a long period of germination, regional planning in Scotland has proved to be relatively short-lived.

National planning policy

As in England and Wales, the essential characteristic of the Scottish planning system is that it is a system of discretionary development control operating within a framework of indicative policy guidance. There are, however, some quite significant differences in the nature of the policy guidance on both sides of the border. In this respect, attention is generally drawn to the Scottish experience with national planning guidelines.

The Nuffield Report, *Town and Country Planning* (1986), asserted that a central input into the planning process is essential, noting: 'Central government should produce and publish concise and consistent statements of national policy where national interests are at stake in questions of land use and development' (para.9.35). The authors go on to state that they were impressed by the Scottish example of national planning guidelines. They recommended their use, suitably adapted, in both England and Wales.

National planning guidelines (NPGs) were first introduced in Scotland in 1974. They arose from a recommendation of the Select Committee on Land Resource Use in Scotland (1972), which was inquiring into the usage of land resources in the rural and urban areas of Scotland. Concern was expressed that Scotland had suffered from insufficient national policy guidance in the past. If Scotland was to be in a position to compete for industry on favourable terms with other European countries, an indicative plan was required, said the Committee, on a national scale showing how it was intended to utilize the land for urban, industrial and recreational purposes (para.63). It recommended the preparation of a national structure plan.

The government, in its response to the Select Committee report, acknowledged the need for a more explicit top-down approach to land-use planning, but rejected the notion of a rigid national structure plan as impractical. The same benefits could be achieved, it was asserted, by building up as quickly as possible '. . . a set of guidelines on those aspects of land use which should be examined for Scotland as a whole' (HMSO, 1973a). These guidelines would become in due course '. . . a compendium of all that can usefully be said about the national framework for land use planning'. Guidelines were subsequently issued over a period of twelve years on topics such as coastal planning, aggregate working, skiing developments, high technology sites, the location of major retail development and agricultural land. Their principal characteristics have been identified as follows (Rowan-Robinson and Lloyd, 1987, 1992):

- the guidelines were based on a Land Use Summary Sheet which contained information about the land resource in question, described its national significance and indicated the prognosis for change;
- the guidelines tended to follow a Summary Sheet only where changes in the land resource were thought likely to have national significance. In other words, there was a discernible client requirement for strategic guidance;
- the guidelines were prepared, up to a point, in a consensual manner with planning authorities and other agencies signalling requirements and assisting in formulation;
- most of the guidelines identified land resources of national significance and sought to safeguard the resources from or for development;
- some of the guidelines indicated development planning priorities where land use issues were thought likely to have a national dimension;
- there was an emphasis on implementation by planning authorities through structure and local plans and through the development control process;
- the guidelines were not planning policy blueprints. They changed according to national planning priorities and were refined through subsequent action by planning authorities and other government agencies.

By indicating the circumstances in which a proposed use or development might have national significance, the guidelines enabled the secretary of state to disengage from day-to-day planning decisions. The minister simply directed that he should be notified of the submission of an application for development having national significance (as defined).

The degree of consensus in the preparation of policy guidance is worth emphasizing as it has been a feature in Scotland. This is not to suggest that there has been unanimity between the Scottish Office and planning authorities on policy matters; there have been important areas of disagreement. But the scale on which the planning system operates in Scotland allows for good liaison between the Scottish Office Development Department and planning authorities. As Lyddon (1980), former chief planner at the Scottish Development Department, commented:

> ... there is no doubt that the difficult process of drafting the guidelines was made easier, perhaps only made possible, by the ease of formal and informal contact with those likely to be affected. The ability to discuss with one local authority association, one society of directors of planning or twelve regional directors of planning covering the whole country, illustrates this. (Lyddon, 1980, p.66)

A similar point has been made by Mackenzie (1989), Lyddon's successor as chief planner: 'The size of the country, the structure of government and the relative ease of contact between the planners, the public, representative bodies and agencies means it is relatively simple to get relevant parties round the table to consider key issues, exchange ideas and to agree on how best to proceed' (Mackenzie, 1989, p.10).

The guidelines were an essentially reactive, problem-solving instrument (Rowan-Robinson et al., 1987). They were a response by the government to occasional conditions of uncertainty. Inevitably, given this reactive approach, the guidelines never became the 'compendium' of all that can usefully be said about national land-use planning. As Wannop (1980) observed, 'There are no guidelines for power generation resources or for land defence purposes. Financial resources for urban renewal and change are not covered – not surprisingly, but not consistent with any intention to make the guidelines a comprehensive framework for regional and district planning' (Wannop, 1980, p.64).

In August 1991, the Scottish Office Environment Department published a consultation paper reviewing the arrangements for strategic planning in Scotland. The paper proposed a number of changes, the most significant of which were the clarification of the different roles of guidelines and circulars and the gradual replacement of the national planning guidelines by national planning policy guidelines (NPPGs). The new guidelines would provide statements of government policy on nationally-important land-use and other planning matters, supported where appropriate by a locational framework. In other words, they would continue to fulfil broadly the same role in the planning system as NPGs but without the reliance on Land Use Summary Sheets. Circulars would, in future, be used to give guidance on policy implementation through legislative or procedural change. At the time of writing, what appear to be the key guidance notes are almost complete. Eleven NPPGs have been issued. They have focused on such issues as 'The Planning System', 'Land for Housing' (subsequently revised), 'Land for Business and Industry', 'Retailing' and 'Planning and Waste Management'. A draft NPPG has been issued on 'Transport and Planning'. The indications are that the identification of land resources having national significance which need to be safeguarded from or for development is now regarded as of less importance than issuing more general policy guidance on land-use issues of national importance. In this respect, the guidelines seem similar to the Planning Policy Guidance series in England and Wales and have moved away from building up the sort of national indicative plan that the Select Committee had in mind.

Regional reports

Regional reports provide a second illustration of the distinctive form of the Scottish framework of indicative policy guidance. The Local Government (Scotland) Act 1973 not only provided for a regional structure of local government (above) but introduced regional reports. Section 173 stated that a regional or general planning authority might at any time prepare and submit to the secretary of state a 'regional report' consisting of planning policy proposals. The report was not subject to procedural requirements and, although it has to be submitted to the secretary of state, is not subject to his or her approval. The minister is, however, required to make observations on each report submitted to him or her. The regional report was peculiar to Scotland. There has been no corresponding provision in the legislation for England and Wales.

The regional report has been described as a 'eureka' happening (McDonald, 1977). That is probably unfair. The genesis of the format of the report appears to lie, not in a flash of inspiration, but in a response to the drive for corporate plans in the build up to local government reorganization in 1975 (Crammond, 1989). The legislation is unclear about the precise purpose of such reports. During the committee stage of the Local Government (Scotland) Bill, George Younger, then under-secretary of state at the Scottish Office, said that regional reports might provide '. . . a basis for discussion between the Secretary of State and regional or islands councils on general development policy'. Alternatively, they might provide '. . . a basis of guidance for the preparation or review of structure plans'. Or, in the absence of structure plans or if a structure plan was out of date, a regional report might provide 'a guide to district planning authorities and, indeed, to developers on up-to-date policy trends'. The report was, therefore, envisaged as a flexible tool.

Crammond (1989) states that a combination of the emphasis in the Patterson Report (HMSO, 1973b) on a corporate approach to the management of the new local authorities and the preparations for local government reorganization being carried forward by the Scottish Office Co-ordinating Group resulted in an early call by the secretary of state for an initial round of regional reports. SDD Circular 4/1975 gave advance notice of this requirement and guidance on the expected content of the reports. Because of a decision to postpone the commencement of the new development plan system in Scotland until after reorganization in May 1975 (see below), the secretary of state indicated that he would require a first round of regional reports to be submitted to him by 15 May 1976. The reports were to be short statements of the main policies and priorities carrying implications for land use which had been adopted by the regional councils. They were, according to Forbes (1983), to be a 'state of the region' statement, together with an assessment of the region's perceived priorities for policy in the near future:

> While it was hoped that the reports would form a policy basis for the subsequent statement of land-use implications in the Structure Plans, the preparation of the Reports propelled the new Regions into a necessary corporate frame of mind. The Regional Report was unavoidably a corporate document, drawing upon the expertise and calculations of many different departments, and consciously relating policy ideas to forecasts of resources of both finance and manpower. (Forbes, 1983, p.106)

The result, as McDonald observed, was that '. . . within some 15 months of reorganization Scotland had achieved almost complete coverage by policy documents offering indications of priorities over broad policy areas backed up by statements of priorities for physical planning action' (McDonald, 1977, p.215). The reports set out the broad policy framework within which structure and local plans would be prepared, and enabled the secretary of state to advise authorities that structure plans should concern themselves with land-use issues and should be problem orientated (Young and Rowan-Robinson, 1985). Mackenzie (1989) states that the transition from the old-style development plan to structure plans was eased both by the effort that had gone into regional planning in Scotland (see above) and by the requirement for each regional council to produce in the first year of their existence a regional report setting out their overall policies.

In his report on the advisory and monitoring functions of the Scottish Development Department with respect to planning authorities, J. S. B. Martin recommended that the secretary of state should consider calling for regional reports on a regular basis as this would lead to better integration between planning and other policies (Young and Rowan-Robinson, 1985). The secretary of state declined to take up this recommendation, ostensibly because the problems associated with local government reorganization had been largely overcome, a range of planning policy instruments had been developed and good progress was being made with structure and local plans. Gillett (1983), however, suggests that there were difficulties in inviting a second round of regional reports because the implication of the legislation is that they were to be preliminary to structure plans. Whatever the explanation, the secretary of state made no further calls for regional reports. Although a few of the regional councils took the opportunity to update their reports, most did not and the reports became less useful with the passage of time. The result, suggest Begg and Pollock (1991), is the loss of an opportunity to continue with the forms of co-ordinated working within authorities which the process of preparing the first regional reports did much to encourage.

The Local Government etc. (Scotland) Act 1994, s.180 and Schedule 14 repealed s.173 of the 1973 Act. This brought to an end the experiment in Scotland with regional reports and removed another of the features which has distinguished the Scottish planning system from that in England and Wales.

Development plans

In this section, attention turns to the role of the development plan as part of the indicative policy guidance. Planning authorities in Scotland, like those in England and Wales, are under a duty to prepare a development plan for their area.

Following criticism in the early 1960s of the 'old-style' single-tier, map-based development plan, the Town and Country Planning (Scotland) Act 1969 followed legislation south of the border in introducing a new two-tier plan, comprising a structure plan and local plans. The structure plan, which comprises a written statement with a key diagram (but not a map) is to provide the strategic planning framework for an area; local plans are drawn up within the framework of the structure plan and set out detailed planning policies and proposals on a map base. The provisions for the new development plan were subsequently incorporated into Part II of the Town and Country Planning (Scotland) Act 1972. The new two-tier development plan system was intended to avoid the narrow focus and procedural delays inherent in the old style plan and to separate strategy from detail.

The provisions for two-tier development planning were introduced at a time when a unitary system of local government was under consideration in England and Wales. The reform of local government in Scotland produced a largely two-tier administrative structure (as above). The result was the separation of responsibility for structure planning (a regional planning authority function) and local planning (a district planning authority function) in all but the three rural regions and the islands areas in Scotland. A similar separation occurred in England and Wales.

The Local Government (Scotland) Act 1973 recognized that, with the separation of development planning functions in the two-tier areas of Scotland, it was necessary to give regional planning authorities the power to intervene to safeguard the structure plan from actions and decisions by district planning authorities that might work to its prejudice. In this respect, the planning system was the only local government function in Scotland where one tier of the new administrative structure was subordinated to the other. The Act achieved this in several ways. First of all, because of anticipated delays in preparing and approving structure plans, district planning authorities were given power to prepare a local plan in advance of a structure plan. Indeed, unlike the position in England and Wales, s.176 of the 1973 Act *required* district and general planning authorities as soon as practicable to prepare local plans for all parts of their area. However, the same section required district planning authorities to obtain the prior consent of the regional planning authority to prepare a plan in advance of the approval of the structure plan for the area. Furthermore, where a structure plan has been prepared, there is requirement that the local plan should conform to the structure plan as it stands at the time (1972 Act, s.9(9)).

The safeguards were not confined to the local plan-making process. Although planning applications in the two-tier areas of Scotland were made to and, in the great majority of cases, determined by district planning authorities, regional planning authorities, in contrast with the position of county councils in England and Wales, had reserve power to safeguard the structure plan. They could, under s.179 of the 1973 Act, call in a planning application from a district planning authority where the proposed development did not conform to the approved structure plan or where it raised a major planning issue of general significance. The secretary of state indicated that he expected the call-in powers to be used only in exceptional circumstances. Experience in practice showed, however, that some regional councils interpreted this power more widely than others (Young, 1979; Keating and Boyle, 1986).

In 1986 Nicolas Ridley, then secretary of state for the Environment, issued a green paper on *The Future of Development Plans* in England and Wales. It criticized structure plan preparation as unacceptably slow and structure plan policies as often over-detailed and irrelevant to strategic planning interests. The green paper proposed an end to structure plans south of the border and a move back towards unitary development plans with county councils preparing self-adopted statements of policy bearing some resemblance to the Scottish regional reports.

Shortly after, the Scottish Development Department issued a consultation paper stating that the government had no plans at that time to dispense with structure plans in Scotland. As Malcolm Rifkind, then secretary of state for

Scotland, commented '. . . by and large the complex arrangements for preparing, consulting on and submitting structure plans have been well-handled in Scotland, with the result that the system enjoys a better reputation than it does south of the border' (Rifkind, 1989, p.5). Part of the explanation for the better reputation lies in the delay in the introduction of the two-tier development plan process until after local government reorganization in May 1975. This enabled Scotland to learn from the experience of the first generation of English structure plans. Begg and Pollock (1991) observe that, with regional reports covering economic and social considerations, Scotland was able to avoid the difficulties which had occurred in England and Wales over the scope of structure plans. 'The way was left clear', they continue, '. . . for structure plans to evolve as comparatively simple documents, dealing with land-use planning only and confined to key issues of genuinely strategic importance' (Begg and Pollock, 1991, p.8). Their review of structure planning experience showed that the plans had been prepared relatively quickly and had not emerged as the cumbersome and inflexible documents which characterized the English system. They found that the average length of time required for the preparation and approval of the 'first round' structure plans in Scotland was three years and six months, compared with an equivalent figure of about eight years in England. Many of the first round plans were also approved without an examination in public, a factor which Begg and Pollock suggest reflected, in part, the degree of dialogue and consensus between the Scottish Office and regional councils over key strategic land-use issues.

It is important not to overstate the success of the new structure plan system in Scotland. There has at times been friction between the Scottish Office and regional councils. Roe (1989), for example, points to a lack of dialogue and consensus between the Scottish Office and Strathclyde Regional Council over the 1989 Review of the Regional Council's structure plan.

Differences between Scotland on the one hand and England and Wales on the other have been less marked with regard to local plans. One difference, however, was the requirement at the outset for total local plan coverage in Scotland. Reference was made earlier to s.173 of the Local Government (Scotland) Act 1973, which requires district and general planning authorities as soon as practicable to prepare local plans for all parts of their area. There is nothing in Scotland corresponding to a 'local plan scheme' (Town and Country Planning Act 1990, s.37). District and general planning authorities have discretion in deciding whether to cover their area with one district-wide plan or with two or more area plans. A structure plan may indicate local plan priorities. The trend at present is towards district-wide coverage (Collar, 1994). Local plan preparation in Scotland has taken longer than expected. Collar observes that '. . . despite this requirement being twenty years old, only 81% of Scotland is covered by an adopted local plan' (Collar, 1994, p.52). Begg and Pollock attribute the delay partly to the requirement that local plans should conform generally to the structure plan and partly to the time taken to prepare a district-wide plan. They suggest, however, that the percentage of local plans adopted is much greater than in England.

Local government reorganization in April 1996 has had implications for the development planning process in Scotland. Twenty-nine unitary authorities have replaced the current two-tier arrangement of regional and district councils. The new councils exercise all local authority functions, including all planning functions (development planning and development control) for their area. The three islands councils of Orkney, Shetland and the Western Isles continue to exist and to perform all functions. The most important change, and the one that has given rise to some concern, is the provision for structure plans. A new s.4A has been inserted into the Town and Country Planning (Scotland) Act 1972. It confers power on the secretary of state to designate structure plan areas. The district of every planning authority will be included in such an area. Where the designated structure plan area falls wholly within the area of the authority there should be no problem, although where that area differs from that for which a structure plan is currently in force, the new planning authority will have to prepare a structure plan for the new area and submit it for approval. A designated structure plan area may, however, extend to the district or part of the district of more than one authority. Where it does so, the planning authorities concerned are jointly to carry out the structure plan functions.

The new structure plan areas were notified to planning authorities by the Scottish Office in September 1995. There are to be seventeen such areas. Of these, eleven coincide with the boundaries of new authorities. The remaining six areas cross the boundaries of two or more of the new authorities. The concern is over the efficiency, and indeed the prospects for harmony, of joint working arrangements. The legislation anticipates possible problems by providing that, at the request of the constituent authorities or of his or her own volition, the secretary of state may establish a joint board to discharge structure plan functions.

The abolition of regional planning authorities in April 1996 brought to an end the arrangement described above whereby one tier of local government could call in a planning application from another in order to safeguard the structure plan. The secretary of state, however, continues to be able to call in a planning application if it touches on matters of national interest and could do so where a planning authority are minded to grant planning permission contrary to the terms of an approved structure plan.

Development control

The essential characteristic of the Scottish planning system was described earlier in this chapter as a system of discretionary development control operating within a framework of indicative policy guidance. Having considered the framework of policy guidance, it is appropriate to turn now to the process of discretionary control.

When Lyddon's colleagues in the Department of the Environment described planning in Scotland as a significantly different system to that in England and Wales (above), it is probable that they had in mind the administrative structure of the system and the policy framework rather than development control. The process of development control is broadly the same on both sides of the border. It is in essence a conventional licensing system. Development is prohibited in the absence of a grant of planning permission. 'Development' is comprehensively defined. In deciding whether to grant permission for development, the planning authority must have regard to the development plan and to all other material considerations. Sanctions are available in the event of a breach of planning control. None the less, there are considerable differences of detail, differences which could trip up the unwary practitioner. The process of control operates under separate legislation and against the background of a different legal system. The Royal Commission on the Constitution (1969–73) noted that the Scottish and English legal systems '. . . remain separate and – a unique constitutional phenomenon within a unitary state – stand to this day in the same juridical relationship to one another as they do individually to the system of any other foreign country' (HMSO, 1974). None the less, the differences are not as great as this separation might suggest. Development control is a creature of statute and, although Scotland enjoys separate legislation, the legislation has tended to follow and to be modelled on that operating in England and Wales. It is not possible in this section to describe all the differences; many of them in any event are very minor. Instead, attention will be drawn to the role of the courts and to the more important of the differences in the legislation.

The role of the courts

The Outer and Inner Houses of the Court of Session in Scotland fulfil a similar function to that of the High Court and the Court of Appeal in England and Wales. There is a right of appeal from the Inner House to the House of Lords. Although the amount of planning litigation in Scotland has increased in recent years, far fewer such cases, relative to population, come before the Scottish courts than is the position in England. Wade and Forsyth (1994) say of the position in England '. . . of all the administrative controls and services which multiply in the modern state, the one which generates most litigation in the courts is town and country planning' (Wade and Forsyth, 1994, p.183). It has been suggested that there are two reasons for the relatively limited activity in Scotland (Rowan-Robinson and Young, 1987). First of all, until comparatively recently the Scottish courts appeared to afford little encouragement to those seeking to challenge the decisions of administrative authorities. Secondly, development pressures have tended to be less strong in Scotland so that there may be less financial incentive to challenge decisions in the courts.

Because of the volume of litigation in this field in England and Wales, and because of the similarity of the legislation, decisions by the courts south of the border, although not binding in Scotland, are likely to be persuasive. There is, none the less, potential for judicial divergence. It has been suggested, for example, that some Scottish judges have shown themselves particularly concerned to protect private rights, perhaps to a greater extent than has been evident in England (Young and Rowan-Robinson, 1985). This may be illustrated by reference to the decision in *British Airports Authority* v. *Secretary of State for Scotland* [1979] SC 200 in which the Court of Session accepted the proposition that a condition which was unnecessary was *ultra vires*, a proposition that had been rejected by the English courts. And the Court of Appeal in England in the case of *R* v. *Greenwich London Borough Council, ex parte Patel* [1985] JPL 851 declined to follow what might fairly be described as a 'private rights'-orientated interpretation of the Court of Session in *McDaid* v. *Clydebank District Council* [1984] SLT 162. The cases turned on similarly worded legislation dealing with the jurisdiction of the courts to question the validity of enforcement notices.

Publicity for planning applications

The development control process is intended to be an open, objective licensing process. For a while, the most notable difference between the processes on both sides of the border focused on the publicity requirements for planning applications. This is an area where differences still remain. In 1975 the categories of 'bad neighbour' development – development which has to be the subject of public notice because it is potentially injurious of amenity – were substantially extended in Scotland following pressure for this from bodies such as the Scottish Law Commission, the Scottish Committee of the Council on Tribunals, the Select Committee on Scottish Affairs and the Law Society of Scotland. The Town and Country Planning (General Development) (Scotland) Order 1975 added five categories of development defined not by the type of development but by their impact on the locality. These included the construction or use of buildings which will affect residential property by reason of fumes, noise, vibration, smoke, artificial lighting or the discharge of any solid or liquid substance; will alter the character of an area of established amenity; will bring crowds into a generally quiet area; will cause activity and noise between the hours of 8p.m. and 8a.m.; and will introduce significant change into a homogeneous area. These categories reappear in the new Order of 1992. The effect is to subject to a public notice requirement a considerably larger number of planning applications than is the case in England and Wales.

In 1977 the Scottish Development Department issued a consultation paper entitled *Review of the Management of Planning*. In a section headed 'What do we want from Planning?', the paper noted that planning can operate as a 'neighbour protection service'. The paper went on to suggest that 'at this level planning is doing little more than providing a conciliation and arbitration service between neighbours. It makes a lot of work for planning authorities' (SDD, 1977, p.5). It went on to suggest that if this role were to be reduced staff could be set free for arguably more important tasks. Many of the responses to the paper, however, endorsed the role of planning as a neighbour protection service and urged that it should be strengthened. As a result, a neighbour notification requirement was introduced. A similar requirement had previously existed in the building control legislation. However, many objections received to building warrant applications related not to the construction of the building but to the principle of development. The neighbour notification requirement was accordingly switched from the building control legislation to the development control process. The Town and Country Planning (General Development) (Scotland) Order 1981 introduced a requirement for an applicant for planning permission to serve notice on a person having a notifiable interest in neighbouring land.

It was some time before England and Wales followed suit. In *R* v. *Secretary of State for the Environment, ex parte Kent* [1988] JPL 706; [1990] JPL 124 the court rejected the suggestion that there was any general duty of notification. Eventually, during the passage of the Planning and Compensation Bill through Parliament, an undertaking was given by the government that all planning applications should receive publicity. The Town and Country Planning General Development (Amendment) (No. 4) Order 1992 subsequently introduced a requirement in England and Wales to notify any adjoining owner or occupier of a planning application which is not otherwise the subject of publicity.

Planning agreements

Curiously for a licensing system, the development control process has always allowed room for negotiation. Section 50 of the Town and Country Planning (Scotland) Act 1972 provides that a planning authority may enter into an agreement with any person interested in land in their area, in so far as the interest of that person enables him to bind the land, for the purpose of restricting or regulating the development or use of the land. Once recorded in the Register of Sasines or in the Land Register for Scotland, an agreement is enforceable by the planning authority against singular successors.

For many years, the legislative provisions relating to agreements on both sides of the border were similar. Notwithstanding this, it seemed likely that the potential scope of agreements in Scotland was wider than in England and Wales. In particular, questions about the enforceability of positive obligations in agreements against successors in title has never been an issue in Scotland.

For a while, there was much discussion south of the border of the question of the enforceability of positive covenants contained in planning agreements. A number of English commentators took the view that the corresponding English provision could not be interpreted in isolation from the common law background. At common law, positive covenants relating to land can bind the person who originally undertakes the obligation but can never bind successors in title. Restrictive covenants can bind successors in title but only if the covenants conform to the strict requirements spelt out in the case of *Tulk* v. *Moxhay* [1848] 2 Ph 774. Amongst other requirements, the covenants must be taken for the benefit of the adjacent land and the person seeking to enforce them must be in possession of the adjacent land. It was argued by the commentators that the intention of the English provision relating to planning agreements was to give the planning authority the same standing as an adjacent landowner. In other words, they could enforce restrictive but not positive covenants. This difficulty was eventually overcome by an express statutory provision in s.126 of the Housing Act 1974 which provided that positive covenants could be enforced against successors in title. That provision was subsequently replaced by s.33 of the Local Government (Miscellaneous Provisions) Act 1982 and that, in turn, has been overtaken by s.12 of the Planning and Compensation Act 1991 (see below), which makes specific provision for positive as well as restrictive planning obligations which may be enforced by a local planning authority against successors in title.

In Scotland it has always been the case that obligations, positive or restrictive, may, if properly constituted, run with the land so as to bind successors in title. The scope of s.50 of the 1972 Act dealing with planning agreements simply turned on an interpretation of the words 'restricting or regulating' the development or use of the land. Although the word 'restricting' would seem to have negative connotations, it was thought that 'regulating' could be construed to encompass positive obligations. As SODevD Circular 12/1996 observes, provided the overall purpose of the agreement is to restrict or regulate the development, an agreement can incorporate positive obligations (Annex 2).

The Planning and Compensation Act 1991 subsequently changed the format of the provision in England and Wales and introduced the term 'planning obligations' in place of agreements. The changes had been canvassed by the Department of the Environment in a consultation paper, *Planning Agreements: Consultation Paper and Draft Guidance* (1989). The paper proposed, first of all, that the consensual basis of planning agreements should be retained but that provision should be made for unilateral undertakings. This would allow a developer to offer to take on certain obligations where an authority had refused to enter into an agreement. That undertaking would then be a material consideration in an appeal and if planning permission was granted following the appeal, the undertaking would bind the developer. Secondly, it proposed that provision should be made for application to the secretary of state to discharge planning obligations after a specified period if the obligations serve no further useful planning purpose. The somewhat limited jurisdiction of the Lands Tribunal in such matters would be ended. These changes were introduced in the 1991 Act which, together with DoE Circular 16/91 *Planning Obligations*, also defined more clearly the purposes which planning obligations could fulfil.

No such changes have been made in Scotland. The term 'planning obligations' has not been introduced, there is no provision in the legislation for unilateral undertakings, planning agreements may still only be employed to restrict or regulate the development or use of land, and there is no provision for reviewing agreements unless such provision has been built into an agreement. The Lands Tribunal for Scotland has never had jurisdiction with regard to reviewing obligations in an agreement. Although the provision for review might be useful, there has been no pressure in Scotland for any further change in the law relating to agreements (Rowan-Robinson and Durman, 1992).

Notwithstanding these differences in the law, it would seem that agreements have been used on both sides of the border for broadly similar purposes (Grimley *et al.*, 1992; Rowan-Robinson and Durman, 1992). They have been used to remove obstacles to the grant of planning permission, to secure tighter control over development and to deal with the distribution of infrastructure costs. There is little evidence on either side of the border of the pursuit by planning authorities of benefits which are wholly unrelated to the development proposed.

Enforcement

A system of regulation requires to be supported by an enforcement regime and development control is no exception. The changes in the enforcement regime introduced in the Planning and Compensation Act 1991 have helped to bring the Scottish system more closely in line with that in England and Wales. Uncertainty about the availability of interdict (the Scottish equivalent of an injunction) as a remedy for a breach of planning control has now been resolved; and the failure to comply with an enforcement notice requiring steps to be taken other than the discontinuance of a use of land is now an offence in Scotland, as it always has been in England.

There remain some differences in practice, in particular with regard to the employment of the criminal law. Scotland has its own very distinctive system of criminal justice and procedure. This affects enforcement in two ways (Rowan-Robinson and Young, 1987). First of all, Scotland has a system of independent public prosecution. If a planning authority wishes to prosecute someone in the Sheriff Court for a breach of planning control, it has to refer the papers to the procurator fiscal. The fiscal is not obliged to prosecute a case which is referred by a planning authority; he or she has a discretion. Notwithstanding the resolution of the authority to invoke the criminal law, the fiscal may decide, having regard to the relative seriousness of the case or to alternative methods of disposal, not to proceed. Local authorities have, from time to time, suggested that fiscals are reluctant to prosecute planning cases (SDD, 1984; Rowan-Robinson and Ross, 1994). Whatever the substance of this criticism, the consequence is that planning authorities may be reluctant to refer cases for prosecution. This can have consequences for the operation of the enforcement regime as a whole. Attention is focused instead on attempting to negotiate a settlement of the breach of control, a settlement which may result in some compromise of planning standards (SDD, 1984).

Secondly, the position in Scotland is that '... no person can be convicted of a crime or a statutory offence ... unless there is evidence of at least two witnesses implicating the person accused with the commission of the crime or offence with which he is charged' (*Morton* v. *HM Advocate* [1938] JC 50. An SDD (1984) research report on *The Enforcement of Planning Control in Scotland* commented on the extent to which this requirement for corroboration can create problems for planning authorities. If nothing else, it is likely to make prosecution a more expensive business in Scotland than in England and Wales.

The problems encountered by planning authorities in enforcing planning control in practice seem to have been much the same on both sides of the border. There was ample opportunity for those intent on resisting control to do so (Rowan-Robinson and Young, 1987; Jowell and Millichap, 1986; Carnwath, 1989). It is likely, however, that the changes brought in by the Planning and Compensation Act 1991 will have gone some way towards tightening up the regime.

Development in the countryside

Broadly speaking, development control applies to the countryside in much the same way as it applies to urban areas. On both sides of the border, considerably more activities in the countryside are exempted from control than in urban areas and there are some minor differences between urban and rural areas in the operation of control. It is with regard to countryside designations that Scotland differs from England and Wales. Designations are important as they can influence development control decisions.

Scotland's countryside is generally acknowledged to be magnificent. There are, however, no national parks; nor is the designation 'area of outstanding natural beauty' employed. The desirability of introducing national parks has been debated from time to time (Countryside Commission for Scotland, 1974, 1991). Instead, the secretary of state in 1948 issued a number of National Park Directions, requiring all planning applications in five areas of outstanding scenic importance to be notified to him so that he could decide whether they should be called-in.

In 1978, the Countryside Commission for Scotland published a survey of Scotland's scenery. It identified forty areas of outstanding landscape, termed national scenic areas, which could form the basis for a new framework for landscape conservation. The new framework came in SDD Circular 20/1980. The circular acknowledged that special measures were 'justified in respect of areas of high quality scenery of national interest to ensure that due consideration is given to the protection of this national resource' (para.1). The National Park Directions were replaced by a new regime which required planning authorities to notify the Countryside Commission for Scotland on receipt of planning applications for certain classes of development (generally all developments of any scale) in national scenic areas. If a planning authority proposed to grant permission for such development against the advice of the commission, the authority had first to notify the secretary of state who could decide whether to call-in the application.

The Countryside Commission for Scotland was replaced by Scottish Natural Heritage (SNH) in 1992. The Natural Heritage (Scotland) Act 1991, s.6 provides for a new designation – a natural heritage area. Natural heritage areas will be designated by the secretary of state on the recommendation of SNH. No such areas have yet been designated. These areas must be considered by SNH to be of outstanding value to Scotland's natural heritage and to justify special protection measures. Natural heritage is defined to include the flora and fauna of Scotland, its geological and physiographical features and its natural beauty and amenity (s.1). No new national scenic areas will be designated, but those already designated will continue unless replaced by a natural heritage area designation. The notification regime will continue and planning authorities are now required under s.262C of the 1972 Act to pay special attention to the desirability of preserving or enhancing the character or appearance of a natural heritage area when exercising its powers under the 1972 Act with respect to land within such an area or a national scenic area.

Conclusion

The conclusion from this discussion must be that, following local government reorganization, Scottish planning will no longer be a significantly different system from that operating in England and Wales. At the time of writing, it seems that differences in the administrative structure of the two systems are likely to remain. The distinctive tier of regional councils in Scotland has, however, disappeared. The regional report has also disappeared – it had already done so for all practical purposes. Scotland has lost the benefit of an integrated approach to strategic planning and key infrastructure provision – a loss which will bring it into line with England and Wales. National planning guidelines are giving way to national planning policy guidelines which are similar to the planning policy guidelines south of the border and both systems have come closer together in their approach to structure and local plans. Scotland retains its own distinctive legal system and the differences which arise from that for the development control process will remain. But these differences, and other divergences in the legislation, are not significant. Perhaps the most notable remaining difference will be the closer liaison that is possible in Scotland because of the relatively small number in the planning community.

Legislation from the European Union may also be a force for convergence between the systems. At present, the impact of the EU on the planning process is limited. EC Directive 85/337 on the assessment of the effects of certain public and private projects on the environment has been the most significant piece of legislation to affect the control of development. Others, such as EC Directive 90/313 on the freedom of access to information on the environment, have had a more indirect effect on the planning process.

A greater degree of conformity between the two systems will eliminate confusion. That is to be welcomed. However, two questions arise. First of all, do the differences that have developed over the years between the two systems reflect an attempt to apply Scottish solutions to Scottish problems? The answer is that, for the most part, the differences identified in this chapter reflect Scottish solutions to problems which are, or have been, common to both systems. The best administrative structure for the management of change, the need to identify and safeguard land resources of national significance, and the most effective approach to development planning are questions which have required answers on both sides of the border.

The second question is whether the solutions attempted in Scotland have anything to offer the planning system in England and Wales. The answer is yes – up to a point. There is room for differing views about the benefits of regional planning, but the integrated and co-ordinated approach, including the integration of key infrastructure provision, which it offers to the management of change has advantages, advantages which are likely to be missed in Scotland following local government reorganization. National planning guidelines provided a useful mechanism for identifying and safeguarding land resources of national significance and the benefits of this have already been harnessed in England and Wales, although in diluted form, in the planning policy guidance notes. The narrower scope of structure plans and the drive for area-wide local plans are initiatives that are now being pursued in both systems.

Reference was made at the beginning of this chapter to Scottish Office autonomy in policy-making in areas where there is no cross-border spill-over. This autonomy remains and it is to be hoped that it will continue to be employed from time to time to develop Scottish solutions to planning problems from which both systems may learn.

References

Begg, H. M. and S. H. A. Pollock 1991. 'Development plans in Scotland since 1975', *Scottish Geographical Magazine*, Vol.107, No.1, p.4.
Carnwath, R. 1989. *Enforcing Planning Control* (London, HMSO).
Collar, N. 1994. *Planning* (Edinburgh, W. Green and Son Ltd.).
Countryside Commission for Scotland 1974. *A Park System for Scotland* (Perth, CCS).
Countryside Commission for Scotland 1978. *Scotland's Scenic Heritage* (Perth, CCS).
Countryside Commission for Scotland 1991. *The Mountain Areas of Scotland* (Perth, CCS).
Crammond, R. D. 1989. 'Regional reports: a unique Scottish planning initiative', in *A Celebration of Planning in Scotland: Essays to Celebrate the 75th Anniversary of the Royal Town Planning Institute in Scotland 1914–1989* (Edinburgh, RTPI).
Forbes, J. 1983. 'A view of planning in Scotland, 1974–1984', *Scottish Geographical Magazine*, p.104.
Gillett, E. 1983. *Investment in the Environment* (Aberdeen, Aberdeen University Press).
Grimley, J. R. Eve in Association with Thames Polytechnic School of Land and Construction Management and Alsop Wilkinson, Solicitors, 1992. *The Use of Planning Agreements* (London, HMSO).
HMSO 1963. *Central Scotland: A Programme for Expansion*, Cmnd 2188 (London).
HMSO 1966. *The Scottish Economy 1965–1970: A Plan for Expansion*, Cmnd 2864 (London).
HMSO 1969a. *Royal Commission on Local Government in Scotland*, Cmnd 4150 (London).
HMSO 1969b. *Royal Commission on Local Government in England 1966–1969*, Cmnd 4040 (London).
HMSO 1972. Select Committee on Scottish Affairs Session 1971–2, *Land Resource Use in Scotland* (Edinburgh, Select Committee on Scottish Affairs).
HMSO 1973a. *Land Resource Use in Scotland: The Government's Observations on the Report of the Select Committee on Scottish Affairs*, Cmnd 5428 (London).
HMSO 1973b. *The New Scottish Local Authorities: Operation and Management Structure* (London).
HMSO 1974. *Report of the Royal Commission on the Constitution, 1969–1973*, Cmnd 5460 (London).
Jowell, J. and D. Millichap 1986. 'The enforcement of planning law: a report and some proposals', *Journal of Planning and Environmental Law*, 482.
Keating, M. and R. Boyle 1986. *Remaking Urban Scotland* (Edinburgh, Edinburgh University Press).
Lyddon, D. 1980. 'Scottish planning in practice – 2: influences and comparisons', *The Planner*, Vol.66, No.3, May/June.
Mackenzie, A. 1989. 'The Scottish planning system', *The Planner*, February, 8.
McDonald, S. T. 1977. 'The regional report in Scotland: a study of change in the planning process', *Town Planning Review*, Vol.48, p.215.
Midwinter, A., M. Keating and J. Mitchell 1991. *Politics and Public Policy in Scotland* (London, Macmillan).
Nuffield Foundation 1986. *Town and Country Planning* (London, Nuffield Foundation).
Rifkind, M. 1989. 'Planning in Scotland since 1979', in *A Celebration of Planning in Scotland: Essays to Celebrate the 75th Anniversary of the Royal Town Planning Institute in Scotland 1914–1989* (Edinburgh, RTPI).

Roe, E. 1989. 'Structure planning and the Scottish Office: the Strathclyde experience', *Scottish Planning Law and Practice*, Vol.28, p.72.

Rowan-Robinson, J. and R. Durman 1992. *Section 50 Agreements* (Edinburgh, Scottish Office Central Research Unit).

Rowan-Robinson, J. and M. G. Lloyd 1991. 'National planning guidelines: a strategic opportunity wasting away?', *Planning Practice and Research*, Vol.6 No.3, p.16.

Rowan-Robinson, J., M. G. Lloyd and R. Elliott 1987. 'National planning guidelines and strategic planning: matching context and method', *Town Planning Review*, Vol.58, No.4, p.369.

Rowan-Robinson, J. and A. Ross 1994. 'Enforcement of environmental regulation in Britain: strengthening the link', *Journal of Planning and Environmental Law*, p.200.

Rowan-Robinson, J. and E. Young 1987. 'Enforcement – the weakest link in the Scottish planning control system', *Urban Law and Policy*, Vol.8, p.255.

Scottish Development Department 1984. *The Enforcement of Planning Control in Scotland, Consultant's Report by J. Rowan-Robinson, E. Young and I. McLarty* (Edinburgh, SDD).

Wade, H.W. R. and C. Forsyth 1994. *Administrative Law* (Oxford, Clarendon Press).

Wannop, U. 1980. 'Scottish planning in practice: four distinctive characteristics', *The Planner*, 64.

Young, E. 1979. 'Call in of planning applications by regional planning authorities', *Journal of Planning and Environmental Law*, 358.

Young, E. and J. Rowan-Robinson 1985. *Scottish Planning Law and Procedure* (Glasgow, Wm. Hodge and Co. Ltd.).

4

Land-Use Planning in Wales: The Conflict between State Centrality and Territorial Nationalism

MARK TEWDWR-JONES

Introduction

The land-use planning system in Wales is now facing a number of challenges. The structural reform of local government may undermine the effectiveness of strategic planning and increase the role of both the Welsh Office and the non-elected quasi-autonomous national governmental organizations in determining strategic priorities. Similarly, the last four years have witnessed a great deal of uncertainty on the development control process operated by some district authorities, with alleged malpractices being implemented by decision-makers deliberately to frustrate a system devised in England that does not, in their opinion, reflect socio-political nuances existing in Wales.

Nevertheless, while there has been considerable progress in the efficiency and effectiveness of the planning system, commentators have suggested that this success has resulted from a unique partnership between the key actors in the Welsh planning process and a consensus between central and local government. Land-use planning in Wales is poised between a distinctive socio-political formation and the centralized legal and bureaucratic apparatus of the British state. This chapter focuses on the implications of this juxtaposition for the planning system in the Principality, by examining the structure and operation of the Welsh planning system at both a national and local level. The principal research area assessed is the extent to which the Welsh Office in its administration of the land-use planning system reflects regional and, to some extent unique, political realities or reinforces wider policy- and decision-making intervention originating in England.

Planning's legislative and administrative structure

The similar legal and administrative planning arrangements that exist in the two countries tends to support the assumption that, from purely a land-use perspective, Wales is merely a western extension of England. Constitutionally as part of the United Kingdom, 'Welsh' planning has an identical legal but subtly different policy approach to the land-use system. Although the planning process has been considerably amended over the years, the key statute governing 'planning' in both England and Wales is the singular 1990 Town and Country Planning Act, as amended by the 1991 Planning and Compensation Act. The 1990 Act sets out the framework for the preparation of structure and local plans and the administration of the development control system.

Until the introduction of the 1991 Planning and Compensation Act, one of the main things that distinguished Welsh planning was the lack of mandatory prepared district development plans; local plan coverage was sparse throughout the country. This is only now starting to be addressed, albeit very slowly, through a requirement in the 1991 Act enforcing district authorities in Wales to prepare district-wide local plans. The 1991 Act also introduced section 54A to the 1990 Act further strengthening the status of development plans for development control purposes; this clause applies equally to England as it does to Wales, and Scotland has an identical provision. Other statutory planning requirements identical to England include the requirement for county councils to approve structure plans, and the content of the use classes and general permitted development orders. Indeed, overall there are far more similarities than differences between planning legislation west and east of Offa's Dyke. However, the statutory planning process is arguably more distinctive, particularly at the national all-Wales level. There are several reasons for this that relate to the good relations that have existed between agencies of governance in Wales, the strategic planning guidance exercise that has been developed since 1990, and underlying these two initiatives, the particular socio-political characteristics existing in the country. In assessing each of these distinctive arrangements in more detail, it is possible to examine the issues of territorial nationalism to illustrate the distinctive features of the land-use planning system in Wales by reference to political and cultural aspects of administrative implementation.

The reorganization of local government in Wales in 1974 introduced a two-tier system of eight counties and thirty-seven districts. All of these authorities existed autonomously and had specific powers. The planning framework that was operated by this structure of local government was the 1971 Town and Country Planning Act, subsequently consolidated by the 1990 Act. The land-use planning system in Wales comprised: legislation and central government Planning Policy Guidance and circulars at the all-Wales level; structure plans providing key strategic direction at the county council level; and local plans providing detailed local policies at the district council level from which the development control process is operated. Although minor changes have occurred to this broad framework, the administrative structure of the planning process in Wales remained broadly unchanged for a twenty-year period until the implementation of the 1994 Local Government (Wales) Act completely modified the local government structure and, in turn, the planning system operated by it.

The 1994 Act created a new form of local government structure in Wales with the abolition of the eight counties and thirty-seven districts and their replacement with twenty-two 'all-purpose' unitary authorities. In England, local government is undergoing an uncertain future, with restructuring planned for certain areas and retention of the status quo for others. The principal reason for this difference was the decision by the government to progress local government reorganization separately in each of the three countries of Britain. Scotland and Wales were dealt with by the respective secretaries of state, while in England the Department of the Environment established an independent Local Government Commission to consider the scope for reorganization in different areas. Although the reorganization in Wales marked a true separation from Department of the Environment's proposals, the nature of local governance in the principality has developed characteristically separate to England. As the Council for Welsh Districts state, 'Wales is different. It has a distinctive cultural, linguistic and political environment. The distinctive circumstances of Wales make clear the case for a vibrant system of local government that can respond to local needs and differences' (CWD, 1991, para. 10.1).

Hambleton and Mills (1993) also highlight a number of structural and administrative differences in local government in Wales compared with the English picture, portraying the governance framework prior to 1994 as a 'picture of stability and consensus' (p.46). While Boyne *et al.* (1991) maintain that central government through the Welsh Office has been prominent in transforming relations between central and local government by fostering, with a key but relatively small number of local authorities, a system of 'good government' (p.12). They conclude that the distinctive characteristics of Wales effectively amount to a separate Welsh local government system.

The contents of the Local (Government) Wales Act 1994 were essentially derived from the Welsh Office's white paper *Local Government in Wales: A Charter for the Future* published on 1 March 1993 (Welsh Office, 1993b). The Act introduced twenty-two unitary authorities to replace the existing forty-five councils from 1 April 1996 with shadow political elections occurring one year previously. The Welsh Office's reasoning for restructuring local government in Wales was contained in two often-quoted key paragraphs within the white paper:

> The Government believes that the present system of local government in Wales is not widely understood, nor does it sufficiently reflect people's identification with their own communities and loyalties. Moreover, a two-tier system of counties and districts contain within it a potential for friction between

authorities – and for duplication of administration – which reduces the ability of the system to deliver services economically, efficiently and effectively. And there is little public understanding of the responsibilities of each tier, a situation which undermines the direct accountability to local people upon which good local government should be based (Welsh Office, 1993b, paragraphs 1.2, 1.3).

The principal issues for the land-use planning system in Wales caused by the reorganization process relate to three areas, and each of these effectively introduces a very different planning approach to that operating in England (Harris and Tewdwr-Jones, 1995). How will Welsh Office planning policy guidance be expressed and delivered to the new unitary authorities? How will the planning process operate in a unitary, as opposed to two-tier, local government structure? And what effect will reorganization have on the future delivery of strategic planning policy? In addition to these procedural questions, other theoretical issues are raised: for example, to what extent will the new administrative and planning framework truly reflect those distinctive social-political and cultural territorial differences?, and will the new planning map alter, reduce or reinforce the system of perceived good government in the Principality?

The emergence of territorial and nationalistic planning

Following the establishment of the Welsh Office as a separate government department in 1964, an attempt was made to create a distinctive planning policy framework that looked at the future social and economic development needs of Wales. The Welsh Office blueprint, *Wales: The Way Ahead*, published in 1967, sought to provide a clear regional economic plan for the Principality that local authorities could work to in progressing their development policies for local areas (HM Government, 1967). The debates surrounding the economic development and future of Wales were facilitated at this time by a parallel political discourse that began emerging as a powerful influence on public and political perceptions of how the nation would develop. The election in 1966 of a member of the Welsh nationalist party, Plaid Cymru, to the House of Commons signalled the importance within both the communities and in political circles of debate surrounding the future growth of Wales. Arguments about the future planning of Wales were thus indecorously bound up in social and political dialogue. The political programme espoused by Plaid Cymru, centering on the principle of decentralizing political authority and the preservation of Welsh culture, together with issues relating to future economic growth, created a distinct agenda for the people and governance of Wales. Although Plaid Cymru, as a pressure group, may have initially attempted to influence future Welsh Office thinking and policies on the economic growth of Wales, once their manifesto gained stronger public support across the country, the Welsh Office's policies following *Wales: The Way Ahead* were subsumed under a wider debate initiated by Welsh nationalists. Plaid Cymru's agenda therefore developed into a stronger political force across Wales.

As the Welsh Office's planning agenda began to be determined by the nationalists' lead, who in turn created the discourse and support among wider sections of Welsh society, the pressure placed on central government to formulate appropriate policy responses was not met. This led to a perception within Welsh political circles and the wider community that the issues under discussion were failing to be addressed in any official or systematic way. Thus, as the Welsh Office was criticized for not setting the broad planning agenda (that is, those contentious policy areas brought forward by the nationalists), a statutory policy vacuum began to develop at an all-Wales level. This lack of national planning only began to be addressed in 1988 with the release of central government Planning Policy Guidance Notes (PPGs), twenty-one years after the publication of *Wales: The Way Ahead*. But in the intervening years, the lack of an effective all-Wales tier of planning policy precipitated strong territorial political mobilization to counteract the perceived intrusive extension of metropolitan (and English or non-Welsh) institutions and policies. This political force, termed 'opposition planning' by Clavel (1983), parallels the 'official planning' of land-use administration operated by the Welsh Office, and created the conditions for a divergent range of planning issues to be debated within Welsh political communities and wider social networks. These issues were predominantly centred on housing, the Welsh language, and economic development; core areas of official planning around which territorial opposition emerged. Although the planning agenda was led by agencies other than the Welsh Office throughout the 1970s, this induced a 'regional consensus' in the Principality (Rees and Lambert, 1979) where the views of the Welsh Office, the local authorities and elements of the nationalist agenda (promoted in the most explicit sense by Plaid Cymru) were debated to ensure that the interests of Wales and the future prosperity of the country were paramount.

The Welsh Office did not completely retreat in agenda-setting for planning and development in Wales. Through a variety of government agencies such as the Welsh Development Agency, the Land Authority for Wales and the Development Board for Rural Wales, in addition to central government initiatives (such as urban policies and funding from the Inner Urban Areas Act 1978 and the Valleys Programme 1988), the Welsh Office created the conditions for the renewal of both urban and rural areas. The difference was that these policies were often implemented outside the official land-use planning system, although there can be no doubt that structure plans of the county councils were viewed by central government as a strategic co-ordinating level for the plethora of initiatives in place. Land-use planning issues that existed outside these areas were not comprehensively dealt with and it is in this arena that 'opposition planning' fostered.

An example of the way the Welsh Office's land-use planning procedures were counteracted by the opposition during this time is in the proposals for new towns at Newtown-Caersŵs in mid-Wales and Llantrisant in Glamorgan. Although proposals for a third town, at Cwmbran near the English–Welsh border, did succeed and the town itself was designated and built, the two other designations were abandoned following a concerted campaign against a policy that was viewed as reflecting British, as opposed to Welsh, interests (Edwards and Thomas, 1974). This abandonment reflects the failure on the part of the Welsh Office systematically to enforce a Welsh element within the wider institutional or state planning system.

The Welsh Office's position on the provision of an overview planning policy for Wales, to update and replace the 1967 *Wales: The Way Ahead*, was one of consistently rejecting the need for broad strategic policies and a reliance instead on strengthening existing structure plans as a means through which changing social and economic circumstances could be co-ordinated. They were also used to co-ordinate an informal partnership and joint collaboration between the Welsh Office and local government. Even in 1978, the then secretary of state for Wales continued to reject the principle of all-Wales planning guidance:

> My preference in the field of economic planning is not the imposition of a grandiose all-Wales plan from on high, but rather to approach the needs of Wales area by area and to collate the proposals drawn from the experience of those nearest to the problem. This is what democracy is about'. (John Morris, MP, Welsh Office Press Note 16, February 1978)

An ideological debate developed in opposition political circles relating to the most salient issues for central government intervention. The official policy vacuum that existed throughout this time created on the one hand an informal national planning response, and on the other a broad consensus among Welsh public organizations for the development of 'good government'. The underlying conditions that created this regional and territorial nationalism to respond on planning matters in Wales were: the Welsh language; a Welsh nationalist tradition; and, perhaps more distinctly, a Welsh cultural homogeneity.

Wales presents two distinctive phenomena: the interaction of national centrality and local development. On the one hand, the Welsh Office as a central government department reflects the policies of the British government as they can be applied to Wales and reinforces the institutional characteristics associated with land-use planning. On the other, the Welsh Office operates for Wales as a regional office, ensuring the interests of the Welsh public are paramount in future economic, environmental and social decisions. The Welsh Office is thus juxtaposed between operating within an institutional framework widely recognized as 'British', while protecting territorial and cultural concerns that are acutely 'Welsh'. Given this contraposition, at frequent intervals in the planning history of Wales particular forces and groups in society possessing defined political viewpoints against a 'British' institution have felt isolated from policy-making arenas, antagonistic towards central government politicians and officials, and independent from laws and policies that may have originated outside Wales. The land-use planning system is located at the centre of this disunion and provides an example of how territorial opposition and nationalism, combined, can form an underlying rationale for policy discourse.

Developing a Welsh planning agenda

During the 1980s, as the land-use planning system in Britain became market-orientated and embraced Thatcherite political ideology to the detriment of state planning controls (Thornley, 1993), the very purpose of planning was questioned. The state's role in co-ordinating a planning system was debated, and attempts were made by the Conservative governments in the mid-1980s to weaken the development plan process (such as through *The Future of Development Plans* white paper, HM Government, 1989). As the professional debate ensued over what role planning should take in facilitating future development requirements of the market, other contemporary commentators advocated a stronger planning or institutional top-down policy framework (Bruton and Nicholson, 1985). This would involve setting planning policies in a hierarchy from national to local, with each level of policy conforming to the preceding level. The committee of inquiry appointed by the Nuffield Foundation also recommended a strengthening of the national level of planning policy in order to provide some strategic co-ordination at the regional, county and district tiers of government (Nuffield Foundation, 1986). As Jeremy Rowan-Robinson highlights in Chapter 3, the committee were particularly impressed by Scotland's system of National Planning Guidance Notes (NPGs) and suggested the application of a similar series of documents for England and Wales.

In 1988, in recognition of the need for a national level of planning policy, the government introduced the first in a series of Planning Policy Guidance Notes (PPGs) for England and Wales. The first eight documents, dealing with such substantive issues as development control, housing, industrial development, retailing and the countryside, were released under joint authorship between the Department of the Environment and the Welsh Office. The documents dealt with detailed land-use planning issues rather than acting as broad statements of national policy. The Nuffield Inquiry's recommendations, therefore, cannot be viewed as the intellectual foundation for the introduction of PPGs (Tewdwr-Jones, 1994c). Over the past seven years, the provision of national planning guidance to shape local policy and procedures in England and Wales has been one of the most important planning trends introduced by the government and has taken on some degree of significance with the introduction of the pro-planning or 'plan-led' system in the Planning and Compensation Act 1991. The influence of the PPGs is considerable, not only in the drafting of strategic and local planning policies but also in the co-ordination of regional planning guidance and the development control process (Tewdwr-Jones, 1994a, b). However, the exact role of national policy guidelines remains uncertain, since they can often appear as mandatory rather than advisory and this has political consequences for the means through which central government in Wales (in other words, the Welsh Office) has implemented national planning policies.

The Welsh Office has not attempted to implement a radically different policy approach to the planning system in Wales from that operating by the Department of the Environment in England. Both central government departments have released circulars and Planning Policy Guidance Notes under joint-authorship over a long period of time, thus reflecting the government's view of the planning system being essentially identical in both countries. Central government's planning policy is delivered through a mixture of circulars that focus on legislative changes, and PPGs that deal with policy issues that are of direct relevance to the formulation and implementation of development plans. Occasionally, however, some circulars and PPGs have been issued separately in Wales from the policy documents in England, either on topics that have a distinct Welsh flavour, or because legal and administrative systems in the two countries are, in these instances, separate.

Until 1995, the Welsh Office introduced very few separate planning policy statements distinctive from the Department of the Environment, although these are worth mentioning briefly. These documents were additional to the plethora of circulars and Planning Policy Guidance Notes issued jointly by the two departments. Circular 61/81 *Historic Buildings and Conservation Areas* was released separately in Wales to reflect the distinct historical and administrative arrangements in the Principality (Welsh Office, 1981). Circular 30/86 *Housing for Senior Management* was introduced as part of the Welsh Office's drive to stimulate local economies and inward investment in Wales. In particular, the then Welsh secretary, Nicholas Edwards, was of the opinion that the lack of an adequate pool of housing attractive to and suitable for senior managers and senior technical staff was a possible disincentive to business people who might otherwise be prepared to invest and develop in Wales. The circular outlined the policy request for each local planning authority in Wales to allow for the designation of additional development sites for new houses or low density groups of houses to allow for the encouragement of commerce and industry 'in and adjoining towns and villages (as well as in proposals for new settlements)' (Welsh Office, 1986, para.1). While Circular 53/88 *The Welsh Language – Development Plans and Planning Control* (Welsh Office, 1988b) outlined how the

Welsh language should be treated as a material consideration in planning policy formulation and implementation, and is particularly relevant as a distinctive policy approach. (This circular is subject to a detailed commentary by Clive James and Colin Williams in this book.) The latter two circulars reflect what is probably the most distinctive policy difference between land-use planning in Wales compared to that for England, and although welcomed by relevant Welsh organizations are limited compared to the plethora of other guidance that has been jointly released.

Following the introduction of the Planning Policy Guidance Notes in 1988, most documents were released jointly by the Department of the Environment and the Welsh Office. This reflected the operation of a common legal and policy planning system across the two countries and, as a consequence, was devoid of spatially specific policies. Although a system of Regional Planning Guidance Notes would translate the British national planning agenda into spatial regions after 1990, critics of the PPG system in Wales – especially rural political representatives – have highlighted the inadequacy of strong national (Welsh) planning guidance for local authorities in the Principality. This, they argue, gives free rein to an alien set of planning policies that are inappropriate for Wales since they fail to take into account geographical, cultural and social considerations distinctive to Wales. This particular issue was debated at length in the Parliamentary Welsh Affairs Select Committee's sessions in 1993 for their report *Rural Housing* (House of Commons Welsh Affairs Committee, 1993).

A political leader of Ceredigion District Council, an area of mid-Wales where a strong opposition planning element exists, complained in evidence of the imposition of English policies at the Welsh local level: 'The secretary of state has gone so far to say that the local communities and local people should decide where and what sort of development to take place in their areas. We are guided by the policy guidance note' (ibid., para.23). The member then went on to justify the local authority taking an opposing view to national guidance, preferring instead to rely on 'local knowledge' provided by the area ward representative in determining individual planning applications. The uncertainty over the application of non-spatially-specific Welsh planning guidance at the community level has also been raised by members of the planning profession. The director of planning of Montgomeryshire District Council in commenting on the role of PPGs in Welsh planning stated that although the guidance contained an increasing 'Welsh flavour', 'the basic policy in relation to developing the countryside is still very much a national [British] one' (ibid., para.26). The amount of criticism put forward at the parliamentary session of central government guidance failing to reflect the particular characteristics of Welsh rural communities and the Welsh countryside was so strong, it led the committee to recommend to the Welsh Office the amendment of policies:

Although we recognise that many of the calls for increasing Welshness to the guidance are, in effect, calls for greater relaxation of controls over developments in the countryside, it is also true that guidance which reflects the settlement patterns of the home counties is unlikely to be equally applicable to rural Wales. (ibid.)

What is clear in this evidence and in almost all of the central government circulars and Planning Policy Guidance Notes issued jointly with the Department of the Environment (some seventeen PPGs) is the lack of a distinctly Welsh policy dimension, and it is questionable why so many other policy topics were not considered appropriate to warrant the issuing of separate policy guidance appropriate for a Welsh audience. In addition to the policy guidance on the countryside and the rural economy, other substantive planning issues covered by these common policies included industrial development, retailing, telecommunications, recreation, coastal planning, tourism, renewable energy, and mineral extraction, and were some of the more politically sensitive issues within the planning system operated in Wales. These issues are located within a wider debate, precipitated by critics of the state, on the role the planning system should take in Wales and whether the core planning areas of concern were at the time being addressed by a Welsh – as opposed to English – central government department. It led the political opposition to label the Welsh Office dormant in the face of Department of the Environment initiatives and to question the extent to which the Welsh Office was sufficiently interventionist in planning issues in the country. This emphasizes the distinct and difficult role for the Welsh Office between operating as a centralized bureaucratic agency of the British state while attempting to implement and co-ordinate planning policy that reflects distinctive socio-political traditions. It also reinforces a belief that central government was still largely ineffective in defining clear planning policy statements (that is, in 'official planning'), thereby causing the development of an alternative planning agenda organized within new territorial coalitions such as rural areas (through 'opposition planning').

The provision of central government planning guidance, therefore, has been more contestly debated in Wales than in England, since the planning issues addressed in the documents have often been closely identified with a state political agenda. In the 1980s and early 1990s, the political role of the Welsh Office in relation to planning was one of centrality with the Department of the Environment. On occasion, separate planning agendas emerged, causing political embroilments throughout national and local political circles on such issues as rural housing, windfarms, opencast mining, economic development and retailing, but these debates were initiated through reactionary politics. Although Peter Walker, the secretary of state for Wales between 1987 and 1990, was widely applauded for his interventionist role in facilitating an urban programme for the Valleys (Welsh Office, 1988a), the methods employed by the Welsh Office to progress and encourage economic change and urban renewal were outside the land-use planning system, and relied on a combination of central government grants, government agencies (such as the Welsh Development Agency and the Land Authority for Wales), private sector investment, and political co-operation across government agencies. The role of both the land-use planning process in co-ordinating development in Wales and of the Welsh Office in providing a national planning policy framework, was not apparent. Although it is possible to suggest that the Welsh Office failed in this respect, it might also have been a deliberate move on the department's part to recognize the diverse and varied nature of planning for different areas within Wales. A system of all-Wales guidance may not, therefore, have been appropriate. An alternative system to all-Wales policy advice could have focused on distinct spatial localities, such as urban, rural and valley areas. Whether the Welsh Office, in its determination to strengthen strategic policies through county councils' structure plans, was indicating a spatial approach to planning through the 1970s and 1980s, is difficult to assess. Certainly, with the benefit of hindsight, there are grounds to describe the spatial approach as inadequate.

The uncertainty over the Welsh Office's land-use planning agenda was exacerbated further in 1993 by the appointment of John Redwood as secretary of state. A change in Welsh Office policy caused principally by personal political ideology on the part of the minister resulted in no further Planning Policy Guidance Notes being released in Wales. Following the publication of a PPG on retailing and town centres jointly by the Department of the Environment and the Welsh Office in July 1993 (Department of the Environment/Welsh Office, 1993), the minister refused to sanction the release of any further planning documents. Many joint-department PPGs remained in draft format at the time and were scheduled for release over the following two years. But the withdrawal of the Welsh Office from the planning policy guidance exercise resulted in Wales (and Welsh local authority planners) undergoing a period of disillusionment and the creation of a policy vacuum that was more devastating for planning's role in Wales than at any time in the 1970s or 1980s. Indeed, the Welsh Office, which had never particularly believed in promoting an independent planning policy approach in the Principality, now found itself slipping behind on those planning policy issues initiated across the border in England. Between 1993 and 1995, five PPGs were released by the Department of the Environment that normally would have applied equally to Wales. The five documents covered: Nature Conservation; Transport; Planning and the Historic Environment; Planning and Pollution Control; and Planning and Noise. The refusal on the part of the Welsh Office to release the PPG on transport resulted in a separate policy approach between the Welsh secretary and the Environment secretary in England on controlling transport in urban areas, protecting the environment, and encouraging more investment in public transport, some of the more rational areas for the planning system's intervention in the 1990s. However, this separatist policy movement was not acted upon by opposition planners to promote an alternative planning agenda for Wales, distinct from that of England. Professional opinion was more concerned with the lack of the same planning guidance, in terms of quantity and detail, as that existing for English local planning authorities (Tompsett, 1994).

Throughout John Redwood's period as Welsh secretary, the Welsh Office was left in a planning timewarp as policies and decisions in England kept apace with the new planning framework, leaving the development industry and local planners in Wales without a comprehensive national planning framework. The exact reasons why Redwood refused to release the 'missing PPGs' (as they became known) have never been critically assessed. The refusal was based on an ideological conviction against the imposition of higher-tier guidance on the activities of lower-level state functions, and a belief that the guidance that was being released was unnecessarily detailed and cumbersome, reflecting (ironically) the same areas of complaint as political opposition groups in rural authorities of Wales. This fuelled a political row between central government and local government, and also between professional planning officers and the political members they served. Planners felt uncomfortable without official planning guidance, since it presented the possibility of a weakening of local authorities' policies against opportunistic developers. Local politicians, on the other hand, whilst condemning the Welsh Office's failure to act on the planning agenda, recognized an opportunity to implement a more discretionary planning system that could cater for local community needs and foster greater territorial politics independent of central government control. The secretary of state and the local politicians were at opposite ends of the political spectrum in ideological terms, but believed in the concept of 'local choice', decisions to be taken at the lowest possible political level. In the rural areas of Wales, this conflict has further allowed the planning system to be used by opposition groups to implement non-planning decisions difficult to justify in planning terms for the benefit of territorial nationalism and a precipitation of local capacity in planning that would otherwise have been dealt with by a strong central government department. The territorial nationalism was not mobilized in any party political sense. Most of the rural authorities are run by independent political representatives lacking strategic direction and who are spatially fragmented, a common feature of local politics (Saunders, 1984). The nationalist configuration did, however, possess some powerful ideas.

The position of the Welsh Office in the planning system during this period of time therefore evolved further. Combined with the requirements of the pro-planning legislation (the 1991 Planning and Compensation Act), the Welsh Office has fostered a degree of harmony among planning professionals with a stable policy framework and a local authority-led development control process. The national planning guidance in place has been welcomed by the professionals who feel they have the necessary policy parameters to implement a local planning system for communities. But the local politicians have not been so easily convinced.

Following the appointment of William Hague as secretary of state for Wales in July 1995, and in one of the last acts sanctioned by John Redwood as Welsh secretary, two new draft Planning Policy Guidance Notes were released that, at the time of writing (September 1995), are at public consultation stage. The two documents, *Unitary Development Plans in Wales* and *Planning Policy Guidance (Wales)* incorporate the 'missing PPGs', but the contents and format of the two drafts is radically different to the joint English/Welsh planning guidance previously released. The principal change in the two draft documents compared to former Welsh advice and current English counterparts centres on the number of PPGs that will in future provide the Welsh national planning policy agenda. The Welsh Office intends to replace all the existing PPGs – some seventeen documents – together with a number of circulars and other government statements with just the two revised PPGs.

Unitary Development Plans in Wales concentrates on preparing UDPs in the reformed unitary local government system in the Principality after April 1996. The guidance does go further, however, and includes detailed advice on plan procedures within the national parks and on transitionary arrangements between the old and new planning systems. The second document, *Planning Policy Guidance (Wales)* is far more interesting, and reduces the advice in the existing seventeen PPGs to 200 paragraphs of guidance. The format, contents and even wording of this PPG is extremely different to past Department of the Environment planning statements. It is apparent that the Welsh Office has accepted the need for change in its planning policy guidance as highlighted by the parliamentary Welsh Affairs Committee in 1993, with the emphasis now on developing policy separately from that in England.

The PPG provides definitive statements that concentrate on strategic issues in recognition, most probably, of the lack of co-ordinating strategic planning agencies in Wales once the county councils are abolished in spring 1996. Some agencies in Wales have already criticized the government for the brevity of the guidance, but have themselves failed to appreciate what the Welsh Office is attempting to achieve. For once, the government is restricting its policy guidance to national and strategic issues at an all-Wales level, a broad framework that permits individual local authorities and developers a greater amount of discretion to determine local issues. The general role of national planning policy has not been amended, however, and local authorities are still required to take account of Welsh Office guidance in preparing development plans and in determining planning applications. But the interpretation of PPGs, where local authorities have the ability to formulate policies and take decisions that are broadly in conformity with the secretary of state's advice, is left for the local authorities themselves to determine, espousing the concept of local choice that the former secretary of state for Wales, John Redwood, supported.

On the whole, the draft PPGs do begin to reflect the particular nuances of Welsh social, economic and environmental concerns. But several important questions remain unanswered. Given the change in nature of the PPGs to cover issues of more strategic concern, Welsh local authorities may well feel as though they are entering another policy vacuum, in much the same way as the uncertainty of the 1970s and early 1980s. The former PPGs dealt with many issues in great detail, to the extent that practically all planning matters were covered by the guidance. Local authorities only had to interpret and adapt national policies to suit their own circumstances. The strategic draft PPGs will leave local authorities with a greater interpretative and policy formulation role, and this may not be welcome in some quarters. Advice on detailed matters will not totally be excluded from the Welsh Office's remit, however. Technical issues will be covered in a series of supplementary Technical Advice Notes for Wales or 'TANS(W)'. However, no indication has, as yet, been made on what issues will be included in TANS or when they are likely to be published.

The language of the new planning policy guidance is, for the most part, simple, concise and clear – a vast improvement on the former PPG documents. Given the lack of detailed guidance, there may also be a temptation for policy and decision makers to look at the contents of the old PPGs for further advice. This would need to be carefully managed since planners will not be able to use the displaced PPGs as material considerations. There may also be a tendency for Welsh local planners to look at English PPG equivalents on particular topics, especially where the amount of advice between the old and the new documents has been reduced significantly. For example, the PPG dealing with coastal planning (Department of the Environment/Welsh Office, 1992) is replaced in the new draft PPG(W) by one single paragraph. This will be a particular concern for planning inspectors who frequently work in both England and Wales – they will now have to be guided by two different sets of policy documents. Local authorities and the inspectorate will need greater clarity and explanation on the implementation of the new framework, although the criticism of the new format from professional representatives in Wales might cause the Welsh Office to reconsider its proposals.

The planning system in a Welsh context

Strategic planning delivery

Although the provision of national planning policy guidance has existed in Wales, albeit tangentially allied to the English Department of the Environment system, Welsh local authorities have attempted to implement a separate strategic all-Wales system of planning advice. Below the national tier of Welsh Office planning policy, local authorities have been central to the development of a strategic planning guidance (SPG) exercise for the Principality to inform the preparation of strategic development plans of the county councils. SPG is similar in content and scope to the regional planning guidance operated in the English regions and reflects Wales' position as both a nation and a region. The distinction between Welsh Office national planning policy guidance and all-Wales strategic planning guidance has become unclear during the 1990s, since both exercises attempt to deal with similar issues. The 1995 draft versions of national planning policy guidance released by the Welsh Office are an important first step in co-ordinating the two separate but interdependent tiers.

The Welsh Office in conjunction with the Assembly of Welsh Counties, has gone some way towards facilitating a 'sub-national' or regional planning framework for Wales below the national tier (AWC, 1992). The government white paper, *The Future of Development Plans*, published jointly in the names of the secretaries of state for the Environment and for Wales, had recognized: 'the particular administrative and planning circumstances in the Principality, especially the multi-functional role of the Welsh Office, [that] required a distinctive approach to the development of regional planning guidance' (HM Government, 1989). Jarvis (1996) identifies two important features of the strategic planning guidance (SPG) in Wales documents that make the exercise distinctive from that in England. First, it is seen as essentially all-Wales aspatial guidance, whereas the regional planning guidance exercise in England has a distinctive spatial element. Secondly, county councils were given the task of co-ordinating and preparing the guidance for submission to the secretary of state for Wales for his approval, liaising with the district authorities, national parks and other interested public-sector organizations in the country. This, argues Jarvis, has led to a major collaborative planning exercise between the various governmental and non-governmental agencies to produce a coherent set of policy documents to guide the physical regeneration and development of Wales in the future.

At the same time, the Welsh Office made it clear that the contents of the SPG exercise should be confined to those matters necessary to enable county and district planning authorities to prepare their statutory plans. The emphasis, therefore, is on physical land-use planning, rather than a broader social and economic planning exercise similar to the *Wales: The Way Ahead* white paper that had been issued in 1967 (HM Government, 1967). Nevertheless, this did not prohibit the county councils from establishing seven broad objectives for the development of the SPG exercise in their report entitled *Strategic Planning Guidance in Wales – Process and Procedures* (AWC, 1990) that were devoted to wider social, economic and environmental problems being experienced in Wales. The objectives set out are to:

- ensure that Wales can enjoy a quality of life at levels comparable with the best in the European Community;
- develop land-use planning policies that reflect the principle of sustainable development;
- protect and enhance the natural and built environment;
- recognize the distinctive language and culture in Wales;
- improve the economic health of the Principality;
- improve access to housing; and
- secure public and private investment in transportation and infrastructure.

When the final report was submitted by the Assembly of Welsh Counties in 1993 it called for a comprehensive strategic policy statement for Wales that would embrace urban, rural, coastal and transportation issues, and allow the future development of land-use planning to be integrated more successfully. Additionally, although the role of the Welsh language had received greater acknowledgement as a material consideration in the planning process in Wales through the publication of Circular 53/88, it was felt that further issues required to be addressed, especially assessing the significance and impact of development on the Welsh language communities.

Above all, the AWC were particularly concerned to give the Strategic Planning Guidance exercise a sub-regional focus within an all-Wales context, to acknowledge the different economic, environmental and cultural circumstances within different areas. These sub-regional requirements, it was argued, could ensure the proper integration of land-use planning and transportation, provide a detailed framework for the preparation of development plans, integrate the policies and programmes of other agencies (such as the Welsh Development Agency and Land Authority for Wales), and act as a means of promotion to the private sector of development opportunities.

Although county and district planning authorities in Wales generally supported the strategic planning guidance (SPG) exercise, some groups have been disappointed by the lack of originality in the process. The Royal Town Planning Institute (RTPI) claims that SPG in Wales has so far been 'no more than an amalgamation of existing county structure plans' (RTPI, 1993). But a strategic planning framework for Wales is necessary if the preparation of development plans by the new unitary authorities is not to be delayed and if decisions are not to be made 'on the grounds of local political expediency' (AWC, 1991, para.5.9.2). This is particularly the case following local government reorganization. The primary concern for policy-makers is to establish which agency will formulate and issue this strategic framework – without the existence of the county councils – in a reorganized system of Welsh governance: joint working between unitary authorities, the Welsh Office, or regional government.

Joint working or co-operation between unitary authorities is the means by which the Welsh Office prefers to see strategic planning guidance operated, but, as Boyne and Law (1993) point out, the establishment of joint arrangements runs counter to the basic principles of democracy since the joint board members are appointed and not democratically elected. The government acknowledges this defect in its policy guidance to the Local Government Commission in England and in the reports of the Commission itself (DoE, 1992). The creation of joint boards undermines the principle of unitary authorities being clearly accountable to the local electorate, may result in difficult decisions being shelved, and may lead to decisions at the level of the lowest common denominator (Boyne and Law, 1993). The RTPI does not consider that voluntary co-operation between unitary authorities can provide the necessary strategic planning framework for Wales. Instead it calls for legislative measures to establish new groupings of authorities on a sub-regional basis. The response of the Welsh Office has been to encourage the voluntary system of joint-working but to emphasize the all-Wales strategic policy element through the contents of its new draft Planning Policy Guidance. The two papers attempt to combine both national (Welsh) planning advice and sub-regional strategic guidance in one set of documents.

Development plan coverage

The first structure plan to be approved in Wales was for Gwynedd in July 1977, with the last being approved in 1983, thereby completing structure plan coverage in Wales. Welsh structure planning has been characterized by a similar process to that of England and Scotland: ongoing replacement and modification. At the more detailed level, complete coverage of Wales by local plans was required by 1996 (Roderick, 1994), but this has been much slower. This has been mainly caused by a move towards the production of district-wide plans. In some areas, such as the more rural authorities where no form of statutory local plan may have previously existed, this has led to administrative uncertainty and delay in the planning system. The Welsh Office had estimated in 1993 that all but one of the thirty-seven districts would achieve district-wide local plan coverage by 1996, with most authorities adopting their plans well in advance (in evidence to the House of Commons Welsh Affairs Committee). Although over half the population of Wales was covered by adopted local plans at this time, only three districts had achieved district-wide coverage: Rhondda, Swansea and Wrexham Maelor. Some other authorities possessed local plans covering only minor parts of their administrative areas, whereas six authorities had yet to start preparing local plans: Carmarthen, Ceredigion, Glyndŵr, Montgomeryshire, Preseli-Pembrokeshire and South Pembrokeshire. For these authorities, centred in the rural areas of Wales, their only statutory policies were contained in the relevant structure plans. With the enhanced status afforded to development plan policies under the terms of section 54A of the Planning and Compensation Act 1991, it was imperative for all district authorities to progress statutory local plan coverage as soon as possible to provide a firm basis for development control decisions.

In the two years to 1995, the progress of approved district-wide local plan coverage in Welsh authorities has improved but not at the rate the Welsh Office had hoped. Some areas are still without any local plan coverage after twenty years, with no progress having been made to publish even draft plans in thirteen districts. While some of these cover remote rural areas where there are likely to be limited development pressures, in particular large parts of Dyfed and Clwyd, there are also a significant number of urban and South Wales valley authorities where plans have not yet been published. The lack of district-wide local plan coverage by April 1996 will result in the new unitary local authorities starting to prepare a different type of statutory land-use document: the unitary development plan (UDP); indeed, this might be one reason why some existing authorities have decided not to progress the current 'old-style' local plans. Plan preparation time remains complex and long-winded, with some authorities not progressing plan approvals following Public Local Inquiries. For example, final local plans for Cardiff, Islwyn and Wrexham Maelor have yet to be approved, despite publishing deposit versions in 1992. Those plans that have been adopted were formulated pre-1991, are out-of-date and do not necessarily reflect current social and economic circumstances proving weak as development control tools under section 54A of the Planning and Compensation Act (Welsh Office, 1995).

The Welsh Office has attempted to deal with the time delay problems by producing advice that has stressed the advantage of rapid and attractive plan production and the need for plans to concentrate more upon land-use issues (Welsh Office, 1992, 1993a). While this has begun to have an impact, it is paradoxical that the implementation of section 54A of the 1991 Planning and Compensation Act and the lack of all-Wales national planning guidance between 1993 and 1995 may have lengthened the time taken for local plan inquiries, thereby undermining the Welsh Office's attempts to speed up plan production. The increased status afforded to local plans may mean that developers, and others with an interest in land use, are now more interested in influencing the content of the plans to ensure that policies that favour their interests are adequately reflected. The problems with local plan uncertainty in Wales may also reflect a view in some local planning authorities, from both officers and members, that the statutory, institutional or 'official' planning system may be irrelevant in addressing the problems facing these communities, especially if these are ones of social and cultural erosion or economic decline. This has undoubtedly resulted in a reliance in some areas of Wales on non-statutory plans and so-called supplementary planning guidance. Local planning authorities have placed non-land-use planning policies (as defined by planning law and central government) outside the statutory plan but within supplementary documentation and then used these documents to facilitate the addressing of community needs. Topics addressed by supplementary plans have included social housing (White and Tewdwr-Jones, 1995).

Controlling development

To complement the new statutory development plan provisions enacted in the 1991 Act, the Welsh Office decided that some form of quality assessment guidance for the implementation of planning policies would be worthwhile, and released its *Development Control – A Guide to Good Practice* document in the summer of 1993. The aims of the booklet are to assist local authorities in improving their development control procedures and increasing the quality in public-sector service delivery (Welsh Office, 1993a). The guide, produced as part of the Citizen's Charter initiative, relates to the standard of service expected of development control sections by emphasizing the right every citizen has to expect efficiency in the local development control service. In addition to providing advice on quality and efficiency in Welsh authorities' work, the booklet also attempts to respond to the parliamentary Welsh Affairs Committee's recommendations in its report on the planning system within the Principality concerning bad procedures and malpractice within Welsh rural authorities. In particular, the report highlighted the actions of planning committee councillors in basing decisions upon the personal circumstances of the applicant, commenting that, 'Many of the most disturbing aspects of the evidence we have received have related to the conduct of members of planning committees' (House of Commons Welsh Affairs Committee, 1993, para.56). The report quotes the evidence of the Director of Planning at Ceredigion District Council in which he remarked that the planning system in the locality had 'become personalised to the extent that the circumstances of the applicant are frequently considered to be more important than the planning merits of the application' (ibid.).

The politicization of land-use planning, as identified by the Welsh select committee, is occurring as a result of the actions and decisions of the elected members of certain authorities. As a direct consequence of the imposed rigidity of national policy parameters, some local politicians are becoming frustrated with their inability to apply local interpretation of national guidance in local circumstances. The professional officers are conforming to the policy planning constraints, but the elected members are reluctant to follow imposed central government guidance. This reluctance to conform is, in turn, resulting in occasions when the local members reject professional advice, downplay central government planning policies, and thereby contribute to reports of misrepresenting the purpose of the land-use planning system (Tewdwr-Jones, 1995). An unfortunate aspect of this localized opposition to the planning system is an anti-incomer dimension. Although this is part of a political reaction, it is especially difficult for a planning officer to deal with. The professional has to recognize and manage politicians' requests to implement an anti-institutional decision-making process against the imposition of central government policies for everyone in the authority's area. It is one thing for local politicians deliberately to ignore established government planning policies for the benefit of everyone in the authority's area, but quite another matter when the opposition is enacted only when it benefits people born in the locality.

Some parallels can be drawn here between the local political configurations of the Welsh rural authorities and the report of maladministration in the operation of the development control function of North Cornwall District Council, a local authority in the rural south-west of England (Department of the Environment, 1993). Many issues highlighted by the members of parliament in Wales are similar to the contents of the North Cornwall report. The key questions emerging from both studies are: why is the operation of the planning system in rural, traditionally Independent, areas not corresponding to the policy framework advocated by central government? how do the political representatives of these authorities perceive the planning system? and do the policy- and decision-makers in these rural areas possess clear views of what role 'planning' should take?

Authorities in both the Welsh 'heartlands' of west, mid- and north Wales and North Cornwall reflect to some extent the same socio-political characteristics. These authorities are politically Independent, are centred on remote rural areas, and possess broadly similar social and economic conditions, such as economic deprivation, and lack of affordable local housing. Additional to these societal problems is a cultural phenomenon. In rural Wales, the erosion of Welsh identity and the threat to the Welsh language is mirrored in Cornwall where Kernow, the Cornish language, is staunchly defended and where the 'threat' is perceived to come from non-local people migrating to the area and eroding both the low supply of housing stock and the distinctive cultural circumstances. The political representatives of both regions are attempting to take decisions that meet the needs and problems of the communities they serve while territorially conserving the cultural nuances that are identified as distinctive from the rest of the country. While it is questionable whether this forms the basis of a rural local state (Cloke and Little, 1990), planners in these areas are faced with a problem of local politicians refusing to enact central policies institutionalized and backed by a legal system. The decision-makers view with great suspicion the imposition of outside policies or guidance that have not been formulated at the local level. They also do not believe that policy solutions devised by anyone other than local people can truly reflect the problems being experienced or create sets of conditions that are appropriate for their own constituencies. Local government and local political representatives are viewed as the best actors to respond to local needs (Jones and

Stewart, 1983). In the place of national policies, they develop a local capacity for non-official planning that, while not politically strong in UK terms, responds to powerful and passionate beliefs held by the wider community in particular localities.

Conclusions

Rural Wales' decision-makers expect the land-use planning system to take on a role that in Britain it was never designed to perform, namely defending territorial nationalism and dealing with wider social and economic problems directly. Perhaps this, more than any other aspect of Welsh planning, separates the land-use system in Wales from that operating in England since the nationalistic dimension can be more readily identified. It should be remembered that not all of these characteristics can be identified in all parts of Wales. And there will be regions in both England and Scotland that possess similar social and economic concerns. But the passion with which opposition planners in Wales debate both nationalistic concerns and how the planning system should respond to changing social and economic conditions as they affect specific spatial areas, reflects a territorial condition that has not been identified so markedly in other parts of Britain. Central government's planning role must be to reflect the separate socio-cultural circumstances of the regions it serves and to be recognized for acting on this distinctiveness. This is an area that requires further research before any firm conclusions can be drawn. The dilemma for the land-use planning system is how to ensure national planning policies reflect regional territorial and cultural differences, since it is these issues that will determine the ultimate success and applicability of all planning policies at the local level.

References

Assembly of Welsh Counties 1990. *Strategic Planning Guidance in Wales: Process and Procedures* (Cardiff, Assembly of Welsh Counties).
Assembly of Welsh Counties 1991. *The Structure of Local Government in Wales: The Assembly's Response to the Consultation Paper Issued by the Secretary of State* (Cardiff, Assembly of Welsh Counties).
Assembly of Welsh Counties 1992. *Strategic Planning Guidance in Wales: Overview Report* (Cardiff, Assembly of Welsh Counties).
Boyne, G., P. Griffiths, A. Lawton and J. Law 1991. *Local Government in Wales: Its Role and Functions* (York, Joseph Rowntree Foundation).
Boyne, G. and J. Law 1993. 'Bidding for the local government franchise: an evaluation of the contest in Wales', *Local Government Studies*, Vol.19, No.4, pp.537–57.
Bruton, M. and D. Nicholson 1985. 'Strategic land use planning and the British development plan system', *Town Planning Review*, Vol.56, No.1, pp.21–40.

Clavel, P. 1983. *Opposition Planning in Wales and Appalachia* (Cardiff, University of Wales Press).

Cloke, P. and J. Little 1990. *The Rural State? Limits to Planning in Rural Society* (Oxford, Clarendon Press).

Council of Welsh Districts 1991. *The Structure of Local Government in Wales: Response to the Welsh Office Consultation Document* (Cardiff, Council of Welsh Districts).

Department of the Environment 1992. *Policy Guidance to the Local Government Commission for England* (London, Department of the Environment).

Department of the Environment 1993. *Enquiry Into the Planning System in North Cornwall District* (London, HMSO).

Department of the Environment/Welsh Office 1992. *Coastal Planning: PPG20* (London, HMSO).

Department of the Environment/Welsh Office 1993. *Town Centres and Retail Development: PPG6* (London, HMSO).

Edwards, J. A. and W. Thomas 1974. *Llantrisant New Town: The Case Against* (Heads of the Valleys Standing Conference).

Hambleton, R. and L. Mills 1993. 'Local government reform in Wales', *Local Government Policy Making*, 19(4), 45–55.

Harris, N. and M. Tewdwr-Jones 1995. 'The implications for planning of local government reorganisation in Wales: purpose, process and practice', *Environment and Planning C: Government and Policy*, Vol.13, No.1, pp.47–66.

HM Government 1967. *Wales: The Way Ahead* (London, HMSO).

HM Government 1989. *The Future of Development Plans* (London, HMSO).

House of Commons Welsh Affairs Committee 1993. *Rural Housing* (London, HMSO).

Jarvis, R. 1996. 'Structure planning policy and strategic planning guidance in Wales', in M. Tewdwr-Jones (ed.), *British Planning Policy in Transition* (London, UCL Press).

Jones, G. and J. Stewart 1983. *The Case for Local Government* (London, Allen and Unwin).

Nuffield Foundation 1986. *A Committee of Inquiry Appointed by the Nuffield Foundation on the Town and Country Planning System* (London, Nuffield Foundation).

Rees, G. and J. Lambert 1979. 'Urban development in a peripheral region: some issues from South Wales', paper presented at the Centre for Environmental Studies conference on Urban Change and Conflict, University of Nottingham, January 1979.

Roderick, P. 1994. 'Central Government Planning Policy', paper presented to the 'Planning Policy in the 1990s' conference, Department of City and Regional Planning, University of Wales College, Cardiff.

Royal Town Planning Institute 1993. *Local Government in Wales: A Charter for the Future – Memorandum of Observations to the Welsh Office on its White Paper* (London, Royal Town Planning Institute).

Saunders, P. 1984. *Urban Politics: A Sociological Interpretation* (London, Hutchinson).

Tewdwr-Jones, M. 1994a. 'Policy implications of the "plan-led" planning system', *Journal of Planning and Environment Law*, Vol.46, No.7, pp.584–93.

Tewdwr-Jones, M. 1994b. 'The development plan in policy implementation', *Environment and Planning C: Government and Policy*, Vol.12, No.2, pp.145–63.

Tewdwr-Jones, M. 1994c. 'The Government's Planning Policy Guidance', *Journal of Planning and Environment Law*, Vol.47, No.2, pp.106–16.

Tewdwr-Jones, M. 1995. 'Development control and the legitimacy of planning decisions', *Town Planning Review*, Vol.66, No.2, pp.163–81.

Thornley, A. 1993. *Urban Planning Under Thatcherism* (London, Routledge).

Tompsett, R. 1994. 'English welsh on guidance for Wales', *Planning Week*, Vol.2, No.41, pp.10–11.

Welsh Office 1981. Circular 61/81, Historical Buildings and Conservation Areas – Policy and Procedure (London, HMSO).

Welsh Office 1986. Circular 30/86, Housing for Senior Management (London, HMSO).

Welsh Office 1988a. *The Valleys Programme* (London, HMSO).

Welsh Office 1988b. Circular 53/88, The Welsh Language: Development Plans and Development Control (London, HMSO).

Welsh Office 1992. *Development Plans and Strategic Planning Guidance in Wales: PPG12(W)* (London, HMSO).

Welsh Office 1993a. *Development Control – A Guide to Good Practice* (Cardiff, Welsh Office).

Welsh Office 1993b. 'Local Government in Wales: A Charter for the Future' (London, HMSO).

Welsh Office 1995. 'Development plan position at March 1995', Personal correspondence to the author.

White, S. and M. Tewdwr-Jones 1995. 'The role and status of supplementary planning guidance', *Journal of Planning and Environment Law*, Vol.48, No.6, pp.471–81.

5

The Fallible Servant: Evaluating the Welsh Development Agency

KEVIN MORGAN and DYLAN HENDERSON

Introduction: rethinking regional policy

Regional authorities throughout the European Union are coming to realize that they can no longer depend on a steady flow of transfer payments to underwrite their regional economies. Over time, the European Union will embrace the poorer countries of central and eastern Europe, leaving less resources for the peripheral regions of the current Union. In the UK, regional policy expenditure has been reduced by some 75 per cent in real terms since 1979. In other words, neither Brussels nor London can be relied upon to provide an endless flow of external support. Although regional aid still has a role to play in facilitating economic renewal – providing it is flanked by complementary measures to promote innovation and development – such aid is far less important than a stock of innovative firms, a skilled and versatile workforce and a robust networking capacity. In short, regions will have to do much more to help themselves in the future.

The regional level is assuming more importance in discussions of economic development today, and there are two reasons for this. First, a good deal of innovative activity in Europe and North America takes the form of regional clusters, as firms agglomerate in certain locations to reap the benefits of external economies and innovative milieux. Second, public policy analysts are coming to the conclusion that the regional level may be the most appropriate at which to design and deploy innovation support programmes for firms, especially for small and medium-sized firms, because central government is too remote to have good local knowledge (Cooke and Morgan, 1993).

These points are understood in most European countries, where there is a well-developed institutional capacity at the regional level in the form of regional assemblies, development agencies and a host of other bodies. Slowly, but surely, the English regions are realizing that their institutional deficit at the regional level has become a major handicap, making it that much more difficult to develop a region-wide perspective on urban renewal, planning and economic development in general. Even the Conservative government, which is totally opposed to the creation of regional institutions in England, has conceded that there is a problem here. To help alleviate the institutional deficit in the English regions, the government felt obliged to create Integrated Regional Offices, which bring together the hitherto separate offices of four Whitehall departments in each English region – a form of 'regionalism from above'.

If Wales lacks institutional capacity relative to regions like Baden-Württemberg in Germany, it is well-endowed in comparison with the English regions. Whatever the shortcomings of the Welsh Office and the Welsh Development Agency (WDA), these two bodies have played a major part in modernizing the Welsh economy. In recent years, however, these bodies have been ensnared in controversy, so much so that the very future of the WDA has been called into question. To look at these issues in more depth, this chapter will examine: (i) the structure of the WDA; (ii) key aspects of its current economic development strategy; (iii) the regulation of the Agency; and (iv) future scenarios of the WDA as a regional animateur.

The structure and resources of the WDA

With an annual budget of £157 million in 1994/5, and around 380 staff, the WDA is one of the largest and most experienced regional development agencies in the EU today. Founded in 1976 the mission of the Agency has remained largely unchanged, which is to: 'raise the level of prosperity and quality of life in Wales by stimulating enterprise and indigenous business growth, by attracting high quality investment and by enhancing the environment' (WDA, 1993a).

This mission statement stems directly from the WDA Act (1975), which empowered the Agency to promote Wales as a location for inward investment, to provide finance and otherwise assist the growth of indigenous businesses, to provide and manage premises for commercial use, to reclaim derelict land and to enhance the built environment. To execute these functions, the Agency has experimented with a number of different structures and here we propose to focus on two of these forms: the *centralized* structure which was in place until recently and the *devolved* structure which is currently being implemented.

As we can see from Figure 5.1, the centralized structure involved a small number of key posts: apart from the Board, there was the chairman, the chief executive and six executive directors, each of which managed one of the Agency's divisions. All these posts were based on the eighteenth floor of the Agency's headquarters in Cardiff, an important point because such physical concentration of power sometimes fostered a bunker-like mentality, leaving the Agency open to the charge that it was removed from the clients it sought to serve in the field. What compounded this problem was the fact that the regional directors, who managed the six regional offices, suffered a progressive loss of

The Centralized Structure

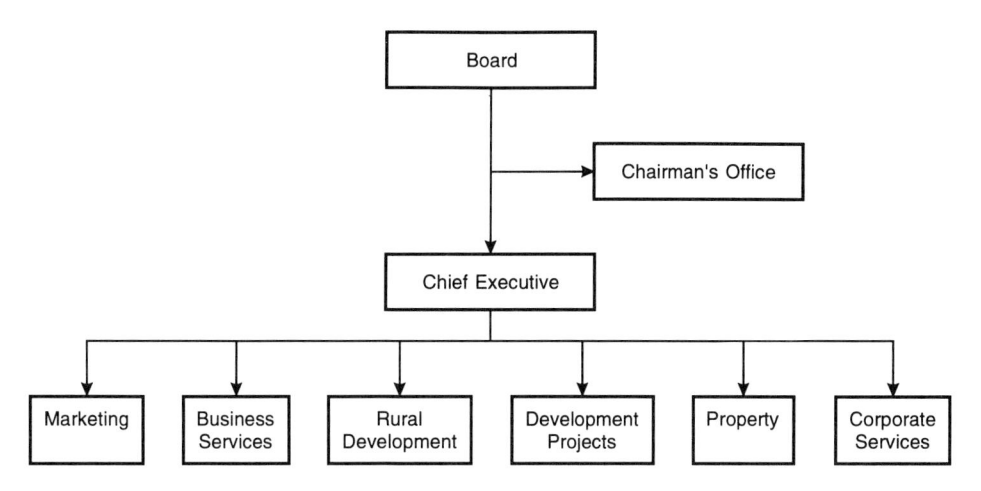

```
                    ┌─────────┐
                    │  Board  │────▶ Chairman's Office
                    └────┬────┘
                         ▼
                  ┌──────────────┐
                  │Chief Executive│
                  └──────┬───────┘
    ┌──────┬──────┬──────┼──────┬──────┬──────┐
Marketing  Business  Rural   Development Property Corporate
           Services Development Projects          Services
```

The Decentralized Structure

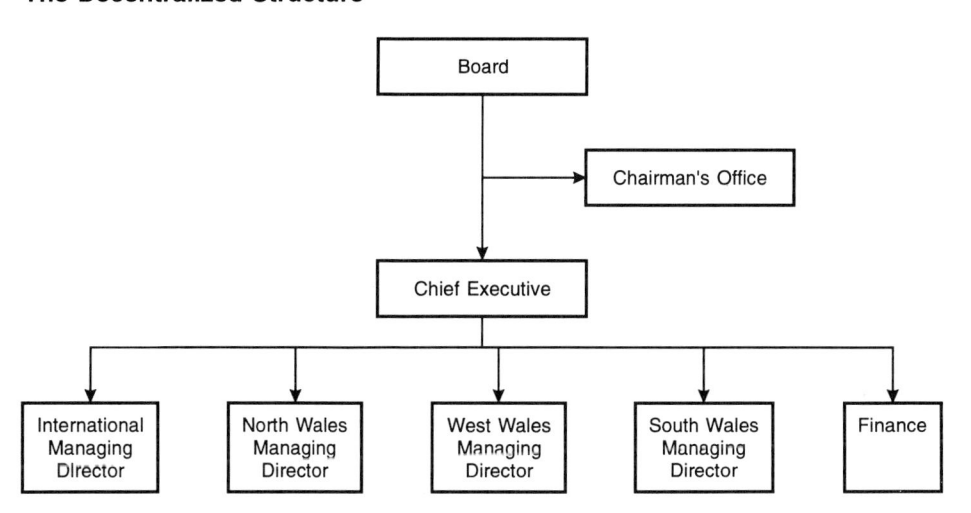

```
                    ┌─────────┐
                    │  Board  │────▶ Chairman's Office
                    └────┬────┘
                         ▼
                  ┌──────────────┐
                  │Chief Executive│
                  └──────┬───────┘
    ┌────────────┬───────┼──────────┬────────────┐
International North Wales West Wales South Wales Finance
Managing     Managing   Managing   Managing
Director     Director   Director   Director
```

Figure 5.1 The changing structure of the WDA

status during the 1980s. This was unfortunate because these regional directors were the main ambassadors of the WDA in the field and, as such, they were potentially well-placed to keep the Agency earthed in and networked to the communities in which the WDA operated. Over time, these regional directors felt more and more excluded from the key decision-making process in Cardiff.

Aside from the communication problems, the restructuring of the Agency had become essential for political reasons. As we shall see below, a series of debilitating internal scandals had fuelled speculation that the Agency was 'out of control'. In technical terms, however, the main rationale for the change was to localize the delivery of programmes, thereby bringing the Agency closer to its customers in the field.

To this end, the six former regions have been amalgamated into three larger, more autonomous regions, each of which is headed by a person of managing director rank. These new 'super regions' are designed to operate as distinct, self-contained units with the authority to design their own regional business plans and deliver the full array of WDA services. As we can see from Figure 5.1, the regional offices are now on a par with the prestigious international division (responsible for inward investment) and they report directly to the chief executive, a move designed to reduce the communication problems associated with the old structure.

A more devolved structure also offers greater potential for cost savings, and this was another motive for restructuring the Agency in this way. By streamlining the central administration the Agency's total staff is being reduced from 440 to around 380 employees and this, in turn, is expected to shave some £1.5 million off the management running costs (MRC) budget, which amounted to £15.1 million in 1993/4. The overall financial position of the WDA is shown in Figure 5.2.

While the resources of the Agency appear to be healthy, the financial picture is far more fragile than it seems. In recent years, the Agency has been forced to raise a growing proportion of its budget from self-generated funds (that is, from sales of its land and property portfolios and from property rents and business service fees). During the tenure of the right-winger John Redwood as the secretary of state for Wales, this process was accelerated to the point where the Agency was forced to raise £180 million through property and land sales in just two years, so that the Welsh Office could reduce the level of grant-in-aid (GIA). While this formula allowed a lower GIA in 1995/6 and 1996/7, it implied a significantly greater level of GIA in 1997/8 if the WDA's total budget was to remain at a similar level.

By this time, of course, the Agency would have little or no capacity to generate internal funds because it would have disposed of its land and property assets. In other words, the WDA faces a coming financial crisis unless it secures a commitment to higher than usual levels of GIA in the future. Not surprisingly, the (unpublished) corporate plan for 1994/5 said that this

Receipts 1994/95
£157.2m

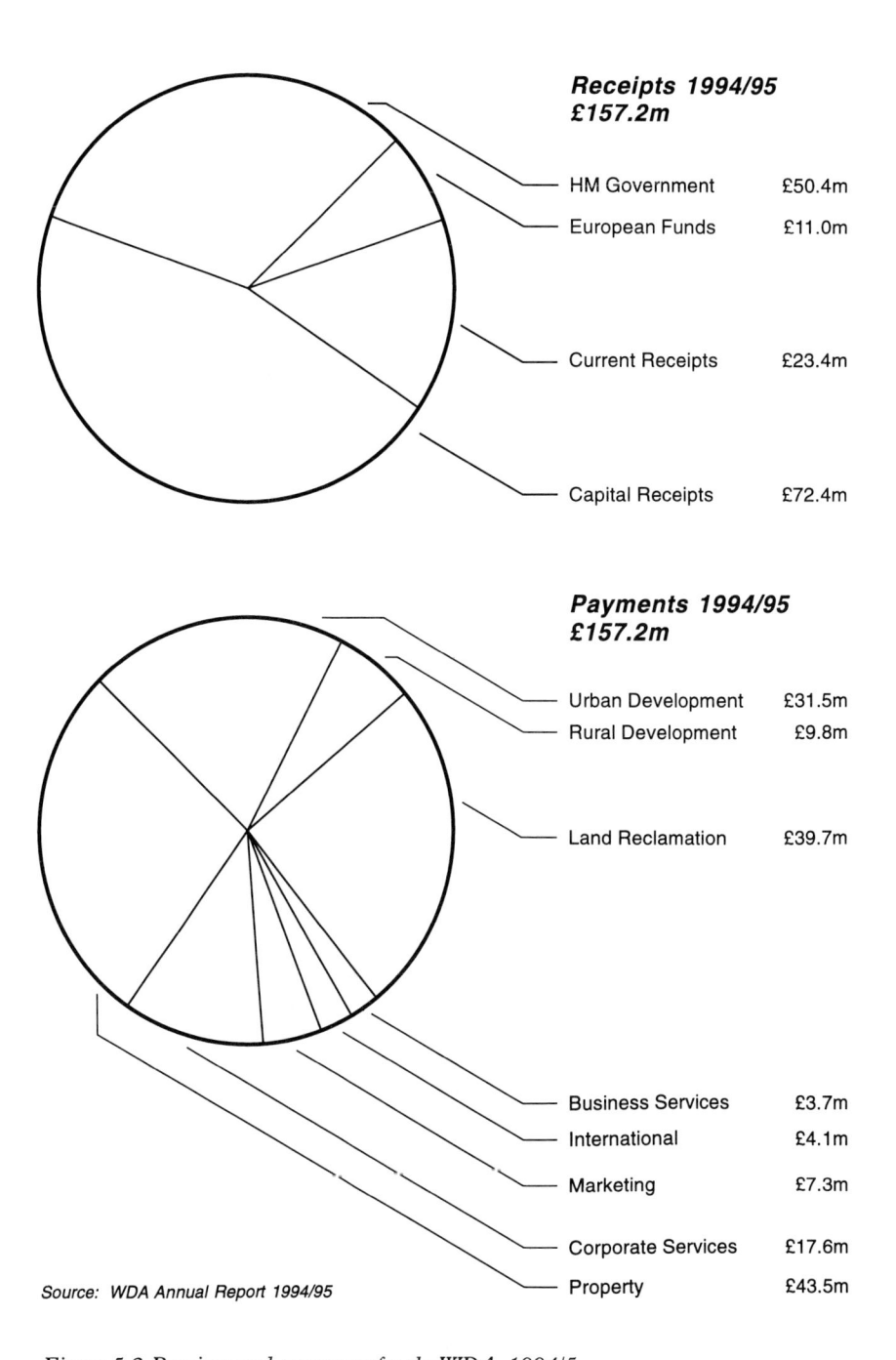

HM Government	£50.4m
European Funds	£11.0m
Current Receipts	£23.4m
Capital Receipts	£72.4m

Payments 1994/95
£157.2m

Urban Development	£31.5m
Rural Development	£9.8m
Land Reclamation	£39.7m
Business Services	£3.7m
International	£4.1m
Marketing	£7.3m
Corporate Services	£17.6m
Property	£43.5m

Source: WDA Annual Report 1994/95

Figure 5.2 Receipts and payments for the WDA, 1994/5

'increased reliance on GIA remains a cause for concern for the Board' (WDA, 1994).

The Agency as animateur: evaluating the strategy

During its early years, the WDA was effectively engaged in a fire-fighting exercise: advance factories were being built at a frenetic pace in the hope of attracting new jobs to compensate for the haemorrhage of traditional jobs in the coal and steel industries. More recently, it has placed a higher premium on the 'soft' infrastructure of business support services, technology transfer and, most crucially of all, paid far more attention to the needs of existing firms, both local SMEs and foreign-owned plants. The aim of this section is to evaluate the WDA's strategy in two key areas: foreign inward investment and business services.

The inward investment strategy: beyond screwdriver plants?

Few parts of the UK have been so dependent on inward investment as Wales. Deprived of an indigenous development capacity when the coal and steel industries collapsed in the inter-war period, the regional development authorities were left with no option other than to attract investment from other regions in the UK and overseas.

There can be no doubt that Wales has been extremely successful in attracting foreign manufacturing investment in recent years. As we can see from Table 5.1, between 1982 and 1992, Wales topped the UK regional table with respect to both investment projects and jobs, so much so that a recent evaluation concluded by saying that 'in the early 1990s Wales remains the number one performing region, attracting around 20 per cent of total new foreign projects entering the UK annually' (Hill and Munday, 1994). With only 5 per cent of the UK population, then, Wales has been securing around a fifth of all foreign projects that have been reported.

If Wales has done well with respect to the *quantity* of foreign investment, what of the *quality* of this investment? The standard critique of the role of foreign investment in Wales is that it has been driven by the search for cheap labour, that it involves low-skill, low-paid activities and that the indirect benefits are minimal because of the weak local multiplier effect – all of which is said to be an inevitable result of the 'branch-plant syndrome'. Although these criticisms carry some force, they are too sweeping to do justice to the nuances within the overseas-owned manufacturing sector in Wales, moreover they do not allow for the incremental changes that are underway in this sector.

The stereotype of the branch-plant in Wales is that of a screwdriver facility which is wholly engaged in semi-skilled assembly functions. While this was

Table 5.1 Regional performance index of foreign investment

Region	Average 1982–92 Project Index	Region	Average 1982–92 New Jobs Index
Wales	3.82	Wales	3.71
North	2.03	Scotland	2.68
Scotland	1.77	North	2.33
West Midlands	1.65	West Midlands	1.48
North West	1.10	North West	0.72
Yorks/Humberside	0.71	East Midlands	0.69
East Midlands	0.65	South West	0.66
South West	0.42	Yorks/Humberside	0.56
South East	0.41	South East	0.30

Source: Hill and Munday (1994).

certainly true in the past, many of these plants appear to be upgrading their facilities into fully-fledged manufacturing operations with a growing brief for design and development and, in a number of cases, for research as well. It is surely significant, for example, that the rate of growth of managers and professional engineers in the electronics and motor component industries has been well above the UK average in the twelve years to 1990 (Lawson and Morgan, 1991). Occupational upgrading of this kind is totally inexplicable if these plants are indeed just assembly – or screwdriver – plants, hence the stereotyped image of the overseas-owned sector needs to be revised.

Given its unpropitious industrial inheritance, Wales has done remarkably well in attracting inward investment and the WDA can legitimately claim to have been in the vanguard of this process. Looking to the future, however, it is not at all certain that Wales will continue to do so well on the inward investment front. Nor is it clear that the WDA is geared up to play as effective a role in the future as it played in the past. Why is this? To highlight the challenge facing Wales as a whole, and the WDA in particular, let us consider how the inward investment process is changing and what this means for regional development policy in Wales.

First and foremost the *mode* of inward investment is changing. Most development agencies in Europe, the WDA included, are still geared to the classical mode of inward investment, that is the new start at a greenfield site. But, as we can see from Table 5.2, this mode of investment is not as important as expansion or re-investment within the existing stock of inward investors, which accounted for 45.6 per cent of all projects between 1984 and 1991.

What this means is that the initial attractions (like the one-off, up-front grant for example) offer no guarantee that the firm will continue to find its existing site sufficiently attractive to commit new rounds of investment at that site. Indeed, the grant factor will be less important to innovative firms than

Table 5.2 Mode of foreign direct investment to the UK, 1984–91

Type of foreign direct investment	Percentage
Expansion	45.6
New Start	37.6
Acquisition	11.6
Joint Venture	5.2

Source: PIEDA (1993).

factors like the quality of labour, the calibre of local suppliers and the networking capacity of the public and private sector organizations.

To illustrate this, local managers at Sony's Bridgend plant found themselves in stiff competition with their colleagues at Sony's Stuttgart and Barcelona plants for the new R&D facility that was eventually secured by the Bridgend plant. To win this re-investment project, the Bridgend managers had to convince Sony's Japanese HQ that South Wales was a location which offered a *sustainable* competitive advantage. In other words the key here was not the one-off, up-front grants which are quickly exhausted, but the fact that Sony found continuing reasons for building on its local achievements in Bridgend – in this case, a committed workforce and trusted local suppliers (Price, Morgan and Cooke, 1994). The moral of this story is that if regions wish to capture these new rounds of investment they must be able to *sustain* their locational attractions and the latter may – and invariably do – change over time.

If regional development agencies are to keep abreast of the changing requirements of key inward investors (or better still to anticipate them), they will need to have more robust *aftercare* programmes than they have today. It would be unfair to say that the WDA is not alive to the growing significance of aftercare. Indeed it claims to have reinforced its aftercare programme so that it visits each inward investor at least once a year to keep abreast of 'its changing business requirements, including wider issues such as training, sourcing opportunities and labour recruitment' (WDA, 1993a). What causes concern, however, is the fact that many WDA managers are not at all clear where the responsibility for aftercare lies – is it a central function or a regional function? Furthermore, who is responsible for ensuring that aftercare information is passed from the inward investment team to the business services team? This issue needs to be resolved as a matter of urgency because the boundary between inward investment and business services functions has become so blurred that an integrated approach is more essential than ever.

The responsibility for aftercare clearly extends beyond the boundaries of the WDA. Because the Agency does not have a major brief for training it is all the more important for it to collaborate with those bodies which do have training as their main responsibility – the Training and Enterprise Councils (TECs) and the Further Education colleges. Fortunately, such collaboration is beginning to happen, but nowhere near the scale that is necessary.

To summarize, we can say that while the WDA has indeed been very successful in attracting inward investment up to now, it will certainly have to improve its aftercare service if it wants to secure re-investment at existing foreign-owned plants. Equally significant, the Agency will have to ensure that an integrated aftercare approach is more than a rhetorical device if it wants to attract high-quality inward investment projects in the future. The key point to remember is that innovative inward investors are no longer content to operate in low-wage, semi-skilled locations: increasingly they are looking for 'an educated, skilled and committed workforce, combined with a social and physical infrastructure capable of generating high productivity' (UNCTAD, 1994). Wales, in other words, needs to reinvent its locational attractions if it wants to stay in the race for foreign inward investment and a whole panoply of organizations, not just the WDA, have a role to play in this process.

The business services strategy: helping firms to help themselves?

All the truly dynamic regional economies in Europe are able to draw upon a wide array of business support services which are designed to enable firms to keep abreast of new technologies, global markets and changing skill requirements. Although these services are particularly important for small and medium-sized enterprises (SMEs), many of which do not have sufficient in-house expertise, these facilities are not unimportant to the larger branch-plants, indeed the latter often cite the local business support environment as a factor in the internal competition for new rounds of investment. These innovative regions, regardless of their political hue, are united in the view that the market is not a sufficient mechanism for promoting either technological innovation or regional development, hence the emphasis on a robust business support system (Cooke and Morgan, 1993).

Although the WDA has been the key factor in the business support scene in Wales for nearly twenty years, it was not until recently that business services received the priority that was always given to land reclamation, property development and inward investment. The elevation of the Agency's business services function is largely due to two factors. First, the Agency was criticized for devoting too much attention to inward investment, and too little attention to indigenous firms. Second, it became clear that at a time when large firms everywhere seemed to be 'downsizing', the main hope for generating jobs lay with SMEs, a sector which had been relatively neglected. Today, the Agency can reasonably claim to have overcome its traditional bias towards inward investment.

The aim of this section is to examine three key areas of business support: (i) sourcing and supplier development; (ii) technology support; (iii) skills development.

One of the most innovative of all the WDA's business services is the *Source Wales* programme, which was originally designed by the Welsh Office and transferred to the Agency. Local sourcing campaigns are nothing new of course, but what differentiates the Source Wales service is that it is first and foremost a supplier development programme. One of the standard criticisms of inward investment in the past was that branch-plants were impervious to local sourcing. The plants themselves claimed that the quality of local suppliers was too poor to risk a local source. To overcome this vicious circle the Source Wales programme, which is buyer-driven, aims to raise the level of local sourcing by working with key customers in the first instance, a route which renders potential suppliers that much more receptive to the WDA's service offerings.

If greater local sourcing is the ultimate aim, the Agency tries to achieve this by fostering long-term partnerships between the buyer and its suppliers. One of the mechanisms for achieving these partnerships is via the Supplier Association, a forum for regular seminars, workshops and development activities where skills, knowledge and techniques are transferred to and from buyers and their key suppliers. Although the Source Wales service has only been fully operational since 1992 it has managed to identify nearly £80 million of sourcing opportunities in 1994/5 and has been well received by both buyers and suppliers in Wales (Henderson, 1994). The key point about the programme is that it does not exhort major customers to 'buy local', rather it aims to achieve this goal as a by-product of a strategy designed to promote high-calibre local suppliers.

A second category of business service is the *technology support* programme which aims to strengthen both product and process technology, especially in the SME sector. One of the ways in which the Agency delivers this service is through an on-site technology audit which identifies the strengths and weaknesses of each firm. These audits, which are part-funded by the European Commission's STRIDE programme, covered 250 SMEs in 1994/5, an increase on the 204 firms audited in the previous year. Apart from working on a one-to-one basis, the Agency also tries to improve the infrastructure by promoting centres of technical expertise within the Welsh academic establishment. These technical centres, which number twenty-two in all, are designed to offer specialized assistance to Welsh-based firms. One of the problems with these centres, however, is that they need to develop a more professional, more commercial approach to the marketing of their services because in too many cases the corporate sector is simply unaware of their existence. In other words, a *supply-side* policy is simply not enough: if firms do not utilize the services then the centres are like cathedrals in the desert.

The Agency has learned that the best business support initiatives are those in which firms are helped to help themselves. A good example of this kind of initiative is the sectorally-based technology club which was pioneered in the Welsh medical sector, and which is now being created in other key sectors. As

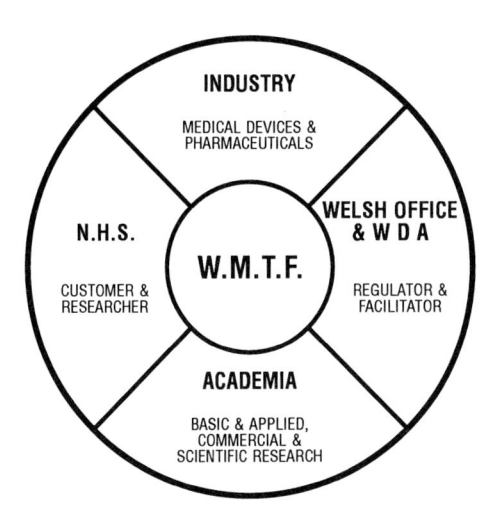

```
                    INDUSTRY
              MEDICAL DEVICES &
              PHARMACEUTICALS

   N.H.S.                        WELSH OFFICE
                   W.M.T.F.         & W D A

  CUSTOMER &                      REGULATOR &
  RESEARCHER                      FACILITATOR

                    ACADEMIA
              BASIC & APPLIED,
              COMMERCIAL &
              SCIENTIFIC RESEARCH
```

The mission of the Forum is:

→ **To improve the competitiveness of the Welsh medical sector.**

→ **I gryfhau gallu cystadleuol y sector meddygol Cymreig.**

and the objectives are:

- To enable Welsh health care companies to become more profitable.
  I alluogi cwmniau gofal iechyd Cymreig i fod yn fwy proffidiol.

- To promote and enhance the research capabilities of Welsh medical technology.
  I hybu ac ehangu'r gallu i wneud ymchwil mewn technoleg meddygol yng Nghymru.

- To enhance interactions between research organisations and industry in Wales.
  I ehangu'r cydweithrediad rhwng sefydliadau ymchwil a diwydiant yng Nghymru.

Figure 5.3 The Welsh Medical Technology Forum

we can see from Figure 5.3, which highlights the strategy and structure of the Welsh Medical Technology Forum, the aim of these clubs is to network the disparate sources of expertise in each sector so as to create the conditions for collaborative learning, a process which is driven by the needs of the firms and facilitated by the Agency.

The third category of business service is *skills development*, where the WDA once again plays the role of animateur rather than direct provider because the main responsibility for training provision lies elsewhere, primarily with the TECs. The most notable training initiatives to date have been designed to overcome the barriers which SMEs face in gaining access to affordable and customized training services. In partnership with the TECs and the Further Education colleges, the Agency has helped to form a number of training consortia: working in concert, these firms are able to specify their common requirements and spread the cost of training between themselves, the TECs and the WDA. These consortia involve new forms of collaboration between providers and users and, through better iteration, this helps to integrate the demand and supply sides of the labour market. Thus far the training consortia concept, which aims to provide joint solutions to common problems, has been used to deliver specific training packages in the information technology and automotive industry, and new consortia are being planned to provide technician grade skills in the manufacturing sector as a whole (WDA, 1992, 1993b). Although it is too early to assess the effects of this initiative, the training consortia concept has been successful in SME-dominated regions throughout Europe and North America.

Any dispassionate evaluation of the WDA's record to date could not fail to conclude that, in the face of adverse circumstances, it has played a very positive role in promoting economic renewal. With very few exceptions it is clear that the Agency is evolving from a position which entailed the direct provision of services – in property and in investment for example – to a point where it increasingly plays the role of *animateur*: that is facilitating, partnering and brokering the activities of a wide array of public and private sector bodies.

This is as it should be because no single organization, no matter how large, has the resources, the competence or the credibility to regenerate the Welsh economy on its own. As we shall see in the next section, it will become more and more difficult to evaluate the role of the WDA as a discrete entity because its success will increasingly come to depend on the complementary actions of its partners, like the local authorities in urban regeneration, the TECs in training, and the Business Connect network in enterprise support. Because of the political crises that have engulfed the WDA during the early 1990s, however, it is difficult to know in which direction the Agency will evolve in the future or, taking the worst scenario, whether it has a future at all. To understand these problems let us turn to consider the origins and consequences of these political crises.

Regulating the Agency: the dilemmas of governance

Development agencies the world over have to contend with a fundamental problem: on the one hand they are charged with the task of regional renewal, which is necessarily a long-term endeavour, but on the other hand they must satisfy the short-term electoral cycle which is uppermost in the minds of their political masters. Where there is a strong regional consensus, in which politicians and officials subscribe to a broadly agreed strategy, this problem is less debilitating; where there is not, the problem can actually undermine the regional strategy itself. Development agencies like SPRI in the Basque country and ERVET in Emilia-Romagna are just two examples of agencies which have recently grappled with this problem. But few agencies in Europe have had to contend with the political problems, both internal and external, which have beset the WDA in recent years.

What exacerbates this problem in Wales is the fact that the political masters at the Welsh Office are Conservatives, a minority political party in Wales with just six of the thirty-eight parliamentary seats and a negligible presence in Welsh local government. Unlike many of the strongest regions in Europe, which have elected regional governments which reflect political opinion in the regions, the political masters in Wales are completely at odds with the vast majority of the Welsh electorate. In other words, the dominant political culture in Wales – the culture of Labourism – has little influence on the Welsh Office, a phenomenon which would not arise in the federal systems of the European Union.

Party differences, however, should not be exaggerated, indeed they are too crude to capture the nuances of Welsh politics. At bottom Wales is a corporatist society, a culture which sets a high premium on collaboration between management and labour in the economy and between the public and private sectors in general. Previous Conservative secretaries of state for Wales, like Peter Walker and David Hunt, felt able and willing to work within this culture because they were Disraelian Tories, a Conservative tradition akin to Christian Democracy in Western Europe, and one which accepts that the state, in partnership with the private sector, has a positive role to play in social and economic renewal. The recent crisis in the WDA stemmed from the fact that John Redwood, the former secretary of state for Wales, came from a radically different Conservative tradition. Thatcherite in essence, hence resolutely pro-market, this tradition embodies a deep ideological aversion towards the public sector.

As we shall see, this pro-market philosophy is now being applied to the WDA, so much so that the Agency is being challenged to justify its very existence. As the WDA is still trying to recover from its own self-inflicted wounds, this political *volte-face* only exacerbates the problems within the Agency.

Fallible servant: the failure of self-regulation

As a non-departmental public body (NDPB), the WDA is subject to the regulations which govern these NDPBs – bodies popularly known as quangos. While these quangos are not subject to day-to-day direction from their sponsoring departments, they are obliged to agree their strategic aims with their political masters (Welsh Affairs Committee, 1993).

By and large, the Agency has always been responsible for regulating its own behaviour, albeit within the parameters laid down by the Welsh Office. This convention of self-regulation makes it all the more important that the chairmanship of the WDA, which is arguably the second most powerful post in Wales after the secretary of state, is occupied by someone who is alive to and respectful of the public service ethos of the Agency. Yet given the status of this post, the flamboyant managerial style which was encouraged by Dr Gwyn Jones, chairman of the Agency from 1988 to 1993, was clearly at odds with the public-service ethos of the WDA.

Projecting himself as a dynamic entrepreneur bringing private-sector practices to a staid public-sector bureaucracy, Dr Jones seemed beyond reproach, especially when, in November 1989, Mrs Thatcher expressed her personal admiration for his work, saying 'what a marvellous chap they've got at the WDA'. This style was clearly anathema to the public service ethos, and for many it was at the heart of scandals exposed between 1990 and 1992. Among other things it was found that:

- the Agency had lost £1.4 million through making irregular redundancy payments to its staff in a scheme which was not notified to the Welsh Office
- it failed to identify professional fees to consultancy firms amounting to £308,000 for 'Operation Wizard', a project which among other things considered the possible privatization of parts of the Agency
- it had incurred £33,000 in irregular payments on a car scheme which allowed Board members and senior executives to be subsidized for private motoring. (Committee of Public Accounts, 1993)

Why did the system of self-regulation within the Agency fail to detect and correct these irregularities? Why, in other words, did the Board fail to live up to the standards of public probity expected of it? It may be that it was simply unfamiliar with the rules and regulations. If this is indeed the case then it exposes the limitations of a policy which extols the use of private sector personnel who are unfamiliar with the conventions of public sector bodies.

These and other issues were exposed to the full glare of public scrutiny in 1992, when the Public Accounts Committee interrogated the WDA. In its report the Committee concluded by saying that it was particularly concerned:

that the Agency have permitted poor management practices to develop, both for personnel matters and financial control. Overall, we consider that the matters covered in this report have demonstrated that the standards of the Agency have been well below what this Committee and Parliament have a right to expect . . . we regard it as unacceptable that the Welsh Office took no action against anyone in the top echelons of the Agency who presided over a catalogue of serious and inexcusable breaches of expected standards of control and accountability. (Committee of Public Accounts, 1993)

Stung by this damning indictment, the Welsh Office quickly appointed a new, more mature chairman. Today, not a single senior executive of the 1988–1992 era remains in post, even though some of these executives were not implicated in the scandals and could have offered some continuity. Although this clean sweep was deemed necessary to placate an embarrassed Welsh Office, it means that the Agency is now being run by a management team which has little or no experience of regional economic development, little knowledge of the public sector and no experience at all of dealing with the Welsh Office. Indeed, with one exception, the new senior management team has been recruited entirely from the private sector and from outside Wales. While this emphasis on new faces is clearly welcome to the Welsh Office, which is eager to show that it has tamed the leading Welsh quango, it means that the new managers face a formidable learning curve at a time when the Agency's stock of political capital is at an all-time low. While this is certainly a problem for the WDA, it is treated with equanimity in the Welsh Office, indeed it helps the latter to re-assert control over the Agency, its fallible servant.

Political master: the fallibility of the Welsh Office

Founded in 1964 with a staff of just 225 civil servants, the Welsh Office currently employs some 2,400 people and had a budget of £6.3 billion in 1993/4, over a third of which was spent via a network of quangos, with the WDA being the largest and most influential. As a multifunctional government department, the Welsh Office has grown as more and more functions have been devolved to Wales from Whitehall, a positive step save for the fact that its politicians are appointed by central government rather than elected by the people of Wales. As a territorial department, the Welsh Office has a somewhat schizophrenic role: while it is first and foremost an outpost of central government, it is also supposed to defend the interests of Wales in central government, where the secretary of state has a seat in cabinet.

Compared to the Scottish Office, which was created in 1885, the Welsh Office lacks a tradition of autonomy; it is therefore not so independently minded, it has fewer locally-bred civil servants in its upper ranks and it is more inclined to accept central government policy initiatives with just minor local variations (Rhodes, 1988). While this view is broadly correct, it tends to underestimate the potential, however modest, for developing policy initiatives in Wales which are not part of the Whitehall 'template'. To a certain extent, the stature and politics of the secretary of state can make a difference. We might recall the way in which Peter Walker used the Welsh Office as a platform to develop his own brand of Conservative philosophy, stressing the 'partnership approach' as opposed to the free-market nostrums of Thatcherism. Recall, too, the way in which David Hunt, who was strongly pro-European, encouraged the WDA to promote Wales in Europe in a way that was unthinkable during the Euro-sceptical regime of John Redwood.

As a key member of the neo-liberal faction in the government, John Redwood has little in common with his two predecessors at the Welsh Office. His appointment in May 1993 was received in Wales with a mixture of disbelief and apprehension, not least because it was generally believed that the Welsh Office was an outpost for interventionist Tories. Given the deeply embedded Labourist traditions in Wales, John Redwood was looked upon as a somewhat bizarre, not to say exotic, political creature who had been transplanted to an alien habitat. With a reputation for being personally involved in the minutiae of policy-formation, he had an unnerving effect on the key Welsh institutions, including the Welsh Office itself, by extolling the market and by being less than effusive about the role of public-sector bodies like the WDA.

Redwood entered the post at a time when the series of scandals had already damaged the Welsh Office's credibility, leaving it open to the charge that the Welsh quangos were 'out of control' (Perry, 1993). Although the WDA scandals proved to be the most embarrassing of all, the Agency was just one of a number of NDPBs which appeared out of control, and these problems added to the sense of malaise. For example, during a review of mismanagement at the Development Board for Rural Wales (DBRW), the Welsh Office readily conceded that control arrangements had not worked effectively.

The political controversies surrounding 'quangoland' have been compounded by the fact that some of the senior posts in these quangos have been given to people who are closely identified with the Conservative Party, fuelling speculation that this minority political party is trying to further its influence through the unelected state because it cannot achieve power through the ballot box in Wales (Morgan and Roberts, 1993). For all these reasons, there is a growing demand for more democracy and more accountability in the governance of Wales, especially for a directly-elected Welsh Parliament, which would mean that the Welsh Office was rendered more accountable to the electorate in Wales (Osmond, 1994).

Against this political background it is easy to understand why the Welsh Office is so anxious to reassert control over the WDA. As we have seen, however, it is not feasible for the Welsh Office to exercise day-to-day control because it does not have the time, the resources or the competence. Indeed, all that it can do is to appoint the Board and define the strategic path which the Agency is expected to follow. In practice, what this means is that the Agency must gain annual approval for its corporate plan and the Secretary of State meets the Board twice a year in order to review past performance and consider priorities for the future.

Tension, however, is ever-present in Welsh Office–WDA relations. In 1994, the Welsh Office rejected the draft corporate plan and informed the Agency that it should go back to the drawing board to justify its very existence. How can we explain this crisis? There were two factors at work. Firstly, the Welsh Office was subject to intense Treasury pressure to reduce public expenditure, hence it was looking for potential savings. Secondly, the corporate plan was presented in a rather amateurish way, which is not surprising when one considers that the newly installed management team was totally unfamiliar with the game of political bargaining. Whatever the reasons, the fact remains that the WDA has been seriously weakened, with the result that staff morale has never been lower.

The networking challenge: a future scenario

Assuming the WDA retains its present functions, what does the future hold? There can be no doubt that it deserves to have a future. Notwithstanding its past management problems, the Agency has played a very positive role in modernizing the Welsh economy and enhancing the environment. For all that has been achieved, however, Wales continues to lag behind on a number of key economic indicators: GDP per head is the lowest in mainland Britain; earnings are well below the UK average; income per head is also the lowest in mainland Britain; and Welsh activity rates have a similar status. In other words there remains a major developmental challenge ahead and the WDA is an important ingredient in the recipe for economic renewal in Wales. For all these reasons, the WDA deserves to have a future. Indeed, it seems surprising that there should be any question at all about its future when the English regions are striving to create their own versions of the WDA.

If the WDA is to meet the challenges ahead it will have to learn the lessons of the past, not an easy task at the best of times, but especially difficult with a totally new management team that understandably wants to distance itself from the past. Forging a capacity for learning, in which information, knowledge and expertise is rapidly diffused throughout the organization, as opposed to being hoarded at the top, is the hallmark of the innovative institution, be it a private firm or a public-sector agency. A robust learning capacity depends on networking, which simply means the disposition to collaborate to achieve mutually beneficial ends (Morgan, 1995b).

Deceptively simple in theory, networking can be extremely demanding in practice because it involves sharing information, exchanging knowledge and pooling resources, all of which requires trust. And trust, as we know, cannot be bought. On the contrary, it has to be earned through collaborating and delivering on agreements, some of which may be tacit, and therefore not easily covered by a contract. Far from being a throwback to some pre-industrial age, qualities like trust, mutuality and co-operation nowadays play a vitally important role in innovative institutions and in dynamic regions (Sabel, 1992; Putnam, 1993). Whatever the difficulties associated with networking, then, the potential prize is too great for either firms or regions to recoil from the challenge.

What does this mean for the Agency today? It means that one of the lessons which the WDA must learn from the past is that it needs to develop better networking skills within the Agency and in its dealings with cognate bodies in the field or regional development. In other words, there is both an *internal* and an *external* dimension to the networking challenge.

As regards the *internal* networking challenge we have seen how the Agency, during its centralized era, was unable to share information across different divisions. In other words, it found it difficult to engage in inter-divisional networking. This problem could be even more debilitating under the new devolved structure because the regional divisions, with far more autonomy than ever before, could so easily develop a bunker mentality, making it that much more difficult to exchange information between the regions and the centre.

It will take time for WDA staff to acclimatize themselves to networking in a federal structure, especially for the senior staff in the hierarchy, who might well feel that devolving responsibilities down the line denudes them of power and status. This is the dilemma of innovative organizations today. As one of the more perceptive management experts puts it:

> In the federal structure hierarchies are limited and local; you relate to people in the wider organisation because their role is relevant to your needs not because their status in the organisation requires it. Forget the hierarchy, use the network. (Handy, 1994)

Unnerving as this may be for managers schooled in the multilayered hierarchies of traditional organizations, public or private, the networking ethos is essential if one wants to tap the collective intelligence of the organization and make this knowledge accessible to all, rather than it being the preserve of a managerial élite. Creating a culture in which decentralized learning and decision-making are encouraged and valued is the secret of the innovative organization (Sabel, 1992). This is the internal networking challenge which the WDA must meet if it wants to refashion itself along innovative lines and make the most of its resources.

The *external* networking challenge presents an even stiffer test because it involves changing the way the Agency relates to cognate bodies as well as getting the latter to reciprocate this new networking ethos. The analogy from the corporate world would be the way in which major firms and their key suppliers are making the transition from an adversarial relationship, based on mutual distrust, to a high-trust partnership in which there is a greater sense of shared destiny. Large firms are not embracing this new model for the love of it, but because it is more effective, not least in facilitating a better flow of knowledge between buyer and supplier.

Just as firms are networking to achieve mutually beneficial ends, so development agencies are trying to fashion networks in the private and public sectors to promote regional development (Cooke and Morgan, 1993). The rationale for these networks is very simple: regional development is an ever more collective endeavour and, because no single organization has a monopoly of wisdom, a networking approach helps to disseminate best practice to each member of the network far more rapidly than if each organization acted alone.

A robust networking culture is far from being a reality in Wales today, and this is exacerbated by the uncertainty that has been injected into the economic development policy arena by local government reorganization on the one hand and by changes in the WDA on the other. As the European Commission noted:

> Many of the partners see partnership in a horizontal sense in which equal partners work towards common ends. Central government has tended to see partnership in vertical terms in which the Welsh Office plays the decisive role with any alternative model viewed as unacceptable . . . Working relationships in industrial South Wales, although reasonably good, are limited in scope. (1991, quoted in Morgan, 1995a)

The vertical model to which the Welsh Office is committed is far removed from the networking ethos which innovative organizations are embracing today. If networking is not practised at the very top, then it is less likely to be valued and adopted by the myriad bodies which interact with the Welsh Office.

But the potential dividends of a robust networking approach are too great for bodies like the WDA to content itself with the limited partnerships which exist at present, hence the need to stimulate the networking ethos from the bottom-up. Wales is not a homogeneous entity, a point which has finally been recognized in the WDA's new regionalized structure. One of the main reasons for adopting this devolved structure was to create a better 'fit' between the Agency and the new unitary local authorities in the hope that more effective partnerships might be encouraged. In the words of a recent corporate plan, 'The new regions will be well placed to provide strategic hubs for localities and help co-ordinate economic development plans. Indeed, a key element in the Agency's restructuring programme is the perceived need to localise policy and delivery mechanisms' (WDA, 1994).

Since each of these Welsh sub-regions has its own nuances, its own threats and opportunities, these can be addressed in a more strategic manner than was possible in the past, not least because the WDA regions now enjoy some real autonomy. In the field of urban regeneration, for example, it is now possible for the WDA, in concert with local authorities and other cognate bodies, to consider the needs of the sub-region as a whole, rather than focusing on discrete towns, which is what tends to happen with the urban joint venture approach. In short there is a new opportunity for strategic partnerships to be formed in these sub-regions, between the agencies themselves and between the public and private sectors.

Paradoxically, one of the biggest question marks about the future concerns the WDA itself. Being pro-active was never a problem in the past, save for the arrogance which characterized the Agency in the 1980s. However, the combination of internal scandals and political humiliation seems to have chastened the Agency to the point where it lacks the self-confidence to play a proactive role in forging new developmental coalitions. Having paid for its 'sins' so to speak the Agency should lose no time in reinventing itself as the key interlocutor for the public and private sectors in each of its sub-regions, where the overriding need is for strategic partnerships which are locally empowered to design and deliver a range of services.

Unfortunately, there seems to be a growing polarization of political opinion concerning the WDA's future, to the point where the Welsh Office appears unsure as to whether it ought to have a future at all. This polarization comes at a time when there is mounting evidence that what will separate the more from the less successful regions in the 1990s is not the level of grants and subsidies, but the degree of political consensus on the one hand and the calibre of a region's networking capacity on the other. Wales has the potential to secure both of these ingredients, but only time will tell if Welsh politicians have the stature and the skills to respond to the challenge.

References

Committee of Public Accounts 1993. *Welsh Development Agency Accounts 1991–92* (London, HMSO).

Cooke, P. and K. Morgan 1993. 'The network paradigm: new departures in corporate and regional development', *Environment and Planning D: Society and Space*, Vol.11, pp.543–64.

Handy, C. 1994. *The Empty Raincoat: Making Sense of the Future* (London, Hutchison).

Henderson, D. 1994. 'Innovation support services in Wales', Unpublished M.Sc. Thesis, Department of City and Regional Planning, University of Wales, Cardiff.

Hill, S. and M. Munday 1994. *The Regional Distribution of Foreign Manufacturing in the UK* (London, Macmillan).

Lawson, G. and K. Morgan 1991. *Employment Trends in the British Engineering Industry* (Watford, Engineering Industry Training Board).

Morgan, K. 1995a. 'Reviving the valleys? Urban renewal and governance structures in Wales', in R. Hambleton and H. Thomas (eds.), *Urban Policy Evaluation: Challenge and Change* (London, Paul Chapman Publishers).

Morgan, K. 1995b. *The Learning Region: Institutions, Innovation and Regional Renewal*, Papers in Planning Research No.157 (Cardiff, Department of City and Regional Planning, University of Wales).

Morgan, K. and E. Roberts 1993. *The Democratic Deficit: A Guide to Quangoland*, Papers in Planning Research No.144 (Cardiff, Department of City and Regional Planning, University of Wales).

Osmond, J. (ed.) 1994. *A Parliament for Wales* (Llandysul, Gomer Press).

Perry, S. 1993. 'Quangos out of control', *Western Mail*, 9 July.

PIEDA 1993. *Inward Investment Trends and Prospects* (London, Department of Trade and Industry).

Price, A., K. Morgan and P. Cooke 1994. *The Welsh Renaissance: Inward Investment and Industrial Innovation*, RIR Report No. 14 (Cardiff, Centre for Advanced Studies, University of Wales).

Putnam, R. 1993. *Making Democracy Work* (Princeton NJ, Princeton University Press).

Rhodes, R. 1988. *Beyond Westminster and Whitehall: The Sub-Central Governments of Britain* (London, Unwin Hyman).

Sabel, C. 1992. 'Studied trust: building new forms of cooperation in a volatile economy', in F. Pyke and W. Sengenberger (eds.), *Industrial Districts and Local Economic Regeneration* (Geneva, IILS).

UNCTAD 1994. *World Investment Report 1994: Transnational Companies, Employment and the Workplace* (Geneva, UN).

Welsh Affairs Committee 1993. *The Work of the Welsh Office* (London, HMSO).

Welsh Development Agency 1992. *Collaborative Training for the IT Industry* (Cardiff, WDA).

WDA 1993a. *Annual Report and Accounts* (Cardiff, WDA).

WDA 1993b. *Collaborative Training for Quality in the Automotive Industry* (Cardiff, WDA).

WDA 1994. *Working for Wales: Corporate Plan 1994* (Cardiff, WDA).

6

The Politics of Regional Development Strategy: The Programme for the Valleys[1]

GARETH REES

Introduction: Valleys images

Penrhys perches high on the mountain which separates the main Rhondda Valley from its smaller off-shoot, the Rhondda Fach. Unmistakably a local authority development, it was built in the 1960s to rehouse families from the older settlements strung along the valley floors, whose economic fortunes were even then in doubt, as the first major wave of post-war colliery closures in south Wales began to bite. From the beginning, Penrhys has evoked a powerful, if contradictory, social imagery, produced and reproduced through the media, and embedded in popular perception. Predominantly, it has been represented as a south Wales variant of a 'sink estate', crystallizing the widely perceived links between unemployment, poverty and the social problems of family break-down, a 'drugs culture' and other forms of crime and lawlessness. A graphic example of this theme was provided by a recent television programme, whose account of Penrhys not only emphasized the debilitation of social life brought about by extensive, long-term unemployment, but also dwelt upon some of the more exotic accommodations made by residents to their circumstances: the frequent appearances of a pet iguana contributed to a portrayal of what must have seemed to network viewers as literally a 'foreign' – and exotic – place (BBC2, 1995). Such was local hostility, however, that BBC Wales commissioned a second programme in which local residents and community workers were able to present an account of Penrhys which drew upon a contrasting set of social images. Here, the emphasis was upon the – at least partially successful – attempts of families and neighbours to pull together to develop means of improving not only community life, but also job prospects and the economic environment more generally (BBC Wales, 1995).

These television programmes and Penrhys itself exemplify some of the complex, indeed contradictory, ways in which the industrial Valleys of south Wales more widely have been represented popularly. Novels, films, as well as newspapers, radio and television, have all both reflected and reproduced particular (pre)conceptualizations of the social and economic structure of the Valleys.[2] On the one hand, there are those which focus upon 'community' strengths. If these accounts are deconstructed, it is clear that they embody notions of social cohesiveness, cemented in powerful bonds of kinship, neighbourliness and general patterns of mutual exchange and support. These dense networks of social interaction provide the basis for highly 'efficient' forms of social organization; those who are vulnerable in ill-health, disability, old-age and so on are cared for within the community. An active citizenship is integral and fostered through education and informal associations (clubs, societies, etc.), as well as the formal institutions of politics and the wider labour movement. More recently, whilst it is acknowledged that economic changes have exerted a toll on these characteristic social relations, even the residue constitutes a significant resource with which to combat economic adversity. In contrast, there are equally powerful representations of the Valleys which elaborate their social *disorganization*. In its contemporary form (from the inter-war years), this set of images stresses the social and economic problems arising from an outmoded, 'smoke-stack' economy. The disintegration of the established structures of a 'traditional' society, rooted specifically in the purported certainties of 'coalmining communities', is held to be accompanied by the excrescence of social pathologies. And there are powerful moral overtones here. Economic 'backwardness' is represented as deriving from a lack of initiative and 'entrepreneurial spirit'; an inability to compete economically as a result of industrial intransigence and political extremism. Family breakdown, educational under-performance and crime derive straightforwardly from individual failures to measure up to accepted standards of behaviour.

These social constructions of the Valleys themselves echo a wider imagery of coalfield areas in Britain and elsewhere. Indeed, the tensions between an emphasis upon 'community' strengths, on the one hand, and social pathology and moral degeneracy, on the other, are characteristic of discourses about the working class more generally, and only take on an especially virulent form in the context of the coalfields.[3] Nevertheless, there are also specifically national, Welsh dimensions to this social imagery of the industrial Valleys. Most obviously, the images are expressed in forms which reflect the particularities of the south Wales coalfield: general constructs are realized in concrete terms which draw upon a highly specific historical experience. Moreover, this history has bulked so large in Welsh national development more generally, that the social imagery which reflects it has itself come to constitute a central element in popular constructions of the wider Welsh identity. In ways which have no real parallel in, say, England, an integral part of such popular constructions embodies a powerful set of images of the social relations characteristic of the industrial Valleys; images, I have argued, which emphasize not only a rootedness in working-class 'communities', but also the precariousness of their future social and economic development.[4]

What is most pertinent to the themes of this chapter, however, is that these same images of the south Wales valleys, precisely because of their powerful popular resonances, have come to constitute a significant resource which has been drawn upon in the political processes through which characteristic forms of development strategy for the region have been generated. Hence, central government policies – as well as those of other state agencies – for regional economic development in south Wales have universally been couched in terms which take as *axiomatic* the need to regenerate the economy of the Valleys, despite the collapse and, by the 1980s, the virtual disappearance of the region's initial economic *raison d'être*. Moreover, these strategies have been presented and subsequently debated in terms which stress both the powerful justification for economic regeneration provided by even the residue of strong community relations, as well as the essential contribution which the latter make to achieving it. Whilst there are clearly parallels elsewhere, it is the special vibrancy and popular currency of the social imagery of the Valleys which, in no small part, accounts for the effectiveness of this presentation. What this indicates, therefore, is the significant role played by this imagery in the *politics* of regional development strategy.

In what follows, these rather diffuse propositions are elaborated by means of an examination of regional development strategy in industrial south Wales, focusing on its most recent phase, the Programme for the Valleys (PFV), which was initiated in 1988. The intention, then, is to develop – albeit in a preliminary form – an analysis of regional development strategy which pays due attention to the political processes through which specific policies are formulated and presented and, in particular, the ways in which a characteristic social imagery of the Valleys is implicated here. This emphasis on political processes is by no means intended to substitute for more conventional analysis aimed at evaluating the real impacts of policies on economic and social conditions. It should be recognized, however, that the latter is inherently inconclusive, given the inevitable difficulties in isolating the effects of given policies from those of other factors. Certainly, the uncovering of the forms and conventions of regional development strategy generates important new insights which have been underexplored in urban and regional analysis hitherto.

'Regionalist consensus' and post-war development strategy in south Wales

The PFV is, of course, only the most recent in a series of regional initiatives by central government aimed at tackling the perceived social and economic problems of the south Wales coalfield. Although it is not possible to explore the details here, this history can be traced back at least to the inter-war period (and, in somewhat different forms, even earlier[5]). It was the economic crisis of these years which marked out south Wales as a 'problem region' of 'Outer Britain': a designation which persisted into the post-war decades. With increasing urgency from the mid-1950s onwards, as the coalfield went into increasingly precipitate decline, the quest was for a regional development strategy which would deliver new – and 'modern' – forms of economic activity, generating employment to replace the jobs which had been lost for ever. For a brief time, the region's steel industry, apparently revitalized in post-war reconstruction, provided the focal point for this quest; before it too fell victim to shifts in world markets and the vagaries of government policy, forcing it to embark upon its own programme of retrenchment after the 1960s (Harris, 1987). Thereafter, it was other forms of manufacturing which were held out as the life-line, with inward investment from other parts of Britain and from abroad playing an increasingly important role in official thinking and the debates about appropriate forms of regional growth (Morgan, 1981).

Perhaps the most tangible expression of these currents was the 1967 white paper, *Wales: the Way Ahead* (Welsh Office, 1967). The development strategy for south Wales which was presented here embodied three elements. Firstly, it was argued that the 'modernization' of the regional economy was all but complete. The state had 'rationalized' the coal and steel industries; encouraged the growth of new manufacturing industry to absorb those made redundant; and had dramatically improved the communications infrastructure and the physical environment generally. Indeed, even a (by now notorious) *Times* leader of 1963 had been able to conclude: 'The redevelopment of south Wales has been one of the great success stories of the past 30 years.' Secondly, the continued development of Cardiff was essential, not only to provide jobs in commerce, administration and cultural services, but also to provide the region and Wales as a whole with an *appropriate* capital city (cf. Thomas, 1992). And thirdly, the major remaining problems were seen to be concentrated in the Valleys '. . . where much of the original economic base has gone and only been partially replaced by new industry' (Welsh Office, 1967, p.102). Given the acknowledged difficulties of attracting manufacturers to the coalfield, the solution offered was to use the financial and other incentives available through regional economic policy to develop planned 'growth centres' at the mouths of the valleys (and, to a more limited extent, at the valley heads), thereby capitalizing on the supposed locational advantages to firms, whilst enabling Valleys residents to commute to the prospective new jobs.

Wales: the Way Ahead, then, was the apotheosis of post-war thinking about development strategy in south Wales. In its thoroughgoing dependence on the efficacy of state intervention to bring about improvements in the region's economic and social infrastructure, it clearly reflected the conventions of the wider 'social democratic consensus' which characterized successive governments up until the 1980s. More specifically, however, it expressed what has been termed elsewhere a 'regionalist consensus' about the problems confronting south Wales, as well as their most likely solutions. To an overwhelming extent, the political parties, trades unions, employers' organizations and professionals were in agreement that south Wales's trajectory of economic and social development was *sui generis* and that, therefore, particular policies were required to tackle the remaining problems, not least through the continued devolution of administrative functions to specifically Welsh institutions, of which the Welsh Office itself and, from the 1970s, the Welsh Development Agency (WDA) were clearly the most significant (Rees and Lambert, 1981).

Although this was an analysis and prescription shared across the political spectrum, it was especially strongly represented within the 'Labourism' which dominated the 'regionalist consensus' and, in particular, the political life of the Valleys themselves. Paradoxically, despite the emphasis on the need to 'modernize' south Wales – and the coalfield, more specifically – there were powerful conservative elements here too. The essential point of reference was the regional crisis of the inter-war period (or, more accurately, a social perception of it); new policies were required as much to avoid any return to the privations of those years, as to promote any positive vision of a new economic and social structure for the region. Whilst the commitment to a future for the Valleys was unequivocal (there was never any serious consideration given to an official policy of 'planned decline' of the kind implemented in west Durham (Bulmer, 1978)), as the 1967 white paper made quite explicit, the primary rationale for addressing the outstanding problems of the coalfield was the unquestioned social benefit of *preserving* the 'communities' of the Valleys. Moreover, whilst the human relationships of kinship and neighbourliness which they embodied provided, as has been suggested, a powerful popular appeal, they also fostered highly particularistic and ascriptive forms of social exchange; the 'who you know' syndrome was a real mechanism through which access to scarce jobs, houses and other goods could be rationed (cf. Bulmer, 1977).

Perhaps most tellingly, however, whatever the popular appeal of the strategy encapsulated in *Wales: the Way Ahead*, it is much more difficult to identify clear effects which flowed from it. Undoubtedly, the economic and social structure of south Wales continued to change very dramatically after the 1960s. Little of this, however, can be attributed unequivocally to state strategy; and certainly the fortunes of the coalfield continued to decline (Rees and Lambert, 1981). For precisely these reasons, new initiatives were required in the radically changed environment of the 1980s.

Markets and the regeneration of the Valleys

As has been frequently remarked, the 1980s witnessed a radical shift away from the previously dominant 'social democratic consensus', as central government, in particular, sought to redefine the state's role by privileging *markets* as the central mechanism for shaping economic and social life. In south Wales, however, it is arguable that the impacts of these changes were in some (limited) respects restricted, as a result of the willingness of successive secretaries of state to pursue a somewhat more interventionist agenda than was possible elsewhere in Britain, utilizing the institutions of 'regional government' – and, most significantly, the Welsh Office itself and the WDA – to achieve their aims. Moreover, especially after the industrial crises of the earlier 1980s (see below), remnants of the 'regionalist consensus' were able to reassert themselves around a strategy of renewed 'modernization' of the south Wales economy. Indeed, by the end of the decade, it had once again become part of the hegemonic analysis of the region's economic fortunes that this 'modernization' had been substantially completed successfully (Rees and Morgan, 1991).[6]

The cornerstone of this analysis were the record levels of inward investment, especially from abroad, which were achieved, with a number of large-scale, high-prestige projects understandably making the headlines. This went hand-in-hand with substantial sectoral diversification, especially after the mid-point of the decade, as key manufacturing industries and financial and business services grew strongly, particularly in the east of the region. Moreover, not only did unemployment rates in south Wales fall appreciably relative to those in other parts of Britain, but also there were *some* indications of a shift away from the routine assembly and 'back-office' jobs which had predominated in earlier inward investment, with a growth of jobs requiring intermediate and higher levels of skills and qualifications (Rees and Thomas, 1994). Certainly, the need to create a 'clever region', based on high-skill employment and technologically sophisticated production of goods and services, became a key element within the wider strategy of 'modernization'.

The downside of this account of regional 'modernization', of course, was the massive loss of jobs from steel during the early 1980s and the almost complete elimination of the deep-mined coal industry in the aftermath of the 1984–5 strike. This collapse of the region's traditional industries was presented as an inevitable consequence of failures to cope with the rigours of international markets and, indeed, a necessary corollary of the development of new, 'sunrise' industries in south Wales. Nevertheless, again in an apparently unconscious echoing of earlier analyses, it was recognized that these traumatic changes had given rise to residual problems of adjustment, concentrated in the hardest-hit part of the region, the Valleys. In particular, pockets of high and long-term unemployment in some areas were acknowledged, along with wider problems of poor labour-market opportunities, low earnings and depressed rates of economic activity. These were exacerbated by poor educational performance and inadequate training and, in turn, contributed to significant social disadvantage, albeit concentrated into localized pockets. What was required, therefore, was another special initiative for the industrial Valleys, aimed at mopping up these outstanding difficulties. It is within this analytical (or ideological) context that the PFV should be located.

The Programme for the Valleys

The PFV was introduced in the summer of 1988 by the then secretary of state for Wales, Peter (now Lord) Walker. It was originally intended to run for three years, but in July 1989 it was extended until 1993, producing a five-year first phase. In March 1993, a second phase of the PFV, running for a further five years, was announced by Mr Walker's successor at the Welsh Office, David Hunt. This was subsequently confirmed and elaborated, in October 1993, by John Redwood, who had recently been appointed to succeed Mr Hunt.

In spite of the media fanfare which accompanied its announcement, the first phase of the PFV was remarkable more for its continuities with existing government policies, rather than anything which was truly innovative. On the directly economic front, in line with a key dimension of the official conventional wisdom, much play was made of the development of new small businesses through improved loans schemes and training and support services for (potential) entrepreneurs. Similarly, a great deal was expected from the enhanced operation of the *existing* machinery of regional economic policy to attract major inward investment and facilitate the expansion of existing firms. The WDA and the local authorities were to continue to build advance factories and workshops. And the drive to transform the Valleys into a major tourist attraction was to be extended. More generally too, there was much that was familiar in the proposals for creating a 'total environment' more conducive to economic growth and revival. In particular, improved educational facilities and training provision were intended to raise the quality of the skills available within the Valleys labour force, although again through the intensification of existing policies rather than wholly new initiatives.

Nevertheless, conventional questions as to what effects the PFV actually had still remained; and a considerable amount of analysis and debate was devoted at the time to the attempt to resolve this. Clearly, even an initiative which implied substantial extra investment on fairly traditional policies could exert a significant effect on the problems of the Valleys; and this was certainly the impression which had been fostered at the launch of the programme. Hence, one of the persistent areas of debate was whether the PFV did involve the commitment of *new* funds, as opposed to the redirection or even re-labelling of existing ones. It should be emphasized that this is a highly controversial issue, which even the House of Commons Committee of Public Accounts failed to sort out entirely. In fact, it is a moot point as to whether it is especially profitable to get embroiled in this debate at all. As the official evaluation report shows, although substantial elements of the PFV did simply bring together and give the appearance of coherence to existing expenditures, there were some – albeit limited – additional funds made available; and private investment may well have been increased by the public prioritization of the Valleys (Victor Hausner and Associates, 1993). Perhaps more significantly, however, this fell some way short of the expectations which had been widely raised at the instigation of the programme and by the manner of its announcement.

Moreover, this mixing together of existing and new expenditures meant that there were even greater difficulties than is usual in evaluation research in trying to separate out what had happened in the Valleys *as a consequence* of the PFV from what would have taken place in any case. Certainly, it seems desirable to avoid the tendency of central government spokespeople to claim the credit for all the good things which have occurred, whilst denying any responsibility for the undesirable things which have taken place during the same period. Much has been made, for example, of new investments in the Valleys, whilst very little has been said about factory closures. (Although, in fairness, see Welsh Office, 1993a.) Some of these general issues can be illustrated by reference to specific elements within the Programme.

New investment and the reduction of unemployment

One of the principal areas for action identified initially in the PFV was the stimulation of new industrial investment through the operation of the Regional Development Grant (RDG) scheme and Regional Selective Assistance (RSA). In fact, the only *specific* commitment to employment creation was associated with this element of the Programme. Indeed, there is a sense in which the goal of economic regeneration was detached from that of achieving anything approaching full employment, in sharp contrast to at least the publicly expressed objectives of previous state initiatives. However, it was suggested that:

> . . . on past experience, Government commitments of Regional Development Grant and Regional Selective Assistance on the scale anticipated for the next three years are likely to create additional private investment of well over £1 billion and lead to the creation of 25-30,000 jobs. (Welsh Office, 1988, p.7)

This, in turn, was related to a projected substantial reduction in unemployment, although no precise figures were given here.

In reality, it would appear that employment in manufacturing in the PFV area *fell* by some 11 per cent (from 59,460 to 53,090) between 1988 and 1992 (compared with the equivalent fall for Wales as a whole of 7 per cent). Moreover, the opening of 73 new manufacturing plants and increased employment in a further 203, needs to be set against the closure of 138 existing ones and the decrease of employment in 205 (Welsh Office, 1993a). Nevertheless, unemployment did fall during the period between June 1988 and June 1993, but by only some 0.8 of a percentage point. This compares very favourably with the experience of Britain as a whole (where unemployment rose substantially), and is slightly higher than the decrease which occurred in the total Welsh economy during this period (from 10.1 to 9.9). This is to say that the disparities between the Valleys and elsewhere in Wales closed somewhat. However, whilst Welsh unemployment as a whole fell to levels close to the UK average, unemployment in the Valleys remained very substantially higher – and male unemployment actually increased during the period of this first phase of the programme.

Moreover, changes in unemployment figures are only one of the indicators relevant to this kind of assessment of the PFV. Equally salient are the data on shifts in employment during the relevant period. More specifically, a much more complex analysis of flows into and out of employment would be required before a proper picture of changes in the Valleys labour market and the opportunities available in it could be established. In particular, it would be important to know what kinds of people are moving into and out of employment, as well as the nature of that employment. Unfortunately, given existing data sources, it is not possible to construct such an analysis. Therefore, official claims that additional private investment during the initial Programme period 'involved' 24,000 jobs should be treated with some caution, as this estimate certainly obscures key distinctions between full-time and part-time jobs, those which have been newly created and those which have been preserved and so on. Moreover, the increasing gaps between male activity rates in Wales and those in Britain, as well as between Welsh average earnings and British ones, reinforce this note of caution.

What is more, even if a complete labour market analysis were available, it would still be necessary to establish the relationship between the changes taking place and the Regional Development Grant Scheme and Regional Selective Assistance. What is most ironic here is that, in line with wider government imperatives, total regional aid to the PFV area was substantially *reduced* over the Programme period. Regional Development Grants (some £17.2 million in 1988/9) were phased out. Actual expenditure on Regional Selective Assistance fell by almost 40 per cent (from £11.6 million to £7.1 million) during the first three years of the Programme, before rising again to over £15.2 million in 1992/3. The overall effect of these changes was a fall in total expenditure (RDG plus RSA) of some 45 per cent (from £28.8 million to £16 million). This is not to suggest, of course, that the effects of these policies were non-existent. However, it would appear difficult to sustain an argument which attributes anything more than a contributory influence on employment generation. Indeed, it seems most likely that the changes in employment and unemployment in the Valleys during this period primarily reflect wider influences than the PFV.

Regional initiative and national policies

The latter point illustrates a key issue with respect to the PFV. Although itself introduced by a department of central government – the Welsh Office – the PFV inevitably operated in an environment structured by wider policy imperatives. Hence, as has been seen, whatever the Programme's intended impacts on regional assistance to the Valleys, these were swamped by the more general aim to cut government expenditure on regional aid, in line with the wider neo-liberal agenda. Moreover, more recent changes have cut regional assistance to the Valleys even further (cf. Rees and Morgan, 1991).

Exactly similar arguments can be made in respect of other key elements of the PFV. For example, considerable emphasis was initially attached to raising the quality of the workforce through improved vocational education and training (VET). Yet government support for the Training and Enterprise Councils (TECs), which since 1989 have had responsibility for the organization and implementation of VET in local labour markets, has been *cut* in successive years. This implies that the TECs' activities have been constrained and the delivery of *statutory* training programmes for the adult long-term unemployed (Employment Training, now Training for

Work) and unemployed 16- and 17-year-olds (Youth Training) has been a much greater element of their work than was initially envisaged. Certainly, given these financial restrictions, there has been relatively little scope to develop programmes of training for those who are already in employment. This has been especially harmful in areas such as the south Wales Valleys, where the need for high quality VET is acute and where employers are frequently both unwilling and unable to invest in such programmes for their employees. Not surprisingly, therefore, levels of participation in training and the acquisition of qualifications continue to lag behind those in more prosperous parts of Wales and Britain generally (Istance and Rees, 1995). The lesson, therefore, is apparently a simple one: regional initiatives, such as the PFV, cannot operate independently of wider policy priorities.

What is, perhaps, most striking here is that this obvious tension between different elements of state policy was wholly ignored in the public presentation of the first phase of the PFV. The latter was ostensibly to be no less than the means by which a revitalized economic and social structure for the Valleys was to be generated. The unquestioned commitment to ensuring the Valleys' future – characteristic, as has been seen, of the whole of the post-war period – was publicly guaranteed. What were different, however, were the terms on which this commitment was made. The government's wider privileging of market relations in economic development entailed a much more explicit emphasis than hitherto on the responsibilities of *individuals* to revive the economic fortunes of the Valleys: to be effective entrepreneurs, skilled employees, successful students and so forth. Likewise, it was for individuals as consumers to structure effective social provision, within a context set by rather traditional family relationships; and so on. Indeed, the success or otherwise of these marketized approaches to the problems of the Valleys provided something of a 'test case' with much more general applicability, precisely because of the Valleys' collectivist political legacy (cf. Rees and Thomas, 1991).

Much more explicitly than with previous strategies, therefore, the PFV was initiated in terms which stressed the popular conceptualization of the south Wales Valleys as economically out-of-date and socially disorganized; and which, more explicitly than at any time since the inter-war years, attributed this to the failings of individuals. A *moral* dimension was at the top of the agenda. All of this, it might appear, sits rather uneasily with the alternative – and previously dominant – social imagery of the Valleys, based upon their 'community'-based strengths and capacities for collective and collaborative action. Paradoxically, however, the PFV, more latterly, has sought the best of both worlds and has simultaneously been couched in terms of the social resources on which strong communities can draw.

Facing the future: the PFV second phase

The second phase of the PFV was announced in April 1993. Its tone was certainly rather different from that of its predecessor. Given the inevitability of continued stringency with respect to public expenditure in Britain as a whole, it is perhaps not surprising that the emphasis was less upon new and additional public investment and more on 'maximizing existing resources'. Possibly, the lessons of the earlier controversies over whether new funding had actually been made available had been absorbed. Moreover, there was a much greater acknowledgement of the positive role to be played in regional development strategy by collaborative and collective forms of action.

Even during the latter years of the first phase of the programme (1991–3), it began to be acknowledged that one of the most positive features of the initiative was the potential which it offered for developing *institutional partnerships* or *networks* which could better direct available resources at alleviating problems in the Valleys. As it was officially put in 1991: 'In assessing the achievements so far, it has become clear over the life of the Programme that the key to its success has been the partnerships it has engendered, between central and local government, the public and private sectors, employers and unions' (Welsh Office, 1991, p.3).

What was being highlighted, then, was that the active participation of local authorities, the social partners and so forth was a necessary element of achieving the PFV's objectives. To put this in other terms, the 'regionalist consensus' around a 'modernization' strategy – which was described earlier – was recognized explicitly by the state and, thereby, it was presumably hoped that its contribution would be cemented. It should be remembered too, of course, that it was becoming increasingly part of the conventional wisdom of regional development strategy that the influence of institutional networks of this kind have been a key element in the economic success of a number of regions in Europe and elsewhere (see, for example, Cooke and Morgan (1993)). Moreover, 'partnership' is very much the language of the European Union (EU); and a *sine qua non* of obtaining EU funding.

What remains much more of a moot point, however, is the extent to which this recognition was translated into practical institutional mechanisms. Certainly, the evidence of the official evaluation report in this regard is somewhat equivocal; there seems to be a considerable gap between the conclusions with respect to facilitating partnerships within the Programme and the actual evidence of their development (Victor Hausner and Associates, 1993). Moreover, to the extent that such institutional partnerships have been developed, they have assumed characteristic forms. Hence, they tend to be markedly vertical in structure, reflecting the fact that they have been instigated by the institutions of regional government in Wales, especially the Welsh Office. The linkages within networks therefore tend to be formalized and restricted in scope and focused on the achievement of closely defined goals. Because of this, they constrain the establishment of trust and partnership-building among the various players because relations assume a dependent rather than interdependent flavour.[7] The conclusion of a European Commission evaluation of partnership arrangements in south Wales is instructive in this regard:

> Many of the partners see partnership in a horizontal sense in which equal partners work towards common ends. Central government has tended to see partnership in vertical terms in which the Welsh Office plays the decisive role with any alternative model viewed as unacceptable . . . Working relationships in industrial South Wales, although reasonably good, are limited in scope. (1991)

In Hausner's (1994) terms – in a discussion of economic development in Central and Eastern Europe – the strategy has been 'imperative' rather than 'interactive'. The objectives and rules of network participation have been laid down by the central authority – the Welsh Office, in this case – rather than where, '. . . the central authority, initiating and directing the changes, takes on the role of participant and treats the other participants as independent agents, whose behaviour can only change as a consequence of mutual interaction' (p.1).

In the light of these arguments, it is ironic that the second phase of the PFV takes this ostensible commitment to collaborative approaches a step further. It stresses not only collaboration at the level of institutions, but also the significance of what are termed: 'local strategies, responding to the needs and opportunities of local communities, and increasingly driven by those local communities themselves' (Welsh Office, 1993b).

What this seems to imply, therefore, is a commitment to increased democratic participation in the development and implementation of the second phase of the PFV, harnessing local initiative and resources. In more general terms, it may be argued that there has been a shift from a programme whose *raison d'être* was presented in terms of providing new sources of public investment in the Valleys to one whose essence is the development of new forms of local governance (and this, incidentally, is what is suggested in the official evaluation report (Victor Hausner and Associates, 1993)).

This appeal to the efficacy of 'community'-based solutions to the problems of the Valleys is, of course, a familiar one. As has been argued throughout this chapter, it draws upon a deeply-rooted set of social images of the strengths of Valleys 'communities', which, in turn, constitutes a significant element in a wider national Welsh consciousness. For these reasons, therefore, a regional development strategy couched in these terms inevitably strikes a powerful, popular chord in south Wales. At present, what remains to be seen, however, is the extent to which this persuasive rhetoric will be translated into practical policies which impact meaningfully upon economic and social life in the Valleys; especially where to do so will require overcoming the effects of a hostile general policy environment. The history of previous regional initiatives in the south Wales Valleys indicates that considerable scepticism is warranted here. Whilst securing a viable future for the Valleys remains a widely shared objective in Wales, its achievement remains as far away as ever.

Notes

[1] This chapter draws in part on research funded by the Economic and Social Research Council (grant number L311253058), whose support is gratefully acknowledged. This research was carried out jointly with Shari Garmise and Kevin Morgan, although responsibility for the views expressed here are mine alone.

[2] This is not the place to develop these arguments more fully. However, it is stereotypical and sentimentalized versions of 'coalfield communities' which have been presented most frequently in popular culture, best illustrated in Hollywood films such as 'How Green Was My Valley' (Berry, 1994, pp.160–6). The alternative, darker accounts have more frequently featured in 'documentary' forms – such as television and newspapers – but can be traced in novels and films too. For an interesting exploration of very similar themes, see Humphrys (1995).

[3] For an insightful development of these themes, see Metcalfe (1988).

[4] Of course, popular constructions of Welsh identity embrace other elements too. The intention here is not to provide a complete account, but simply to indicate the significance of social constructions of the industrial Valleys. It is also conceded that this discussion is somewhat speculative. However, it is at least consistent with what little survey data there are available: see, for example, Balsom (1985).

[5] Before the crisis of the inter-war period, greatest concern was expressed over the need to control the effects of excessive growth in the south Wales coalfield, in terms of both the need to provide proper housing and to plan urban development coherently, as well as to curb the perceived effects of rapid social transformation.

[6] The analysis is well expressed in much of the marketing literature produced by the WDA. A more extended account in this vein is given in Cole (1990), *The New Wales*, a collection of essays brought together by a well-known journalist on behalf of the WDA. Alternative accounts of regional development were of course offered, but failed to achieve a comparable impact.

[7] These points are elaborated in Garmise, Morgan and Rees (1995).

References

Balsom, D. 1985. 'The three Wales model: the political sociology of Welsh identity, recent electoral trends, pressures for change', in J. Osmond (ed.), *The National Question Again* (Llandysul, Gomer).

BBC2 1995. 'Mad Passionate Dreams', *Nice Work series*, 14 November.
BBC Wales 1995. 'The Way It Is', December.
Berry, D. 1994. *Wales and Cinema: The first hundred years* (Cardiff, University of Wales Press).
Bulmer, M. 1977. 'Tammany Hall beside the Wear', *New Society*, 24 November.
Bulmer, M. (ed.) 1978. *Mining and Social Change* (London, Croom Helm).
Cole, D. (ed.) 1990. *The New Wales* (Cardiff, University of Wales Press).
Cooke, P. and K. Morgan 1993. 'The network paradigm: new departures in corporate and regional development', *Society and Space*, Vol.11, pp.543–64.
European Commission 1991. *Ex-Ante Evaluation of Community Support Programmes and Dependent Programmes for the Objective 2 Areas of South Wales and Bremen* (Brussels, European Commission).
Garmise, S., K. Morgan and G. Rees 1995. 'New Structures of Local Economic Governance', *End-of-Award Report to the ESRC*, mimeo.
Harris, C. 1987. *Redundancy and Recession in South Wales* (Oxford, Blackwell).
Hausner, J. 1994. 'Imperative vs. interactive strategy of systematic change in Central and Eastern Europe', *Review of International Political Economy*, Vol.2.
Humphrys, R. 1995. 'Images of Wales', in T. Herbert, and G. E. Jones (eds.), *Post-War Wales* (Cardiff, University of Wales Press).
Istance, D. and G. Rees 1995. 'Education and training in Wales: problems and paradoxes revisited', *Contemporary Wales*, Vol.7, pp.6–26.
Metcalfe, A. 1988. *For Freedom and Dignity: historical agency and class structures in the coalfields of NSW* (Sydney, Allen and Unwin).
Morgan, K. 1981. 'State policy and regional development in Britain: the case of Wales', Unpublished D.Phil. Dissertation, University of Sussex.
Rees, G. and J. Lambert 1981. 'Nationalism as legitimation? Notes towards a political economy of regional development in south Wales', in M. Harloe (ed.), *New Perspectives in Urban Change and Conflict* (London, Heinemann).
Rees, G. and K. Morgan 1991. 'Industrial restructuring, innovation systems and the regional state: south Wales in the 1990s', in G. Day and G. Rees (eds.), *Regions, Nations and European Integration* (Cardiff, University of Wales Press).
Rees, G. and M. Thomas 1991. 'From coal-miners to entrepreneurs? A case-study in the sociology of re-industrialisation', in M. Cross and G. Payne (eds.), *Work and the Enterprise Culture* (Lewes, Falmer Press).
Rees, G. and M. Thomas 1994. 'Inward investment, labour market adjustment and skills development: recent experience in south Wales', *Local Economy*, Vol.9, pp.48–61.
Thomas, H. 1992. 'Redevelopment in Cardiff Bay: state intervention and the securing of consent', *Contemporary Wales*, Vol.5, pp.81–98.
Victor Hausner and Associates 1993. *The Programme for the Valleys: An evaluation* (London, Victor Hausner & Associates).
Welsh Office 1967. *Wales: the Way Ahead*, Cmnd. 3334 (Cardiff, HMSO).
Welsh Office 1988. *The Valleys – a Programme for the People* (Cardiff, Welsh Office).
Welsh Office 1991. *The Valleys – Partnership with the People* (Cardiff, Welsh Office).
Welsh Office 1993a. *Programme for the Valleys: A Statistical Profile 1993* (Cardiff, Welsh Office).
Welsh Office 1993b. *The New Programme for the Valleys* (Press Release) (Cardiff, Welsh Office).

7

Structure and Culture: Regional Planning and Institutional Innovation in Scotland

M. G. LLOYD

Introduction

Regional planning is a specific form of intervention in the spatial and institutional economy. It attempts to provide an integrated approach to the management of economic, social and physical change in defined geographical areas. In general, regional planning operates at a sub-national scale of administration thereby providing a strategic framework for agenda-setting, resource allocation and decision-making at the local level by local authorities, public-sector agencies and the private sector. In practice, regional planning is caught between the national policy agenda for the management of industrial restructuring and economic change and the local outcome and response to that change. Not surprisingly, perhaps, the experience of regional planning in Britain has been a relatively chequered one (Glasson, 1993). Furthermore, the rise and fall of regional planning has reflected emerging economic priorities and political pressures associated with arguments concerning the relative efficiency and effectiveness of intervention and markets. Notwithstanding these powerful influences, however, regional planning has been described as representing 'an enduring but inconstant feature of public affairs' in post-war Britain (Wannop and Cherry, 1994, p.52).

Regional planning provides a means of securing a strategic perspective on the management of change in defined geographical regions. It can facilitate greater consistency in decision-making by different interests and provide an agenda for the implementation of local and regional development initiatives. In short, regional planning can provide a more realistic strategic context for addressing localized economic, social and land-use planning circumstances. Reflecting this optimism, Diamond (1979) has asserted that it is important to acknowledge that such a strategic planning approach is capable of assuming a variety of forms which may be deemed appropriate to prevailing circumstances. In Scotland, for example, there is a long established tradition of regional planning which has attempted to reconcile the priorities and concerns of a national agenda for economic growth and development with local circumstances and opportunities for the management of change. Regional planning has deployed a strategic approach to policy implementation for local and regional economic development in Scotland and this has involved a diversity of structures and cultures. In institutional terms, for example, regional planning in Scotland is facilitated through a complex network of organizations and agencies which are dedicated to different aspects of the managed change of defined localities. This enables an appropriate response to the specifics of such areas as the Highlands and Islands, the Central Belt or the major urban centres. As a consequence, the bodies involved have defined responsibilities, jurisdictions and resources and include central government departments, local authorities, semi-autonomous agencies and local public and private interests.

Binding the institutional structure together, however, is a culture of intervention which is generally corporatist, and which acknowledges the need for integrated action to address Scotland's specific needs and circumstances (McCrone, 1994). This culture, which would appear to posit a collectivist agenda, is a consequence of Scotland's economic and political history. Since the Act of Union 1707, for example, whilst being part of the British polity Scotland has retained a number of distinctive features that give it a special identity – including its legal system, the arrangements for education and religion and a corporatist tradition of intervention in economic matters. The latter characteristic reflects a combination of a number of factors. These include the relatively poor performance of the Scottish economy relative to that of Britain, a convergence of interests of the governing élites in Scotland which resulted in a consensus for development intervention (McCrone, 1994) and a political arena which acknowledged the economic and physical circumstances in Scotland at different times throughout the post-war period and which encouraged political support for the creation of regional development agencies (Wannop, 1984; Damesick and Wood, 1987).

This chapter examines the nature of regional planning in Scotland to identify the extent to which it is part of the British-wide response to the processes of modernization and spatial restructuring and to what extent it exhibits a Scottish distinctiveness. The chapter identifies and describes the nature of the regional planning framework in Scotland with reference to its origins, evolution and achievements.

Regional planning and development agencies in Scotland

There are two principal and complementary economic reasons for the established history and experience of regional planning in Scotland which continues to adapt to changing circumstances. Firstly, on the one hand, throughout the post-war period the Scottish economy has tended to underperform relative to the national average in terms of unemployment, incomes and expenditure, lower rates of new firm formation and indigenous economic development (Randall, 1987; Danson, Lloyd and Newlands, 1992). At different times this has been reflected in political concern with the degree of divergence between the Scottish and national economies (McCrone, 1993). In the earlier part of the post-war period it tended to result in government intervention through the provision of regional industrial policy assistance. Between 1971 and 1982, for example, the whole of Scotland was designated an 'Assisted Area', with incentives provided to encourage inward investment and indigenous growth and diversification. More recently, the political environment has led to a subsequent erosion in the extent of geographical coverage of the policy assistance and the levels of financial support to industry. Notwithstanding the differentials in economic performance, however, it is important to acknowledge that Scotland is 'a miniature, though highly internally differentiated version of Britain as a whole' (Kendrick, Bechhofer and McCrone, 1985, p.85). Thus, as a specific geopolitical region of Britain, Scotland is exposed to the same processes of social and economic restructuring that affect other regions such as Wales and Northern Ireland. Secondly, and on the other hand, it has been acknowledged at different times that Scotland is not a homogeneous region and is characterized by internal sectoral and spatial differentials in economic performance and constraints (Ashcroft, 1983; Regional Studies Association, 1983; Danson, Lloyd and Newlands, 1993). Thus attention can be drawn to broad urban–rural contrasts, to peripheral and ex-urban rural areas, to industrial decline in the central belt and technology and oil-related growth along the eastern seaboard.

Regional planning has been a response to both the general economic context and the specific circumstances of localities within Scotland. As a consequence, Scotland is noted for its distinctive form of regional development agency intervention such as the Highlands and Islands Development Board and the Scottish Development Agency (Danson, Lloyd and Newlands, 1993). These bodies in particular, together with their successors – Highlands and Islands Enterprise and Scottish Enterprise – have attracted considerable attention as exemplars of such institutional forms.

The Highlands and Islands Development Board (HIDB) reflects these influences. It was established in 1965 as a specific response to the economic and social problems associated with the relatively remote

Highlands and Islands of Scotland (Grassie, 1983). The HIDB was put into place to complement the then existing framework of regional industrial policy assistance. Its objectives were clear: to assist the people of the region to improve their economic and social conditions and to enable the area to play a more effective part in the economic and social development of the national economy. Thus, against the backdrop of a relatively disadvantaged Scottish economy, the Highlands and Islands region exhibited a number of specific problems which included population loss through out-migration, limited employment opportunities and inward investment and restricted indigenous economic activity. It was suggested at the time that the HIDB had been given a formidable task that was seen as the most difficult regional development problem then prevailing in Britain involving a long-established process of economic and social decay (Carter, 1974). To address the problems of the region, the HIDB was given a wide range of powers, including the ability to provide financial assistance by way of grant, loan and equity; to carry out commercial activities itself; to undertake research and promotion; to provide advisory management and training services; and to acquire land, erect factories and provide equipment to firms. There was an additional aspect to its work which has proven to be an enduring and distinctive feature of regional intervention in the area. Since its inception, the HIDB was given the primary responsibility for ensuring both the economic and social development of the region. This balance of responsibilities reflected the fragility of individual communities throughout the region.

The HIDB put into place a planning framework deemed appropriate to the locational and structural features of the regional economy. An industrial development strategy sought to encourage traditional economic activities, such as agriculture and fishing. It also sought to complement this with a strategy of attracting manufacturing investment into the region. Since this early strategy, the HIDB has committed itself to a policy of higher per capita assistance in the more fragile communities of the region's periphery. In the 1970s and 1980s, there was a reversal of net migration from the region. This overall process of change obscures a redistribution of population within the Highlands and Islands. There has been, for example, a significant movement of population away from the north and west to the Moray Firth sub-region reflecting an agglomeration of industrial investment and activity. The HIDB provided a strategic context to the work of the local authorities and other organizations in the region – such as the Crown Estate (Scotland), tourist boards and craft groups (Black and Lloyd, 1993).

This model of regional planning was examined in 1985 by the Scottish Affairs Committee which conducted a detailed investigation of the functions, impact and cost-effectiveness of the HIDB. This was an important test of the political acceptability of the HIDB given the very different ideology of government and attitudes to intervention and planning then in place. This may be contrasted with the ideas prevalent at the setting up of the HIDB. The review, however, acknowledged the case for an agency-led regional planning approach to economic and social regeneration in the Highlands and Islands. Reflecting the political shifts that had occurred this support was qualified to embrace some changes to the HIDB's work. On the one hand, for example, it was recommended that certain additional areas be included in the Board's jurisdiction. On the other hand, however, it was recommended that the proportion of public-sector resources to the HIDB be reduced further so as to further encourage the involvement of private-sector activity and finance in the Highlands and Islands. It was argued also in this respect that HIDB Board members should have business and commercial experience so as to ensure the appropriateness of its policies on industrial development (Scottish Affairs Committee, 1985). The sharpening of the HIDB's role to conform more closely to the prevailing ideas about the balance of state and market was subsequently extended. In 1987 the Industry Department for Scotland and the Treasury conducted a further critical review of the HIDB. This study recommended that the HIDB be given specific objectives which reflected the emphasis on private sector responsibility and activity. The modified remit for the HIDB was to encourage the growth of entrepreneurship in the region, to assist in the creation of a viable economy and to build confidence within the area as a generator of wealth for Scotland and the UK; to assist in the diversification of the economy of the area and to identify opportunities for new development; to foster increased private-sector involvement in the development of the area and to work constructively with other public-sector bodies operating in the Highlands and Islands; to offer advice to ministers on the opportunities for development in the Highlands and Islands; and to dispose of land, property and investments when the opportunity arises. It is important to note, however, that the social dimension was retained in that the HIDB was to continue to help stabilize the level and improve the structure of the population of the area.

These objectives clearly indicate the increasing tendency to the commercialization of the HIDB's activities and which were subsequently reflected in the corporate strategy of the HIDB. The market-led approach to the recapitalization of the Highlands and Islands was further underlined by the statement that the

> continuing rationale for the Board and its activities must reflect the government's general approach to intervention in the economy and its aim of creating a self-sustaining economy and society in the longer term. As a general rule public intervention should offer the prospect of long run real

benefits to the regional (and national) economy, should support activities that are additional to the area and do not involve displacement (except in line with stated geographical objectives), should be based on a clear diagnosis of the root cause of the problem it seeks to overcome and should be aimed at rectifying the underlying market failure . . . the Board, in pursuing any intervention in the market, should aim to encourage the private sector wherever possible, should justify the costs of any intervention against specified objectives and should aim to share in rewards as well as risks. (Industry Department for Scotland 1987a, p.8)

In 1975, another regional planning approach was initiated for the remaining geography of the Scottish economy. The Scottish Development Agency (SDA) was introduced to further economic development; to provide, maintain and safeguard employment; to promote industrial efficiency and international competitiveness and to further the improvement of the environment in lowland Scotland (Wannop, 1984, 1990). The emphasis of the SDA was primarily economic in character and changed in response to emerging problems and opportunities. Initially, the SDA developed a regional planning framework based on an industrial development strategy which emphasized the performance of key sectors such as high technology. This was complemented by an inward investment strategy, implemented through *Locate in Scotland.* Subsequently, however, the SDA put into place a portfolio of area-specific initiatives which were intended to address the internal circumstances of localities within the Scottish economy. The SDA's approach emphasized the development of competitive and efficient enterprise, economic diversification and the leveraging of private investment into local development schemes. The SDA offers an interesting example of how a regional planning and development body can evolve to meet changing circumstances. Thus, over the period 1975 to 1979 the SDA tended to concentrate on its industrial role taking lowland Scotland as a whole. In this context, it operated primarily as an investment bank and its activities included a strong emphasis on the acquisition and provision of land and buildings. Not surprisingly, perhaps, the focus of the SDA's industrial strategy on existing activity and securing the conditions for associated growth tended to concentrate on urban localities. This outcome marked the beginning of an interest by the SDA in area-based initiatives which it subsequently began to introduce as the mainstay of its regional economic planning strategy in 1981. The initial operating emphasis on industrial development and company restructuring was effectively downgraded and, in terms of expenditure, was overshadowed by the rising investment and interest in the physical renewal of selected areas in Scotland. In a relatively short period of time, area initiatives became a distinctive policy approach of the regional planning approach associated with the SDA (Gulliver, 1984). The SDA stated that 'emphasis will be placed on economic and industrial regeneration and the crucial criterion in the selection of areas will be their potential for improved performance. Thus while the programme will focus on areas where current performance is poor, it will not exclude initiatives in relatively prosperous areas where substantial development opportunities are identified' (Scottish Development Agency, 1984). The local schemes put in place by the SDA, including the Dundee Project for example, offered a pragmatic approach to local economic development. The SDA was attempting to address the performance of defined localities which were experiencing severe economic decline by establishing a regional planning context for the appropriate policies and programmes of all bodies involved in improving the local economy (Moore and Booth, 1986). Regional planning in this context was more managerial in attempting to secure an ordered and consistent approach to local economic regeneration.

This specific form of intervention was not immune to political change. As with the HIDB, the SDA's remit was subsequently modified to conform with government priorities. This resulted in a relatively more explicit emphasis on the commercial aspects of its work. In particular, the SDA's activities were expected to highlight a selective form of indirect intervention and, more significantly, to involve the private sector as far as is possible in its specific development policies. In 1981, for example, government modifications removed the SDA's obligations to maintain and safeguard employment and to promote industrial democracy. In 1986, the priority on private-sector involvement in local economic regeneration was confirmed in a review of the SDA carried out by the Industry Department for Scotland, which made a considerable number of recommendations as to the detailed operation of the SDA. Interestingly, in the light of prevailing political ideas, the outcome of the review was not to propose changes to, or a reduction in, the scope of the SDA's functions and responsibilities. It is possible to interpret this as a vote of confidence in the model of regional planning represented by the SDA. In practical terms, the review expressed a vote of confidence in the SDA as a means of effecting a private-sector-led, market-oriented approach to regional and local economic development. This rested on the principal idea that the public sector should only be involved where the market alone will not produce the outcome desired by policy; and its intervention should wherever possible seek to achieve its ends by improving the working of the market and should not create dependence (Industry Department for Scotland, 1987b). Thus the review pointed to the necessity for the phased withdrawal of the SDA from the provision of premises to the private sector in circumstances where the market itself could ensure an adequate supply of premises. The review confirmed the consistency of the SDA's economic development strategy with the government's overall economic and industrial strategy.

It is clear that a distinctive feature of regional planning in Scotland has been the tradition of development agencies operating in defined geographical areas. These established a broad strategic context for public and private sector activity and investment. More importantly, as in the case of the SDA in particular, the model of regional planning advocated and rested on a defined partnership of public-sector agencies in an attempt to define policy and spending priorities in specific localities.

A wider tradition of regional planning

In Scotland, however, regional planning does not rest simply on the activities of the development agencies. The regional development agency approach is only one facet of the Scottish tradition of regional planning that is effected in a variety of ways. Arguably, the broader acceptance of regional or strategic approaches to specific problems stems in part from the particular and distinctive form of administration in Scotland. The Scottish Office, for example, plays a key role in this respect. It discharges the policies and functions of central government in Scotland thereby forming an integral part of the British system of government and public administration. Whilst, however, the activities of the Scottish Office are bound closely to Westminster, it commands sufficient autonomy and discretion to respond positively to the changing economic and social circumstances within Scotland. Indeed the history of the Scottish Office shows it to be perceived as a national (Scottish) rather than a functional government department. It has also adapted to change in an innovative way defining its own identity (Kellas, 1980). This contrasts the Scottish Office with the arrangements in Wales, for example, which is more closely bound to the detailed workings of Westminster.

The Scottish Office has subsequently developed as a multifunctional department with activities devolved from central departments to the responsibility of the secretary of state for Scotland. Its main aim is to create an environment in which public and private sectors work together to improve the economic, social and environmental conditions within which people in Scotland live and work. In general terms, the Scottish Office comprises the departments of Agriculture and Fisheries, Development, Education, Home and Health and Industry. A distinguishing feature of the Scottish Office, however, is the extent to which its policies are co-ordinated rather than being centrally determined and simply reflecting the autonomy and priorities of individual departments. This provides the basis for a more collective appreciation of issues and the devising of a strategic or regional dimension to its activities. Whilst the Scottish Office continues to evolve in terms of its particular administrative structures (Parry, 1992), it retains the responsibility for the strategic overview of the management of the Scottish economy and its physical infrastructure with a strong regional emphasis involving the integration of economic and land-use matters.

The Scottish Office has, over time, initiated a number of regional planning measures in this strategic tradition. At a relatively broad geographical scale, for example, sub-regional planning studies have been conducted. The Gaskin Report (Gaskin, 1969) on the economic development potential of the north-east of Scotland prior to the advent of oil-related development activity confronted the management problems associated with a highly-fragmented local government structure. It led to the creation of a specific regional planning organization – the North East of Scotland Joint Planning Advisory Committee – which was set up in the early 1970s prior to local government reorganization in order to consider the strategic issues which confronted all the constituent areas of the broad geographical region. At a more local level, the Scottish Office has initiated an urban policy framework which was set in place to address the administrative and policy mismatch between broader regional industrial concerns and local land-use planning matters. Attention has been focused also on new towns which have played a critical role within regional policy in Scotland, land-use planning policies of slum clearance, peripheral housing estates and the planned redevelopment of retailing and commercial centres.

In addition, the Scottish Office has provided an innovative form of strategic planning guidance for local authorities in the formulation and implementation of development plans. The strategic guidance was also of benefit to private-sector interests. Thus the National Planning Guidelines, and more recently the National Planning Policy Guidelines (NPPGs), have provided a form of regional planning through the explicit bringing together of regional policy and economic development concerns with the responsibilities of the physical land-use planning system (Rowan-Robinson, Lloyd and Elliot, 1987). The origins of the National Planning Guidelines rest on a recommendation of the Select Committee on Land Resource Use in Scotland in 1972. This advocated the need to adopt a regional approach to planning in Scotland which was based on the explicit integration of industrial and economic development with the operation and responsibility of the land-use planning system. In what may be seen as a radical line of argument, the select committee supported the case for the preparation of an indicative plan for Scotland to be conducted at a national scale. Within this, a regional dimension would be secured by demonstrating how it was intended to utilize the land for urban, industrial and recreational purposes. The select committee thereby recommended what was in effect a national structure plan which would embody a national industrial strategy with a comprehensive and integrated regional planning system of land-use zoning and land allocation policies. In the event, however, the government, in its observations on the select committee report acknowledged the need for more explicit central strategic guidance to land-use planning, accepted the need for more effective liaison between those involved in the processes of land use, planning and development in Scotland but rejected the notion of a national structure plan as impractical and proposed a set of guidelines on those aspects of land use which should be examined for Scotland as a whole (Lloyd, 1994).

From 1974 on, National Planning Guidelines represented a specific approach to regional planning practice in Scotland. The guidelines were issued for a number of selected land-use matters where there was considered to be a national interest in its development or protection. By the mid–1980s, the National Planning Guidelines were established as a significant source of strategic planning policy guidance in Scotland. There was an acceptance of national physical land-use planning priorities with information about local and regional circumstances. Significantly, the guidelines rested on the importance of explicit links between agencies involved at the national and local levels of administration. This was complemented by a selective approach to those issues which required strategic guidance which balanced national priorities with regional and local strategic planning issues. In the specific context of the strategic guidance issued for the necessary management of the onshore infrastructure required for North Sea oil- and gas-related developments it has been suggested that the Scottish Office acted in a reticulist manner (Fischer, 1981). This involves the creation of decision-making networks which are devised to overcome any jurisdictional boundaries which impede an effective response by an organization to a specific problem. In order to manage the complex interface between development and the environment in the context of onshore oil-related facilities, the SDD had developed communication networks amongst those concerned so as to reach a consensus on the handling of this interface (Fischer, 1981). This in effect represented a strategic approach through the managed and co-ordinated framework for change which is a form of regional planning practice. Up until the late 1980s, the measure was unique to Scotland but as a consequence of favourable and critical attention (Nuffield Foundation, 1986) it gained wider applicability in a modified form in England and Wales. This took the form of Planning Policy Guidance Notes (PPGs) produced by the Department of the Environment and which have been held to have made an important contribution to planning practice in England and Wales (Tewdwr-Jones, 1994). Today, NPPGs are prepared by the Scottish Office Environment Department in order to identify land resources having national significance in Scotland which should either be safeguarded from or for development.

The tradition of a regional planning perspective extended also to the work of local government. The Local Government (Scotland) Act 1973 created a two-tier institutional structure of regional councils and district councils. This established a division of responsibility between strategic functions, such as water and sewerage, roads and transport and structure planning, and the more local functions of housing, development control and licensing. There were variations on these arrangements. The unitary authorities (Orkney, Shetland and the Western Isles) and the general planning authorities (Highland, Borders and Dumfries and Galloway), for example, reflected a sympathy for the specific demographic and economic circumstances of their localities and a better match to appropriate functions. The Local Government (Scotland) Act 1973 introduced also the concept of regional reports to facilitate the creation of a regional level of local government in Scotland (McDonald, 1977). Regional reports were intended to provide the policy context to the subsequent preparation of structure plans (by regional authorities) and local plans (by district authorities). Regional reports were therefore intended to provide a structure and a process for strategic planning at a time of unprecedented change in Scottish local government. By May 1976, the required regional reports had been submitted to the secretary of state for Scotland. The regional reports were primarily economic in character, being concerned with development strategies which were based on the promotion of industry and the reconciliation with land-use priorities. In this respect, the regional report concept made a significant contribution to the regional planning tradition in Scotland led by the local authorities.

Scottish Enterprise and Highlands and Islands Enterprise

Since 1991, the arrangements for the Scottish regional development agencies have been dramatically overhauled. New bodies – Scottish Enterprise and Highlands and Islands Enterprise – have replaced the SDA and the HIDB respectively and have assumed the responsibility for the integrated delivery of economic and business development initiatives, the provision of training and the implementation of measures to secure the improvement of the environment in Scotland (Danson, Lloyd and Newlands, 1989). Scottish Enterprise and Highlands and Islands Enterprise represent a radical development in the Scottish tradition of regional planning for economic development by bringing together the key factors of capital, labour and land. The institutional restructuring involved may be considered representative of the general shift in economic policy-making and governance from managerialism to an approach based on entrepreneurialism (Harvey, 1989). This had already started with respect to the regional development agencies in Scotland and was now taken forward more forcibly.

In formal terms, Scottish Enterprise and Highlands and Islands Enterprise are charged with the responsibility of stimulating self-sustaining economic development and the growth of enterprise, securing the improvement of the environment, encouraging the creation of viable jobs, reducing unemployment and improving the skills of the Scottish workforce. The delivery of the integrated enterprise and training services is sub-contracted by Scottish Enterprise and Highlands and Islands Enterprise to a network of local enterprise companies (LECs). LECs are not statutory bodies *per se* but are private companies constituted under the Companies Act 1985

> to bring a direct knowledge and understanding of the needs and opportunities of the local economy to the delivery of the Government's enterprise, environment and training programme, and to engage the commitment, experience and entrepreneurial flair of senior members of the private sector. (Scottish Affairs Committee, 1995, p.v)

In practice, the LECs provide a delivery framework for the specific services associated with training, enterprise and business development and environmental improvement. The training programmes comprise the delivery of national schemes and the design of customized measures to reflect local circumstances throughout Scotland. The LECs implement government-funded training programmes in their individual areas; assess local requirements for industrial property and for environmental improvement or land renewal schemes and investigate and recommend new local initiatives in respect of training and economic and social development. The LECs operate in defined geographical areas and within the strategic context established by the parent organizations. The Scottish arrangements are distinctive: they differ considerably in their remit and their potential for securing an integrated development framework when compared with the institutions in England and Wales.

The new bodies have a much broader and more integrated role to play than their predecessors. In practice, Scottish Enterprise and Highlands and Islands Enterprise provide strategic policy guidance and expert advice to the LECs on individual economic sectors; undertake major projects or research activities which extend beyond the areas of individual LECs; provide individual LECs with a range of central support services which will initially include administrative, accounting and property services; undertake marketing and inward investment programmes for the areas in question; undertake major environmental improvement and land renewal programmes, in consultation with the LECs involved; and monitor the progress of the LECs in implementing their plans and achieving their objectives.

Following an established theme, Highlands and Islands Enterprise is charged with the social aspect of its developmental responsibilities, and this is reflected in a particular approach to its development strategy for the region. The strategy provides a hierarchical management context to the devising, financing and implementation of local initiatives by the LECs which of necessity embrace economic development and training schemes tailored to the individual circumstances of localities within the region. Highlands and Islands Enterprise has set out a strategy for the development of enterprise in order 'to enable the people of the Highlands and Islands . . . realize their full potential by means of: stimulating business development; encouraging training and learning; strengthening communities; enhancing the environment and raising the quality of life' (Highlands and Islands Enterprise, 1992). Highlands and Islands Enterprise has established three principal operating principles which are: to afford a pre-eminent role to private capital and entrepreneurship in the implementation of its development ethos and strategy; the decentralization of the administration and decision-making involved in the delivery of the strategic services; and the minimization of red tape. This ethos is a familiar expression of the government's philosophy and is clearly evident throughout the Highlands and Islands Enterprise initiative. It demonstrates that the process of agency restructuring has involved a marked realignment of the public and private sector interests involved in local economic development schemes in the Highlands and Islands.

The Highlands and Islands Enterprise regional planning strategy is translated into a number of specific objectives. These are to increase the personal benefits for the people of the area; to increase the number and profitability of private-sector businesses in the area; to improve the quality, availability and volume of training and learning opportunities in the area; to create conditions in which successful and lasting development provides the basis for long-term economic growth in the area; to strengthen and diversify the economic base of individual communities in the area; to improve further the attractiveness of the area's natural and man-made heritage; to maintain and develop the social, community and cultural values of the different parts of the area. Highlands and Islands Enterprise's objectives embrace social, economic and environmental considerations within an integrated approach to development. This is supported by an area framework which categorizes the Highlands and Islands into different priority areas. Firstly, the 'fragile remote areas' fall into two possible types. On the one hand, areas that exhibit long-term problems of population decline, lack of employment opportunities, poor infrastructure and social problems. The Western Isles is a case in point. On the other hand, there are areas which are smaller in scale and population and which are vulnerable to sudden crisis such as the closure of a plant or service. The island of Colonsay is held to be representative of this type. The 'fragile remote areas' are accorded a high priority within the overall development strategy. Secondly, 'areas of employment deficit' are localities created by a major closure or plant rundown and the category may change according to circumstance. Localities likely to have been or to be in this category include Fort William, Caithness and Easter Ross. These areas are held to be of high strategic priority and would require immediate action by Highlands and Islands Enterprise. This would include the promotion of inward investment and the provision of floorspace for development by way of compensation. Thirdly, the defined 'intermediate areas' are held to be of medium priority and are areas of mixed need. Most of the Highlands and Islands would fall into this category. Finally, Inverness and its hinterland is designated as an area of low priority as it is considered to be the principal centre in the region in terms of the geographical concentration of economic activity (Black and Lloyd, 1993).

The new institutional arrangements for enterprise and training have attracted critical attention from the Scottish Affairs Committee which sits to examine, *inter alia*, the expenditure, administration and policy of the Scottish Office and its associated public bodies. The Committee undertook an investigation of the enterprise network in Scotland although it was considered to be too early to give 'a comprehensive evaluation of the efficiency and effectiveness of the (LEC) network in achieving its overall objective: that of helping to generate jobs and prosperity for the people of Scotland' (Scottish Affairs Committee, 1995, p.vi). The principal concern, however, of the Scottish Affairs Committee was the accountability of the Scottish Enterprise and Highlands and Islands Enterprise arrangements both in terms of the relationship of the LECs to the parent organizations and the relationships of the LECs to their communities for which they were responsible. The recommendations and conclusions of the Committee reflected this concern with the need to enhance accountability of the enterprise network, particularly in the context of the relationships between LECs and their respective communities and localities. In this context, the Scottish Affairs Committee recommended that the geographical coverage of the LECs in the Scottish Enterprise network be reviewed to ensure coterminosity between their boundaries and those of local authorities. Further, the Committee wished to see local authorities and others in the public sector being fully involved with the development of the LECs' training strategy. The theme of accountability was pursued also through a recommendation that there be greater openness in the letting of contracts by LECs to local contractors – a policy already developed by Highlands and Islands Enterprise. Finally, the Committee drew attention to the importance of facilitating mandatory consultation by LECs of local authorities to replace the present discretionary arrangements. Whilst the principal attention of the Committee was directed to the issues of accountability and of securing a greater legitimacy for the enterprise networks in Scottish local governance and communities, it stressed also the need for a strategic perspective to be developed with regard to a comprehensive skills strategy for Scotland which could be linked to sectoral targets in partnership with industries. The point here is that an aspect of accountability is the way in which the enterprise networks are responding to the problems of the Scottish economy as a whole (Fairley and Lloyd, 1995).

Change and the regional planning agenda

The regional planning tradition in Scotland continues to evolve in response to emerging and changing circumstances. Constitutional debates, for example, about the future governance of Scotland will affect the nature of regional planning in Scotland. The economic and political outcomes of the relative autonomy of the Scottish institutions will inevitably involve opportunities and constraints to future policy options (Paterson, 1994; Bell and Dow, 1995). The regional development agencies are already being confronted with political pressures and concerns about their accountability to the communities for which they have responsibility. At the same time, other forces for change are emerging. The issues associated with the operation and accountability of the enterprise network of the regional development agencies, for example, are thrown into sharper relief because of the process of local government reorganization in Scotland.

The Local Government (Scotland) Act 1994 put into effect the reorganization of local authorities from a two-tier structure of regions and districts into a unitary system of councils. The drive to institutional reorganization forms part of the restructuring of local government initiated under Mrs Thatcher and which has been maintained by Mr Major through the increased scope for compulsory competitive tendering of local authority services, tighter financial stringency and administrative changes to key functions such as community care and education (Young, 1994). The legislation introduces a streamlined, single-tier market-oriented enabling system of local governance comprising thirty-two councils which have responsibility for a number of defined responsibilities such as structure planning, local planning and development control, social services and economic development. The principal function of the councils will be to enable the delivery of the defined services rather than automatically assuming the responsibility for delivering (Lang, 1994). Local government reorganization will impinge directly onto the regional planning tradition in Scotland. This will have a number of likely effects.

Firstly, the nature of the reorganization will erode the regional character of Scottish local government through the fragmentation of administrative units (Alexander and Ou, 1994). Thus in place of the twelve regional councils which had discharged a strategic role for the management of change there will be a larger number of councils which will require special arrangements for joint working to be put into place to secure a holistic perspective of the strategic issues confronting given geographical areas. This erosion of space is not even across Scotland, but it will impact on certain areas such as Strathclyde and Tayside. Furthermore, the strategic arrangements for regional planning will be diluted because of the transfer of water and sewerage responsibilities from the councils to three new centralized public water authorities. This will erode the ability of councils to secure the strategic management of change and the provision of services for land and property development (Black, 1994).

Secondly, the role of the structure plans may be displaced in the process of reorganization (Goodstadt, 1994; Jarman, 1994). As the established structure plan areas are broken up, as in Strathclyde, Central and Tayside, there will be a move away from a regional strategy (Hayton, 1994). At the very least, there can be little doubt, for example, that the creation of single-tier authorities will create pressures on the relationships between structure and local plans. The new councils will be responsible for the delivery of both documents in direct comparison to the established tradition of defining different geographical scales for strategic and local planning matters. The smaller councils will likely place greater emphasis on the local plans but this raises questions as to whether this will be sufficient for future planning requirements. The local plans may have to become more strategic and/or become more specialized or subject-specific. There are related concerns such as the implications of the likely effectiveness of designated structure plan areas which have been nominated by the secretary of state for Scotland – some of these correspond to existing structure plan areas such as Highland, Fife and Borders. Others do not and will involve considerable adjustments to the needs of providing within short order a strategic context to local planning and development (Hayton, 1992; Kerley and Ou, 1993).

Finally, in some areas where fragmentation takes place it is evident that the LECs will become de facto regional planning agencies. This would represent a significant shift in responsibility for regional planning and raise the concerns relating to accountability and representation identified by the Scottish Affairs Committee. Allied to this is the provision in the enabling legislation for Scottish councils to undertake economic development initiatives. There is an established tradition of local economic development activity in Scotland (McQuaid, 1992), but this will be taken forward divorced from the activities of the enterprise agencies and within different institutional arrangements for structure planning. It is likely that this will cause concern as reorganization unfolds fully.

Local government reorganization involves a centralizing effect in the responsibility of services such as water and sewerage, together with the enhanced role of the LECs. This is also evident in the activities of other bodies which none the less maintain the tradition of regional planning in Scotland. Scottish Homes, for example, was established under the Housing (Scotland) Act 1988 to bring together the Housing Corporation in Scotland and the Scottish Special Housing Association. Scottish Homes operates as a national housing development agency to enable and fund projects to improve the quality of choice of housing in Scotland. It was an attempt to address the complex housing system in Scotland which has changed rapidly in scale, structure and in terms of moving to more market-oriented forms of provision. Its role has become more important as local authorities have experienced controls on capital and revenue expenditure thereby limiting new house building programmes and modernization of the housing stock. In practice, Scottish Homes acts alongside the enterprise agencies in their regional planning role. Similarly, Scottish Natural Heritage was established in 1991 as a consequence of the Natural Heritage (Scotland) Act 1991 to secure the conservation and enhancement of the natural heritage of Scotland, and to foster understanding and facilitate the enjoyment of the natural heritage of Scotland. Its responsibilities include the encouragement of the natural heritage, promotion of responsible public access and the encouragement of environmental sustainability in economic development (Ross, Rowan-Robinson and Walton, 1995). It takes on a regional planning dimension to its work such as the Firths Initiative to promote the integrated management of the natural resources of Scottish firths (Scottish Natural Heritage, 1994). In practical terms it seeks to facilitate co-operation among the users and statutory authorities involved in the estuarine areas. The Firths Initiative, for example, has been described as 'the most comprehensive attempt to address the estuarine and coastal resource issues throughout Scotland' (Burbridge and Burbridge, 1994, p.123). The Firths Initiative is a response to the increasing and cumulative effects of development pressures on the Scottish Firths and the fragmented or piecemeal management arrangements. This has resulted in a continuing conflict between economic development activities and the environmental qualities of the areas. The Initiative seeks to promote the integrated management of natural regions. Finally, a regional planning role will be discharged by the Scottish Environmental Protection Agency which will assume responsibility for controlling defined forms of pollution in Scotland, including integrated pollution control, air quality and radioactive waste, the prevention and control of water pollution and the regulation of solid waste disposal. It will bring together the present regulatory bodies under an integrated structure and take a strategic approach to preventing pollution of the environment. SEPA will be a single, independent agency with executive powers which will assume the pollution control responsibilities of three sets of existing bodies: the river purification boards, the district and island councils and HM Industrial Pollution Inspectorate (Lloyd and Ross, 1994).

Conclusions

Scotland has an established structure and culture of regional planning. This was born out of its economic history, its culture, its polity and power structures and its experience with interventionism. Regional planning practice has been effected through the work of dedicated regional planning and development agencies but this has been complemented by activities in other spheres. A regional ideology has been carried forward by the Scottish Office and local government as well as other agencies. There can be little doubt, however, that regional planning in Scotland has changed over time in response to circumstances and political pressures. That change will continue with the constitutional debate and, although there is an emerging shift away from the local government role, it is to be expected that Scottish regional planning will continue to evolve into the millennium.

References

Alexander, A. and K. Ou 1994. 'The reform of Scottish local government', *Public Money and Management*, Vol.14, No.1, pp.33–8.
Ashcroft, B. 1983. 'The Scottish region and the regions of Scotland', in K. Ingham and J. Love (eds.), *Understanding the Scottish Economy* (Oxford, Martin Robertson), pp.173–87.
Bell, D. and S. Dow 1995. 'Economic policy options for a Scottish Parliament', *Scottish Affairs*, No.13, pp.42–67.
Black, S. 1994. 'What's happening to water and sewerage services in Scotland?', *Scottish Affairs*, No.6, pp.25–34.
Black, J. S. and M. G. Lloyd 1993. 'Highlands and Islands Enterprise – strategies for economic and social development', *Local Economy*, Vol.8, No.1, pp.69–81.
Burbridge, P. R. and V. Burbridge 1994. *Review of Scottish Coastal Issues* (Edinburgh, Scottish Office, Central Research Unit).
Carter, I. 1974. 'The Highlands of Scotland as an under-developed region', in E. de Kadt and G. Williams (eds.), *Sociology and Development* (Tavistock, Tavistock Press), pp.279–311.
Damesick, P. and P. Wood 1987. 'Public policy for regional development: restoration or reformation?', in idem (eds.), *Regional Problems, Problem Regions and Public Policy in the United Kingdom* (Oxford, Clarendon Press), pp.260–6.

Danson, M., M. G. Lloyd and D. Newlands 1989. 'Scottish Enterprise: towards a model agency?', *Regional Studies*, Vol.23, No.6, pp.557–64.

Danson, M., M. G. Lloyd and D. Newlands 1992. 'Scotland', in R. Martin and P. Townroe (eds.), *Regional Development in the 1990s. Britain and Ireland in Transition* (London, Jessica Kingsley Publishers).

Danson, M., M. G. Lloyd and D. Newlands 1993. 'The role of development agencies in regional economic development', in M. Hart and R. Harrison (eds.), *Spatial Policy in a Divided Nation* (London, Jessica Kingsley Publishers), pp.162–75.

Diamond, D. 1979. 'The uses of strategic planning: the example of the National Planning Guidelines in Scotland', *Town Planning Review*, Vol.50, No.1, pp.18–25.

Fairley, J. and M. G. Lloyd 1995. 'Economic development and training: the roles of Scottish Enterprise, Highlands and Islands Enterprise and the Local Enterprise Companies', *Scottish Affairs*, No.12, pp.52–72.

Fischer, D. W. 1981. *North Sea Oil: An Environment Interface* (Norway, Universitetsforlaget).

Gaskin, M. 1969. *North-East Scotland: A Survey of its Development Potential* (Edinburgh, HMSO).

Glasson, J. 1993. 'The fall and rise of regional planning in the economically advanced nations', in R. Paddison *et al.* (eds.), *International Perspectives in Urban Studies 1* (London, Jessica Kingsley Publishers), pp.182–209.

Goodstadt, V. 1994. 'Local government reorganisation', *The Scottish Planner*, No.37, p.4.

Grassie, J. 1983. *Highland Experiment: The Story of the HIDB* (Aberdeen, Aberdeen University Press).

Gulliver, S. 1984. 'The area projects of the Scottish Development Agency', *Town Planning Review*, Vol.55, No.3, pp.322–34.

Harvey, D. 1989. 'From managerialism to entrepreneurialism', *Geografissker Annaler*, Vol.71B, pp.3–17.

Hayton, K. 1992. 'The impact of local government reform on local economic development', *Frazer of Allander Quarterly Economic Commentary*, Vol.18, No.2, pp.57–60.

Hayton, K. 1994. 'Planning and Scottish local government reform', *Planning Practice and Research*, Vol.9, No.1, pp.55–62.

Highlands and Islands Enterprise 1992. *A Strategy for the Highlands and Islands* (Inverness, HIE).

Industry Department for Scotland 1987a. *Review of the Highlands and Islands Development Board. Report to the Secretary of State for Scotland* (Edinburgh, Industry Department for Scotland).

Industry Department for Scotland 1987b. *Review of the Scottish Development Agency. Report to the Secretary of State for Scotland* (Edinburgh, Industry Department for Scotland).

Jarman, D. 1994. 'Strategic planning after reorganisation: threat or opportunity?', *The Scottish Planner*, No.40, p.8.

Kellas, J. 1980. *Modern Scotland* (London, Allen and Unwin).

Kendrick, S., F. Bechhofer and D. McCrone 1985. 'Is Scotland different? Industrial and occupational change in Scotland and Britain', in H. Newby *et al.*(eds.), *Restructuring Capital* (London, Macmillan), pp.63–104.

Kerley, R. and K. Ou 1993. 'Joint arrangements in Scotland', *Local Government Studies*, Vol.19, No.3, pp.309–18.

Lang, I. 1994. 'Local government reorganisation', *Scottish Affairs*, No.6, pp.14–24.
Lloyd, M. G. 1994. 'Innovative strategic land use planning: National Planning Guidelines in Scotland', *Scottish Affairs*, No.6, pp.84–100.
Lloyd, M. G. and A. Ross 1994. 'Pollution control and the Scottish environment', *Scottish Geographical Magazine*, Vol.63, No.7, pp.223–34.
McCrone, D. 1993. 'Regionalism and constitutional change in Scotland', *Regional Studies*, Vol.27, No.6, pp.507–12.
McCrone, D. 1994. *Understanding Scotland. The Sociology of a Stateless Nation* (London, Routledge).
McDonald, S. T. 1977. 'The regional report in Scotland', *Town Planning Review*, Vol.48, pp.215–32.
McQuaid, R. 1992. *Local Authorities and Economic Development in Scotland* (Edinburgh, COSLA).
Moore, C. and S. Booth 1986. 'Urban policy contradictions: the market versus redistributive approaches', *Policy and Politics*, Vol.14, pp.361–87.
Nuffield Foundation 1986. *An Inquiry into the Town and Country Planning System* (London, Nuffield Foundation).
Parry, R. 1992. 'The structure of the Scottish Office', in L. Paterson and D. McCrone (eds.), *The Scottish Government Yearbook 1992* (Edinburgh, Edinburgh University Press), pp.247–55.
Paterson, L. 1994. *The Autonomy of Modern Scotland* (Edinburgh, Edinburgh University Press).
Randall, J. 1987. 'Scotland', in P. Damesick and P. Wood (eds.), *Regional Problems, Problem Regions and Public Policy in the United Kingdom* (Oxford, Clarendon Press), pp.218–37.
Regional Studies Association 1983. *Report of an Inquiry into Regional Problems in the United Kingdom* (Norwich, Geobooks).
Ross, A., J. Rowan-Robinson and W. Walton 1995. 'Sustainable development in Scotland: the role of Scottish Natural Heritage', *Land Use Policy*, Vol.12, No.3, pp.237–52.
Rowan-Robinson, J., M. G. Lloyd and R. Elliot 1987. 'National Planning Guidelines and Strategic Planning: Matching context and method', *Town Planning Review*, Vol.58, No.4, pp.369–81.
Scottish Affairs Committee 1985. *Highlands and Islands Development Board. Volume 1. Report and Proceedings of the Committee* (London, House of Commons).
Scottish Affairs Committee 1995. *The Operation of the Enterprise Agencies and the LECs* (London, House of Commons).
Scottish Development Agency 1984. *Annual Report* (Glasgow, SDA).
Scottish Natural Heritage 1994. *The Firths Initiative* (Edinburgh, SNH).
Tewdwr-Jones, M. 1994. 'The government's planning policy guidance', *Journal of Planning and Environment Law*, February, pp.106–15.
Wannop, U. 1984. 'The evolution and roles of the Scottish Development Agency', *Town Planning Review*, Vol.55, pp.313–21.
Wannop, U. 1990. 'The Glasgow Eastern Area Renewal Project: A perspective on the management of urban regeneration', *Town Planning Review*, Vol.61, pp.455–74.
Wannop, U. and G. Cherry 1994. 'The development of regional planning in the UK', *Planning Perspectives*, Vol.9, pp.29–60.
Young, K. 1994. 'Local government', in D. Kavanagh and A. Seldon (eds.), *The Major Effect* (London, Papermac), pp.83–98.

8

Planning Capital Cities: Edinburgh and Cardiff Compared

CLIFF HAGUE and HUW THOMAS

Introduction

A capital city is a symbol which can assume a particular significance in the consciousness of nationalists in multinational states. It provides a reaffirmation of the reality of nationhood for all nationalists, while for separatists it prefigures a shift in power (either devolution or total independence), when a seat of government will be needed. The capital city can also be a convenient – because 'proper' – location for the wide range of institutions which have accompanied the growth of a distinctively modern nationalist consciousness in the nineteenth and twentieth centuries: national libraries, universities, museums, and so on need a home, or a headquarters, and the capital is the likely first choice. Of course, in turn these institutions underpin the significance of the capital as a locus of 'cultural hegemony' in a particular territory (King, 1993), so those wishing to boost the capital city need the institutions as much as the institutions may gain in prestige, or legitimacy, from a capital city location. The claim of the capital to house a given institution may be challenged, and, periodically, is. Recently, the need to develop a national sports stadium in London has been questioned, for example; and the twentieth-century history of Cardiff and Edinburgh is punctuated by competition with other cities for national institutions. However, the background to, and nature of, that competition is very different, and reflects the distinctive histories of the cities and the countries of which they are a part.

This chapter will compare the planning of Edinburgh and Cardiff, concentrating especially on the implications for planning of their being capital cities. It will ask to what extent do we need to be aware of the significance of capital city status in Scotland and Wales in order to fully understand the planning and spatial development of the two cities? Reviews of international experiences confirm the significance of state intervention in shaping the urban form of capital cities through the production of administrative and other buildings (often in symbolically significant civic spaces), the sponsoring of public art aimed at presenting a particular message about the national identity, and the creation or sustaining of particular kinds of communication links with the remainder of the country (Sutcliffe, 1993). However, it has also been argued that the contemporary significance of capital city status is increasingly ambiguous as ideas of nationhood are brought into question by globalization (however interpreted) and the growing political significance of a variety of sources of personal and group identity (King, 1993; Meisel, 1993). Against this complex background, the two case studies suggest that there have, indeed, been important ways in which being capital cities have impinged on planning, though in both Cardiff and Edinburgh there have been tensions between political agendas sensitive to local concerns and those which have sought to project the cities on larger stages.

But a comparison of the two cities reveals not only the significance of capital city status, but also the very different ways in which this has influenced planning as a consequence of the different histories of the two countries. The union of Scotland and England in the early eighteenth century was one of two nation-states (albeit unequal in power); Edinburgh was already a capital city with a distinctive social and economic character. Its status as capital was not challenged as Glasgow flourished with the growth of Empire and industrialization. The city's politics – well into the twentieth century – was dominated by a view which counterpoised the civility (and planned environment) of being a capital city to the dirt, sprawl and disorder of an industrial city like Glasgow. In Cardiff, by way of contrast, the acquisition of capital city status was the culmination of decades of civic boosterism largely guided by a middle class which had developed during the city's explosive growth in the late nineteenth century. The lobbying for the title 'city', and, later, 'capital city', were bound up, then, with a project of civic aggrandizement whose foundation, and ultimate justification, was the kind of regional economic dominance regarded with such disdain by Edinburgh's élite.

These historical contingencies (among others) made a real difference to the planning and spatial development of the city up to the 1980s. A question which the case studies pose is whether the differences have become less prominent in the late 1980s and 1990s as both cities are marketed to an audience of footloose property developers, tourists and financiers; and, if so, why that should be. The remainder of the chapter is divided into three sections – one each on Edinburgh and Cardiff, followed by a conclusion which returns to the question of contemporary similarities and differences in a period of global economic restructuring.

Planning a capital for north Britain

Edinburgh's position as capital city has been uncontested within Scotland in modern times. What has that status meant in terms of the city's planning and development? Have the parameters of capital-building been set at a local level, or through conscious reference to a Scottish, UK or European context? The development of the New Town in the eighteenth century answered these questions so well that it inspired but also atrophied thinking for 200 years. Because the nation and the definitive development of the capital were in the past, Edinburgh's planning has been about preservation not boosterism.

The Union of the Scottish and English Parliaments in 1707 offered Scotland a fast track to economic development fuelled by the wealth and larger markets of its southern neighbour. In the short term, though, there were disbenefits, and 'Edinburgh, capital as well as largest city, suffered probably more than any' (Youngson, 1966, p.22). The trappings and populace of nationhood, and the business associated with it, migrated to London. Thus the issue in Edinburgh was not competition with other Scottish cities but the relation of the capital to London and beyond that to European capital cities.

The failure of the Jacobite Rebellion of 1745–6 removed uncertainty about Scotland's constitutional future. Agriculture and industry underwent startling 'improvements', and the Scottish economy prospered as never before. Wealth was created which could be invested in urban development, while in turn the new economy required new buildings for its new functions.

An anonymous pamphlet in 1752 took the gracious houses, parks and squares being laid out in London as the model of modernity. In contrast Edinburgh, 'the metropolis of Scotland when a separate kingdom, and still chief city of NORTH BRITAIN' was still a medieval town; confined by a town wall, 'the houses stand more crowded than in any town in *Europe*'. The 'meanness of EDINBURGH' was 'a reproach to SCOTLAND'. Proposals 'to enlarge and beautify the town' were therefore advanced by 'the magistrates and town council, the college of justice and several persons of rank'. The avowed purpose was to make Edinburgh a real alternative to London, and to achieve this, inspiration was drawn from new town developments in Turin and Berlin. The timing and the comparators were quite different from developments designed to assert Cardiff's claims as a capital.

An Improvement Act was passed in 1753, which *The Scots Magazine* supported on the grounds that 'The certain consequence is general wealth and prosperity', a path along which the rest of Scotland could follow the capital's example (quoted in Mears and Russell, 1938, p.180). This must be the earliest statement of growth pole theory! In 1766, the Town Council launched a competition for a plan for a New Town to extend the city. James Craig's entry, inspired by the lay-out for Nancy in France, won. It was a formal, regular and spacious development, the physical expression of the Age of Reason. Edinburgh was now 'The Athens of the North', a leading centre of the European Enlightenment: 'There is not a city in Europe . . . that enjoys such a singular and noble privilege . . . Here I stand at what is called the *Cross of Edinburgh*, and can, in a few minutes, take fifty men of genius by the hand' (William Smellie, quoted in Daiches, 1978, p.151).

The planning and the building of the New Town, which continued until the 1830s, was of fundamental significance to the development of Edinburgh. Economically it was an important investment and boost to the wider Scottish economy; socially it defined and housed a national élite; culturally it placed town planning and architecture at the centre of Edinburgh's achievement in establishing itself as an alternative to London, a European capital city. The city's élite positively embraced change to construct an urban environment giving expression to Edinburgh as the capital of North Britain, a twin capital for the wealthiest nation in the world.

The city as capital of Scotland: beware of town planners

Edinburgh's star shone relatively briefly in the European firmament. Eclipsed at home not just by London, but by the industrial growth that made Glasgow second city of the Empire, Edinburgh became provincial. 'The Athens of the North' became part of that nostalgia for a romantic tartan past captured in Sir Walter Scott's novels, and the Scottish Baronial architecture that characterized much of the late nineteenth-century spread of tenements and villas. Reviewing the planning and development of the city, from the nineteenth-century Improvement Acts through to the halting progress of statutory planning schemes during the inter-war years, Hague (1984) stressed the significance of localized and class-based political conflicts. A significant professional planning community developed in the city, inspired by the visions of Patrick Geddes, and his argument that the ordered planning of the New Town marked a pinnacle from which laissez-faire industrialism had descended to create a haphazard environment and bland bungaloid suburbia. In opposition were people like Sir Louis Gumley, proprietor of a major estate agency, and Lord Provost in 1938, when he told the Edinburgh and District Master Plumbers' Association,

> Some of our buildings are not, perhaps, beautiful, but if we had not had the bungalows we would have been short of very many happy households. People . . . are very happy in their £400 or £500 bungalows. I hope some

more builders will come forward to build them. (quoted in Hague, 1984, p.186)

The nationhood of the past might be preserved in the city's monuments but practical, commercial concerns dictated modern development. The town council consistently set its face against any comprehensive planning of the city, until 1943, when, with the prospect of peace and central government enthusiasm for planning, they set up an advisory committee on city development, to 'report on the general considerations governing the development and redevelopment of the City as the Capital of Scotland' (City and Royal Burgh of Edinburgh, 1943, p.3). An exhibition was held at the National Galleries to seek public views, at which the Lord Provost, Sir William Darling, asked citizens to consider what kind of city they wanted, 'one developed in the industrial plan or on the plan of a great capital city' (quoted in *The Scotsman*, 23 July 1943).

In Edinburgh's sophisticated language games, 'the industrial plan' could be decoded as Glasgow, a working-class city, the negation of Edinburgh's proud middle-class institutions, the destruction of a romantic and historic city. The threat was real, with the expectation of major coalmining development on the edge of the city which Sir William saw as unlikely to create 'a graceful attribute'. Edinburgh had no aspiration to be a 'Coal Metropolis'.

The advisory committee report observed that Edinburgh now had 'a rendez-vous with destiny' (p.10). Its response was preservation, not boosterism. It urged the creation of a green belt, and stronger planning controls in the New Town (as well as the conversion of large houses into flats because of the increasing shortage of domestic servants). A complete survey of the Old Town was required to safeguard the historic buildings. The authors cannily warned against the threat that town planning evangelists would pose:

Fired with enthusiasm for the new science of planning they lay aside all financial considerations, they urge the adoption of the 'broad view', they talk of 'aiming high', and they recommend the approval of idealistic and often revolutionary proposals, which they fondly hope can be realised fifty or a hundred years hence. (City and Royal Burgh of Edinburgh, 1943, p.6)

These were prophetic words. Was Edinburgh as capital best served by maximizing continuity with the past, while addressing contemporary needs like the servant problem, or did a capital city need the kind of revolutionary vision sweeping through a Europe grasping for a new post-war world? Was town planning to be a vehicle to force modernization or to contain it? The Town Council got it wrong. They wanted no change; but against the advice of their Burgh Engineer, they appointed Sir Patrick Abercrombie to produce the master plan.

The preamble to Abercrombie's Civic Survey and Plan states:

> A Plan for Edinburgh must needs be a hazardous undertaking: there can be few cities towards which the inhabitants display a fiercer loyalty or deeper affection . . . Even its blemishes are venerated . . . The planner who dares to propose improvements must go warily . . .

The Plan's proposals included: blasting tunnels through the Old Town and under Calton Hill to carry a new dual carriageway; making Princes Street two tier by building a new road beneath the existing street level and open to the famous gardens; various other roads cutting through established residential areas; complete clearance of housing from Leith to make the area an industrial zone ('a bit on the drastic side', Abercrombie conceded – *The Scotsman*, 3 October 1947); comprehensive redevelopment of an area off Princes Street for a new Festival Theatre; and building flats on the playing fields of private schools and in middle-class neighbourhoods to house those displaced by slum clearance. What further 'improvements' might have been propounded but for the need to 'go warily'?

Abercrombie's minimalism was too much. The correspondence columns of *The Scotsman* fizzed: 'sacrilegious proposals', 'scandalous expense', 'desecration', 'impossible of execution', 'an outrage' . . . The Lord Provost drily observed that the proposals were 'so radical and so far reaching, and . . . involve much expenditure' (all quoted in Hague, 1984, pp.210–11). Destiny left, to tryst with admirers elsewhere. Denmark's capital, Copenhagen, produced its celebrated Finger Plan in 1948. Stockholm, another small capital city in a peripheral north European country, produced a plan in 1952, basing city growth on an underground public transport system, with satellite growth directed to high density nodes around the stations. Edinburgh's planning reverted to type, albeit a development plan was eventually produced to meet the statutory requirements of the 1947 Act.

'Nivertheface'

The celebrated writer Muriel Spark (1993) claims that 'nevertheless' has been the most used word in Edinburgh:

> . . . my whole education, in and out of school, seemed . . . to pivot around this word. My teachers used it a great deal. All grades of society constructed sentences bridged by 'nevertheless'. It is my own instinct to associate the

word, as the core of a whole thought pattern, with Edinburgh particularly
. . . The sound was roughly 'nivertheface' and the emphasis was a heartfelt
one.

This attitude had seen off the alien Abercrombie. It infused planning in the city. Edinburgh's council remained under the control of the political right through the 1950s and 1960s. They kept down the rates (the old system of local property taxation), they kept up the rents of council houses (at least relative to the low norms of urban Scotland), and above all they venerated the traditions of the city. The dominant ethos was caution verging on complaisance, an attitude of mind which became cemented into the city's local government bureaucracy. The real success stories of Edinburgh planning during these years were the things that did not happen. The ambitions of the city engineer to build urban motorways were thwarted; Glasgow built the highest council flats in Europe, Edinburgh did not. Nor did it build the Festival Theatre needed to stage effectively opera at the International Festival but 'nivertheface' going to cost a lot of money. Nationhood, and the image of the capital city associated with it, was in the history and romantic topography of the city, it was not about defining a future. De facto London was *the* capital; within Scotland, Glasgow would bluster, but what did it matter? Edinburgh had no ambition to become a Glasgow. And that was that: there were no other comparators.

Scottish Office attempts to create modernization of the Scottish economy focused on the lagging areas dominated by extractive and manufacturing industries. Branches of the motor industry were transplanted from the English Midlands to Linwood to provide jobs for those leaving Clydeside's shipyards, and to West Lothian where the mining and oil shale industries were in steep decline. Central government created five New Towns in Scotland, and by the late 1960s one of them, East Kilbride, was the sixth largest town in the country. The New Towns were the key to the growth of the new electronics industries. In all of this, the significance of Edinburgh's service industries to Scotland's economy was under-appreciated. Regional policy in the 1950s and 1960s actually disadvantaged Edinburgh, by grant-aiding moves of manufacturing companies from the city to locations outside its boundaries. The most ambitious modernization project sponsored by central government in Scotland in the 1970s and 1980s was the Glasgow Eastern Area Renewal Project. True the Scottish Office did sponsor an Edinburgh traffic study by Colin Buchanan. He was brought in at the end of the 1960s, when an impasse had been reached over road plans for the city centre (see Hague, 1984); his proposals were rejected by local politicians of all parties.

Between the 1950s and 1980s, Edinburgh's city centre remained largely unchanged, except for the 'mind-numbingly awful prefabricated concrete

St James shopping centre' (Sudjic, 1994), built on the site earmarked by Abercrombie for a Festival Theatre. The problems of Clydeside dominated Scottish Office policy-making. Within Edinburgh local boosterism on the political right was constrained by caution and penny-pinching thrift. Edinburgh's middle class was made up of lawyers, the pensions and life insurance industry, civil servants and university teachers – people living comfortably in a beautiful historic city, not 'muck is brass' industrial entrepreneurs.

Edingrad

Local government reorganization in 1975 imposed a new regional-scale council. This modernization downgraded the status of the city itself to a mere district, stripped of responsibility for strategic planning and transport, as well as key services such as education and social work. It also challenged the very basis by which the capital nature of Edinburgh had been defined – that is through civic continuity and tradition. There was much angst (see, for example, Gray, 1980).

The early 1980s saw the most intense period of economic change and political conflict in the city in modern times. While Edinburgh's service-based economy was less devastated by manufacturing closures than were the traditional cities of production, unemployment still rose to levels never experienced since the 1930s. Hard drugs became a serious problem for the generation denied the chance of a job, and living in the peripheral council housing estates (for example, see Craigmillar Festival Society, 1983). The Conservative-controlled Edinburgh District Council's sale with vacant possession of over 700 council houses in the deprived West Pilton area provoked bitter protests as house waiting lists lengthened (Hague, 1985). Rates increased dramatically as Lothian's controlling Labour group sought to improve public services and the Conservative government imposed penalties for overspending. The Chamber of Commerce and RAGE, the Ratepayers' Action Group of Edinburgh, pilloried the regional council, and fondly looked back to the days when the city's local government had not been politicized.

As Mrs Thatcher's shrill English voice hectored the nation, Conservative support in Scotland shrank. Labour surprised everyone, including themselves, by winning control of Edinburgh District Council in 1984. Under a 'Hard Left' leadership they had campaigned against the latest plans to build an opera house. There would be no pandering to effete middle-class tastes or false consciousness about the capital city and nationhood. Council housing and recreation services topped the list in the struggle for socialism. The activities of the planning department excited little interest; building conservation, elevation controls and local plans seemed unpromising avenues for socialist transformation. The red flag fluttered on the mast of the City Chambers above the Royal Mile. Fly stickers appeared on the streets bearing Edinburgh's heraldic coat of arms and saying 'Welcome Comrades to Edingrad – Once a Festival City'.

Edinburgh's Capital

Edinburgh's Capital was the response to this political crisis. It was a report,

> ... initiated by the Chamber of Commerce and supported by a group of Edinburgh companies in response to a growing concern within the business community that Edinburgh has failed, in recent years, to take full advantage of its full potential for development ... The decision to commission this study was also influenced by the experience where the private sector has taken a lead in proposing a strategic programme for city development and renewal. The most prominent examples of this type of initiative come from the United States and include Baltimore, Atlanta and Dallas, although there are also other overseas examples, notably Osaka in Japan. (Edinburgh Chamber of Commerce and Manufacturers, 1985, paras.1.1 and 1.3)

The title communicated three messages. It was the view of business, capital, in Edinburgh; Edinburgh is Scotland's capital; and special, a 'capital' place to live and invest. The two words of the title overturned the previous association of the capital city with preserving the past, and changed town planning into marketing.

High technology and knowledge-based industry, financial services, tourism and leisure and retailing were identified as the sectors with most growth potential. *Edinburgh's Capital* set out a list of projects, including development of a conference centre and attraction of a major hotel, better promotion of the Castle and enhancement of the Royal Mile, and provision of high amenity sites for industrial development. The Structure Plan's policies restricting parking provision in new office developments and limiting office development in the city centre were 'a relative failure' (para. 12.5). The call was for 'relaxations' to help small and medium-sized firms, together with larger-scale office development on the western edge of the city centre. The report called for increased release of land for housing development, while also floating the idea of improvement for sale of public-sector housing. The other main challenge to strategic physical planning policies was in the field of transport, where the call was for the building of a major new approach road through the west of the city, reviving a proposal Labour councillors had bitterly opposed. It criticized the planning controls which had made 'modest' city centre retailing redevelopment difficult to achieve because of the emphasis on townscape and conservation (para.11.7), and also called for 'controlled expansion of out-of-town shopping' (para.11.22).

Edinburgh's Capital looked beyond statutory land-use plans. It called for reductions in the rates (local taxes) levied on industrial and commercial enterprises. It considered the need for training to better match the supply and demand of labour skills. Above all, it sought promotion of the city and a multi-agency public–private partnership model as the way ahead. Its projects and programmes were intended to benefit 'Edinburgh and its citizens' (para.1.7). It was the first real recognition of the context of international competition.

'Count me in'

While the red flag flew in the capital, Mr Happy, a character from children's books, beamed 'Glasgow's Miles Better' from Britain's billboards. Douce stickers replying that 'Edinburgh is slightly superior' appeared in the capital. The announcement that derelict docks beside the River Clyde would be the venue for the 1988 International Garden Festival brought knowing smiles. Glasgow's new art gallery to house the Burrell Collection was conceded to be something of an achievement. Glasgow gave homes to the Scottish National Orchestra and Scottish Opera; a pity that Edinburgh never built its opera house. Glasgow, not the capital, not the Festival City, was named European City of Culture for 1990!

Edinburgh's Chamber of Commerce hired Michael Kelly, the man behind the 'Glasgow's Miles Better' campaign. The result was 'Count Me In':

> an exciting campaign . . . giving the people of Edinburgh a chance to show their commitment to the Capital's future.
>
> Masterminded by the Chamber of Commerce, the idea is to get people working together for the good of the city and to change the attitudes that are holding it back.
>
> It is a campaign seeking civic involvement and civic unity; it is designed to give Edinburgh folk the chance to demonstrate pride in our city. (Thomson, 1987)

Urban planning and development were marginal to the Hard Left but central to the 'Count Me In' agenda. Kelly called for action 'within a few weeks' on the conference centre proposed in *Edinburgh's Capital*. He urged tenants to realize that while their houses 'may not be repaired for a couple of years because the money is being spent on a conference centre', real benefits would come in the form of extra jobs and investment (*Edinburgh*

Evening News, 6 April 1987). Other proposals concerned gap sites on the Royal Mile, improvements to the Castle, and an opera house (to be funded by 'big business').

By the late 1980s the attitudinal changes sought by the Chamber of Commerce had largely been achieved; the councils co-operated with the private sector and the government's quango the Scottish Development Agency (and then its successor, Lothian and Edinburgh Enterprise Limited) around a programme very similar to that advocated in *Edinburgh's Capital*. 'Count Me In' did not ignite an unstoppable popular movement demanding a new consensus. Labour remained in control in both the region and the district, but the 1987 General Election was a watershed, not just locally but for the New Urban Left councils throughout the UK. For example, Labour's leader in Islington, Margaret Hodge, confessed 'The days of flying banners from town hall windows and hoisting up red flags on the roof are over' (quoted in Wolmar, 1987). There were no loopholes left for creative accounting, and no prospect of rescue by a Labour government.

The only escape from ratecapping and the poll tax led into the market place. Development and sale of land and property assets could boost local authority income without recourse to increased local taxation. The property boom, stoked by financial de-regulation and easy credit as the Conservative government paved the way to its election victory, came to the aid of the beleaguered councils. In this changed situation, key individuals on both sides of Edinburgh's divide began to build bridges, notably Councillor Kerevan (chair of the District Council's Economic Development and Estates Committee), Mark Lazarowicz (Leader of the District Council) and Professor Jack Shaw, the executive director of Scottish Financial Enterprise, the 'trade association' of the city's financial community. The Scottish Development Agency worked hard as matchmaker, avoiding the kind of antagonisms that imposition of an urban development corporation might have enflamed. The strength of the land and property market in the city (in part a result of the restrictionist planning policies challenged by *Edinburgh's Capital*) also reduced the need for a UDC-style body.

By 1990, Edinburgh Vision had been set up as an independent company limited by shareholding, and funded by the district council, the Chamber of Commerce and the Scottish Development Agency. They tried to project Edinburgh thirty years into the future. The vision was:

To further develop Edinburgh as a great, international capital city,

With pride in itself, its services and its unique character;

Creating an environment where wealth creation, culture and quality can prosper;

Where all sectors of our community can participate in and be committed to its success.

A European capital city

Europe was an important reference point to cement the coalition between Labour councils and business interests. As Mrs Thatcher's antipathy to Europe grew, Europe became one of a number of platforms around which Scots of all parties (except the dwindling Conservative and Unionist Party) could unite. Constitutionally, economically and politically Europe was a way of by-passing the kind of English nationalism that enthralled Westminster. Scotland's role in Europe, and therefore Edinburgh's status as capital and flagship, could be rethought, at last liberated from the backward-looking, parochial gaze that had shackled the city's thinking about development for so long. Councillor George Kerevan spearheaded Edinburgh's attempts to market itself as a European city. While the property market was still buoyant in 1989, he pushed the vision:

> We should be ready to take advantage of the Single European Market, selling the city as hard as possible and creating employment opportunities. We wanted a strategy which would bring balanced development and prosperity to the capital city of Scotland, not just the piecemeal approach to planning ... (*Edinburgh Evening News*, 10 January 1989)

Gap sites owned for a generation by the local authority were developed as flagships for the new Euro-capital, and as revenue earners for the council. The 'hole in the ground' which had awaited an opera house for a quarter of a century was developed by Scottish Metropolitan Properties as the Scottish Financial Services Centre, with 130,000 square feet of office space, together with a new base for the Traverse Theatre. A Festival Theatre has finally been achieved, through conversion of a former Bingo Hall, funded by Lothian and Edinburgh Enterprise Limited (LEEL) and the local authorities, not Michael Kelly's 'big business'. The 1200-seat Edinburgh International Conference Centre, designed by the internationally renowned architect Terry Farrell, opened in 1995, is the centrepiece of an 800,000-square feet office development, again on land owned by the district council.

A similar high profile was sought on the edge of the city for a business park development. Again local authority land ownership was a key factor in producing a 185-acre site, for which a £450m development was put together, by the District Council and the Miller Group. They formed a new company, New Edinburgh Ltd., to carry through the scheme. In a clear declaration of intent to go for a scheme of international quality the developers brought in the American architect Richard Meier, a designer with a global reputation, who had undertaken major commissions in Antwerp, Paris, Munich and Frankfurt as well as in the USA. Significantly this was his first British project.

A research park with facilities for research and development was part of Meier's plan, as was a production and service area for high technology industries. A 'teleport' will provide advanced communications and business services for the whole of Scotland; through fibre optic cables and satellites Scottish business will be plugged in to international communications networks without needing to go through London. This vision of Edinburgh as the 'high tech' city was expressed in the planning application:

> The City of Edinburgh has several key advantages attractive to high technology firms including good communications, the proximity to the airport, and the proposed park being a key element. Edinburgh has two major universities with a combined annual research budget in excess of 18 million pounds, excellent teaching hospitals, a secondary and tertiary education system that is nationally renowned, the second largest financial centre in Europe after London, existing high technology firms which are world leaders in their field and a continuation of scientific endeavour since the Enlightenment, all located within one of Europe's most beautiful and vibrant cities.

Keith Miller, chairman of Miller Developments, spoke of the development as being the most important in the city since the eighteenth century New Town. He said:

> We believe it will be pivotal to our vision for a new Edinburgh, which will be attractive to international as well as British companies seeking an appropriate headquarters location. It will enable Edinburgh to compete with other major cities throughout Europe . . . (*The Scotsman*, 21 December 1990)

European marketing has also infused thinking about tourism. In 1989 Peat Marwick McLintock produced a tourism report for Edinburgh that had been commissioned by the Scottish Tourist Board, the regional and district councils, the Chamber of Commerce and the Scottish Development Agency. Such a study would not have been seen as necessary before 1984, and in 1984–6 such collaboration between the public and private sectors would have been inconceivable. The report found that:

> Edinburgh is perceived by potential visitors as being somewhat sedate and unexciting, with a limited variety of things to do, inadequately packaged and

without a distinct identity from the rest of Scotland . . . Edinburgh's history and setting is not well presented and interpreted compared to other European destinations such as Salzburg, Munich and Florence . . . If it is to be seen as a European destination, Edinburgh needs to be seen as a cosmopolitan capital city.

A series of measures have followed, including improvements to restrict traffic on the Royal Mile, and better presentation of the castle.

The key reference-points for the restructuring of planning and development in Edinburgh in the early 1990s were regional, national at the Scottish level, and finally European. The regional stimulus was Glasgow's presumptuous promotion. The national influence was the recurrent image of the Scottish capital, most evidently mobilized in *Edinburgh's Capital*, but thereafter a bridge joining different sides of the class divide. Finally, and firmly linked to Scotland's national identity, came the awareness of Edinburgh in a European context. Central government was significant directly through its agency the Scottish Development Agency and then Lothian and Edinburgh Enterprise Limited. Ironically, though, it was the unpopularity of the English nationalist image of central government that really produced change. It achieved what political demography suggested was impossible – it delivered political control of Edinburgh to the Labour Party, and created a local version of a wider Scottish consensus that saw Europe as a positive alternative to the crypto-English British nation-state.

'Nivertheface' . . . the rediscovery of Edinburgh as a European capital has actually made it a less distinct capital. All capital cities now have their MacDonald's, the same international hotel chains, the conference centre, the shopping mall, the Manhattan skyline of cathedrals to capital. Has the resolution of the crisis of Edinburgh's capital identity been resolved in a way that actually destroys its urban identity? Of course the romantic topography of hills and water are still there; the landmarks, the stone and the cobbles, the grain and texture still make the Old Town and the New Town urban environments unsurpassed by any other British city. But even here the vitality of the city centre is under threat. The new office and conference centre complex has emptied the elegant Charlotte Square of its office users. Eventually the New Town will revert to residential use, but it is likely to be a slow and dispiriting process, cluttered by 'To Let' signs. The retail park adjacent to the new edge of city business park offers a view of the classical city skyline, but otherwise could be anywhere. As a gateway to the city it contributes nothing, but it threatens the city centre's retailing dominance. The City By-pass, constructed in the 1980s, combined with increased car ownership and growing congestion, has changed patterns of accessibility, decisively favouring the periphery. Local government reorganization in 1996, forced on Scotland for no better reason than to reduce the number of anti-Conservative local authorities, creates an all-purpose authority for the capital, but will also damage strategic planning in the city region around Edinburgh, further accentuating pressures for urban spread, and undermining the distinctiveness of the free-standing city.

'The meanness of EDINBURGH has been too long an obstruction to our improvement, and a reproach to SCOTLAND', said the 'Proposals' of 1752. That statement held true for many long years after the blaze of the Scottish Enlightenment faded. The playwright Tom Stoppard was able to dub The Athens of the North 'The Reykjavik of the South'. A new European identity, cast by new political structures and the creaking of the antique British state, has opened possibilities for a capital revival. Edinburgh could become a demonstration capital showing how a small nation can live within its resource base, how cities can be made more socially and ecologically sustainable. That, not retail parks and multiplex cinemas strung around and beyond the edge of the city, is what a European capital city should be in the twenty-first century. There are some encouraging pointers. In late 1995 a Capital City Partnership of Scottish Homes, LEEL and the Regional and District councils produced an urban regeneration strategy which aims to 'reduce the stark inequalities of income and opportunity across the city and so increase markedly the quality of life for those experiencing unemployment, poverty and hardship'. The partners say that the strategy seeks to realize a vision for the city in which:

> Edinburgh will be a place where all will prosper and no one is excluded from the city's unique advantages, where opportunities in the worlds of work, education, leisure and housing are readily available to all citizens. It will be a truly Capital city attractive to investors and visitors alike, and equally accessible to all who live here. It will be a city of distinct, integrated and balanced communities located in an environment free from congestion and the dangers of pollution.

Of course there are going to be structural barriers to realizing these fine words, but it is the best vision for what Scotland's capital could be that we have had for over 200 years.

Cardiff: capital development?

The purpose of this section is to examine the extent to which the planning of Cardiff – focusing for the most part on the post-1945 period – can be understood fully only if set within an account of the politics of Welsh nationalism which involves, *inter alia*, claims to 'capital city' status.

It is certainly the case that city boosterists have traded on capital city status. Typical recent examples would be the successive tourism strategies for the city. For example, the Cardiff Tourism Study, undertaken by consultants Tibbalds Colbourne Partnership for the city council, recommended the reinforcement and promotion of Cardiff's capital city status as one of six strategic objectives (Karski, 1988). But, going beyond this it appears that the politics of planning and development in the city has been skewed in ways not seen in comparable regional centres in England (such as, say, Nottingham or Sheffield). The section begins by reprising some important features of the account of Welsh identity and nationalism set out in the introductory chapter of this volume; the relationship of Cardiff's local politics to the project of creating (and recreating) a national identity is then discussed; and, finally, the manner in which the development of the city's built environment has been implicated in these is set out.

The rise to dominance

In a discussion of Cardiff as capital city, the most significant fact is the city's newness as a capital, and its relative youth as a major settlement. Wales has not been a nation-state, and until the mid-twentieth century has not had a capital. As Carter (1986, pp.171–2) puts it, '. . . the country has never formed unequivocally an independent political unit . . . [and] never achieved a political identity and its concomitant administrative apparatus, which might have generated a capital city'. Indeed, so profound was the political and economic fragmentation of the country before and during industrialization it would even be difficult to draw up a *short* (as opposed to long) list of places with some kind of historic claim to capital city status. And so dramatic were the social and economic changes created by the industrial revolution that even many candidates on a long list would now appear far fetched: could Whitland, in rural Dyfed, be a serious candidate, even if it was once home to the court of Hywel Dda, one of the country's great law givers; or Aberffraw, though it was the historic seat of the kings of Gwynedd (Davies, 1993)? The process of industrialization introduced and exacerbated a range of social divisions, one manifestation of which was contested conceptions of what being Welsh involved. So, though there might be no *historic* rivals for the role of capital city of Wales, it was by no means uncontentious which town deserved that kind of symbolic status when a Welsh nationalism – that is, a promotion of the idea of Wales as a nation – became influential in the (then hegemonic) Liberal politics of the late nineteenth century.

The first college of the University of Wales was founded in Aberystwyth, a town which also bid successfully for the National Library; Cardiff secured its own college of the University in 1883, and also won the political fight for the National Museum (in gaining the latter, a decisive factor was the availability of a splendid site in Cathays Park as part of a civic complex being built in accordance with strict restrictive covenants on land donated to the city by the Marquess of Bute, the greatest local landowner (Evans, 1985)). By 1905, when Cardiff was granted the status of city, its economic dynamism and rapid growth made it stand out among Welsh towns, but the fact that it was only in 1955 that Cardiff was declared, by Queen Elizabeth II, *capital city* of Wales demonstrates both the degree of contestation of Cardiff's claim to some more general cultural significance and also the struggle which the nationalist agenda faced in making inroads in the British state. Even in the mid-1950s, Cardiff's claims were challenged by Caernarfon, Aberystwyth and Llandrindod Wells who put forward their own bids for being made capital.

The sheer newness of Cardiff as a major settlement (let alone a capital city) is underlined by the fact it acquired its first bank and printing press in the 1870s, at a time when Edinburgh's New Town was long developed (Davies, 1988, p.25). As Daunton (1977) has documented, it was the development by the aristocratic Bute family of Cardiff docks to export first iron and then coal from the south Wales Valleys that formed the basis of the city's growth. Though the first of the modern docks – Bute West – was opened in 1839, it was in the late nineteenth century that trade, and population, exploded. By 1913 Cardiff was a coal exporting port of international significance, a 'Coal Metropolis'. The nineteenth century was a period of economic and social ferment in Wales, and Cardiff was by no means the only boom town. It was as late as 1881 that Cardiff overtook Merthyr as the largest town in Wales; meanwhile Swansea developed as a sub-regional centre for the western coalfield. For those portions of the increasingly powerful middle classes who saw their personal interests tied to the fortunes of their towns boosterism and inter-urban competition was an important aspect of local politics. The use of *capital* city status in Cardiff's civic boosterism is thus only the latest phase of a tradition which extends over a century.

Nationalism and the post-war regionalist consensus

A distinctively nationalist perspective has survived the decline of Liberalism and the rise of a Labour hegemony in Wales. Within post-war Welsh political life, the construction of Wales as a nation with a distinctive set of interests and concerns has been adopted by the Labour movement. It has become an integral part of the justification of a dominant political project which has portrayed the Welsh economy as one in need of 'modernization' with state intervention having a critical role to play in that process by (i) ameliorating the human costs of modernization; and (ii) creating the right conditions for attracting investment in 'modern' industries. Rees and Lambert (1981) argue, persuasively, that this set of ideas has been shared across political parties in Wales, and across levels of government; Pickvance (1985) has commented that the phenomenon is a good example of a spatial coalition – a political project for promoting a particular set of policies in an area, which enjoys support across class and other social cleavages, and finds institutional expression in a number of agencies including those of local, and regional, government. The coalition remained intact in the 1980s, for as the secretary of state for Wales from 1979 to 1987 (the then Nicholas Edwards) has recently remarked to one of the authors of this chapter, he found no difficulty in working with Labour local authorities in Wales (nor did his immediate successor, Peter Walker), partly because he struggled to maintain a commitment to state intervention in the Welsh economy in the face of Cabinet scepticism.

Having a worthy capital city as a shop-window for Wales is an important part of the project. But while this allows planners and local politicians to exploit the tag of 'capital city', the manner in which that status has been manufactured has also legitimized intervention in the city's planning by the 'regional' tier of central government in the form of the Welsh Office, and its predecessors.

From the mid-1950s onwards, it seems that within the regional arm of central government (then, a section of the Ministry of Housing and Local Government; from 1964, the Welsh Office) there was an acceptance that Cardiff – as the largest (and still growing) town in south Wales – offered important economic opportunities, and at the very least needed to be modernized along with the rest of the region. Though a full public expression of the special significance of Cardiff in the strategy of modernization was to come in 1967 in the white paper *Wales: The Way Ahead* (Welsh Office, 1967), nearly a decade earlier central government had taken the initiative in forcing Cardiff City Council to reconsider its development plan for the central area, and encouraging it to use top consultant Colin Buchanan to draw up a development plan worthy of a capital city (Cooke 1980). From that time onwards, as will be seen, the Welsh Office has been supportive of, and at times has prompted, planning strategies which have as their aim the spatial restructuring of areas of the city seen as critical if it is to play a role as not simply a sub-regional centre, but a capital city. In Cardiff's politics, however, boosting the city as a capital and all that entailed in terms of redevelopment and spatial restructuring had to compete for attention with other concerns. Within the Labour movement, ameliorating a housing shortage and securing industrial employment appear to have had consistent attention in the post-war period. However, Labour was rarely in power locally until the mid-1970s, and the Conservatives were certainly committed to boosterism and receptive to government advice on partnerships in city centre development, even if their small-business support (and mentality) occasionally meant they had to be led rather purposefully (as with Buchanan's appointment). In practice, a workable, if sometimes fractious, local consensus emerged in relation to post-war planning policy, which involved on the one hand a commitment to central area redevelopment, to develop Cardiff as 'an administrative and commercial centre and as the Capital of Wales' (letter of the Secretary of State for Wales, March 1969, quoted in Cooke, 1980, p.219). On the other hand, central government supported a programme of municipal housing by the City Council (for example, by supporting its need for peripheral expansion – sometimes in opposition to Glamorgan County Council). Bourne's (1980) analysis of post-war housebuilding finds consistent bipartisan support, though there were differences in relation to council house sales.

From city centre to Cardiff Bay

The process of radically reappraising, and spatially restructuring, the city centre, which began with the appointment of Buchanan in the early 1960s, took twenty years to complete. By the mid-1980s, transport patterns, land uses and the physical structure of the centre had been transformed, largely through 'partnerships', in which the City Council assembled development sites (typically by compulsory purchase) which were subsequently developed by the private sector. It is a measure of the bipartisan support which this project enjoyed that though control of local and central governments changed a number of times over that period any setbacks it had can more plausibly be ascribed to the vagaries of the investment climate than to changes in political will (Cooke, 1980; Hamilton, 1988; Imrie and Thomas, 1993).

The importance of the Welsh Office was illustrated by what it failed to support as much as by what it did. Giving massive urban development grants (of just under £2m, and close to £3m) to 1980s city centre projects (a hotel and 'World Trade Centre' respectively) showed how helpful support could be; nearly twenty years earlier, the failure of the Welsh Office to confirm a compulsory purchase order sunk ambitious plans for a university precinct to complement the restructured city centre.

Planning and spatial development in the city in the 1990s have been dominated by the regeneration of Cardiff Bay. The shift in the focus of planning and commercial development interest to this area has been politically led. This is illustrated by the clear signals to local authorities and developers about the availability of central government assistance given in the early 1980s (Thomas, 1992), and is underlined by the fact that there remained in Cardiff, in the city centre and in some peripheral areas, opportunities for commercial and housing development throughout the 1980s and early 1990s. This was not a developer-led initiative, though speculative ideas from a local developer appear to have drawn the Welsh Office's attention to Cardiff Bay (Thomas, 1992). The kind of future envisaged for this mix of industrial and poorer residential areas in the city's docklands, and the rhetoric with which it is presented, locates the project within the nationalist modernizing Welsh political consensus (Thomas and Imrie, 1993); for example, the mission of Cardiff Bay Development Corporation (set up in 1987) is to:

- unite Cardiff with its waterfront;
- create a superb environment for people to work, live and play;
- achieve the very highest worldwide standards in architectural design;
- create jobs, homes and exciting tourist attractions. (Pickup, 1988)

The two distinguishing features of the politics of development in Cardiff – local cross-party support behind a project of civic promotion and Welsh Office intervention – are evident once more in the Cardiff Bay story.

Welsh Office influence has been especially significant. It was the then secretary of state for Wales, Nicholas Edwards, who, in 1983 signalled that public money would be available to underpin a major shift in planning and development interest from the city centre to the docklands. In a speech in the House of Commons he virtually invited developers and local authorities to put together development packages (an invitation made in the knowledge that there were speculative proposals on the table):

> While I can at this stage make no specific . . . commitment, I have made it clear that I will consider sympathetically for inclusion in any future [programme] any project which commends the support of the local and planning authorities, which attracts investment by the private sector, and which offers a good prospect of viability. (Edwards, 1983)

In 1985, an urban development grant of about £9m was given to a 90-acre mixed-use redevelopment in just the area identified in Edwards' speech. But the secretary of state's ambition to transform Cardiff from a nationally significant city to an internationally recognized one, had been whetted by the prospects for ultimately profitable private-sector redevelopment which the docklands – only a mile from the city centre – held. Interviews conducted by one of the authors with key individuals involved in local politics and local planning at the time make it clear that the secretary of state was intent on creating an urban development corporation as a single-purpose agency for transforming the physical (and hence economic and social) character of the area. Such an agency would underpin (and hence attract) private investment in property development; that development would be for whatever uses were profitable – generally commercial uses of various kinds and private-sector housing. In this way, a bright new 'maritime city' would be created, over fifty years after the decline of the 'Coal Metropolis'.

The agency, at least, has been set up, though not without considerable efforts having to be made to ensure that the broad consensus which has supported the planning of Cardiff for many decades has been retained. This has not been an entirely straightforward task (Thomas, 1992). There have been the natural resentments of a county council and city council towards a well-funded new organization (budget £61.5m in 1996/7). Allowing the city council to retain planning powers within CBDC's area was a conciliatory gesture. Other anxieties have been less easily allayed. The city council's work over many decades in co-ordinating city centre redevelopment has left it with a complex stake – professional, political and financial – in the continuing prosperity of the centre. The initial response by many senior politicians and officers to the winds of change in the 1980s was a concern that any major new development in Cardiff Bay would compete with the city centre. The evident commitment of the Welsh Office (and, especially, the secretary of state) to making something happen in Cardiff Bay has muted political criticism as potentially counter-productive, but the city council (when under Labour control, and when 'hung') has been notably less enthusiastic in its backing than has the county council.

South Glamorgan County Council has been under Labour control since 1982, and dominant within the Labour group has been a set of (male) councillors with an agenda which places as its highest priority securing and increasing employment opportunities for working-class people – especially men made redundant from blue-collar occupations. By the early 1980s, these councillors had come to accept that the nature of contemporary economic restructuring was such that there were few if any new industrial jobs which could be attracted to Cardiff. Consequently, they became more receptive to the prospects of other kinds of development in an area which had hitherto been largely industrial. Any investment was better than none. As the then secretary of the Cardiff Trades Council put it:

> Reluctantly we ask you to consider that the priority can no longer remain with manufacture. The only source from which we can obtain the [jobs] needed is the tertiary sector so it is that sector which should be given priority.

It is unlikely that CBDC – always intended to be a short-term body – will survive beyond 1999. The scale of its achievements (even by its own standards) will depend to quite an extent on the state of the property market and competing options for potential investors. But whatever its legacy (such as the 1.2 km barrage across 'Cardiff Bay' now under construction), it is likely that the political consensus of which it is an expression will remain powerful for a while longer. For some time, for example, South Glamorgan County Council has been promoting the slogan 'Cardiff Euro-capital, 2020'. Cardiff, as a capital city, will continue to be a potent symbol in local politics, and its planning will continue to attract disproportionate attention from central government.

Yet not all Cardiff citizens are dazzled by the glamour of the capital, not all feel themselves benefiting from the city's marketing of itself. There is a deep-rooted anxiety in Butetown, at the heart of Cardiff Bay, that the redevelopment strategy is not intended to bring it any benefits. The more the local press trumpets the virtues of 'revitalization' (Thomas, 1994), the more convinced are long-time residents of this multi-ethnic area that they will somehow be levered out. More generally, authoritative reports on the local economy have recently confirmed the persistence of racial discrimination and disadvantage (CRE, 1993). Racial harassment is also an everyday problem for many of the city's residents (SGCC, 1995). In some areas, local authorities deploy modest budgets in community development in places which have achieved unwelcome notoriety for violence and alleged social malaise (Campbell, 1994). One of the strands in the complex, and confused, discussions about Cardiff Bay's proposed opera house emphasized the concern that an expensive building designed to put the city on the international map would provide few benefits for the local population (*Financial Times*, 1995). The arguments to the contrary of prominent local worthies failed to engage with widespread (though by no means universal) local anxieties that the vision of a 'Euro-capital' had little connection with distributive justice. If these worries persist and become more common they will introduce a new dimension to Cardiff's local politics, in which to date the civic boosterism associated with capital city status has been accepted as providing general benefits. As Keil and Leiser (1992) document with respect to Frankfurt's bid to be a 'global city', consistent and systematic 'selective exclusion' can have an explosive impact on local politics.

Conclusions

Edinburgh and Cardiff are capitals of stateless nations. We might suggest that a capital would be too vital to the trappings of a full nation-state to permit local politics to be a key factor in the development of its capital city.

Paradoxically one could even interpret the damage done to London's development since the mid-1980s by the abolition of a London-wide tier of government in those terms. The Scottish Office and the Welsh Office have clearly exerted influence over the development of Edinburgh and Cardiff, but there have been important differences. We have argued that the Welsh Office has been more concerned to boost, modernize and restructure Cardiff than has the Scottish Office with Edinburgh. This statement should have the status of a hypothesis, for our research has not been able to investigate government records, for example, or to interview all relevant senior civil servants or ministers, past or present. Setting aside this caveat, we might suggest that the explanation for the differences lie in the newness of Cardiff and the antiquity of Edinburgh. Such an explanation is not sufficient. Both the Welsh Office and the Scottish Office were preoccupied by the problems of managing economic restructuring, rather than the political task of stating nationhood through a visible capital city. However, in the Welsh case the promotion of a new capital city, and its attendant nationalist rhetoric and sentiment, was based on a long-standing use of a Welsh nationalism as an ideological support for levering resources from the nation-state as part of managing restructuring. Boostering Cardiff, one time 'Coal Metropolis', was strongly associated with addressing the problems of the decline of south Wales's mining and heavy industry base, in particular, but Cardiff has also provided economic benefits for migrants from all over Wales (Giggs and Pattie, 1992). In Scotland, there was not just a north/south, rural/urban cleavage, as in Wales, but also an east/west divide within the Central Belt. Edinburgh and its service industries competed with Clydeside and its extractive and manufacturing base rather than complemented them. Cardiff has had no such competitor within Wales in the twentieth century.

The wider point we are making is that the development and planning of capital cities is not autonomous at the political level, it is always, and arguably increasingly, fashioned by economic factors, not least by land and property markets and decisions made by investors rather than planners or politicians. In recent years, the essence of major projects in both Cardiff and Edinburgh has been to create the conditions which will attract mobile capital to undertake property development. Indeed the capital city status is one card to be played in this game, implying that the cities provide an entry to wider economic opportunities and are of greater economic and political significance than ordinary provincial competitor cities. Potentially, the other side of this card is the leverage it gives planners to demand quality in new developments, though the case studies show that such a realization is not automatically grasped or readily achieved.

The nation-state is therefore just one of the players in the drama of fabricating the meaning of the capital city and investing in it. Cardiff and Edinburgh show that in stateless nations this nation-state role is itself doubly complicated and potentially contradictory. There is always the potential for tension between the central state and the stateless nation. In Wales, the imposition in recent years of secretaries of state with no personal connections with the country, and political views radically at variance with most Conservatives, let alone the non-Conservative majority, has underscored this possibility. If these circumstances persist then the Cardiff Bay Development Corporation might begin to be read as a negation of the right of the Welsh to determine their own planning of their capital, even if, to date, some measure of local consensus and acceptance has been painstakingly achieved. The comparison with Scotland is fascinating. The capacity of the Scottish Office to massage the tension between Westminster and Scotland to produce a negotiated, voluntary acceptance of the primacy of markets and private sector influence on urban development has been remarkable. The partnership idea is underpinned by a sense of shared Scottishness which for many of the partners is defined by antipathy to the Westminster government.

This brings us directly to issues of local politics and behind them the potential contradictions between class and nationalism as bases of identification and political action. It is clear that local politics matter (as implied above, they probably matter more in stateless nations than in conventional nation-states). However, they are highly contingent, not just on local class structures, party politics, and central/local relations, but also on agency and leadership. In both cities the local development agenda has shifted considerably over the years, not surprisingly. What is important is the vision of the meaning of the capital city and the distributional impact of the class compromise that is arrived at in implementing this vision. The two cities show that there are times when Labour councillors are in favour of development and times they are against it, and the same is true of local councillors from the political right. Likewise the case studies show that there are numerous times in history when there is an opportunity to define a new vision for the capital, and/or when a new grouping of forces can grasp the agenda. Devolution to an elected parliament, let alone independence would necessitate such a new vision.

We would therefore suggest two critical lessons for the development of these cities as we approach the millennium. Firstly, some kind of coalition or consensus is likely to be more fruitful for the cities and their people than is a scenario of heightened local conflict. The nature of inter-city competition, the mobility of capital, the impoverishment of the quality of life for all in cities where poverty and social exclusion stalk substantial minorities, together with the imperative to devise more environmentally sustainable forms of living – all these factors are interconnected and require mutual understanding and concern to achieve a resolution. Secondly, and linked to the former, a vision for the city as capital and for its planning are vital, or put another way, it is not just the coalition that matters but what are its shared aims? Again some broad parameters seem clear – positioning the capital in a European context and thereby making a statement about national identity, planning and developing through partnership, attaching a high priority to quality and design. Ideas of social and environmental sustainability offer even stateless nations the chance to define a dynamic continuity with their past, while creating new roles and relationships for their capitals and nations.

References

Abercrombie, P. and D. Plumstead 1949. *A Civic Survey and Plan for Edinburgh* (Edinburgh, Oliver and Boyd).

Bourne, M. C. 1980. 'A Study of Council House Building Activity in Post War Cardiff', M.Sc. Dissertation (Cardiff, Department of Town Planning, UWIST).

Campbell, B. 1994. *Goliath* (London, Methuen).

Cardiff Trades Union Council 1983. *Comments on South Glamorgan Structure Plan 1983. Employment and the Economy*, Cardiff Trades Union Council Archives 5.13 (Cardiff, University of Wales College of Cardiff).

Carter, H. 1986. 'Cardiff: local, regional and national capital', in G. Gordon (ed.), *Regional Cities in the UK, 1890–1980* (London, Harper and Row), pp.171–90.

City and Royal Burgh of Edinburgh 1943. *The Future of Edinburgh. The Report of the Advisory Committee on City Development* (Edinburgh, City and Royal Burgh of Edinburgh).

Commission for Racial Equality 1993. *Employers in Cardiff* (London, CRE).

Cooke, P. 1980. 'Capital relations and state dependency: An analysis of urban development policy in Cardiff', in G. Rees and T. Rees (eds.), *Poverty and Social Inequality in Wales* (London, Croom Helm).

Craigmillar Festival Society 1983. 'Craigmillar in Crisis', mimeo.

Daiches, D. 1978. *Edinburgh* (London, Hamish Hamilton).

Daunton, M. 1977. *Coal Metropolis: Cardiff, 1870–1914* (Leicester, Leicester University Press).

Davies, J. 1988. 'Aristocratic town-makers and the coal metropolis: the Marquess of Bute and the growth of Cardiff, 1776 to 1947', in D. Cannadine (ed.), *Patricians, Power and Politics in Nineteenth Century Towns* (Leicester, Leicester University Press), pp.18–67.

Davies, J. 1993. *A History of Wales* (London, Allen Lane. The Penguin Press) (first published in Welsh as *Hanes Cymru*, 1990).

Edinburgh Chamber of Commerce and Manufacturers 1985. *Edinburgh's Capital* (Henley-on-Thames and Edinburgh, PEIDA).

Edwards, N. 1983. Statement in the House of Commons, *Hansard*, 10 February, vols.1176–8.

Evans, N. 1985. 'The Welsh Victorian city: The middle class and civic and national consciousness in Cardiff, 1850–1914', *Welsh History Review*, Vol.12, pp.350–87.

Financial Times 1995. 'In praise of élitism', editorial, 27 December.

Giggs, J. and C. Pattie 1992. 'Wales as a plural society', *Contemporary Wales*, Vol.5, pp.25–63.

Gray, J. G. 1980. *The Capital of Scotland: Its Precedence and Status* (Edinburgh, The Edina Press).

Hague, C. 1984. *The Development of Planning Thought* (London, Hutchinson).
Hague, C. 1985. 'Housing privatisation in practice', *Housing and Planning Review*, Vol.30, pp.16–18.
Hamilton, N. 1988. 'The City Centre', in E. Evans and H. Thomas (eds.), *Cardiff. Capital Development* (Cardiff, Cardiff City Council), pp.20–30.
Harvey, D. 1989. 'Transformations in urban governance in late capitalism', *Geografiska Annaler*, Vol.71(B), pp.3–17.
Imrie, R. and H. Thomas 1993. 'The limits of property led regeneration', *Environment and Planning C: Government and Policy*, Vol.11, pp.87–102.
Karski, A. 1988. 'Cardiff – the tourism potential', in E. Evans and H. Thomas (eds.), *Cardiff Capital Development* (Cardiff, Cardiff City Council), p.39.
King, Anthony D. 1993. 'Cultural hegemony and capital cities', in J. Taylor *et al.* (eds.), *Capital Cities: International Perspectives* (Ottawa, Carleton University Press).
Keil, R. and P. Leiser 1992. 'Frankfurt: global city – local politics', in M. P. Smith (ed.), *After Modernism* (London, Sage), pp.39–69.
Mears, F. C. and J. Russell 1938. 'The new town of Edinburgh – Part 1', *Book of the Old Edinburgh Club*, Vol.22, pp.167–200.
Meisel, J. 1993. 'Capital cities: what is a capital?', in J. Taylor *et al.* (eds.), *Capital Cities: International Perspectives* (Ottawa, Carleton University Press).
Pickup, J. 1988. 'Cardiff Bay – the way forward', in E. Evans and H. Thomas (eds.), *Cardiff Capital Development* (Cardiff, Cardiff City Council), p.10.
Pickvance, C. 1985. 'Spatial polity as territorial politics', in G. Rees *et al.* (eds.), *Political Action and Social Identity* (London, Macmillan).
Rees, G. and J. Lambert 1981. 'Nationalism as legitimation? Notes towards a political economy of regional development in south Wales', in M. Harloe (ed.), *New Perspectives in Urban Change and Conflict* (London, Heinemann Educational).
South Glamorgan County Council 1995. *South Glamorgan Race Equality* (Summer issue).
Spark, M. 1993. 'Edinburgh born', in programme for 'The Prime of Miss Jean Brodie', Royal Lyceum Company, Edinburgh, 8–30 January 1993.
Sudjic, D. 1994. 'City of the future?', *The Guardian*, 9 August, Guardian 2, pp.4–5.
Sutcliffe, A. 1993. 'Capital cities: does form follow values?', in J. Taylor *et al.* (eds.), *Capital Cities: International Perspectives* (Ottawa, Carleton University Press).
Thomas, H. 1992. 'Redevelopment in Cardiff Bay: state intervention and the securing of consent', *Contemporary Wales*, Vol.5, pp.81–98.
Thomas, H. 1994. 'The local press and urban renewal: a south Wales case study', *International Journal of Urban and Regional Research*, Vol.18, No.2, pp.315–33.
Thomas, H. and R. Imrie 1993. 'Cardiff Bay and the project of modernization', in R. Imrie and H. Thomas (eds.), *British Urban Policy and the Urban Development Corporations* (London, Paul Chapman Publishing).
Thomson, R. 1987. 'Now let's get a move on!', *Edinburgh Evening News*, 6 April 1987, p.1.
Welsh Office 1967. *Wales: The Way Ahead* (London, HMSO).
Wolmar, C. 1987. 'The fresh face of the capital's politics', *New Statesman*, 18 October 1987.
Youngson, A. J. 1966. *The Making of Classical Edinburgh* (Edinburgh, Edinburgh University Press).

9

Urban Growth Management: Distinctive Solutions in the Celtic Countries?

MARTIN J. ELSON and RODERICK MACDONALD

Introduction

Green Belts are an integral part of the professional and political ideology of post-war planning. Their promotion and defence has long been associated with the affluent south-east of England. What then are we to make of their emergence as professional and political concerns in Scotland and Wales? Are they different instruments masquerading under the same name? The situations of Scotland and Wales make for interesting comparison as there are currently five approved Green Belts in Scotland but none in Wales, although a number of authorities have implemented or are actively moving towards Green Belt-type policies. Scotland is also interesting as it is the only area in the United Kingdom where a Green Belt has been removed, in the case of the City of Dundee.

The aim of this chapter is to review the operation of Green Belts and other forms of urban growth management in Scotland and Wales, concluding as to the contrasts and similarities with the English situation. The chapter draws on work undertaken by the authors for the Department of the Environment and the Scottish Office on *The Effectiveness of Green Belts* (Elson *et al.*, 1993) and *Green Belts for Wales – A Positive Role for Sport and Recreation* (Elson, 1991) for the Sports Council for Wales, together with analysis of recent developments in urban growth management in the two countries.

Scotland

There are currently five approved Green Belts in Scotland, totalling some 165,000 hectares (Scottish Office, 1991) (see Figure 9.1). Over the years,

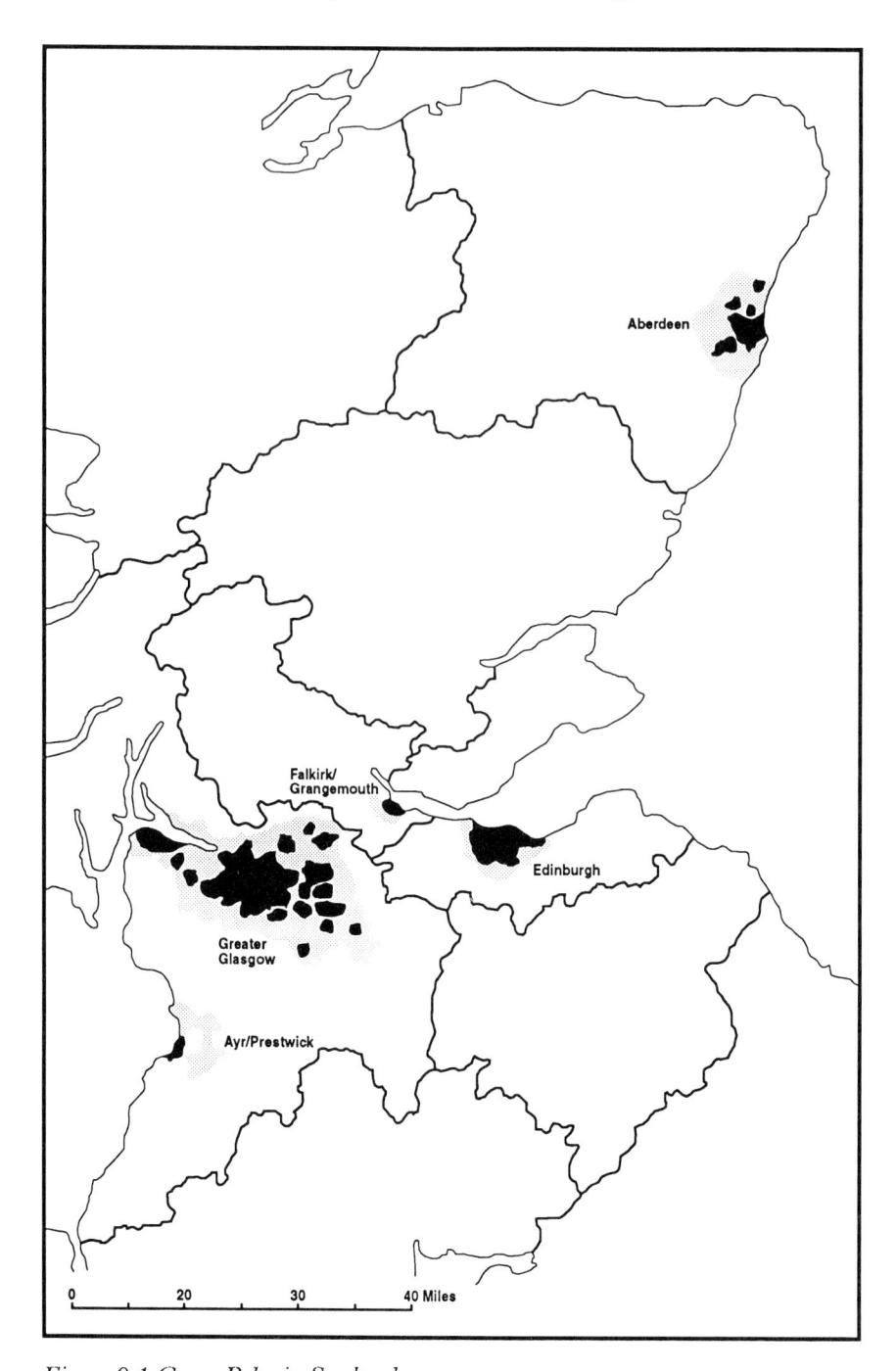

Figure 9.1 Green Belts in Scotland

there have been variations in the total area of Green Belt with abandonment of the Dundee Green Belt in 1978 and reductions in the Aberdeen Green Belt in the 1980s. In 1992, proposals by Central Regional Council for a new Green Belt around Stirling, Dunblane and Alloa were approved. In Strathclyde, the Green Belt has been extended around Ayr, Prestwick and Troon and reduced by exceptional releases for housing and commercial development in the Glasgow conurbation (Elson et al., 1993). Table 9.1 indicates the area of approved Green Belt in 1990.

Table 9.1 Area of Approved Green Belt in Scotland

Green Belt	Hectares
Aberdeen	23,664
Ayr/Prestwick	2,853
Falkirk/Grangemouth	3,495
Greater Glasgow	120,000
Lothian	14,600

Source: Scottish Office (1991).

Following English circulars in the 1950s allowing Green Belts to be designated in areas outside London, Scottish Green Belt policy was codified for the first time by Circular 14/1960, and is currently being operated by Scottish Office Circular 24/1985. This circular, *Development in the Countryside and Green Belts*, sets out the three main purposes of Green Belts in Scotland: to maintain the identity of towns by establishing a clear definition of their physical boundaries and preventing coalescence; to provide countryside for recreation or institutional purposes of various kinds; and to maintain the landscape setting of towns.

Despite Scottish Office involvement in the above-mentioned Department of the Environment research which led to the revision of Planning Policy Guidance (PPG) 2 *Green Belts* in England (Department of the Environment, 1995), no such revision has taken place in Scotland. The Scottish Office is, however, working towards issuing National Planning Policy Guidelines (NPPG) in 1997 examining Green Belt policy. Since local government reorganization in 1975, Green Belts in Scotland have been defined in structure plans by regional councils, whose areas equate to wider areas than counties in England. There is no discussion in the Scottish circular of the precise longevity of Green Belts, nor are there provisions for safeguarded land or similar as in England.

The 1985 circular was introduced at a time when countryside policies in Scotland were seen as too restrictive, noting that maintenance of Green Belts could only be expected where '. . . a balance between containment and growth of urban development can be sustained on a long term basis'

(Scottish Development Department, 1985a, para.6). Planning authorities are therefore expected to revise Green Belts in terms of examining demand for all forms of development and reviewing the locations where such demands can be met. This could involve infilling in Green Belt towns and villages, using derelict or poor agricultural land in Green Belt settlements and identifying land on inner boundaries of Green Belts no longer making a contribution to the Green Belt. While there is strong political support for Green Belts, as in England, changes to it through the structure plan process are not ruled out but these should be in exceptional circumstances. In terms of development control a more limited range of uses are mentioned than in English guidance. Paragraph 4 (iv) of Circular 24/1985 states

> . . . approval should not be given, except in very special circumstances, for the construction of new buildings and the extension or change of use of existing buildings, for purposes other than agriculture, horticulture, woodland management and recreation, or establishments and institutions standing in extensive grounds or other uses appropriate to the rural character of the area.

The future for Green Belt policy in Scotland is, however, somewhat uncertain because of the review of the structure of local government which came into force on 1 April 1996. The new structure is on a unitary basis, with regional councils being abolished along with smaller districts. It is likely, but not at the time of writing confirmed, that strategic planning will be undertaken by groupings of new unitary authorities or by single unitary authorities where a natural structure plan area is evident. The implications for the Scottish Green Belts of these arrangements are not yet fully clear and it is assumed that the NPPG being drafted by the Scottish Office will explain how Green Belt policy will function in the new local government system.

The Glasgow Green Belt

The Greater Glasgow Green Belt, controlled by Strathclyde Regional Council (SRC) and a considerable number of district councils, is the largest in Scotland being of some 120,000 hectares (see Figure 9.2).

The Green Belt can be traced to the Clyde Valley Plan of 1946 and has slowly grown via a succession of development plans since 1958, without recourse to an Examination in Public. The emphasis of the Glasgow Green Belt in terms of renewal of the conurbation is important. As the 1994 Consultation Draft of the Strathclyde Structure Plan Review notes the purpose of the Green Belt is '. . . to complement the process of urban renewal by controlling the growth of built up areas and providing the

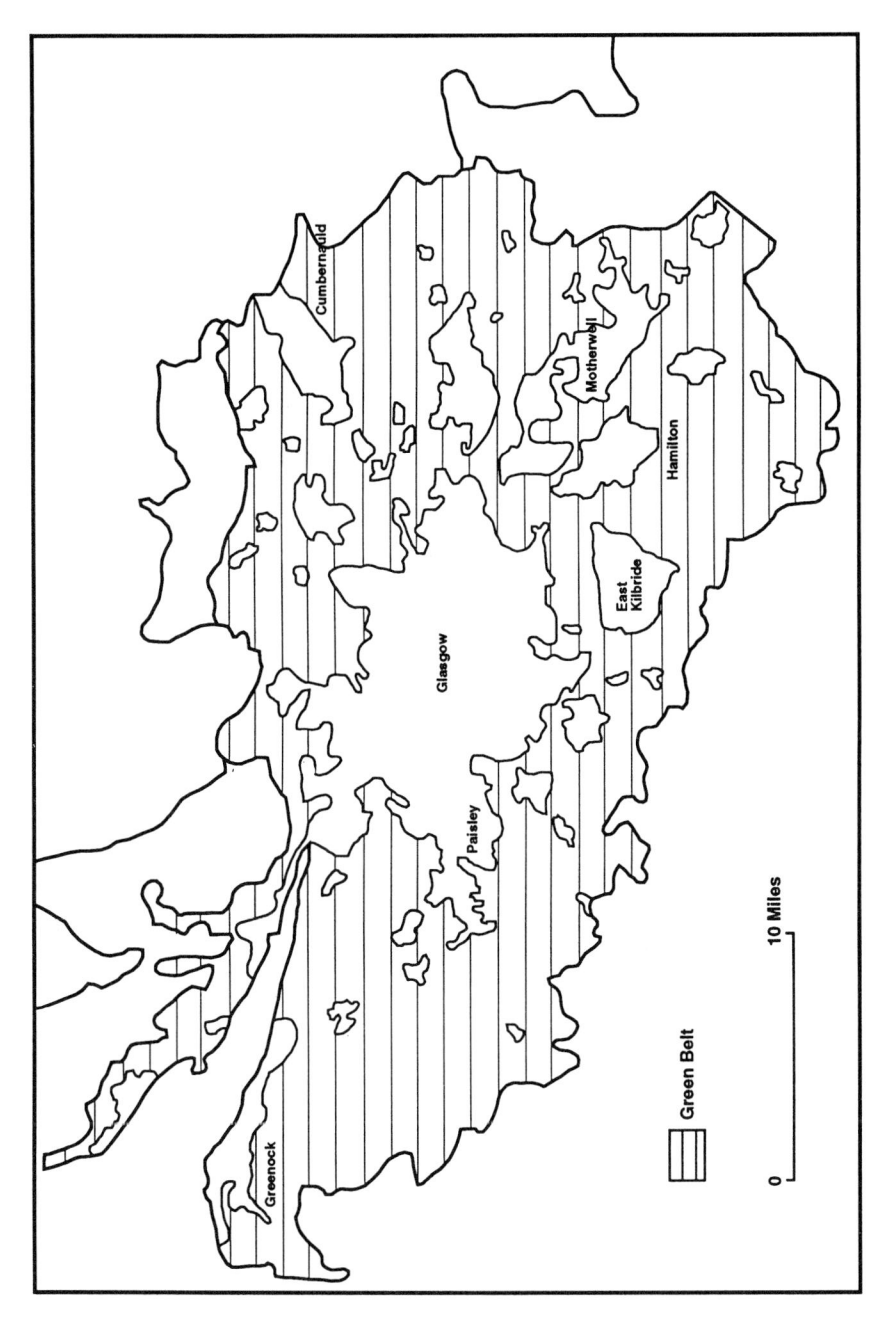

Urban Growth Management: Distinctive Solutions in the Celtic Countries   163

Figure 9.2 The Glasgow Green Belt

necessary stability for its productive use, enhancement and enjoyment' (SRC, 1994, p.39). Since the 1976 Regional Report for the conurbation it has been seen that renewal of the conurbation was necessary to check processes of decentralization. The 1979 Structure Plan therefore set out a strategy of urban renewal with the Green Belt playing a complementary role. This role can be seen in terms of future greenfield land release being related to identified need for new land whilst achieving wider social benefits; controlling speculative pressures for urban expansion into countryside not jeopardizing the process of renewal; and action to improve the urban fringe environment, particularly to ensure an attractive environment for investment (SRC, 1979).

Monitoring evidence from the 1980s suggests the Green Belt was successful in focusing development onto brownfield sites (Elson et al., 1993). The annual release of greenfield land, for example, was around 400 hectares in the 1970s which decreased to around 50 hectares in the 1980s (SRC, 1986). It can be seen that the principle of balance is important with the Green Belt being used as a regulator (Elson et al., 1993). The regional council notes the '... enhancement of the Green Belt makes an important contribution to the economic marketability of the conurbation and the development of the recreation potential of the area is particularly relevant to a number of deprived communities on the periphery of the built-up area' (SRC, 1994, p.39). Overall, a balance has been sought between greenfield (and Green Belt) release for planned expansion and the recycling of brownfield land within the conurbation.

While greenfield land release was not extensive in the 1980s, by 1990 there had been a reduced amount of land recycling because of a reduction in publicly-financed land reclamation projects and an increased demand for housing up to the period 1997. In order to meet such demand for land release the 1990 update of the Structure Plan proposed that the Green Belt should contribute sites for 6000 dwellings from around twenty locations. These releases, selected on a variety of criteria, totalled 200 hectares. Precise site boundaries were to be identified (in some cases reluctantly) by district councils through local plans. The 1992 update Structure Plan however indicated a slowing in trends in private housebuilding and proposed only minor future releases. In terms of strategic policy such releases were not seen to be a change in strategy. The 1994 Consultation Draft on this basis therefore noted that the environment will be protected and enhanced by

> ... ensuring that the continued effectiveness of approved Green Belts is not affected adversely by new development ... when considering the need for any greenfield land release, to minimise environmental impact, and prevent, where possible, loss of Green Belt and other naturally and regionally protected land. (SRC, 1994, p.80)

The balancing role of the Glasgow Green Belt can also be seen in terms of employment site release following production of a National Planning Guideline on high technology industry (SDD, 1985b). This required six sites in Strathclyde, some of which would be in the Green Belt; for example Faulds Park, Inverclyde. In 1987 a site at Erskine received planning permission for a development by the computer company Compaq and in 1992 a further site was proposed in Motherwell District, in response to the closure of the Ravenscraig Steelworks. Smaller amounts of Green Belt land have also been released over the years for industrial and business use.

In Strathclyde there is no 'white' or safeguarded land for long-term development needs, because the regional council consider there would be problems in controlling release and it would undermine proposals for improving the urban fringe. Overall, the Glasgow Green Belt is much more flexible than most English Green Belts. The regional council consider that the Green Belt should provide control 'indefinitely', but that there should be flexibility to move the inner boundary of the Green Belt as the strategy for the conurbation is updated (Elson *et al.*, 1993). However, overall the operation of the Green Belt is not dissimilar to English Green Belts; releases in the early 1990s were not huge when related to the size of the Green Belt. The conurbation-wide view of the regional council has undoubtedly aided the balancing role of the Green Belt and there is a concern that this view will be lost with the move to unitary authorities and the demise of Strathclyde Region. Importantly in Strathclyde the balancing exercise is further developed with the *Greening the Conurbation* strategy which, since 1981, has been a key regional council initiative. It encompasses urban fringe initiatives, river valley strategies and community woodland plans. Working with a variety of partners, including the European Community, the regional council has been seeking to improve as well as protect the Glasgow Green Belt.

The Edinburgh Green Belt

The Edinburgh Green Belt, which is between two and three miles wide, was established in 1956 and aims to limit the expansion of the city; prevent the merging of built-up areas; prevent the use of agricultural land for development; and preserve and enhance the landscape setting of the capital (Lothian Regional Council, 1989). Unusually, the Green Belt contains a number of detached green areas within the city, such as Holyrood Park, which are seen as preserving and enhancing the landscape setting of the city (see Figure 9.3).

Another unusual feature of the Edinburgh Green Belt is the *Green Belt Agreement* which was concluded in 1983. This is basically a code of practice for development control in the Green Belt and provides further guidance

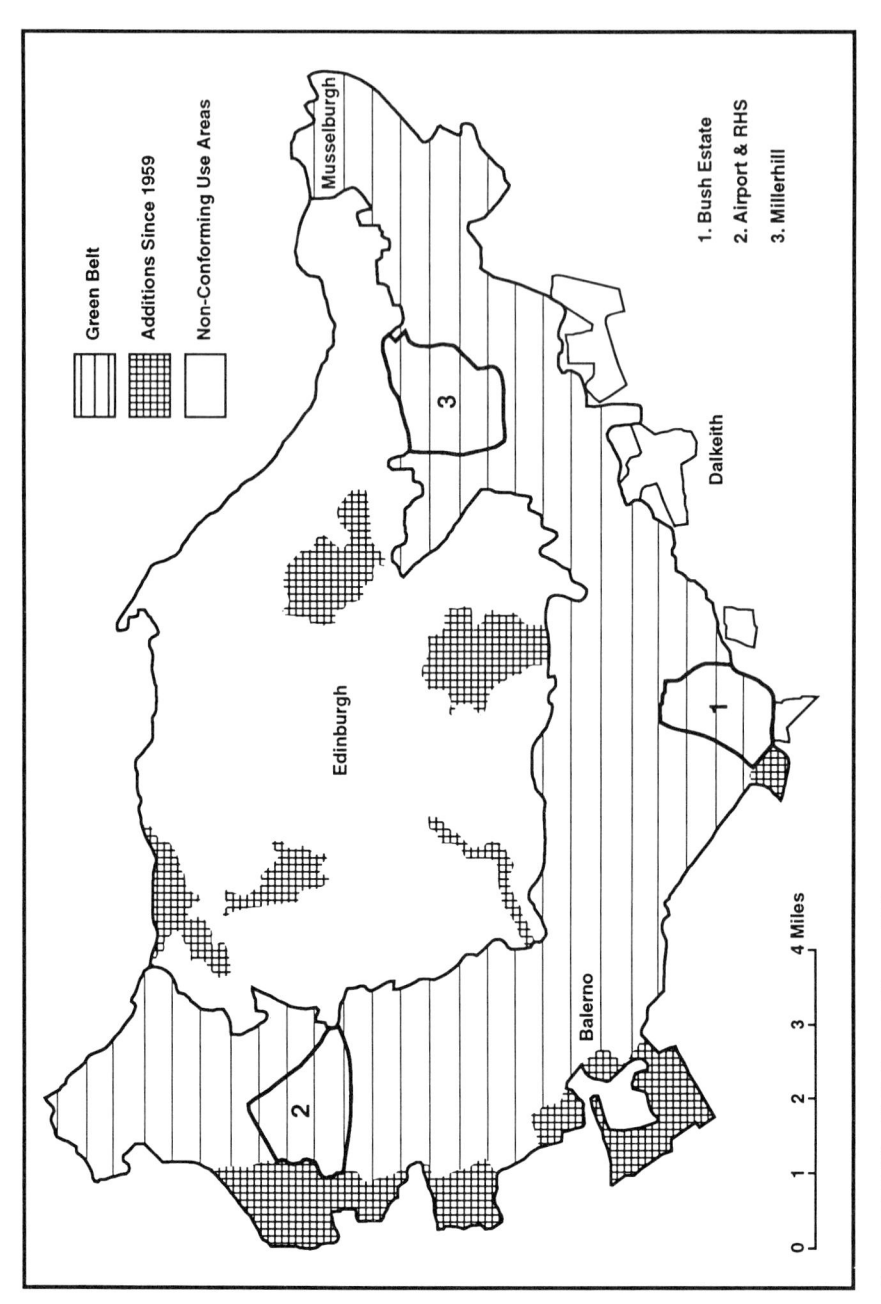

Figure 9.3 The Edinburgh Green Belt

from Lothian Regional Council for district councils. It follows structure plan policy indicating that permission will not be given for new development or redevelopment other than for agriculture, forestry, active recreation or other uses appropriate to a rural area; except those shown as necessary and of strategic significance where no suitable alternative location exists outwith the Green Belt (Lothian Regional Council, 1983). The agreement also deals with improvement of the Green Belt and procedures for non-conforming developments such as at the Heriot-Watt University campus at Riccarton and the Edinburgh University Research Centre at Bush. Importantly, the agreement has allowed the development of a consultation process for development control involving all the relevant districts in the region (Elson *et al.*, 1993).

The first review of the Lothian Structure Plan took place around the time of the publication of Circular 24/1985. In dealing with the period up to 1996 the submitted plan suggested that housebuilding land should be a mix of urban infill and greenfield development beyond the existing urban area. The plan noted that if by 1991 the necessary land supply did not come forward through infill there would be a need for Green Belt land release (Lothian Regional Council, 1985). In order to identify stable long-term boundaries the Scottish Office approval letter for the 1985 Structure Plan allowed a review of Green Belt boundaries to accommodate policy requirements up to 1996. This involved 200 hectares of extensions to the Green Belt and 183 hectares of deletions, particularly on the inner boundaries within the city by-pass.

The replacement for the 1985 Structure Plan was approved in September 1994 by Lothian Regional Council for submission to the secretary of state for Scotland (Lothian Regional Council, 1994). This document, following on from the boundary reviews of the 1985 plan, noted that 'stability and endurance' of Green Belt policies can only be achieved with a balance between containment and urban growth. The council concluded that in order to undertake this some Green Belt land would have to be released. The plan notes that there would then be no further releases following this plan period – which extends up to 2005. This would result in a long-term defensible boundary. While development would be constrained in the west and south of the city, with the exception of some development close to Currie railway station, most development would be concentrated on the south-east of the city. Such a release of land was not considered to compromise the overall integrity of the Green Belt. The Structure Plan notes that such changes would be carried out via local plans (Lothian Regional Council, 1994).

One particular release area is the South-East Wedge Joint Study Area, which the council notes must be planned comprehensively and integrated with surrounding communities, tying in with regeneration activities at

Craigmiller and Niddrie. The idea is a mixed development with swathes of open land creating a more defensible inner boundary in the longer term. The regional council proposed that a joint study involving the relevant district councils be undertaken which would seek to establish development potential, determine layouts, devise a landscape framework and define modified Green Belt boundaries. The overall aim was to achieve a strategic and detailed co-ordinated approach to Green Belt release. In addition, local plans would be required to take into account strategic proposals for land release in the north Midlothian towns, west sector of East Lothian and Currie (Lothian Regional Council, 1994).

The Structure Plan also suggested an extension of the Green Belt in the high pressured areas of Queensbury, Kirkliston and Winchburgh. The improvement and enhancement of the Edinburgh Green Belt has also been encouraged since 1991 with the formation of the Edinburgh Green Belt Trust which aims to protect, enhance and promote enjoyment of the Green Belt. In addition the Regional Council, in conjunction with the districts and Scottish Natural Heritage were seeking to undertake a review of Green Belt recreation including the potential for country parks in Green Belt wedges at Mortonhall/Braids and Craigmiller (Lothian Regional Council, 1994).

In terms of evaluation of the overall policy approach, revision of the Edinburgh Green Belt is seen as likely at each structure plan review, especially as the Edinburgh City Centre Local Plan has an approved anti-intensification policy for residential areas (Edinburgh District Council, 1992). However, these initiatives do not appear to impair the basic purpose of the Green Belt (Elson *et al.*, 1993) and it may be that the boundary set by the 1994 Structure Plan process will endure for a longer period. The importance of high technology and high amenity sites can also be seen in the Edinburgh Green Belt, such as the Heriot-Watt campus which has been allowed to expand and the Royal Agricultural Showground at Ingliston, which the 1994 Structure Plan allows to expand only in the circumstances of maintaining its national status as an attraction. Like Strathclyde, the future of the Edinburgh Green Belt lies in the hands of a new unitary City of Edinburgh Council and a series of unitary authorities surrounding the city – the implications of this, particularly in terms of maintaining a strategic approach to planning for the Green Belt and pressures for economic development on the new authorities, remain to be seen. Arrangements are to be put in place by the Scottish Office for the drawing up of a structure plan for the region.

Summary of the Scottish situation

Both in Strathclyde and Lothian, Green Belts appear to be used as much more of a positive urban growth management tool than in England, with planned releases for housing land and key industrial and employment sites, combined with a greater emphasis on improvement and enhancement of the Green Belt and the provision of recreational opportunities. Research for the Department of the Environment and the Scottish Office on *The Effectiveness of Green Belts* highlighted some of the key aspects of the Scottish Green Belt situation (Elson *et al.*, 1993). The research noted the Green Belt purposes in Circular 24/85 remain limited but have been added to by regional councils. No review of policy has been issued in Scotland in line with the review of PPG 2 in England, although this is being undertaken. The research highlighted the landscape objectives of the policy, which do not exist in England, and may cause problems and conflict in reviewing boundaries. Such issues are perhaps balanced with improvements and enhancement of the Green Belt but may bring problems with the public view that Green Belts are permanent. One reason for attempts to improve Green Belts in Scotland, an activity not so apparent in England, is because of the poor condition of some parts of the Scottish Green Belts, for example in the Lanarkshire conurbation and Midlothian. This approach, however, is also because of the more positive policy attitude in Scotland to the concept as opposed to the more absolutist view taken in parts of England. The role of Green Belts in Strathclyde, in particular in complementing urban regeneration, has reached the most sophisticated level in the United Kingdom. The use of the Green Belt for employment land release can also be seen in the Edinburgh Green Belt. The overview of Strathclyde Regional Council, and the involvement of Scottish Enterprise in land reclamation, indicates what could be achieved in a similar conurbation, such as the West Midlands. The research also stressed the demand for high technology industry sites and that the demand to expand other 'non-conforming' sites in the Green Belt, such as Bush House near Edinburgh which is essentially an office use in large grounds, is set to be a feature of the Scottish Green Belts particularly as their contribution to regeneration is vital, if not contained in Scottish Office guidelines.

Finally, it is important to consider the implications of local government review. As a result of Scottish Office proposals, as opposed to an independent commission in England, a new system of twenty-nine unitary authorities has been set up. This means the abolition of Strathclyde and Lothian Regions. As indicated earlier, in some areas the new unitary authorities will prepare a structure plan if a natural structure plan area exists. In other cases voluntary arrangements will be required or the secretary of state may set up statutory joint boards. In terms of the Green Belt this will mean some authorities may seek to overturn strategic planning policies, seeking greenfield development for the sole benefit of their authority as opposed to a wider conurbation view (Hayton, 1994).

Overall, as Hayton (1994) notes, strategic planning and the integrity of Green Belts may suffer as compromise between neighbouring authorities with different agendas occurs. In preparation for the new system of local government in Scotland, the Scottish Office issued a short document called *Review of the Town and Country Planning System in Scotland: The Way Ahead* (Scottish Office, 1995). This document particularly examines performance and efficiency in the system but also suggests that the Scottish Office would take a 'radical' look at focusing structure plans more. The document has, however, been criticized for not really developing practice (Tompsett, 1996). As indicated earlier, at the time of writing (1996), the Scottish Office was drafting an NPPG discussing Green Belt policy. The future of Green Belt policy in Scotland is therefore somewhat open and it is hoped that the achievements of the policy in the past, particularly balancing the need for environmental protection and economic development, are not lost.

Urban growth management in Wales

A fundamental difference in growth management planning in Wales, compared to both Scotland and England, is that there are no approved Green Belts. Following Circular 42/55 draft proposals were drawn up for certain areas in Wales, including Swansea, Newport and Cardiff. The most advanced, in areas of Flintshire, received approval in principle from the Ministry of Housing and Local Government. Work, however, ceased on Green Belt proposals in the 1960s. In 1973 local authorities were told that the existing sketch proposals were not likely to be approved. Structure plans in Wales have, however, brought forward a variety of growth management policies, but not Green Belts (Welsh Office, 1991).

At the launch of the Environment white paper *This Common Inheritance* (Secretary of State for the Environment *et al.*, 1990) the then secretary of state for Wales, David Hunt, MP, invited the Association of Welsh Counties to examine further the potential role of statutory Green Belts in Wales. Speaking at a conference debating Green Belts in Wales, he noted that although no Green Belts existed there was a set of useful countryside designations including Green Wedges, Green Barriers, Buffer Zones and Special Landscape Areas. He particularly noted that Green Belts should not just be about protecting the countryside but defining settlement patterns and urban structure, helping to accommodate future jobs and housing (Hunt, 1991). The conference highlighted a number of different views on Green Belts. The Campaign for Protection of Rural Wales (CPRW) supported the notion of Green Belts, seeing them as a way of introducing much-needed strategic planning (Caldwell, 1991). The

Countryside Commission, while supporting Green Belts, was concerned to see development pressures assessed generally so as to avoid pressures being merely pushed elsewhere. It also wished to see positive landscape and recreation uses for Green Belts (Fitton, 1991). The House Builders Federation asked why Green Belts were needed and what extra protection they would actually give, also stressing the potential effects on land and house prices (Lewis, 1991). The Country Landowners' Association felt the concept may make local authorities too negative (Bosanquet, 1991). The Welsh District Planning Officers Society stressed that while they wanted to protect the Welsh countryside from gradual erosion, there was concern over the limiting effect Green Belts would have on attracting inward investment (Osborne, 1991). This later sentiment was echoed by the speaker from the Welsh Development Agency, who considered that conventional Green Belt thinking would be counter-productive in terms of Welsh economic development. He did, however, consider there was an opportunity to make development and environment complimentary (Farnsworth, 1991). Importantly, the above indicates the range of opinions on Green Belts of different interests; ranging from the support of the CPRW, the mixed support and reservations of the Countryside Commission, the Welsh district planners association and the more negative views of the economic based interests such as the House Builders Federation, the Country Landowners' Association and the Welsh Development Agency.

Following this conference a study of the role of Green Belts in promoting sport and recreation was undertaken for the Sports Council for Wales (Elson, 1991). This noted that the challenge was to make Green Belt a positive not negative device that could actually promote and sustain sport and recreation opportunities (Elson, 1991). An interim report on Green Belts in Wales was also published in 1991 by the Strategic Planning Advisory Committee, which comprised representatives from the Assembly of Welsh Counties, the Council of Welsh Districts, the Welsh county and district councils and the National Parks committees. This concluded that planning authorities had achieved similar objectives to Green Belts in Wales by the use of 'Green Wedges' and 'Green Barriers'; Green Belts must only be proposed as part of a balanced strategic planning process taking into account long-term development needs; central government policy on Welsh Green Belts may need to vary from England, particularly including a landscape criteria; Green Belts once established should not be reviewed at every plan review; and long-term public acceptance will be greatly enhanced if Green Belts emphasize positive action and improvements (Strategic Planning Advisory Committee, 1991). Despite the continued deliberations of the various local authority groups and other interests, no Green Belts have been approved for Wales – however a number of areas have Green Belts under active consideration through the planning process.

As in the discussion on Scotland, it is instructive to examine a number of individual areas.

South Glamorgan

The 1989 approved Structure Plan of South Glamorgan County Council, which consists of the Vale of Glamorgan Borough and the City of Cardiff, has no Green Belt or similar policies but does have an urban fringe policy which notes that there will be a presumption against development unsuitable in a rural area. The plan also suggests countryside zones where permanent protection will be given to sensitive or vulnerable environments (South Glamorgan County Council, 1989). However in the deposit version of the Replacement Structure Plan produced in February 1995, a Green Belt policy exists. Policy EV3 indicates:

> A Green Belt will be provided to maintain and enhance the environmental setting of Cardiff, Penarth and Barry, to prevent urban sprawl and the coalescence of settlements and to conserve the rural character of the eastern part of the Vale of Glamorgan. Within the Green Belt there will be a presumption against development other than that required for agriculture, forestry and mineral workings, utilities or appropriate informal recreation. Positive countryside measures will be favoured.

The Plan notes that parts of the urban fringe and the open countryside around main settlements were under particular development pressure. The Green Belt for the Cardiff area would be subject to a special study with boundaries detailed in local plans (South Glamorgan County Council, 1995). The Plan notes that:

> The primary purposes of a Green Belt would be to maintain the distinction between town and country, to provide an attractive backcloth to the main settlements. In addition to the controlling function, it would be an opportunity to facilitate appropriate management and enhance the environment in the urban fringe for landscape, recreation, amenity and nature conservation interests. (South Glamorgan County Council, 1995, p.15)

The proposal has the support of Vale of Glamorgan Borough Council and Cardiff City Council. Under local government review, however, both Cardiff City and Vale of Glamorgan have become unitary authorities with the disappearance of South Glamorgan County. Whether the Green Belt policy will survive these changes is unclear. While it is likely the new Vale of Glamorgan Unitary Authority will support the proposals, the Cardiff authority may be under considerable pressure to find new land for housing in the city. The November 1995 Examination in Public of the Structure Plan resulted in a discussion of the concept, where the proposal was supported by the Countryside Council for Wales. At the time of writing the panel had not reported its results, however because of reorganization the Structure Plan will not be changed as a result of the panel report but will be left for the two new authorities to deal with, including the Green Belt issue.

Gwent

The consultation draft of the Gwent Structure Plan 1991 identified a 'Green Spaces' policy which aimed to prevent coalescence of urban areas separating Cardiff, Newport, Caerleon and Cwmbran (Gwent County Council, 1991). The policy prescription for these areas is the same as Green Belts in Scotland and England, that is retaining openness by permitting only agriculture, forestry, recreational uses and other uses which involve no substantial new building. They are extensive areas, take account of long-term development and have a permanence beyond the period of the plan. They are essentially small-scale Green Belts in all but name (Elson, 1991). The local authority, however, noted that these 'Green Spaces' would not preclude the designation of a Green Belt between Newport and Cardiff if that was part of a more extensive Green Belt around Cardiff. With the addition of one additional area the 'Green Spaces' policy has remained in the Gwent Structure Plan. In the modified plan of July 1994 policies C1 and C2 are relevant:

(C1) In order to prevent the coalescence of urban areas throughout the County, 'Green Spaces' will be identified in local plans within which there will be a presumption against urban development. In particular, extensive 'Green Spaces' will be identified between the urban areas of:

i) Newport and Cardiff (county boundary);
ii) Newport and Caerleon;
iii) Malpas and Cwmbran;
v) Bettws and Cwmbran;
vii) Rogerstone and Bettws;
viii) Rogerstone and Risca;

(C2) It is intended that local plans will identify a continuous 'Green Zone' immediately north of the M4 Motorway between Langstone and Chepstow. Within which there will be a presumption against urban development.

Importantly, the county council considered there was a need to prevent coalescence between towns and create a meaningful countryside gap. As indicated above, whether a Green Belt will occur around Cardiff after local government reorganization will depend on the new unitary authorities working together to achieve this.

Clwyd

The First Alteration of the Clwyd Structure Plan continues and extends a policy of 'Green Barriers' (Clwyd County Council, 1990). These aim to control the growth of towns in the county such as Mold, Connahs Quay, Flint and also development from nearby Chester. Boundaries of the Green Barriers are defined in local plans and the policy wording accords with the English guidance on Green Belts (Elson, 1991). The current approved policy is CONS 5 (1990), which identifies a considerable number of areas which the policy protects. It indicates:

> Within Green Barriers there will be a strong presumption against developments that would affect their open character. Developments associated with agriculture, forestry, outdoor sport and recreation, cemeteries, institutions standing in extensive grounds or other uses appropriate to a rural area will be permitted providing they do not detract from the open character of the area.

In approving the First Alteration Structure Plan (1990), the secretary of state for Wales requested that Green Belt designation be considered at the next review of the plan. This was because of the intense development pressures on the area at the time and the proximity of the Chester Green Belt. In the 1994 consultation on the Second Alteration, the council put forward a number of alternatives. These were: to review all Green Barriers to ensure they were necessary and check no new ones were needed; to have a mixture of Green Belts and Green Barriers; or to convert all Green Barriers to Green Belts. The final option, it was noted, would perhaps be inappropriate because the current designated areas are definitely barriers and not continuous Green Belts. In considering these options in the 1994 plan, the council notes that Green Belts are a long-term national designation but also notes that the Barriers policy is well understood and has endured well. Importantly, the council was concerned whether Green Belts were compatible with the still fragile economy of the area.

Following the consultation period for this plan, officers prepared an issues paper on the responses related to the Green Belts/Green Barrier issue; which was noted to raise more discussion than any other (Clwyd County Council, 1995). It was seen that there was strong support for some form of countryside protection, although there was little reference to other aspects of Green Belt and Green Barrier roles; there was popular attachment to the concept of Green Belts from the public; straight conversion to Green Belts was not generally favoured; a mix was seen as acceptable in principle but may be confusing; and professional opinion saw benefits in the flexibility of the Barriers. Importantly, there appeared to be support for a Green Belt around Chester, but less so in other areas. In assessing the comments received, officers considered the best solution was to have a Green Belt to the south and west of Chester in Clwyd as this would match the designation around the rest of Chester, helping to control development in that area. They also noted in order to maintain the value of Green Barriers the development control policies should be the same in both Belts and Barriers. Overall, Belts would be a national policy in large swathes, while Barriers would be a county policy in smaller parts. This approach was considered to meet the issue of controlling development around Chester while maintaining the flexibility of Barriers, particularly for economic development reasons.

Summary of the Welsh situation

The importance of economic development in Wales means that many authorities have not sought to designate Green Belts in the past, particularly in the context of an unsupportive government. However, certain parts of the country have considerable development pressures where Green Belts would be appropriate. A number of authorities have utilized various pseudo-Green Belt policies in order to achieve Green Belt-type aims. Newer plans in Clwyd and around Cardiff are now proposing Green Belts, ironically at a time when local government in Wales is being reorganized. The results of such deliberations will therefore not be clear until local government reorganization has been implemented. This is taking the form of unitary authorities who will be expected to prepare unitary development plans, covering both strategic and local issues, replacing the previous two-tier system of local government and planning.

An important development in planning in Wales is the launch of a consultation version of new planning guidance replacing the existing PPG series (not all of which applied to Wales) with only two documents: *Planning Policy Guidance (Wales)*, which replaces all of the earlier PPGs; and *Planning Guidance (Wales): Unitary Development Plans*, which gives guidance for unitary authorities regarding their development plans (Welsh Office, 1995a, 1995b). Some concern has been expressed at the brevity of the guidance contained in these documents (Packer, 1995), while others have seen them as a step forward in achieving brief and succinct central planning guidance concentrating on strategic planning matters (Romaya, 1995). Importantly, *PPG (Wales)* includes a section on Green Belts, noting that Green Belts should only be considered in the more heavily populated parts of Wales which are subject to significant pressures for development. The guidance notes that Green Belts should be established through development plans and must demonstrate why Green Wedge and Green Barrier policies would not be adequate. The purposes of Green Belts set out in the draft guidance differ slightly from those for England, particularly in not mentioning sprawl but advocating protecting the setting of all urban areas not just those of historic towns. As in England, the guidance notes that local authorities should ensure a sufficient supply of development land is available but differ in noting that Green Belts need not necessarily extend in a continuous band around the urban area. Significantly this is the first time such guidance clearly advocating Green Belts has been issued in Wales and has been welcomed by the Countryside Council for Wales among others.

Conclusions

This chapter started off by asking the question whether Green Belts in Scotland, those proposed in Wales, and other growth management policies in Wales were in fact different instruments masquerading under the name of Green Belt. In many ways they are the same animal as in England, because the key purpose of Green Belts and the other growth management measures in the two countries is to control and manage urban form, particularly responding to the pressures of urban development. Following this line of thought the differences therefore between Scotland, Wales and England are, in principle, not all that significant. However, in terms of using the Green Belt more positively differences can be seen. In Scotland, there is a particular emphasis put on improving the Green Belt which does not exist to the same extent in England. This emphasis on positive use of the Green Belt has also been prominent in the debates on Green Belts in Wales. Green Belts in Scotland also have a role to play in providing housing and industrial land. Both in Scotland and Wales, there is an emphasis on using Green Belts and urban growth management devices generally to assist with the regeneration of problematic economies. This demands a more flexible Green Belt in Scotland and a series of more flexible pseudo-Green Belt policies in Wales.

While similarities exist between Scotland and Wales and the English situation both countries have adopted a distinctive approach in order to reflect the different planning contexts. Generally a less absolutist Green Belt is sought in the Celtic countries, one which can help improve the landscape, provide recreation opportunities and help economic development by selective greenfield releases. These priorities relate in part to the geography and culture of the countries. Positive use of Green Belts in Scotland, and potentially in Wales, can perhaps be related to a different view of the countryside in the Celtic countries than in England. The English 'country garden' and rural idyll idea, particularly apparent in the South of England, can be seen to ensue strong political support for Green Belts, both nationally and locally. In Scotland and Wales, wider areas of the countryside are more accessible than in congested Southern England. It could therefore be argued that there may be less public emphasis on preserving rings of land around cities which may be less than attractive, particularly in the Glasgow case where a considerable amount of derelict land is contained in the Green Belt. The proximity of areas like Loch Lomond to Glasgow means politicians and the public may be less concerned about the absolute protection of the edge of city land, especially when there is a need and demand for inward investment and new housing. This could lead to the comment that the 'NIMBY' factor is less apparent in Scotland than in England, however in certain contexts this is not the case, examples being demonstrations against the M77 highway works and the conservative nature of some of the outer Glasgow districts.

An examination of Green Belts in the West Midlands and around Newcastle-upon-Tyne would reveal similar operations to Scotland and relates to the Green Belt debate in Wales. Many Northern and Midland areas of England view selective release of employment sites in the Green Belt as part of their long-term development strategies. In the West Midlands the regional guidance indicates that local authorities should identify high-technology sites for incoming industry some of which will inevitably be in the Green Belt. In Newcastle-upon-Tyne, there is an acknowledgement that the Green Belt has helped inner-city redevelopment over the years, but that it is now holding back new housing and employment opportunities. Hence in the most recent Newcastle-upon-Tyne Unitary Development Plan process there has been considerable debate over the need to release land for up to 5,000 houses and 120 ha of employment land from the Green Belt up to the year 2006 (Elson et al., 1993). It is, therefore, perhaps only in Southern England where Green Belts operate in a way akin to the public perception of the policy.

It can be seen therefore that Green Belts in Scotland, and potentially in Wales in the future, are in some respects a different animal to those in Southern England but have much in common with those in the Midland and Northern parts of England. Calls for a looser, more flexible form of Green Belt in England (see Cherry, 1992) may be informed by the situation in Scotland and the emerging debate in Wales, particularly where there is a need for both the management of development pressures and economic development. In terms of improving the Green Belt the Department of the Environment has responded to calls for a more positive role for Green Belts in England with a revised more proactive PPG 2 (1995).

The future of Green Belts and growth management policies in Scotland and Wales is developing in a number of ways, including: local government reorganization in both countries; the retention of structure plans in Scotland and the introduction of unitary development plans in Wales; the drafting of a single principal planning policy document for Wales containing Green Belt policy; and the drafting of a new National Planning Policy Guideline for Scotland on the topic. The next few years, because of these developments, may therefore mean considerable changes in the operation of urban growth management policies in the two countries. Green Belt and growth management policies will, however, remain key parts of the planning systems of Scotland and Wales and will hopefully continue to develop in relation to the needs and contexts of the two countries as opposed to being mere clones of the English situation.

References

Assembly of Welsh Counties 1992. *Strategic Planning Guidance in Wales, Topic Report 'Green Belts'* (Cardiff, AWC).

Bosanquet, S. 1991. 'Speech by Mr S. Bosanquet, Country Landowners' Association', in *Green Belts for Wales – Proceedings of Conference held at Welsh Office* (Cardiff, Welsh Office), pp.48–55.

Caldwell, N. 1991. 'Speech by Dr N. Caldwell', in *Green Belts for Wales – Proceedings of Conference held at Welsh Office* (Cardiff, Welsh Office), pp.32–8.

Cherry, G. 1992. 'Green Belt and the emergent city', *Property Review*, December, pp.97–101.

Clwyd County Council 1990. *Clwyd Structure Plan – First Alteration: submitted Written Statement* (Mold, CCC).

Clwyd County Council 1994. *Clwyd Structure Plan Second Alteration Policies and Explanatory Memorandum Consultation* (Mold, CCC).

Clwyd County Council 1995. *Issue Paper 2 – Green Belts or Green Barriers?* (Mold, CCC).

Department of the Environment 1990. *This Common Inheritance* (London, HMSO).

Department of the Environment 1995. *Green Belts*, Planning Policy Guidance Note 2 (London, HMSO).

Edinburgh District Council 1992. *Central Edinburgh Local Plan* (Edinburgh, EDC).

Elson, M. J. 1986. *Green Belts: Conflict Mediation in the Urban Fringe* (London, Heinemann).

Elson, M. J. 1991. *Green Belts for Wales – A Positive Role for Sport and Recreation* (Cardiff, Sports Council for Wales).

Elson, M. J., S. Walker, R. Macdonald and J. Edge 1993. *The Effectiveness of Green Belts* (London, HMSO).

Farnsworth, D. 1991. 'Speech by David Farnsworth, Executive Director,

Development Projects Division, Welsh Development Agency', in *Green Belts for Wales – Proceedings of Conference held at Welsh Office* (Cardiff, Welsh Office), pp.67–71.

Fitton, M. 1991. 'Synopsis of speech given by Mr Martin Fitton of the Countryside Commission', in *Green Belts for Wales – Proceedings of Conference held at Welsh Office* (Cardiff, Welsh Office), p.56.

Gwent County Council 1991. *Gwent Structure Plan: First Alterations, Draft for Consultation* (Cwmbran, GCC).

Gwent County Council 1993. *Gwent Structure Plan 1991–2006 Proposed Amendments to Deposit Plan* (Cwmbran, GCC).

Gwent County Council 1994. *Gwent Structure Plan 1991–2006 Proposed Structure Plan Policies as modified July 1994* (Cwmbran, GCC).

Hayton, K. 1994. 'Planning and Scottish local government reform', *Planning Practice and Research*, Vol.9, No.1, pp.55–62.

Hunt, D. 1991. 'Address by Mr David Hunt, MP, Secretary of State for Wales', in *Green Belts for Wales – Proceedings of Conference held at Welsh Office* (Cardiff, Welsh Office), pp.1–5.

Lewis, D. L. 1991. 'Speech by Mr Don L. Lewis, The House Builders Federation', *Green Belts for Wales – Proceedings of Conference held at Welsh Office* (Cardiff, Welsh Office), pp.39–47.

Lothian Regional Council 1983. *Edinburgh Green Belt Agreement* (Edinburgh, LRC).

Lothian Regional Council 1985. *Lothian Region Structure Plan* (Edinburgh, LRC).

Lothian Regional Council 1989. *Edinburgh Green Belt: Background, Green Belt Information Note 1* (Edinburgh, LRC).

Lothian Regional Council 1994. *Finalised Written Statement* (Edinburgh, LRC).

Osborne, T. 1991. 'Contribution on behalf of the Welsh District Planning Officers' Society by Trevor Osborne, Director of Development, Swansea City Council', in *Green Belts for Wales – Proceedings of Conference held at Welsh Office* (Cardiff, Welsh Office), pp.57–66.

Packer, N. C. 1995. 'Welsh baffled over brevity of draft PPGs', *Planning Week*, 27 July, p.1.

Romaya, S. 1995. 'Leaner and fitter?', *Planning Week*, 12 October, p.15.

Scottish Development Department 1985a. *Development in the Countryside and Green Belts*, Circular 24/1995 (Edinburgh, SDD).

Scottish Development Department 1985b. *High Technology: Individual High Amenity Sites* (Edinburgh, SDD).

Scottish Office 1991. *Scotland: Land Use and Physical Features Fact Sheet 19* (Edinburgh, Scottish Office).

Scottish Office 1995. *Review of the Town and Country Planning System in Scotland: The Way Forward* (Edinburgh, Scottish Office).

Secretary of State for the Environment and Others 1990. *This Common Inheritance* (London, HMSO).

South Glamorgan County Council 1989. *Approved Structure Plan Policies*, (Cardiff, SGCC).

South Glamorgan County Council 1995. *Replacement Structure Plan 1991–2011 Deposit Document* (Cardiff, SGCC).

Strategic Planning Advisory Committee 1991. *Strategic Planning Guidance in Wales – Interim Report on Green Belts* (Cardiff, SPAC).

Strathclyde Regional Council 1979. *Strathclyde Structure Plan* (Glasgow, SRC).
Strathclyde Regional Council 1986. *Structure Plan Update (1986) Written Statement* (Glasgow, SRC).
Strathclyde Regional Council 1992. *Structure Plan Update* (Glasgow, SRC).
Strathclyde Regional Council 1994. *Structure Plan Review Consultation Draft* (Glasgow, SRC).
Tompsett, R. 1996. 'Missing milestone or a high road to reform', *Planning Week*, 11 June, p.10.
Welsh Office 1991. *Green Belts for Wales – Proceedings of Conference held at Welsh Office* (Cardiff, Welsh Office).
Welsh Office 1995a. *Draft Planning Policy Guidance (Wales)* (Cardiff, Welsh Office.
Welsh Office 1995b. *Draft Planning Guidance (Wales): Unitary Development Plans in Wales* (Cardiff, Welsh Office).

10

Contrasting Approaches to Rural Economic Development

CHRISTOPHER L.W. MINAY

Introduction

This chapter explores approaches to rural development in Scotland and Wales and considers the extent to which they differ from those in England. In so far as there are differences, it attempts to assess whether these differences are related to geographical, economic or cultural distinctiveness and whether Scotland and Wales share any features which arise from these factors. This search is approached through an examination of three key questions which are considered fundamental to the assessment of distinctiveness. First, comes an examination of whether rural development has been defined as a distinct concept in each country and whether any such definitions have any features specific to their setting. Second, the institutions involved in rural development are examined, in terms of their role and functions, broad strategy, and resource use. Thirdly, examples of rural development practice are examined to assess the extent to which the problems of individual communities bear out higher level definitions and strategy, and are tackled in ways which reflect both strategy and assumptions about distinctiveness.

Rural development is in itself a nebulous concept, both in terms of its aims and its scope. Indeed, both the words which make it up are themselves problematic. The old dichotomy between 'urban' and 'rural' has seemed less and less relevant in recent years, and the concept of the rural area has recently been subjected, in England particularly, to a process of re-examination (Marsden *et al.*, 1990; Murdoch and Marsden, 1994). Superficially, Wales and Scotland seem to have areas which are more clearly marked out as 'rural' but they are subject to the same processes of global and national change that affect English rural areas, even if their peripheral location might have delayed change – or at least reduced the intensity of pressure for it.

What constitutes 'development' in a rural area is a similarly debatable question (Buller and Wright, 1990). It can be a process of change induced from within or from outside, and it can serve the needs and aspirations of existing residents or those of a variety of outsiders, including immigrants and those who remain 'absentee' interests. The potential conflict between these groups is fertile material for those who allege cultural differences between England, Wales and Scotland, but it is at least questionable whether, for example, there is a real difference between concerns about affordable housing and the effect of its scarcity on 'local' people in remoter upland areas of Wales and villages in the home counties.

Rural development is also an area of government policy in which a number of government bodies have a hand. However, the sectoral divisions which are employed by government to manage its activities only serve to muddy the waters when it comes to defining rural development as a policy area. The principal interests in rural areas in terms of production and land use have long been separated from those with responsibility for settlement planning and infrastructure provision, who are themselves at least partially separated from those concerned with ecological and recreational matters. These divisions, and their consequences on how rural development is viewed, are becoming increasingly problematic in a period when the sustainability of different approaches to development is coming under scrutiny.

The context of rural development in Scotland and Wales

While the rural areas of Scotland and Wales have distinctive characteristics deriving from their individual geographies and histories, the context within which they are currently evolving is shaped by external forces deriving on the one hand from global economic and social processes and on the other from standardizing policies of national (UK) and supra-national government (EU) bodies. The progressive opening-up of regional and national economies to international competition in recent decades has been accompanied by the decline of local markets, the takeover and incorporation of local businesses by national or multinational companies, and the introduction of post-Fordist production methods. To some extent, rural areas have been shielded from the most drastic effects of these changes by their low level of manufacturing activity and small production units: to some extent they have benefitted from the declining importance of raw material and transport costs in production processes, the growth of smaller units as a result of sub-contracting and the dismemberment of unwieldy organizational structures, and the benefits of remote working arising from the growth of telecommunications and computer technology. The importance of a good environment to the new generation of entrepreneurs has favoured remoter locations (Keeble et al., 1992).

The relative importance of primary activities has been a mixed blessing to rural locations. The significance of public support to agricultural production has made rural areas, especially marginal ones, susceptible in a period of public cost-cutting, while internationalization of policy has affected not only agricultural subsidy but also such matters as conservation of fish stocks and the national valuation of forest resources. Compensating changes in public opinion, such as the protection of environmentally-friendly farming and forestry methods, have brought only slow improvements from an economic perspective. Growing resistance to environmental damage in more populous areas could bring 'benefits' in the form of job-creating extraction sites in remoter areas, exemplified by the Harris super-quarry, but these benefits have proved questionable.

These global processes have been accelerated by the free market, deregulatory stance of national government – which has commanded little support in Wales and Scotland – and, to a lesser extent, by European Union membership and its implications. An important contrast exists here between Europe's recognition that the benefits of integration depend on compensating measures to support marginal communities on the Union's fringes, and national government's ideological reluctance to accept subsidy and support. The Thatcher and Major governments have favoured inducements to self-reliance which, while valid to a degree, lead in the extreme case to the further marginalization of those whose location creates a degree of dependence. Ironically, in the debate over Scottish devolution re-emerging at the time of writing, Conservative policy rejects the call from Nationalists for ultimate self-reliance on the grounds that Scotland benefits financially from membership of the United Kingdom.

The other principal element of national policy in the 1980s and early 1990s has been privatization. This promised to impact on Wales and Scotland more severely than on England, partly because both economies relied more heavily on the public sector, directly and indirectly through the importance of special public-sector agencies, and partly because lower income levels and lower dependence on unearned income suggested that they might be less able to participate in the process.

A final – and to some extent contradictory – element in recent national policy is the growing importance of the concept of sustainability. Living closer to nature, rural areas might be expected to be able to absorb this notion into their lifestyle more readily, even perhaps to reflect it in existing practice. On the other hand, the developing emphasis within government thinking in the early 1990s seems to be that sustainability is about the supposed efficiency of relatively high density living, threatening the very idea of the rural community.

These processes and policies will need further examination in the following sections as the organization and practice of rural development in

Wales and Scotland are examined in more detail. Key issues in this review must be the extent of incorporation of the economies of rural Scotland and Wales in the British, European and global systems, and the interaction between the distinctive settlement structures and political contexts of these areas, including the locus of control, the nature of political allegiances, and cultural and conceptual distinctiveness.

Definitions of rural development

As already outlined, the term 'rural development' presents numerous problems. In the United Kingdom, there has been a widely-held view that the development of rural areas is an arena of conflict between competing interests. Some see this conflict as the consequence of the ad hoc way in which public policy has evolved (Select Committee on the European Communities, 1990), addressing specific issues and problems as they arise. Others see the conflict as institutionalized, not merely as an accident of history but as a method of political management, deflecting criticism of government into inter-institutional debate. Thus, not only do private-sector interests face public sector ones, but the latter are themselves sub-divided between socio-economic, landscape and recreational, and wildlife interests, for example. Yet others regard these institutional divisions as surface manifestations of deeper social divisions between different production and consumption interests which harness a variety of perspectives about rural areas and institutional mechanisms to support their own particular objectives and values (Marsden et al., 1993).

In this analysis, Marsden and his associates distinguish areas, particularly in the English lowlands, where anti-development and preservationist attitudes dominate ('the preserved countryside'), areas where local interests still dominate but where incomers increasingly challenge decisions ('the contested countryside'), other areas still dominated by large estates and the like ('the paternalistic countryside'), and remoter areas where an alliance between local economic interests and state agencies creates a 'clientelist countryside'. All these models have relevance to Wales and Scotland, although in each country a distinctive gloss is put on each in popular perceptions. In much of rural Wales, the contested countryside model will be seen as a representation of the conflict between, on the one hand, small farmers and small-town business people, and on the other, mostly English incomers more concerned with landscape, recreation and tourism than with the social and economic fortunes of the local community. Those very incomers, on the other hand, may well see the same issues as indicative of a clientelist alliance between inward-looking Welsh people and state agencies supporting outdated practices and ideas.

In Scotland, large areas have long been viewed as dominated by paternalist interests, particularly but not exclusively the owners of big Highland estates, and the creation of the first true rural development agency – the Highlands and Islands Development Board – as an attempt to alter the balance of power by establishing client groups amongst both local interests like crofters and fishermen and incoming industrialists and tourism operators who would break down old patterns of working and social relations. Meanwhile, there is growing evidence of middle-class environmentalist attitudes similar to those in England impacting on other areas of Scotland as commuters begin to spread into them, for example from Edinburgh into the Borders and Fife.

In response to this conflictual model, there have been numerous attempts by professionals and public-sector bodies to initiate a wide variety of integrative mechanisms to secure a co-ordinated approach to the development of particular rural areas. The EC Integrated Development Projects are a particularly notable example of this movement, but they range from projects concerned with the multiple use of land (see, for example, North Riding County Council, 1975) to co-ordinated programmes of socio-economic development (see Rural Development Commission, 1994) and broader-based rural strategies (Countryside Commission et al., undated). In England the two latter approaches lie closest to a comprehensive and strategic approach to rural development.

The Rural Development Commission (RDC) role is itself a consequence of and limited by the sectoral approach to rural affairs adopted by successive governments. Its remit is confined to the economic and social development of rural areas and, although it is broad enough to legitimize a strategic approach to analysis which can cross institutional boundaries – for example, to encompass changes arising from agricultural and defence industry restructuring in its recent Countryside Employment Programme initiatives – its powers are circumscribed by its remit and responsible Department (Environment). Special programmes in designated Rural Development Areas (about 35 per cent of England) were introduced in 1984 and based on a partnership approach involving the Commission, local authorities, rural community councils, training and enterprise councils (TECs), and, where appropriate, other organizations, including the private sector. From 1994, for each area a strategy covering five to ten years and an operating plan developing a rolling programme for three years are produced, setting out specific projects and proposals covering economic development, local services, help for disadvantaged groups, and complementary environmental improvements.

These priorities are indicative of how the RDC views rural development. The concern is primarily with the economic and social well-being of rural areas, with the strengthening and diversification of the economy, the maintenance or provision of key services and facilities, and the support of those who are disadvantaged as a result of the consequences of rural living. These concerns are complemented by a requirement that the commission's activities maintain or improve the environment, but it views extreme opposition to change as inimical to maintaining a viable countryside.

The call for rural strategies emanated from a co-operative venture by the three English rural agencies – the RDC, Countryside Commission, and English Nature – and manifestly takes a broader view. They seek to develop a shared vision of the future for defined rural areas by bringing together policies for securing environmental objectives, access to and enjoyment of the countryside, as well as the social and economic needs of rural communities. A number of strategies have been produced – mainly for English counties, such as Hampshire, Sussex and Wiltshire.

On the face of it, the integrated nature of government departments in Scotland and Wales should facilitate the development of a more comprehensive and consistent approach to policy formulation than is possible in England, while the importance of extensive rural areas to those two countries should increase the necessity for each to adopt explicit policies for rural development. The Scottish Office has indeed published a *Rural Framework* (Scottish Office, 1992a) and supported it with analytical data (Scottish Office, 1992b). The Welsh Office had produced a policy document on its 'rural initiative' in 1991, but this never seems to have been regarded as very adequate in Wales.

The timing of the Scottish Office documents, and the subject of the secretary of state's opening sentence ('In 1992, rural Scotland is taking its rightful place in Europe'), suggests that the approach was heavily influenced by European integration, although there is no reference to the European Community paper on the future of rural society (EC Economic and Social Committee, 1990). The report does not attempt to define rural development, nor indeed to indicate a pro- or anti-development stance. It recognizes that even within the Scottish Office there are different departmental interests and perspectives and asserts that 'tackling rural issues in a sectoral manner does not work' (Scottish Office, 1992a, p.4). The framework document identifies eight themes in order to 'develop a common language which rural communities and those working in their support can use to build their own ideas for development'. The themes are summarized as community involvement, diversity, quality, local added value, effective service delivery, networks and communications, Europe and sustainability.

There is not a great deal of national distinctiveness here. Apart from a few localized examples, and a recognition that standardized solutions are inappropriate to dispersed and isolated communities, there is little in this rural framework that is different from ideas south of the border.

The secretary of state for Wales produced a policy statement on rural Wales in December 1991 (Welsh Office, 1991). This promised 'a fresh approach' with the long-term objective of creating 'a self-supporting market economy'. The Welsh document reflected sectoral structures, with objectives and sections covering agriculture, small business and new industry, training, tourism, housing, transport, natural heritage and sport. It is difficult to see anything distinctively Welsh about the document apart from some discussion of the development agencies and a very short and inconclusive section on the language. New funding, on the contrary, included a competitive programme of capital projects between local authorities reflecting the national government approach and a new scheme for Welsh farming explicitly based on the 'Countryside Stewardship' scheme in England (but see also chapter 12 below).

Welsh local authorities have provided advice for the secretary of state for Wales on the need for strategic planning guidance in which they criticized the existing guidance (DoE, 1992; Welsh Office, 1992) as failing to provide the integrative approach necessary (Assembly of Welsh Counties, 1992a). The supporting *Topic Report on Rural Wales* refers to the need for a coherent statement of overall policy goals for the Welsh countryside, not simply relating to the language and culture but also to the particular economic characteristics of rural Wales. The Welsh rural heartland is much more dependent on agriculture than most rural areas of England, the scope for diversification into, for example, rural high technological enterprise or leisure varies, and policy needs a Welsh dimension (Assembly of Welsh Counties, 1992b, p.22).

The report is also critical of the inconsistency of 'agency strategies' on which the Welsh Office is said to rely. However, apart from references to the importance of agriculture to both jobs and landscape character, to potential pressure for new or extended reservoirs from south-east England, and to the importance of common land in rural Wales, the report's authors are not very specific about the possible distinctive content of a Welsh rural strategy.

The Welsh language is dealt with in a separate topic report. While it is not seen as an issue only in rural Wales, existing guidance (PPG3 (Wales)) recognizes the language as an aspect of the social fabric of villages and the topic report points to two types of threat to the language in rural locations: from development which involves immigration of non-Welsh speakers; and from the stultifying of appropriate development because of conservation considerations.

The demand for more 'Welshness' in policy guidance has also been taken up by the Welsh Affairs Committee (1993), who have commented that 'guidance which reflects the settlement patterns of the home counties is unlikely to be equally applicable to rural Wales' (Welsh Affairs

Committee, 1993, p.xiv) and see the use of village envelopes as particularly inappropriate. Ironically, then, there is a clearer sense of why a distinct approach to rural policy is needed for Wales, where it is somewhat lacking, than in Scotland, where it has been attempted.

Institutions of rural development

Non-elected government agencies play an important role in rural development in England, Wales and Scotland. The role of the Rural Development Commission in England has already been outlined. There are similar bodies in Wales and Scotland, discussed below. Elected local authorities still command much larger resources, although their powers and resources have both been substantially reduced since 1979. Planning, housing, transport and education are the most important areas of responsibility by which local authorities contribute to rural development, but they also have economic development powers.

Superficially, Wales retains its 'socialist' quangos, created in the mid-1970s, whereas Scotland has had its replaced by 'Tory' quangos created at the beginning of the 1990s. Much of rural Wales comes under the Development Board for Rural Wales (DBRW), created in 1976, while the remainder is assisted by the Welsh Development Agency (WDA), which came into being a year earlier. Each is managed by a board of members nominated by the secretary of state for Wales. The former Scottish Development Agency (also of 1976) and the Highlands and Islands Development Board (HIDB) (1965) were replaced in 1991 by Scottish Enterprise and Highlands and Islands Enterprise (HIE) respectively. Two novel features of the new Scottish arrangements were that the activities of the Training Agency in Scotland were amalgamated with those of the development agencies, and a majority of the resulting functions are discharged through a network of local enterprise companies (LECs). In Wales, as in England, Training Agency functions were taken over by training and enterprise councils (TECs). TECs and LECs draw their memberships largely from the private sector. Privatization of enterprise and training development has therefore proceeded further in Scotland than in Wales.

This picture must be qualified, however. Government agencies, whatever their form, tend to reflect the policies of the government of the day: controls over membership, resources, and spending patterns all ensure this. Furthermore, other changes present a contradictory picture. Both the former HIDB and DBRW had social as well as economic roles in their respective areas, a reflection of the view that economic development would only be achievable if complemented by development of the social infrastructure. HIE has retained this role since reorganization and devolved much of it to the LECs. In contrast, the social role of the DBRW has been diminished as a result of a government review which resulted in some grant-making powers being transferred to local authorities (Hansard, 1994). Thus, in Scotland the private sector in the form of the LECs has been assigned a social role in development whereas in Wales this role has moved back more into the basic, more accountable part of the public sector.

Another important contrast between Scotland and both Wales and England lies in the extent to which the new structures reflect distinctly rural communities. Partly this is a function of geography and the more sharply-defined distinction between urban and rural communities in Scotland, but some of the LECs in the Scottish Enterprise area as well as in the Highlands and Islands are predominantly 'rural'. This, coupled with the devolved budgets and greater powers of LECs (compared with TECs), offers rural communities an opportunity to develop distinctive development strategies which reflect their particular problems and resources.

In Scotland, too, local government reorganization to some extent strengthens the urban–rural split, particularly in the break-up of Strathclyde, although increased commuting from more accessible rural areas like Borders and Fife will ensure that new 'rural' authorities will often be dominated by issues in adjacent urban areas. A somewhat similar picture is presented by local government reorganization in Wales, but the pattern of TECs tends to run across urban–rural boundaries. In England, where the views of the public were sought, a much more chaotic pattern of local government reorganization has emerged, but in many parts of the country local authorities will continue to be dominated by urban communities.

Even before the recent curtailment of the DBRW's role (which affected tourism as well as social development), its powers and range of activities were less extensive than its counterpart in the Highlands and Islands. HIE has adopted a substantial enterprise strategy as well as separate strategies for the environment, social development, and the development of Gaelic (Lloyd and Black, 1993). These documents present a much fuller policy statement about the agency's aims for and attitudes to the area and therefore offer scope for other interests to present and debate alternative views. The DBRW's strategy was much more concise and instrumental rather than conceptual, while the local authorities' strategic approach tends to be confined to land-use planning.

In terms of grant aid from government, Scotland and Wales do well by comparison with England. In 1993/4, for example, the Rural Development Commission received about £22 million, or about £8 per head if only the population in Rural Development Areas (2.75 million, compared to about ten million in the whole of rural England) is considered. By comparison, the DBRW received rather less than £14 million at about £65 per head and HIE £62 million at £168 per head. The WDA claimed to spend 5 per cent of its £70 million on rural areas, representing £34 per head. However, such comparisons are crude in the extreme, not only because need increases with increasing peripherality but because powers and responsibilities vary as between the various agencies.

During the early 1990s, the buzz-word in economic regeneration has been partnership. The concept of partnership is built into the English rural development machinery: preparation of the RDPs already discussed is required to be undertaken by a partnership of local public- and private-sector bodies and on the whole this has been judged to work well (Public Sector Management Research Centre, 1990). DBRW has been seen as more inclined to operate in isolation from local authorities and local community interests, although the WDA has followed RDC practice more closely in its rural work. In Scotland, where local authorities often adopted an active role in economic and social development, considerable concern was expressed about the diminution of their role following introduction of LECs but there is some evidence that effective local partnerships have been developing (Fairley, 1992; HIE, 1994).

European designations and funding have become relatively more important in the 1990s following the reform of the Structural Funds. For the 1994–9 period, the Highlands and Islands has joined the countries of Southern Europe, Ireland, and former East Germany in being designated an 'Objective 1' region, where development is lagging behind the rest of Europe. This will bring an extra £30 to £50 million a year to the area. Other parts of rural Britain are eligible for 'Objective 5b' funding, specifically aimed at the development of rural areas. The significance of Objective 1 designation for the Highlands and Islands is indicated by comparison with the levels of funding from 5b designation in the previous programming period of 1988–91:

Highlands and Islands	£73 million
Dumfries and Galloway	£10 million
Rural Wales	£79 million (incl. 1987–8)

Sources: Bryden *et al.* 1993, pp.50–3; Welsh Office, 1994, Appendix 4.

These figures are in turn put in their place by comparison with just one year of direct subsidies to the agricultural livestock sector from the EC's common agriculture policy: £35 million for the Highlands and Islands, £23 million for Dumfries and Galloway (Bryden *et al.*, 1993). In simple financial terms, therefore, agricultural support is much more significant than payments from the Structural Funds. If the latter succeed in their intended purpose of diversifying the economies of these areas, however, they will in the long term prove the more important.

Turok (1994) has argued that the Scottish Office Objective 1 plan fails to consider how its various elements – infrastructure provision, business support, training and environmental measures – may be integrated, and proposes that the targeting of particular industrial sectors would provide much greater coherence. The Rural Wales Objective 5b programming document has similar weaknesses: despite acknowledging that the area 'remains overly dependent on traditional industries such as agriculture, forestry, and tourism' (Welsh Office, 1994, para.4.1.3), they are the only industrial sectors specifically mentioned in the document. Although a degree of flexibility is desirable, the considerable reluctance in these documents to target efforts is at least questionable and should be justified. This is in contrast to Scottish Enterprise's approach to the Scottish economy as a whole, where the potential of particular industries is under active investigation (Scottish Enterprise, 1994).

Policies and practice of rural development: agencies

The four principal government agencies for rural development operating in Wales and Scotland pursue strategies which have both similarities and differences, in relation to each other and to English practice. All must necessarily follow the broad 'enterprise' path established by the British governments of the 1980s and 1990s, and all have a battery of developmental instruments which include financial packages, property development and infrastructure provision, business advice services, and promotional activities. They all pursue a broad range of economic activities rather than limiting themselves to sectors and firms with a particular 'rural' character; indeed, because, as previously discussed, many rural activities are the province of other government ministries or agencies, their role in such areas as agriculture, forestry and fishing is necessarily limited.

Institutional boundaries are also responsible for some of the major functional differences between these agencies and the nearest English equivalent – the Rural Development Commission. The Commission has a narrower range of functions than any of the Welsh and Scottish agencies, partly because of the resources available to it but primarily because of the complex evolution of political and institutional history in the three countries. The RDC, for example, has played a more limited role in financial support for business and has not become significantly involved in marketing and promotional activities.

One interpretation of these differences between England on the one hand and Wales and Scotland on the other is that the Celtic countries have been able to bring political pressure to bear to obtain a degree of devolution of power through the creation of special development agencies. The introduction of the then Highlands and Islands Development Board in 1965 can well be seen in this way, and its comparative success helped to generate demand for the Development Board for Rural Wales in the 1970s. It also helps to explain the survival of both, if in modified form, through the lifetimes of hostile governments and a variety of specific crises. On the other hand, the creation of government agencies with wide powers in the Celtic countries could also be viewed as a way of ensuring a high degree of control on detailed decision-making for London and the government in power; in England, despite recent reductions in local government's independence of action, more local discretion may be said to remain, at least in principle.

In Wales, a notable feature of rural development strategy has been an area-based approach. From its inception, the DBRW has pursued an explicit spatial strategy based on the classification of the region's small towns into a number of categories and the identification of particular types of development provision with each category. The board's *Strategy for the 1990s* (DBRW, 1989), for example, outlined its spatial strategy in the following terms:

	Category	*No.*	*Assistance*
1.	Growth areas	6	250–325,000 sq.ft.*
2.	Special towns	12	98–150,000 sq.ft.*
3.	Smaller towns in West	–	Small workshops

Note: *Split between categories 1 and 2 not fully specified in all cases.

This spatial strategy has always provoked debate, particularly about the Board's genuine commitment to all parts of its area and the appropriateness of the kinds of development it promotes. The *Strategy for the 1990s* proposes to give more help to the remoter western half of its region, particularly in smaller towns and villages. This commitment remains unquantified, however, in the Board's most recent annual report. On the other hand, there is soft evidence of greater support in the west through involvement in major development projects in Aberystwyth and in the South Gwynedd partnership area affected by the closure of Trawsfynydd nuclear power station, as well as support for more business centres in the west than the east.

Inward investment, mainly from England, has always figured prominently, and this has been seen by some as a threat to Welsh language and culture and as having little to do with the area's rural character. In more recent years there has been some shift in the balance away from reliance on inward investment: for example, in the early 1990s only 10 per cent of business finance provided by the Board went to inward investment projects compared with 28 per cent to local start-ups (DBRW, 1994).

In rural Wales outside the Board's area, the Welsh Development Agency has pursued a strategy which has some similarities. No spatial strategy has been developed as such, but the formation of local development partnerships usually based on a small town and its surrounding catchment area has been encouraged. This has the advantage of being potentially more responsive to local needs and opinions, although the resources and underlying objectives of the government agency remain a powerful steering influence. This need to balance local and national concerns is nicely illustrated by a paragraph from a recent Agency report:

> There are three key principles informing our rural strategy. The first essential requirement is the support and commitment of the local people; then a comprehensive action plan that takes account of all aspects of community life; and, finally, local solutions to local needs. Projects are evaluated for practicality, cost-effectiveness, value for tax-payers' money and the 'fit' with the objectives of the Agency and other public sector bodies. (WDA, 1994, p.25)

No systematic evaluation of the effectiveness of this approach has been published but there is some evidence from individual examples that it has in at least some cases allowed local communities to adopt both policies and styles of operation suited to their particular circumstances.

In both Welsh cases, however, there has been a strong emphasis on a property-led approach, with a considerable reliance on site provision and servicing, together with advance factory construction and environmental improvements. In effect, the aim has been to strengthen the urban base of the area by helping the small towns which characterize it to expand modestly, this being achieved mainly by attracting businesses from elsewhere. Encouragement to indigenous enterprise is available but until recently was much less successful, despite a tradition of small businesses in the area's farming and services.

In Scotland the HIDB had originally also adopted a spatial strategy based around three growth points, but this was quite quickly abandoned in favour of a more flexible strategy with many elements to it. In the more populous and accessible areas, such as the Moray Firth rim and Lochaber, an inward investment approach based on property development and active promotion was followed, with a similar emphasis for tourism development in the Cairngorms. However, the Board had a wide range of powers and these were harnessed to find other solutions for the more fragile areas of the Western Highlands and Islands. Attempts were made to revive fishing as a complement to crofting, employing traditional methods and also by endeavouring to introduce industrial fishing and fish farming. Small remote communities were encouraged to identify opportunities for co-operative businesses and then to implement them, including meeting local service needs and exploiting small-scale tourism and craft opportunities.

From the start the importance – symbolically, at least – of these fragile areas was recognized. The First Report quotes the Board's first Chairman, whose opinion was that '. . . the Board will be judged by its ability to hold population in the true crofting areas' (HIDB, 1967, p.5). This correlation of fragility with the presence of crofting was in part a simplification – crofting is not practised in all remote communities – in part an appeal to the emotional reaction, since crofting is a living reminder of the imposition on Highland social and economic life of the priorities of outsiders in the past. Nearly thirty years on, Highlands and Islands Enterprise continues to promise high priority to fragile areas but is cautious about the definition of fragility and resists any temptation there may still be to equate it with one simple indicator. At the same time they express equal concern about 'areas of employment deficit', usually resulting from the closure or major run-down of a large local firm (HIE, 1991). Ironically, some of these major declines are the result of earlier attempts to bring work to the area and capitalize on indigenous or nearby assets such as North Sea oil; the solutions envisaged may well rely on further inward investment.

One of the weaknesses of the old HIDB was that it was slow to develop a decentralized structure; in remoter communities its headquarters in Inverness was often perceived to be almost as distant as the Scottish Office in Edinburgh or parliament in Westminster. A strength of the SE–HIE organization is the concept of a network of local agencies linked by a smaller core body. This concept recognizes the distinctiveness of individual communities even within a large rural area which has marked characteristics distinguishing it from the rest of the country. The Scottish LECs offer, in principle, scope to customize relatively standardized powers and assistance packages to the particular needs and opportunities of localities. Early reports suggest that genuine benefits are accruing (Bennett et al., 1993), although systematic evaluation remains to be done and some anecdotal evidence in the early years pointed the other way.

One of the advantages of the network structure for observers is that more information is readily available through annual reports for individual LECs. In the HIE area, in particular, it is possible to make comparisons between the performance of different LECs and therefore areas because of a degree of standardization of data collection and presentation. Table 10.1, for example, presents results in terms of job creation and relative cost for the first three years of the HIE system:

Table 10.1 Job Creation and Retention in LEC Areas, 1992–4

LEC	Jobs*	% of Total	% of HIE Population	Cost per Job (£)
Shetland	819	9.64	6.13	3976
Orkney	390	4.59	5.34	3966
Western Isles	1098	12.92	7.95	3101
Caithness & Sutherland	947	11.14	10.76	4826
Ross & Cromarty	1335	15.71	13.46	3646
Skye & Lochalsh	524	6.16	3.21	3437
Inverness & Nairn	756	8.89	20.04	2270
Moray Badenoch Strathspey	692	8.14	9.11	3540
Lochaber	518	6.09	5.24	3756
Argyll & Islands	1421	16.72	18.77	3616
TOTAL	**8500**	**100**	**100**	**3611**

Note: *Jobs created or retained.
Source: Highlands and Islands Enterprise Annual Reports, 1992–4.

This demonstrates that some of the remoter areas (Shetland, Western Isles, and Skye and Lochalsh particularly) have received more than their share of new jobs, although the relative costs are higher than for the main population centres. Although such figures must always be treated with caution since the job estimates of agencies are always optimistic, cost calculations may ignore other sources of funding, and no data is presented on job losses it would be nevertheless helpful if comparable figures were compiled for other rural areas of Britain.

An important feature of HIE is its network strategy, with its relatively detailed economic strategy complemented by strategies for social, environmental, and Gaelic language development. As Black (1994) has observed, HIE is the first British development agency to integrate the concept of sustainable development into its approach, while its strategy for Gaelic is far more explicit than those of the Welsh agencies, even though Welsh is much more widely spoken than Gaelic.

Local policy and practice

Development agencies and local authorities provide the framework of policies and ideas and a source of finance and support, but all development ultimately depends on the imagination, energy and harmonious effort of individuals and communities. The small-scale intimacy of rural areas can facilitate co-operative effort to achieve self-sustaining development based on local resources and potentials, but small communities can also be highly conservative containing inter-family rivalry and suspicion. It is doubtful whether small communities in Wales and Scotland are any different from those in England in this respect, although differences of circumstance can help to account for relative success or failure in different locations. The attempt to develop genuine community co-operation for economic and social development in the Western Highlands and Islands achieved some degree of success, partly because of local state support but also because of the value of sharing the risks in a marginal environment. Its value in building 'morale and self-confidence' (HIDB, referred to by Bryden and Scott, 1990) may have brought unexpected benefits in the longer term, for example through the community *feisean* (Gaelic Arts festivals) which developed in the 1980s (Rennie, undated).

Studies of small community revival in England, Wales and Scotland show many common features (Minay *et al.*, 1995; Minay and Findlay, forthcoming). Much of the initiative comes from outside, via development agencies and local authorities; the ideas are often reshaped by the local community but seldom without considerable wrangling between different local interests. Most are generated by concern about local economic circumstances but effort often becomes translated into environmental or social action: the economic benefits are therefore likely to be somewhat indirect.

In Table 10.2, an analysis is presented based on returns summarized in a recent directory of projects concerned with reviving small communities. The figures are indicative only but present some interesting contrasts between England, Wales and Scotland.

Table 10.2 Most Important Factors in Problem Definition for Small Community Revival Projects (% in brackets)

	England	Wales	Scotland	Total
Decline of local industries	29 (70)	18 (69)	13 (68)	60
Narrow industrial base	13 (32)	7 (27)	13 (68)	33
Level of unemployment	17 (41)	10 (38)	3 (15)	30
Out-migration/depopulation	10 (24)	7 (27)	5 (26)	22
Loss of services	16 (39)	3 (11)	–	19
Ageing population	9 (22)	3 (11)	6 (31)	18
Physical isolation	5 (12)	3 (11)	5 (26)	13
Lack of access to jobs	6 (15)	5 (19)	2 (10)	13
Environmental decay	7 (17)	4 (15)	–	11
Total cases	**41**	**26**	**19**	**86**

Note: More than one factor may be mentioned for each project.
Source: Minay *et al.*, 1995, raw data.

The narrowness of the local industrial base is a proportionally much more serious concern in Scotland, together with an ageing population structure.

In England, the loss of services is viewed as a much more serious problem than in Wales or Scotland, probably because a higher level has been expected and experienced there, though it may be that the remoter communities of Wales and Scotland have found ways of providing services that have not yet been adopted in England. Minor factors not listed on the table also show some interesting variations: high house prices and a growing dormitory/second-home status are seen as proportionally more important problems in Wales; seasonality of employment in Scotland.

These variations in concern can be seen in locally-produced strategy documents. A town study for Knighton, located right on the border between England and Wales, was undertaken – like many for small English towns – by the Civic Trust Regeneration Unit. It stresses local conservation and environmental enhancement linked to tourism development based on Offa's Dyke. It has much in common with similar English studies and shows relatively little consciousness of any distinct Welsh problems or values. In contrast, a strategy for Llŷn in north-west Wales was undertaken for a local development organization whose aim:

is to ensure a thriving future for Llŷn by developing the confidence of the local inhabitants and ensuring:

- adequate and varied employment in relevant locations;
- suitable housing in appropriate locations;
- suitable conditions for the culture and language of Llŷn to thrive;
- the quality of the environment   (Antur Llŷn, 1989, p.11).

Population trends, remoteness, migration patterns and the impact on local housing were particular concerns; a high priority was given to local consultation; but, while the strategy did not appear to reject inward investment, it stressed actions which would stimulate successful establishment and retention of local businesses and activities consistent with local cultural and linguistic priorities. The resulting activities are now focusing on enterprise development in order to stimulate a stronger local economy from within, as well as continuing to give high priority to community animation.

In Scotland, Grampian Region has experimented with a rural development approach under the heading 'Villages in Control'. This is based on a study of Canadian experience and involves a pair of 'development executives' working, mainly with the business community, in selected villages, on a short-term (six months per community) basis. The aim is to generate a self-help group in each village who will develop and take on ideas on their own initiative after the visitors have left. So far two studies have been conducted, one of Laurencekirk (Kincardineshire, population 1740) and the other of Insch (Gordon District, population 1540). The very short time-scale and the business development emphasis provides a strong contrast with most community projects elsewhere, which have found it difficult to generate a self-sustaining process even after a two- or three-year period of support. Although an interesting experiment, this approach has encountered considerable difficulties of this sort. Moreover, many of the projects envisaged as the result of this process seem to involve site development and other physical solutions which require a much longer time-scale and are likely to result in associated work for the local authorities and others for a prolonged period. Indeed, these results are much like projects generated by other processes and in other locations.

A comparison with the slightly earlier North West Fife Rural Initiative (1986–91) is instructive. This pilot rural development initiative covered a predominantly rural part of Fife with a population of about 21,000. There was a strong emphasis on farm diversification because of the then cutback in farm subsidies from the EC, and the initiative explored a variety of projects which might help the area to weather these changes, including food marketing, farm holidays, low-cost golf courses, and field sports development. The initiative argued that there was value in collaborative work of this type because individuals lack time and resources to consider new directions for development but also recognized that, once identified, many projects were best followed up by individuals or individual groups or organizations working on focused tasks. However, five years had been allowed for the development of collaboration and generation of ideas, in contrast with the Grampian example.

Conclusions

Rural economic development as practised in England, Wales and Scotland has a number of common features which suggest that the factors making for conformity are greater than those encouraging cultural distinctiveness. This conclusion is not surprising given the recent preoccupation with the strength of global processes in shaping modern economic development. Regional distinctiveness has everywhere been in retreat in recent decades as international capital has migrated around the globe to exploit opportunities as they occur, and as firms have found new ways of coping with the resultant pressures. The effect of these processes on rural Wales has been nicely illustrated by Day (1991) in the opening paragraph of an excellent chapter from an earlier book in this series, with reference to the mineral water business and car component manufacturers.

Neither of these industries would immediately come to mind in a discussion of rural development – one would look in vain for reference to them in most if not all government policy documents on rural development

– but they are nevertheless constituent parts of that particular rural economy. They therefore illustrate another important point about rural economic development: that it is no easy matter to define what the rural economy is in the last decade of the twentieth century. The 'traditional' components of that economy – agriculture, forestry, fishing – remain important to the appearance and use of rural areas but are of relatively marginal importance to the fabric of rural society. This is certainly *less* true in parts of Wales and Scotland than it now is in much of England, but the contrast is becoming less marked.

The rural economy as a single entity is now highly diversified, in that single industries are becoming less and less significant. This does not alter the fact that individual local economies in rural areas may still have a high degree of dependence on a small number of industries or even firms. Often, as in the Western Isles, there is still a high degree of dependence on the public sector, and in a period of public-sector retrenchment which shows little sign of abating this is as much bad news as dependence on a private-sector business subject to decisions taken hundreds or thousands of miles away.

In many rural communities, a major concern is increasingly the centralization of many services, from retailing through banking to personal services. This is no new process, but it is taking new and unexpected forms which are worrying many small businesses in rural areas as well as members of the general public. In some ways, the remotest settlements have the least to fear from this, since they have learned to manage without many services and they are too far from major centres for the services that remain to face fierce competition. It is the small towns within the orbit of the extended catchment areas of major centres that have most to lose. Investment levels in them have been historically low and they are ill equipped either to cope with competition or to generate and sustain new investment.

Some are seeking salvation through promotion of local heritage features and a consequent reliance on the continued growth of tourism. Not only is this a risky business in which local and global competition is increasing, but it is one which many local people view with considerable scepticism, if not downright hostility. For others, the only hope is to generate new small industries which can survive in less accessible locations through a combination of high-value products, specialist expertise, and reliance on modern telecommunications technology. Few areas can generate these in sufficient numbers, however, to sustain local services, which seem doomed to further decline.

The nature of, and response to, these trends appears more likely to rely on relative remoteness than on cultural or institutional distinctiveness. This may go some way to explain the failure of the policy statements and strategies we have reviewed to encompass distinct characteristics arising either from the separate identities of each country or their individual organizational frameworks. All are essentially tackling the same processes and are constrained by the limited range of techniques and tools at their disposal. Or, to be fair, the quite wide range of techniques and tools, because the narrow technical base which once characterized regional development activity generally has given way to the employment of a diversity of tools. The issue today is less about the range of tools employed than about whether they are being used to maximum effect.

Two interrelated constraints may be said to limit their effectiveness. The first is ideology, both in the sense of political ideology and institutional ideology. It works both directly and indirectly to inhibit innovation, even when it is also helping to innovate. Despite an increased emphasis on partnership, public and private sectors often remain distrustful of each other. The ideology of left and right at national level promotes alternative development models which encourage this distrust. At the European level, ideology is reduced by the need for compromise, at the local level the practical politics of deriving local benefits similarly reduce its significance – although, of course, some local communities remain fundamentally divided by it.

Wales and Scotland may be said to have suffered more than most from recent ideological conflicts because they have been so strongly at variance with English-dominated government. This may well mean that their desire for distinct approaches to rural development has been muted by the need for conformity with government dogma. Organizational changes have been imposed from outside or at the behest of an indigenous minority. However, these organizational changes are not necessarily producing only negative results. The LEC experiment in Scotland does seem to have some potential, particularly in the HIE area where the remit is wider.

This brings us to the second constraint on effectiveness, which is the capacity of local economic communities to determine their own path to development. Although most, if not all, local communities are to some extent divided by a variety of opposing interests, there is also evidence that a degree of consensus can often be achieved through a shared analysis of problems and potential solutions. In most rural areas, however, the scope to implement, or even define, these solutions is distinctly limited without the support of external resources. Persuading those sources to help without compromising local objectives or solutions to suit the rules and regulations of the funders is a major problem. The increased use of competitive bidding could help in this respect if it allowed rules to be relaxed to suit local circumstances, but it appears more likely to produce approaches which try to conform to some pre-ordained model or to result in arbitrary decisions based on purely political considerations. Here again, the LEC model has potential, despite many shortcomings. The development of local economic organizations with their own budgets able to explore locally-appropriate opportunities, but supported by a core organization which provided broad administrative, advisory and research support, would have considerable potential for extension to other rural and mixed urban–rural areas. It would have particular potential in areas, such as the Welsh-speaking areas of Wales, where a culturally-distinct approach to economic development is sought. However, such an organization should have clearer accountability to the entire local community than all the currently 'appointed' agencies do.

References

Antur Llŷn 1989. *A Strategy for Llŷn 1990–2000: Towards a Thriving Community* (Llyn, Antur Llŷn).
Assembly of Welsh Counties 1992a. *Strategic Planning Guidance in Wales: Draft Submission to the Secretary of State for Wales: Overview Report* (Mold, AWC).
Assembly of Welsh Counties 1992b. *Strategic Planning Guidance in Wales: Draft Submission to the Secretary of State for Wales: Topic Reports* (Mold, AWC).
Bennett, R., P. Wicks and A.. McCoshan 1993. *Local Empowerment and Business Services: Britain's Experiment with Training and Enterprise Councils* (London, UCL Press).
Black, S. 1994. 'Environmental and economic development policies in the Highlands and Islands of Scotland', in S. Hardy and G. Lloyd, *Sustainable Regions* (London, Regional Studies Association).
Bryden, J. *et al.* 1993. *Pounds, Policies and Prospects: Rural Scotland and the European Community* (Edinburgh, Scottish Office).
Bryden, J. and I. Scott 1990. 'The Celtic fringe: state-sponsored versus indigenous local development initiatives in Scotland and Ireland', in W. Stöhr, *Global Challenge and Local Response* (London, Mansell for UN University).
Buller, H. and S. Wright 1990. *Rural Development: Problems and Practices* (Aldershot, Avebury).
Countryside Commission, English Nature and Rural Development Commission, undated. *Rural Strategies* (Cheltenham, Countryside Commission).
Day, G. 1991. 'The regeneration of Rural Wales: Prospects for the 1990s', in G. Day and G. Rees, *Regions, Nations and European Integration: Remaking the Celtic Periphery* (Cardiff, University of Wales Press).
Department of the Environment 1992. *The Countryside and the Rural Economy*, Planning Policy Guidance Note No.7 (London, HMSO).
Development Board for Rural Wales 1989. *Strategy for the 1990s* (Newtown, DBRW).
European Communities Economic and Social Committee 1990. *The Future of Rural Society* (Brussels, European Community).
Fairley, J. 1992. 'Scottish local authorities and local enterprise companies: a developing relationship', *Regional Studies*, Vol.26(2), pp.193–207.
Hansard 1994. *Development Board for Rural Wales*, House of Commons Parliamentary Debates, Issue 1661, pp.463–74, 7 July (London, HMSO).

Highlands and Islands Development Board 1967. *First Report* (Inverness, HIDB).

Highlands and Islands Enterprise 1991. *A Strategy for Enterprise Development in the Highlands and Islands of Scotland* (Inverness, HIE).

Highlands and Islands Enterprise 1994. *Third Report 1993–94* (Inverness, HIE).

Keeble, D. et al. 1992. *Business Success in the Countryside* (London, HMSO).

Lloyd, M. G. and S. Black 1993. 'Highlands and Islands Enterprise: strategies for economic and social development', *Local Economy*, Vol.8(1), May, pp.69–81.

Marsden, T. et al. 1990. *Rural Restructuring: Global Processes and their Responses* (London, David Fulton).

Marsden, T. et al. 1993. *Constructing the Countryside* (London, UCL Press).

Minay, C. et al. 1995. *Reviving Small Communities: A Directory of Projects* (Oxford, Oxford Brookes University).

Minay, C. and L. Findlay, forthcoming. *Reviving Small Communities: A Good Practice Guide* (Oxford, Oxford Brookes University).

Murdoch, J. and T. Marsden 1994. *Reconstituting Rurality: Class, Community and Power in the Development Process* (London, UCL Press).

North Riding County Council 1975. *North Riding Pennines Study* (Northallerton, NRCC).

Public Sector Management Research Centre 1990. *An Evaluation of the Rural Development Programme Process* (Birmingham, Aston Business School).

Rennie, F. undated. *Feis Bharraigh*, Case Studies in Rural and Community Development No.1 (Perth, Rural Forum).

Rural Development Commission 1994. *Rural Development Strategy for the 1990s* (Salisbury, RDC).

Scottish Enterprise 1994. *The Network Strategy* (Glasgow, Scottish Enterprise).

Scottish Office 1992a. *Rural Framework* (Edinburgh, Scottish Office).

Scottish Office 1992b. *Scottish Rural Life: a Socio-Economic Profile of Rural Scotland* (Edinburgh, Scottish Office).

Select Committee on the European Communities 1990. *The Future of Rural Society*, Volume 1-Report (HL80-I), House of Lords, Session 1989–90, (London, HMSO).

Turok, I. 1994. 'Targeting sectors to boost Highlands and Islands development', *Town and Country Planning*, Vol.63, February, pp.54–5.

Welsh Affairs Committee 1993. *Third Report of the Committee, Rural Housing*, Volume 1 (HC621-I), House of Commons, Session 1992–93 (London, HMSO).

Welsh Development Agency 1994. *Report and Accounts 1993–1994* (Cardiff, WDA).

Welsh Office 1991. *The Rural Initiative: Putting the Heart into Rural Wales* (Cardiff, Welsh Office).

Welsh Office 1992. *Conservation and Regeneration of the Rural Environment and Economy*, SPGW(S)13 (Cardiff, Welsh Office).

Welsh Office 1994. *Rural Wales Objective 5b: Single Programming Document 1994–1999* (Cardiff, Welsh Office).

11

The Designation of Valued Landscapes in Scotland

JOHN MOIR

Introduction

Whilst the promotion of economic development is a fundamental objective in all advanced Western countries, there is also a strong commitment to the protection of rural landscapes. Such protection can be achieved in a variety of ways (Mather, 1986), but perhaps the best known approach has been through the designation of valued landscapes. In England and Wales, this is exemplified by National Parks, Areas of Outstanding Natural Beauty, Heritage Coasts, Country Parks and, to a lesser extent Nature Reserves and Sites of Special Scientific Interest (SSSIs) – although the latter are primarily for nature conservation rather than for visual or landscape purposes. These designations cover a substantial area of England and Wales (see Blunden and Curry, 1990; DoE, 1992; Evans, 1992; and Poore and Poore, 1987). Protection of the countryside in general and designated landscapes in particular has clearly become a significant part of British planning practice (Cullingworth and Nadin, 1994; Curry, 1994; Gilg, 1978, 1985 and 1991; Hall et al., 1973). Indeed some have suggested that the political strength of rural protection has led to regressive effects (Newby, 1980; Newby et al., 1978), although others point to the weakness of conservation policies and statutory organizations (Green, 1985; Lowe et al., 1986; Shoard, 1980, 1987).

Whilst an extensive literature has now been built up on the policies associated with landscape protection, the focus has been on experience in England with little, if anything, on Scotland. Landscape protection 'north of the Border' is often referred to as a subject meriting further study. Yet relatively little has emerged on this with some notable exceptions, for example, Shucksmith and Lloyd (1983) and Selman (ed.) (1988). The objectives of this chapter are to:

(i) highlight the distinctiveness of the approaches adopted in Scotland to landscape conservation and the designation of valued landscapes;

(ii) explore some of the reasons behind this distinctiveness and some of the issues and conflicts with the Scottish approach to landscape conservation.

Landscape protection and the designation of valued landscapes – similarities between Scotland and England

Although the purpose here is to highlight the *contrasts* between England and Scotland, it is not suggested that the approaches to landscape protection in the two countries are completely different. The principle of protecting the open countryside from sporadic housing development has been and remains strong in both England and Scotland (Moir *et al.*, 1995). The provisions of the 1949 National Parks and Access to the Countryside Act and the 1980s Wildlife and Countryside Acts have led to the designation of large numbers of Nature Reserves and SSSIs in both countries, although significantly, the area covered by both these is greater in Scotland. More recently, European Union (EU) environmental policy is leading to the definition of a network of Special Areas of Conservation and Bird Protection Areas throughout England and Scotland. Finally, although established through different acts, an extensive distribution of country parks has been established both north and south of the 'border'. Nevertheless, despite these similarities, more noticeable perhaps are the differences between England and Scotland in terms of their approaches to landscape protection.

The designation of valued landscapes – differences between England and Scotland

Paradoxically, given the quality of its upland landscapes, there are no national parks in Scotland. This does not mean that national parks have never been contemplated as a way of protecting valued Scottish landscapes. Cherry (1975), Ferguson (1988) and Moir (1991) provide useful accounts of attempts to establish Scottish National Parks. Here it is only necessary to summarize these attempts. Concerns about access to the Scottish mountains can be traced back to the nineteenth century with Bryce's Access to the Mountains Bill and conflicts between landowners and the predecessors of the Scottish Rights of Way Society. Despite the successes of the Rights of Way Society and the inclusion of Scotland in the 1931 Addison Committee's recommendations for national parks, up to the 1940s relatively little had been done to establish national parks in Scotland. Over the last fifty years, however, there have been three main attempts to set up Scottish national parks.

The Ramsay Reports in the 1940s

The creation of national parks was part of the general commitment given to post-war reconstruction in the 1940s. The Scott, Dower and Hobhouse reports are usually associated with providing the impetus for national parks but their recommendations did not apply to Scotland. Scottish rural issues were considered by the Normand and Ramsay committees. Nevertheless, the enthusiasm for national parks was felt in both Scotland and England during the 1940s. As a result, the recommendations of the Ramsay committees on Scottish national parks parallel those of the Dower and Hobhouse committees. Ramsay recommended the establishment of five national parks (Loch Lomond/Trossachs; Cairngorms; Ben Nevis/Glen Coe/Black Mount; Glen Affric/Glen Cannich/Strath Farrar; and Wester Ross) and three 'Reserve Areas' (Moidart/Morar/Knoydart; Ben Lawers/Glen Lyon/Schiehallion; and St Mary's Loch). Whilst a number of Dower's and Hobhouse's recommendations for England and Wales were implemented through the 1949 National Parks and Access to the Countryside Act, the provisions for national parks did not apply to Scotland. The commitment to creating Scottish national parks faltered and by the early 1950s, they were, in effect, dropped from the political and legislative agenda.

Special parks and the park system for Scotland in the 1970s

During the 1950s, there were moves to establish national parks in the Cairngorms and in Loch Lomond. But these were local initiatives and they took place at different times. The next comprehensive attempt to set up national parks throughout Scotland was in the 1970s with the Countryside Commission for Scotland's (CCS's) proposals for 'Special Parks' (CCS, 1974). These parks were intended to satisfy low-intensity national recreational demands and be located in relatively remote and sparsely-populated locations of national and international landscape value. Responsibilities for their planning and management were to be given to special park authorities comprising two-thirds local authority appointees with the other third being 'independent members appointed by the Secretary of State to represent the national interest' (CCS, 1974, p.24). The special park authorities would have had normal local authority planning and countryside functions but the parks would also have been subject to additional controls such as those available in Section 9 of the 1967 Countryside (Scotland) Act. A list of potential locations was not given, but Loch Lomond/ Trossachs, Glen Coe/ Ben Nevis and the Cairngorms were again highlighted for consideration. The term 'national park' was not applied but clearly there were similarities with the English and Welsh national parks. However, again the proposals were not implemented and by the early 1980s, the concept of the 'special park' faded away.

The 1990s – National Parks and the mountain areas of Scotland

Despite the failure of the 'special parks', interest in national parks was soon revived. During the 1980s pressures to develop Scotland's natural resources, notably for skiing and forestry and culminating in several well-publicized conflicts at Craig Meagaidh, the 'Flow Country' and the Cairngorms, led to calls for the adoption of measures to ensure effective conservation of Scotland's upland landscapes. As a consequence, in 1989 the CCS was asked by the Scottish minister for Home Affairs and the Environment to '. . . study management arrangements for popular mountain areas such as the Cairngorms, taking into consideration the case for arrangements on national park lines in Scotland' (CCS, 1990, p.4). The commission's views were produced in 1990 (CCS, 1990). These included wide-ranging proposals for both designated and non-designated mountain areas. Unfortunately many of these proposals attracted less scrutiny than they merited – largely because attention was focused on the commission's view that Scotland should have its own national parks. Four areas were recommended for designation – Cairngorms, Loch Lomond and the Trossachs, Ben Nevis/Glen Coe/Black Mount and Wester Ross – broadly in line with four of the areas recommended by Ramsay forty years previously. Three of the parks would be run on similar lines to those in the Peak and Lake District National Parks in England with independent park boards, comprising local and national members. They would have planning and countryside functions, financial precept powers and support through Scottish Office funding (although higher than central government support in England). A joint committee was put forward as the most appropriate way of administering the proposed Wester Ross National Park. Yet again, however, these proposals in the early 1990s to create Scottish national parks have not led to their establishment. Scotland remains one of the few industrialized countries without national parks.

Scotland's distinctive approach to landscape protection

Despite the absence of national parks, some action has been taken to address concerns about threats to Scotland's rural landscapes. Paradoxically, each of the failed attempts in the 1940s, 1970s and 1990s has been followed by steps to designate the most valued landscapes so that Scotland has evolved its own distinctive approach to landscape protection.

National Park Direction Areas

Although the five areas included in the Ramsay Committee's recommendations never became national parks, in 1948 they were designated as National Park Direction Areas (NPDAs). In these areas, local authorities were directed to furnish the Scottish Office with applications for development submitted under the Town and Country Planning Acts, and if necessary, the secretary of state could 'call-in' any application to make a judgement.

National Scenic Areas

Whilst 'Special Parks' were not put in place, the idea of protecting landscapes of national or international importance was nevertheless accepted. By 1980, forty of these areas were identified and designated as National Scenic Areas (SDD, 1980; 1987a) (see Figure 11.1). National Scenic Areas (NSAs) replaced the NPDAs and the Directions relating to them. Where a planning authority proposed to grant planning permission for any of the following categories of development:

- schemes for 5 or more houses or chalets (unless already included in approved development plans);
- sites for 5 or more mobile homes or caravans;
- non-residential developments over 0.5 ha;
- buildings over 12m high (including agriculture and forestry developments);
- vehicle tracks;
- local authority roadworks (outside existing road boundaries) costing over £100,000

against the CCS's advice, the secretary of state would have to be notified and he or she would decide whether or not to 'call-in' the application. No special administration has been set up for the NSAs. Nor has specific funding been set aside for them. Although the development control measures in NSAs were intended to be complemented by positive planning and management measures, relatively little has been achieved on the latter, with some exceptions (CCS, 1985). Certainly, the circulars associated with the NSAs only dealt with the development control measures. National Scenic Areas are also more limited than NPDAs in terms of the scale and numbers of developments considered by central government. In this respect, they represent a rationalization of 'central' influence over development in scenic areas. Yet central government's influence on development has been extended in two ways. Firstly, in terms of the area of

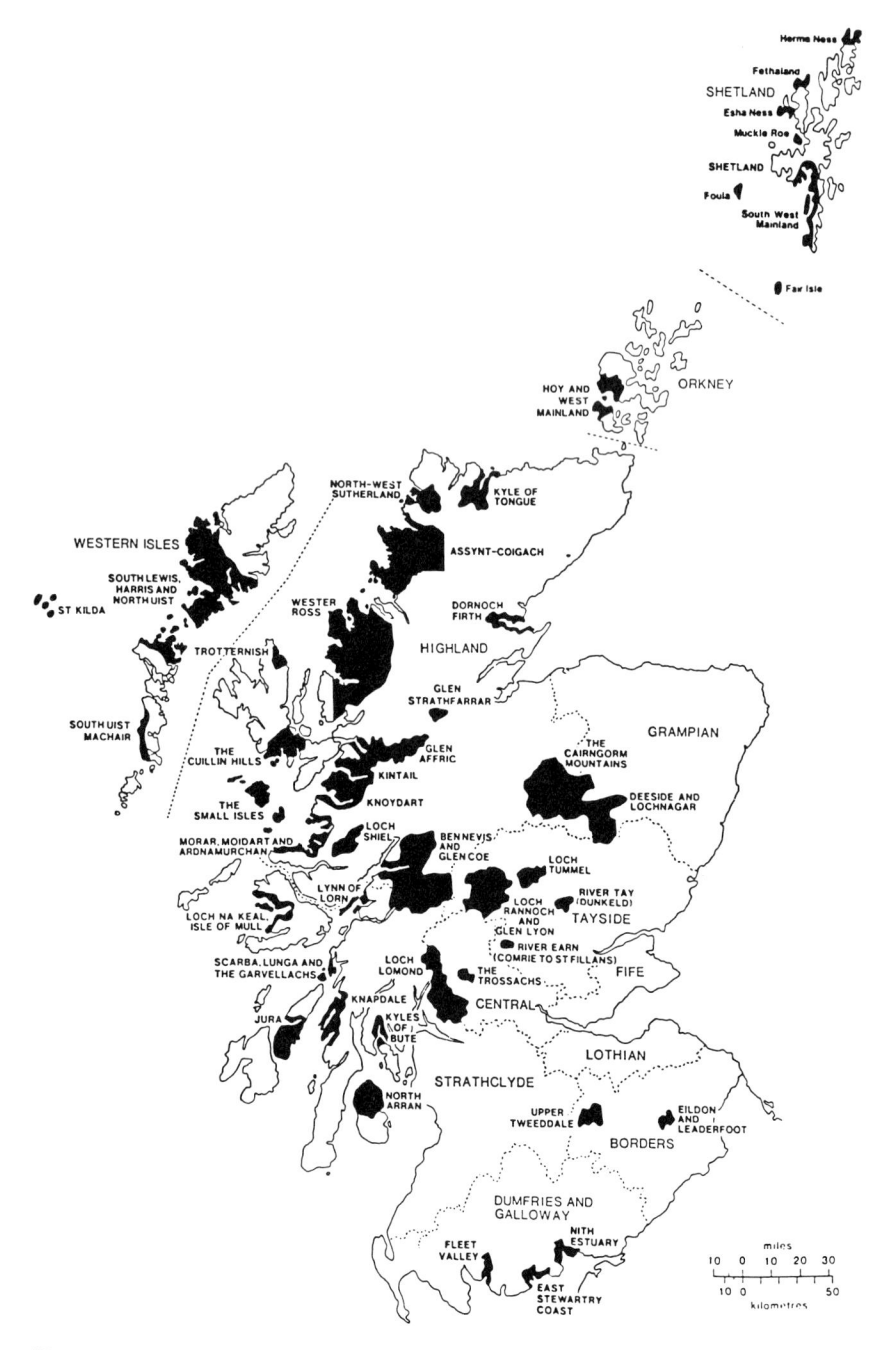

Figure 11.1 National Scenic Areas in Scotland (Source: Countryside Commission for Scotland 1990, Map 9, p. 15)

The Designation of Valued Landscapes in Scotland

valued landscape covered. Some NSAs are contiguous with the NPDAs but in total they cover more of Scotland. The forty NSAs cover 1,026,300 ha or just over 13 per cent of Scotland (see Table 11.1) compared with the NPDAs' 6 per cent.

Table 11.1 Distribution of NSAs in Scotland

Region	Hectarage of NSA	Percentage of Scotland covered by NSA
Borders	15900	0.19
Central	19800	0.25
Dumfries & Galloway	19800	0.25
Fife	–	–
Grampian	62000	0.79
Highland	549600	6.97
Lothian	–	–
Orkney	14800	0.19
Tayside	77200	0.98
Shetland	15600	0.19
Strathclyde	137000	1.74
Western Isles	115600	1.47
SCOTLAND	1026300	13.03

Source: Countryside Commission for Scotland (1978, pp.8–9).

Only 35,700 ha of NSA lie south of the Highland Boundary Fault and many parts of Scotland, especially in the east have no NSAs. Nevertheless, Figure 11.1 and Table 11.1 show that they are widely distributed. Twenty-two per cent of Highland Region comprises NSA (Highland Regional Council, 1990) but they also cover much of the Islands. Secondly, whilst local authorities were no longer required to submit *all* planning applications for the secretary of state's consideration, controls had been extended over track and road developments as well as some agriculture and forestry developments.

Natural Heritage Areas and Partnership Initiatives

National Scenic Areas have been in place for fifteen years but in the 1990s, proposals have been forwarded for two additional measures to conserve landscapes of national and international significance – Natural Heritage Areas (NHAs) and Partnership Initiatives for the Cairngorms and Loch Lomond. Neither of these were included in the CCS's recommendations for Scotland's mountain areas. They emerged soon afterwards and could be interpreted as responses to the recommendations, especially those for National Parks.

NHAs were intended to address criticisms levelled at both SSSIs and NSAs: the former being inappropriate for effective nature conservation when applied to large areas such as the Flow Country; the latter being '... widely misunderstood and ineffective' (Scottish Office Environment Department, 1991, summary page). They would be appropriate for large areas and would act as a framework for integrated heritage management. As such, they were seen as having broad-based conservation objectives encompassing nature and landscape protection, land management and recreation. They could act as a substitute for SSSIs and might replace NSAs, but equally they could be used as a framework designation providing a general level of protection over large areas subsuming other conservation designations, with the latter being used to give a higher level of protection to sites of special importance.

Fundamental to the implementation of the NHA would be a Management Statement which would include a long-term strategy and a short-term operational plan, both agreed by the organizations involved with and affected by the NHA. These statements would inevitably vary from area to area, but it was expected that they would be founded on the concepts of sustainable development and environmentally-sensitive land management. It was intended that existing structures would be relied on for the administration of NHAs. However, SNH would likely play a co-ordinating role in their designation and management. But it would not act alone in this. SNH would probably set up a working party for each NHA to assist in its designation and the preparation of the Management Statement. This approach to planning and management points to the emphasis which the Scottish Office felt should be placed on co-operation and partnership in all NHAs (Scottish Office Environment Department, 1991, 1992). It was envisaged that NHAs could be designated in both upland and lowland Scotland. No list of potential NHAs has been defined to date, although the Cairngorms, the Flow Country of Caithness and Sutherland, North-West Sutherland and even parts of Central Scotland have been cited as potential examples.

Whilst there has been consultation on the NHA and the Scottish Office has produced a paper on its implementation which indicated that SNH would prepare criteria for the designation of NHAs (Scottish Office Environment Department, 1992), little progress appears to have been made since then. Certainly, there have been no designations – not even in the Cairngorms despite early suggestions that this was an obvious choice and despite the recommendation from the Cairngorms Working Party (1992a and b) that it should be designated an NHA. Similarly the Loch Lomond and the Trossachs Working Party (1993) supported the concept in principle but did not make a firm recommendation for its adoption. What has unfolded over the last three years since it was first mooted implies that, as with Scottish National Parks, the Natural Heritage Area may simply remain a tantalizing but unattainable concept.

Although the NHA concept has not been taken far, more progress has been made on the Cairngorms and Loch Lomond/Trossachs Partnership Initiatives. These initiatives represent the most recent steps taken to conserve nationally valued landscapes and if successful could act as models for other parts of Scotland. Earlier paragraphs have shown that the Cairngorms and Loch Lomond/Trossachs were included in Scottish-wide proposals for national parks in the 1940s, 1970s and early 1990s. But both areas have also been the subject of more localized moves to protect their natural heritage qualities or designate them as national parks (Grampian Regional Council, 1990; Loch Lomond Planning Group, 1986; Loch Lomond Technical Group, 1973; Cherry, 1975; SDD, 1969). Whilst none of these attempts has been successful, both areas' landscape value is clearly indicated by their designation as NPDAs and NSAs. Moreover, in the areas there are a variety of other conservation designations (see Figures 11.2 and 11.3). Interestingly too, there is overlap in the designations within the Cairngorms – a feature which has understandably caused some confusion in the planning and management of the Cairngorms.

Yet despite the fact that these designations include some of the strongest available measures for protecting Scotland's rural environment, many in the conservation movement are not convinced that these are adequate to protect outstanding but vulnerable landscapes such as the Cairngorms (CCS, 1990). Existing measures have been unable to contain the threat of inappropriate developments, especially intensive recreation and commercial forestry, nor do they promote 'sustainable development' and the regeneration of natural environments. Even with the proliferation of protective designations, there has still been deterioration in semi-natural habitats and many would point to the decline in the quality of the visual environment and wilderness experience. In recognition of these problems in the Cairngorms and Loch Lomond, two working parties were set up in 1991 to prepare recommendations on the most effective ways of managing and administering both areas. The reports of the working parties (Cairngorms Working Party, 1992b; Loch Lomond and the Trossachs Working Party, 1993) and the secretary of state's responses to them (Scottish Office, 1994, 1995) set out the approach to landscape conservation which will be adopted in these two highly valued scenic areas for the rest of the 1990s at least.

For both areas, 'environmental sustainability' will be a guiding principle in their planning and management. In pursuing this, integrated management strategies will be prepared and a number of more specific conservation measures will be introduced. The latter include programmes to regenerate the native (Caledonian) woodland; promotion of a diversity

Figure 11.2 Conservation designations in the Cairngorms (Source: Cairngorms Working Party 1992b, Annex 11.7)

of moorland habitats; encouragement of 'environmentally friendly' farming and extension of the current Environmentally Sensitive Areas (ESAs). The Loch Lomond Working Party recommended the ESA should be extended over the whole area whilst the Cairngorms Working Party recommended ESA coverage for all farmland. Both working parties also came out in favour of extension of the NSA Notification System, although the secretary of state has left the final decision on this to the new bodies who will administer these areas in the future.

It is hardly surprising that heritage conservation will be an important aim in the planning and management of the Cairngorms and Loch Lomond, but it will not be the *only* aim. A second guiding principle will be the social and economic well-being of those who live and work in the areas. In the Cairngorms, this is to be achieved through encouraging tourism, small-scale enterprise and affordable housing – and the area's EU Objective 1 and Objective 5b status was viewed as assisting in this. Significantly, whilst neither the secretary of state nor the working party indicated their support for an extension of skiing in the Cairngorms, there was acceptance of skiing as a land use and support for the existing facilities and their improvement where it did not damage the environment. In Loch Lomond, too, importance was attached to the preparation of visitor management and recreational strategies which would cater for recreational and tourist demands and extend the tourist season. The promotion of economic and social development is seen as a priority for both areas. Moreover, even when pursuing landscape protection and conservation measures, reliance will not be placed solely on legal or statutory powers. Non-statutory mechanisms are likely to be emphasized. Reflecting the importance attached by the Scottish Office throughout the 1990s and specifically incorporated into both working parties' remits, voluntary and co-operative principles are embedded in the approach to conservation in both the Cairngorms and Loch Lomond/Trossachs areas.

Whilst there are similarities in the approaches to planning and management of the two areas, there are also interesting differences. The Cairngorms Working Party recommended that its area should be designated an NHA. In Loch Lomond, there was no such outright support. Paradoxically, the secretary of state did not indicate a firm commitment to a Cairngorms NHA although again this perhaps points to a cooling of his enthusiasm towards the NHA concept. A more significant difference relates to the administration of the two areas. Both working parties and the secretary of state were not in favour of independent park authorities as envisaged by the CCS (CCS, 1990). For the Cairngorms, a partnership board comprising local authority and community representatives, land managers, business, tourism, recreational and environmental interests was favoured. The Loch Lomond/Trossachs Working Party rejected the

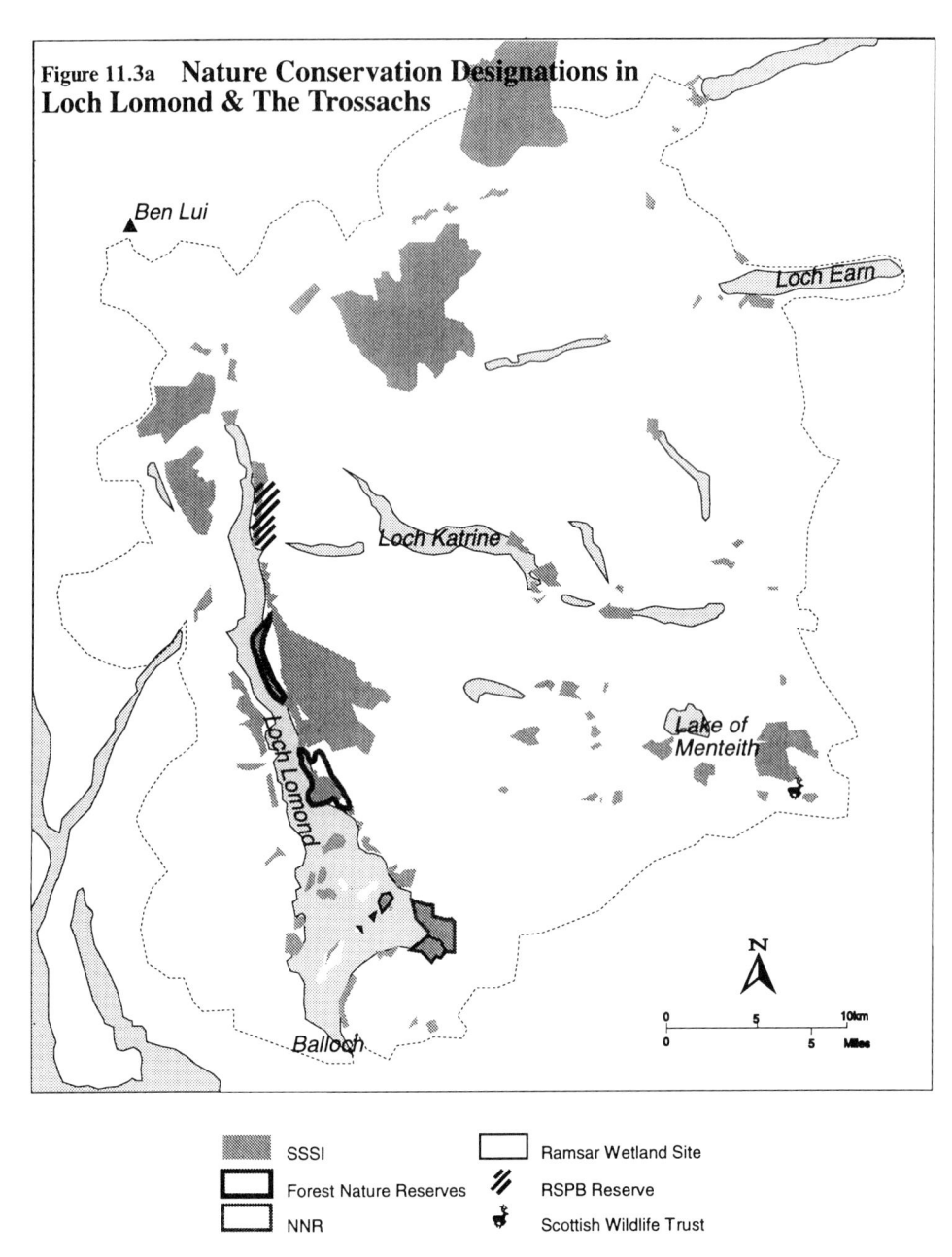

Figure 11.3a Nature conservation designations in Loch Lomond and the Trossachs (Source: Loch Lomond and the Trossachs Working Party 1993)

The Designation of Valued Landscapes in Scotland 215

Figure 11.3b Landscape and Heritage Designations in Loch Lomond & The Trossachs

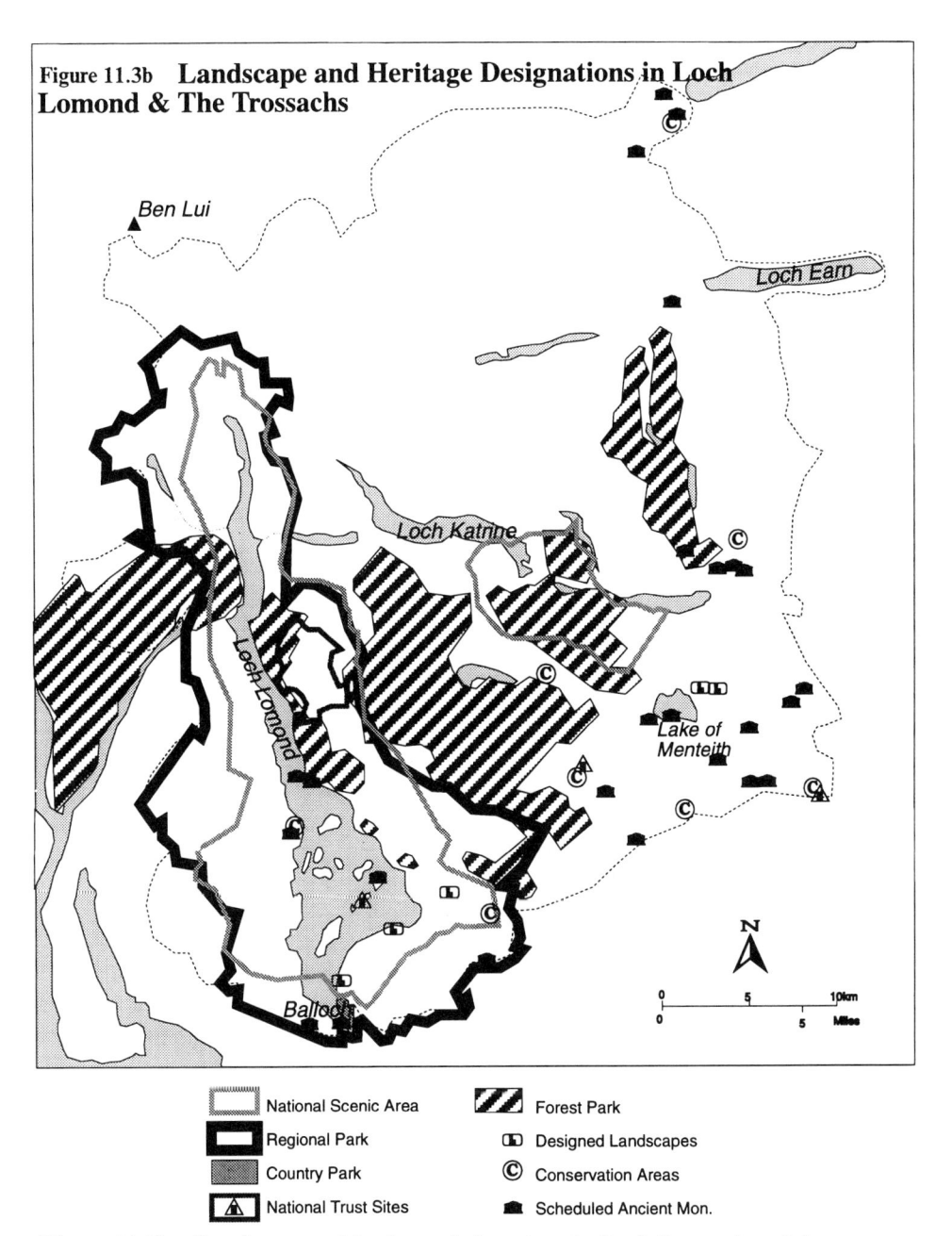

Figure 11.3b Landscape and heritage designations in Loch Lomond and the Trossachs (Source: Loch Lomond and the Trossachs Working Party 1993)

Cairngorms' partnership board model. For a number of years, the Loch Lomond Park Authority, a joint committee of Strathclyde and Central Regional Councils and Dumbarton and Stirling District Councils, has administered Loch Lomond (but not the Trossachs). The working party felt that a joint committee should continue to administer the area, but with strengthened powers so that it had delegated plan-making, development control and countryside functions. The committee would comprise 50 per cent local elected members (compared with the present two-thirds) and 50 per cent from the local community and from local and national farming, land-use, recreation and conservation interests. Three-quarters of its resourcing of about £2.1m p.a. (much higher than the existing park authority) would derive from central government, the remainder from the local authorities. Despite the marked difference from the administrative model to be adopted in the Cairngorms, the secretary of state accepted the joint committee approach advocated for Loch Lomond and the Trossachs and also the balance of the resourcing between central government (SNH) and local authority.

The protection of landscapes of regional and local significance

Areas of great landscape value

In England and Wales, national parks represent the most valued scenic areas, but Hobhouse also envisaged protection for other scenic areas which did not merit national park status. Since the 1950s, this has taken the form of Areas of Outstanding Natural Beauty (AONB) and, more recently, Heritage Coasts. AONBs and Heritage Coasts are designated and partly funded by the Countryside Commission or Countryside Council for Wales although administrative and planning functions are largely in the hands of local authorities (Anderson, 1990; Smart and Anderson, 1990). In Scotland, there are neither AONBs nor Heritage Coasts, but there are designated areas of regional or local landscape significance. Initially, these areas were called Areas of Great Landscape Value (AGLV) although in recent years a variety of terms have been used – Heritage Areas (Borders Regional Council, 1991); Landscape Areas of Regional Importance (Fife Regional Council, 1989); and Areas of Regional Landscape Significance (Grampian Regional Council, 1992). Again in contrast to England and Wales, their designation is by local authorities rather than central government. Several AGLVs were included in the first development plans after the 1947 Act, but from the 1960s they were used more extensively. These 1960s designations have been modified over the last thirty years and some planning authorities, for example, Tayside Regional Council and Angus District Council, have even deleted AGLVs from their development plan policies. Nevertheless, in most regions and districts, they have remained as important elements of policy.

These designations were originally intended to safeguard outstanding scenic areas through inculcating a strong presumption against development. Yet at the same time, proposals for tourist facilities within AGLVs were also to be defined. By the 1970s, the scope had widened beyond tourism into 'conservation strategies' (CCS, 1978, para.4.1) which subsequently have been interpreted by local authorities to include recreation, tourism, landscape enhancement, forestry and even housing development (Cobham Resource Consultants, 1988; Brown, 1995). Therefore, the essence of the AGLV is that it is intended to be a negative (development) control mechanism, complemented by a variety of proactive management or developmental initiatives.

Although included within development plans for several decades, there have been few attempts to estimate the extent of AGLV coverage. Cobham Resource Consultants (1988) estimated that there were 178 regional/local designations (AGLVs or equivalent definitions), covering 1.468m ha or 18.6 per cent of Scotland. More recently, Brown (1995) suggests that the number of AGLVs may have risen to 193. But several of the AGLVs overlap with NSAs. Moreover, since local authorities are responsible for their designation, they vary considerably in their characteristics, landscape quality and purpose as well as their relationship to one another and NSAs. Therefore, there is some validity in the view that there is no 'comprehensive and consistent system of regional landscape designations' (Cobham Resource Consultants, 1988, para.8.45, p.59).

Regional parks

Regional parks are extensive areas of rural land, usually amounting to several thousand hectares. Although landscape protection and recreation are important within regional parks, they are also envisaged to contain a number of different land uses, particularly farming and forestry. Indeed, recreation might be a secondary function, taking place in specific locations such as country parks linked by a path system. Their size and intended purposes clearly differentiate them from country parks which are smaller and primarily recreational. The first regional park was started in the late 1960s by Renfrew County Council. But the idea gained wider recognition when regional parks were included as one tier in the hierarchy of parks which the CCS wanted to establish throughout Scotland (CCS, 1974). The regional park gained a more formal status in the 1981 Countryside (Scotland) Act. This provided the (enabling) mechanism for their establishment and marks a significant departure from English and Welsh legislation which does not include provision for regional parks.

Since the 1981 Act, some local authorities have shown an interest in establishing regional parks (Central Region Council, 1991; Tayside Regional Council, 1988) but only four have been designated: Lomond Hills (Fife); Pentlands Hills (Lothians); Loch Lomond; and Clyde-Muirshiel (Strathclyde). Whilst each is different, a good illustration of the nature and character of a regional park is seen in the Pentlands. Much of its 9000 ha is in long-established agriculture, forestry and even Ministry of Defence uses. Such uses are envisaged to continue. Recreation is also long-established and there are a number of footpaths throughout the hills. Car access and intensive recreational use is focused on a limited number of nodes (for example, country parks). It is clearly not the intention to create a park which is purely recreational. Fundamental to its purpose is the integration of recreation with the other land uses of the park. Given that the basic recreational attraction owes much to the park's scenery, landscape protection and enhancement is an important planning objective. However, landscape policies and programmes are directed towards the agricultural, forestry and Ministry of Defence land and the water surfaces as well as the recreational areas. Once again, the integrative aims of the park come through in its landscape planning and management. To date, regional councils have played a crucial role in administering and funding the regional parks, but local government reorganization has raised concerns about who will take over park responsibilities when the regional councils are disbanded. There are some doubts that the new, smaller unitary authorities with their more limited financial and resource bases will maintain the same commitment to the regional parks. It seems unfortunate that such a significant initiative in multiple and integrated land-use and landscape management should wither because of local government reorganization.

Factors influencing the nature and distinctiveness of Scotland's landscape and its approaches to landscape conservation

The preceding paragraphs have shown that clear differences in approaches to landscape protection and the designation of valued landscapes can be drawn between England and Scotland. Of course, it is relatively easy to set out *what* the differences are, but it is more difficult to explain *why* such differences have emerged. There have been few attempts to do this. Cherry (1975) is an exception, but he only deals with the period between 1940 and 1968. Here a broader and long-term perspective is adopted. Scotland's approach to the designation of its most valued landscapes can be attributed to the interplay of three sets of factors:

1 Physical Factors: Geology, geomorphology and climate have given rise to a scenery which is distinctive, even unique and justifies designation.
2 Historical and Cultural Factors: Landscape is also the product of human impacts and influences. In Scotland, historical and cultural factors have contributed to the visual quality of the countryside and generated a range of landscape features and rural issues which are not encountered (at least to the same degree) in England and which require different policy approaches.
3 Political Factors: These first two sets of factors 'set the scene' but it is the role of and inter-relationships between often divergent political forces over the last fifty years which have ultimately led to the adoption of the particular approaches to landscape protection seen in Scotland today.

The influence of geology on scenery

Perhaps the most obvious physical influence in moulding the Scottish landscape is its geology. Reed (1984) acknowledges that geological structures set the stage for human influences on the landscape. Sissons (1967) stresses the importance of geology on Scotland's landforms because of '. . . the striking correlation in many areas between rock type and scenery' (Sissons, 1967, p.3). Moreover, despite the effect of glaciation on Scotland's geomorphology, he feels that '. . . the main elements of the relief of Scotland were fashioned before the country was overwhelmed by glacier ice . . .' (Sissons, 1967, p.29).

In contrast to a popular view held by many tourists (to an extent perpetuated by the media and tourist brochures), Scotland is not made up of mountains and moors. It is a country of both lowland and upland landscapes. In general terms, Scotland can be subdivided into three physiographic units – the Highlands, Central (Belt) Lowlands and Southern Uplands. Devonian and Carboniferous sedimentary rocks from the Clyde Estuary to the North Sea underlie the extensive Central Lowlands. These include the best of Scotland's farming areas and also coal/shale mining measures from Ayrshire to the Lothians and South Fife. Although the Central Belt represents Scotland's principal lowland region it is not the only one. Lowland landscapes, underlain by Devonian Old Red Sandstone, are found again in the Moray Firth, North-East Caithness and Orkney (all in the 'Highlands'), whilst New Red Sandstones and Carboniferous rocks lie under Solway Firth Lowlands and Tweed Basin in the south of Scotland. Lowland landscapes cover about a third of Scotland's land area. They contain the homes and work places for the majority of Scotland's population. They provide most of Scottish farming's output. Much of the lowland countryside is not seen as meriting landscape designation, although many areas have their own beauty and it is not surprising that writers, poets and artists such as Grassic Gibbon, Burns, Mackintosh Patrick and Morrison have all captured and conveyed the visual quality of rural lowland areas. Nevertheless, it is Scotland's uplands which have been accorded greater scenic significance. As with the lowland landscapes, hills are distributed widely throughout Scotland. Even in the Central Lowlands, hills of considerable local scenic significance punctuate the landscape. The Sidlaws (maximum height, 376 m); the Ochils (720 m); Kilpatricks (400 m); Campsies (586 m) and Pentlands are the largest of these remnants of volcanic activity which stand out within the lower-lying Straths, Howes and Carselands. They are used mainly for hill farming and forestry, but because the majority of Scotland's urban population live within sight of at least one of these hill ranges, they are also important for informal recreation. Parts of the Ochils and the Pentlands are regional parks. Moreover, their scenic importance is reflected in the AGLV designation attached to all of them.

Of course, the hills within the Central Lowlands are limited in area compared to the Southern Uplands and the Highlands. These hill and mountain ranges contain Britain's highest peaks; its most extensive upland and moorland landscapes and some of its most spectacular mountain scenery. The underlying solid geology – tertiary volcanic and seismic activity and the more recent Quaternary (Pleistocene) ice ages – have all contributed to the character of the Highlands and the Southern Uplands. The geological structures and processes which have been so influential in creating these two physiographic regions are not paralleled in England. Nor is the legacy they have left on the landscape seen in many places in England – the Lake District being perhaps the most notable exception. The Southern Uplands and the Highlands are not uniform in their relief and geology. The Southern Uplands are derived from folded Ordovician and Silurian sediments punctuated by igneous rocks. The Highlands comprise a series of complex igneous and metamorphic rocks of different ages but generally older and harder than the sedimentaries underlying the lowlands of both Scotland and England. Millman (1975) and Sissons (1967) draw a distinction between the Highlands which lie east and west of the Great Glen. Granites dominate the geological map (and also the landscape) of the central eastern Highlands. Devonian granite intrusions have broken through their metamorphic 'cap' to culminate in the high ground around areas such as Etive (much of which is included in the Ben Nevis/Glen Coe NPDA and in one of the CCS's proposed national parks); North Arran,

Lochnagar and Mount Keen (all designated as NSAs); and Benachie (an area of Regional Landscape Significance) in Aberdeenshire. Granites and lavas also form the dome mass of Ben Nevis, the highest peak in Britain. The largest Highland granitic intrusion has created the Cairngorms massif – the most extensive, contiguous mountain area over 600 m in Britain.

Granitic intrusions are not confined to the central Highlands. Skye's Red Cuillins (part of the Cuillins NSA) are composed of granite. In Dumfries and Galloway, granites stand above the surrounding (sedimentary) rocks at Criffell (in the Nith Estuary NSA), Cairnsmore of Fleet and Cairnsmore of Carsphairn. In the Borders, the Cheviots are composed of granites and these hills, together with other outcrops of volcanic rocks – for example Eildon, Rubers Law and Dunion Hill – have become attractive touring countryside, although only Eildon and Leaderfoot to the west are NSAs. Paradoxically, granitic intrusions sometimes form extensive lowlands or basins as in Rannoch Moor (part of Ben Nevis/Glen Coe NPDA and NSA) and much of Aberdeenshire and Banffshire. In the Southern Uplands, Loch Doon is in a granite basin surrounded by the metamorphic sedimentary rock mountains of Merrick and Kells Range. Elsewhere in the Highlands, non-granitic rocks have also contributed to the formation of mountains. Metamorphic grits at the junction of the Highlands and Central Lowlands are seen in the peaks of Ben Lomond, Ben Ledi (both in Loch Lomond and Trossachs NPDA, NSA and one of CCS's proposed national parks) and Perthshire's Ben Vorlich, as well as in some of the narrow valleys which extend into the Highlands from the Lowlands (including the River Earn NSA between St Fillans and Comrie and the River Tay NSA at Dunkeld). Hard quartzites have similarly proved resistant to erosion and contribute to Schiehallion (in one of Ramsay's 'Reserve Areas' and the Loch Rannoch/Glen Lyon NSA); the ridge at Killiecrankie and some of the hills in Moray and Banffshire – for example, Ben Aigan (an area of Regional Landscape Significance) near Rothes. Quartzites form the tops of Sgurr a Mhaim, Am Bodach and Binneain Mor (all within the CCS's proposed national park and the NPDA and NSA between Glens Nevis and Coe). Jura, much of which is NSA, is almost wholly composed of quartzite.

The North-West Highlands have some of the oldest rocks in Britain and the erosion to which they have been subjected has created landscapes which are different from those in the Central and Eastern Highlands – and some would say of even greater scenic beauty. Erosional processes over the millennia have worn down the Lewisian Gneiss into a relatively flat hummocky landscape. But overlying the gneiss are remnants of Torridonian sandstone, in places associated with Cambrian quartzite, left as spectacular inselberg-like mountains such as Suilven, Stac Pollaidh, Cul Mor and Quinag. Foinaven and Arkle, composed of Cambrian grits and quartzites and metamorphosed Moine quartzose schistose flags, form the massive inland backdrop to the hummocky Lewisian gneiss around Laxford Loch. To the south, in Coigach and Wester Ross, more massive Torridonian sandstone has left pronounced mountains at Ben More, Coigach, An Teallach, Ben Slioch, Applecross, Torridon and the Coulin Forest. Such rock formations from North-West Sutherland to Wester Ross have helped create an attractive almost unique landscape, and it is not surprising that both Ramsay and the CCS put forward this area for national park status, nor that it contains several large NSAs – NW Sutherland, Assynt-Coigach and Wester Ross (see Figure 11.1).

The basic rock type has not been the only geological influence in the formation of Scotland's mountains. Substantial seismic movement and Pleistocene Ice Age activity have also left their mark. In the late Silurian/early Devonian era, the Caledonian orogeny led to or accentuated the characteristic north-east to south-west alignment in Scotland's physiography. Other more recent mountain-forming phases have reinforced the structural grain and faulting. The resultant fractures and thrust planes prevalent throughout Scotland have contributed to some prominent landscape features seen today. The best-known faults are the Great Glen and Highland Boundary Faults. Other major NE–SW fault-lines in the Highlands are marked by the western side of Loch Tay (part of Glen Lyon NSA and one of Ramsay's Reserve Areas) through Glen Garry (and Loch Tummel NSA) and into Glen Tilt (in one of the CCS's proposed national parks and part of the Cairngorms Partnership area); Loch Long, Loch Fyne, Upper Loch Etive (part of the Ben Nevis/Glen Coe NSA and proposed National Park); Loch Shiel (an NSA and one of Ramsay's Reserve Areas); Loch Carron; the Kyle of Tongue (an NSA); Loch Eriboll; Glen Affric (an NSA and NPDA); and Loch Laggan.

East to west faults mark out Glen Lyon (an NSA); Rannochside (an NSA); Lower Loch Etive (part of Ben Nevis/Glen Coe NPDA); Loch Leven (part of the Ben Nevis/Glen Coe NPDA and NSA and one of the CCS's proposed national parks); Loch Sunart (part of which was in Ramsay's Moidart/Knoydart Reserve Area); inner Loch Hourn and Loch Nevis (both in Ramsay's Reserve Area and Knoydart NSA); Loch Torridon and Glen Torridon (part of Wester Ross NPDA, NSA and in the CCS's proposed National Park). Finally north-west to south-east fault-lines define the orientation of Loch Ewe and Loch Maree (both in Wester Ross NSA, NPDA and proposed National Park); Little Loch Broom (in Wester Ross NPDA); Loch Broom and Loch Laxford (in North West Sutherland NSA). In Quaternary Pleistocene times, glacial activity accentuated many of the features established in earlier geological periods. Moreover, the effects of glaciers on the Scottish landscape were much more pronounced than in England, a substantial proportion of which was periglacial.

A whole range of classic glacial features are in evidence throughout Scotland including glacial troughs, for example at Glen Callater, Glen Clova, Loch Muick (all in the NSAs and AGLVs around Lochnagar) and the Tulla, Moffat Water and the Upper Dee in the Southern Uplands; water-filled rock basins, for example at the Lake of Montieth in the Central Lowlands, Lochs Ness, Morar (in one of Ramsay's Reserve Areas), Lomond (NPDA and NSA), Maree (in Wester Ross NPDA and NSA), Shiel (NSA), Sunart, Etive, Linnhe, Duich (part of Kintail NSA) and Hourn (in Knoydart NSA); corries – found in many locations in the Southern Uplands and the Central Highlands but more numerous in the Western Highlands (Linton, 1959); and meltwater channels, for example between Gifford and St Abb's along the base of Lammermuirs, the Slochd, Burn O' Vat, Killiecrankie (part of Tummel NSA) and the Little Glen between Glens Lui and Quoich in the Cairngorms. All of Scotland displays the effects of glacial activity but there are regional variations due to Pleistocene climatic variations. In the east, the climate was colder but drier; whilst in the west, precipitation was higher and ice activity and rock shattering were more pronounced. As a consequence, the glacial activity in the central and east uplands has produced a more rounded effect whereas in the west, even in the western Southern Uplands, for example around Loch Doon, the ice caused more serrated edges and deeper valleys, but the outcome is more spectacular in scenic terms.

Climatic influences on the landscape

Climate has also exerted a strong influence on Scotland's scenery. Scotland has a climate which is wetter and cooler than the rest of the United Kingdom. It has more snow and snow lies longer. In those areas above 300 m, winter can be extremely harsh. The growing season in Scotland is shorter. Climate (and geology) have contributed to create extensive areas of poor soils. Seventy-two per cent of Scotland's rural land is classed as Grade 5, 6 or 7 and has limited capability for agriculture. A sizeable area of land is even of limited capability for forestry. The east coast lowlands have some of the highest quality agricultural land in the United Kingdom, but much of Scotland has 'Less Favoured Area' status under EU Agricultural Policy. Compared with England, Scottish rural land use displays higher levels of forestry; pastoral farming, especially hillstock-rearing; unimproved land and heather moor, and 'specialized recreational' uses in grouse moor and deer forest.

The peripheral nature of agriculture and indeed the virtual non-productive value of some of the harshest upland environments have contributed to the emergence of some distinctive natural and semi-natural environments. Several upland areas – for example, the Cairngorms,

Caenlochan (in the Deeside and Lochnagar NSA); Beinn Eighe (Wester Ross NSA), Inverpolly and Inchnadamph (NW Sutherland NSA) – support valued arctic, sub-arctic, alpine or specialized mountain flora. Extensive upland peat bogs are found throughout the Highlands but SNH have also drawn attention to the importance of lowland bogs. Indeed, it stresses that Scotland holds two-thirds of Britain's bogland resources (SNH, 1995). The existence of such habitats explains why so much of Scotland has nature conservation designations but they also contribute to the distinctive landscapes especially in the Cairngorms, the 'Flow Country', Wester Ross, NW Sutherland and many of the Islands.

The 'marginality' of the physical environment has also influenced the demographic map of Scotland. Rural Scotland contains some of the most sparsely populated areas in the United Kingdom. Moreover relief, physiography and climate when combined with population density and distance from the main centres of population have led to communication and accessibility problems. At the same time though, especially in the North-West, some of the Islands, Cairngorms, Glen Coe and Rannoch, it is easy to experience remoteness, even solitude. Indeed many feel that such areas justify the label of the last remaining wilderness in the United Kingdom or even Western Europe.

The special character of the physical environment means that Scottish rural planners are confronted, if not by different issues and problems, then at least by different priorities, compared to their English counterparts. These require different approaches to landscape conservation. The most obvious problem may seem how best to preserve the experience of remoteness and wilderness of some of the upland landscapes. Yet the marginality which is a positive aspect of Scotland's rural environment for many tourists and conservationists, is viewed by others as the cause of social and economic problems. Over the years local communities, local authorities and organizations – such as the HIDB, Highlands and Islands Enterprise, the Crofters Commission and the Cairngorms Partnership in the Highlands and Islands and the Development Commission and SICRAS in the Borders (Hodge and Whitby, 1983) – have placed considerable emphasis on improving accessibility and promoting housing development and economic development. Scottish planners, particularly in the most peripheral areas, have sought to reach a compromise between development and protection of the countryside. Such a compromise has clear implications for the nature of landscape protection and conservation adopted. It is interesting that the Cairngorms Partnership was set up not just to protect the Cairngorms but also to achieve an effective and lasting compromise between the objectives of the different and often opposing interests in the mountains.

Historical and cultural influences on the landscape

It is, of course, insufficient to limit an explanation of the influences which have moulded the Scottish landscape to physical factors. Historic and cultural influences have contributed in no small way to the emergence of a landscape which is quite distinct from that south of the Border. Ferguson (1968), Hunter (1976, 1991), Millman (1975), Parry and Slater (1980) and Smout (1969) have provided a detailed view of the historical development of rural society and landscape in Scotland, and when read alongside the works of Derby (1973), Hoskins (1970), Mingay (1986), Reed (1984, 1987) and others which explore similar themes in England, put into perspective the extent to which the social and cultural development of rural Scotland took a different direction from that of England – with important consequences for the landscape seen today. Almost inevitably, it is only possible here to highlight a few of these differences which have special significance for the contemporary rural landscape and perhaps more significantly for the policy issues they raise for planners today.

It is inappropriate to say that Scotland was impervious to the diffusion of ideas or that development imperatives especially capitalist agriculture and industrialization bypassed Scotland. Nevertheless, as Millman (1975) and Reed (1987) point out, Scotland's peripherality in relation to the core of European ideas meant that: the country hung on longer to old ideas; was slower to adapt; and experienced the impact of development later. 'Regional character' was retained or lost more slowly, especially in the more isolated Highlands or Galloway and, to a lesser extent, Buchan. Celtic culture and traditions, for example in terms of social relationships and agricultural practices, were adhered to much longer in the Highlands than in the rest of the United Kingdom. Even in the modern era, remnants of communal Celtic agricultural practices were continued in the North-West Highlands and Islands (Millman, 1975). When change came too, the outcome was often different from the rest of the United Kingdom.

Such differences were obviously most marked in the historic past but their legacy can be seen in the landscape today. Thus the centuries-old colonization of the land which led to extensive clearing of the natural woodland, took place in England and the Scottish Lowlands between 800 and 1600 but started later in the Highlands because of their remoteness and difficulties of access. Indeed, despite the extensive Highland deforestation over the eighteenth century (for ironworking and sheep rearing) and nineteenth century (for sheep and deer), in areas such as Strathfarrar and Glenaffric (included in Ramsay's National Park proposals and currently two NSAs) as well as Strathspey, there are still remnants of the indigenous mixed woodlands of the once extensive Caledonian Forest.

Another difference can be seen in the nature and pattern of rural settlement. The village, so characteristic in rural England, is less a feature of Scottish rural settlement – except in the south-east and parts of east Stirlingshire. A nucleated form of settlement had existed in Scotland for centuries but it was different from the village in origin; in function and in the social and political relationships displayed within it. Burghs were not agricultural but were created for trade, defence and political purposes (Millman, 1975). Outside the burgh, the main type of settlement in Scotland before the seventeenth century was the fermtoun (in the lowlands) or clachan (Highlands/Celtic areas) but again they were not the same as the English village in terms of their organization, tenure and property rights. During the Agricultural Revolution in the lowlands, partly because the limited property rights held by most of the agricultural population facilitated the adoption of new agricultural ideas, the fermtouns were swept away from the landscape to be replaced by a more dispersed settlement (Millman, 1975). New nucleated settlements emerged, for example at Letham, Douglastown and Friockheim in Angus; Longman in Banffshire and Cuminestown in Aberdeenshire, but more dominant in the lowland landscape were the farmhouse and farmworker's cottage. The Agricultural Revolution has, if anything, accentuated the difference in settlement structure and pattern between England and Scotland. This difference has lasted to the present. Scotland still has a more pronounced dispersed rural settlement.

This dominance of dispersed settlement has given rise to different issues for planning in Scotland, and in turn these have required approaches which can be different from these in English rural planning. It is not entirely appropriate to say as many planners since Sharp (1946) have said, that the village is the natural and historic form of settlement and hence that rural settlement policy should channel all housing in the countryside into settlements. This may be economically or financially justifiable but in Scotland, culturally and historically, dispersed settlement is more characteristic of the countryside. This has been used by a number of Scottish local authorities to justify the adoption of a 'flexible' approach to demand for housing in the countryside (Moir *et al.*, 1995). Their policy allows individual houses to be built in the open countryside, even in some valued scenic areas, raising the possibility of significant conflict not only with 'protectionist' groups but also with central government policy on housing in the countryside.

The Agricultural Revolution not only had an impact on the settlement pattern, but also led to the establishment of the enclosed field pattern of the lowland farming landscape. In England, the Agricultural Revolution saw the old open field system being replaced by enclosures – although Hoskins (1970) points out that enclosure had been taking place for several centuries before the Revolution. In Scotland too, the Agricultural Revolution replaced the old field patterns ('infield/outfield' and 'runrig') with enclosures, but Millman (1975) feels that because change was later in the Scottish lowlands, the fields are larger and hence more adaptable to modern farming practices. The lowland Scottish enclosed landscape, especially in the east, has been more stable and less susceptible to change in the post-war period than England. However, recent evidence raises questions about the validity of Millman's views. Tudor *et al.* (1994) have shown that there has been a 37 per cent reduction in hedgerows and a 23 per cent reduction in lowland raised bog throughout Scotland between the 1940s and 1970s alone. The Scottish lowland enclosure landscape has clearly undergone considerable change since the 1940s.

The Agricultural Revolution also had a great influence on form and appearance of the Highland landscape seen today, although the outcome of the agricultural change was quite different from that in the lowlands (Prebble, 1969; Hunter, 1976). Before the eighteenth century, Highland land-use and settlement patterns were based on Celtic traditions and relationships which prevailed in the clan system. After the 1745 Rebellion, the collapse of the clan system, the consequent reorientation in the allegiances of the Highland's élite, the establishment of new social and power relationships and the introduction of new land-use practices all contributed to the emergence of a new rural landscape.

During the eighteenth and nineteenth centuries, in the Highlands, a specialized land-use system was established – sheep pastures, grouse moors and deer forests, all of which cleared much of the indigenous woodland (Millman, 1975). But this land-use revolution, accompanied by the 'Clearances' of the population to the coast (and beyond), left a landscape of extensive sparsely populated, even unpopulated, glens and hillsides – although often houses were left standing so that the remnants of the clachans can still be seen today, for example in Strathnaver and Kildonan. The remoteness and wilderness character of the Highlands referred to earlier is as much to do with social, cultural and political influences as it has to do with the physical environment. Moreover, the emotions and controversy which are stirred even today by the history of the Highlands, play an important part in explaining the attraction of this unique landscape.

The Agricultural Revolution in the Highlands also led to the birth of crofting – a land-use and land tenure system which is confined to the Highlands (Hunter, 1976). Despite criticisms during the 1950s and 1960s that it was a 'dinosaur' doomed to extinction, crofting has proved remarkably resilient and now seems to be undergoing some revitalization (Hunter, 1991). Indeed, in the 1990s it has been held up as a model of 'sustainable land-use'! Crofting is not the dominant source of employment nor the major land-use in the Highlands – although it accounts for 25 per cent of agricultural area and 20 per cent of agricultural output of the seven 'Crofting Counties' (Crofters Commission, 1991). The crofting community does not make up the majority of the Highland population, although crofting households represent about a third of households in landward areas. Nevertheless, its impact on the Highland landscape (and society and economy) can be significant, especially in its core localities in the Islands, North-West Sutherland and West Caithness. The 17,670 crofts in 1990 covered 773,000 ha, 500,000 of which were given over to common grazings. They are essentially based on agriculture (hill sheep and cattle) and/or fishing but employment and land use associated with crofting can be diverse and includes forestry, tourism and craft industries. Moreover, the dispersed nature of crofting communities and 'townships' creates a distinctive visual impact in the Highland scene – a classic example being Trottenish NSA, established in part because of the crofting settlement.

The role of the Scottish Office and its agencies in landscape protection

Whilst history and geography can be used to explain the appearance of Scotland's landscape, the value attached to its scenery and even the rationale for a distinctive approach to landscape protection, explanations for the decisions to adopt such a distinctive approach must be sought elsewhere. Of fundamental importance here has been the relationship between central and local government in rural planning in Scotland and the role played by central government in the planning and management of rural areas.

The influence of central government in urban and regional planning in Scotland is fairly well established (Keating and Boyle, 1986; Carter, 1981; Hood, 1991; Lloyd, 1994; Rowan-Robinson and Lloyd, 1991), but its importance also extends into rural planning – coastal planning and management; agricultural land (SDD, 1974, 1975, 1977, 1981, 1987b and c) – and landscape protection and conservation. The Scottish Office and its agencies, especially the CCS and SNH, have played a pivotal role in the rise and fall of attempts to create Scottish national parks. They have also been active in promoting particular initiatives and controls, exemplified by NPDAs, regional parks, NSAs and even the design of housing in the countryside, aimed and safeguarding Scotland's landscape resources of national, regional and local significance.

The intervention of the Scottish Office in landscape protection extends over the last fifty years. The delay in implementing Ramsay's proposals and putting into place the necessary legislation for Scottish national parks is attributed by Cherry (1975) to the Scottish secretary of state who, in 1948, '. . . did not regard the need for legislation "as one of pressing urgency"'

(Cherry, 1975, p.142) and who eventually (in February 1950) decided 'to propose no [National Park] Bill at [that] time' (Cherry, 1975, p.144). Nevertheless, despite its lukewarm response, the secretary of state did take an unusual, even unique step to protect Scotland's most valued landscapes by using Article 5 of the Town and Country Planning General Development (Scotland) Order 1948 to designate Ramsay's five areas as NPDAs. This required local authorities with planning responsibilities for the NPDAs to furnish the Scottish Office with details of all planning proposals classed as development under the town and country planning legislation.

More recently, it was the Scottish Office who introduced and promoted the concept of Natural Heritage Areas (NHA). First hints that they were considering NHAs were given in the White Paper on Scottish Natural Heritage (SDD, 1990, p.14) but elaboration of the idea came in a 1991 Consultation Paper specifically devoted to the NHA (Scottish Office Environment Department, 1991). It was interesting (and perhaps unfortunate) that the NHA was introduced at the same time as the CCS submitted its proposals for national parks. It is easy therefore to interpret the NHA as an indication of the Scottish Office's lack of enthusiasm for national parks and that the NHA was put forward as an alternative to them. The Scottish Office did stress that NHAs were not intended as a substitute for the CCS's proposals on national parks, but they would be different in function. National parks were seen as measures for recreation and landscape conservation in upland areas. NHAs on the other hand were 'partly' to act as an alternative for nature conservation and more specifically the designation of large areas for SSSI designation. Nevertheless, it was indicated that NHAs would also be '. . . appropriate over a wide range of situations in *upland* [my emphasis] and lowland Scotland' (Scottish Office Environment Department, 1991, para.3) and as a designation which would encompass nature conservation, landscape conservation, land management, access and recreation objectives. As indicated earlier, despite the provision made in the Natural Heritage (Scotland) Act 1991 the designation of the first NHA is still awaited at the start of 1996. The NHA represents one response by the Scottish Office to the most recent debate on national parks and the protection of mountain areas in Scotland. But it has also initiated action taken in relation to two of the areas which the CCS proposed should be national parks: The Cairngorms and Loch Lomond/Trossachs.

Whilst the Scottish Office did not confer national park status on these two areas, nevertheless it did promote the partnership initiatives in the Cairngorms and Loch Lomond/Trossachs as alternatives to national parks (Secretary of State for Scotland, 1991). Moreover, the voluntary and co-operative principles which were built into both working parties' remits, which determined the organizational structure taken by the new

Cairngorms Partnership and the Loch Lomond/Trossachs Joint Committee and which will provide the driving force in their operation, are a direct reflection of the ethos on rural policy held by the Scottish Office throughout the 1990s (Scottish Office, 1992, 1995b).

The Scottish Office has not always played such a direct role in protecting the landscape. At times it has acted as a catalyst for local authority action. The encouragement given by the SDD to local authorities to identify and designate AGLVs is an early example of this (SDD, 1962). In this it was stressed that 'local authorities have a positive duty . . . to consider what must be done . . . to safeguard [their] most outstanding beauty spots' (SDD, 1962, para.2). To fulfil this 'duty', 'Each authority should . . . reach a preliminary view on the particular areas which ought . . . to be delineated . . . as areas of great landscape value' (SDD 1962, para.5). AGLVs appeared in development plans, for example Fife and Aberdeenshire, before the 1962 circular with county planning authorities taking up advice contained in 1949 Technical Broadsheets (DHS, 1949, 1961) but a proliferation of AGLVs appeared after the 1962 circular. Thus, even by January 1963, all thirty counties, and twenty-three out of twenty-six burghs, had responded to the circular (Cherry, 1975).

Of course, the role played by central government in the planning and management of Scotland's valued landscapes is not just attributable to the Scottish Office but also its agencies. The original ideas for both NSAs and regional parks emanate from the CCS (CCS, 1974). Shortly after its establishment, the Commission embarked on a review of the (then existing) arrangements for landscape conservation and outdoor recreation provision. Drawing upon an approach developed by the Outdoor Recreation Resources Review Commission in the United States, the Commission put forward the idea of establishing a four-tier hierarchy or system of parks throughout Scotland (CCS, 1974): the first two tiers or elements of the system, urban and country parks, were already established, but the other two – special parks and regional parks – were new and innovative measures for landscape conservation and recreation provision.

The CCS submitted their proposals for a park system to the secretary of state and although he rejected the need for special parks – partly, as will be shown later because of opposition from some local authorities – he acknowledged that landscapes of national importance should be identified and offered protection. After an extensive survey of Scotland, CCS submitted their recommendation that forty areas, predominantly in the Highlands and Islands (see Figure 11.1) should be accorded special protection and management as National Scenic Areas (NSAs). The secretary of state accepted these proposals and, using two circulars, put in place, special measures to control development (SDD, 1980, 1987a). However the positive management measures which were integral to the

CCS's original recommendations were never adequately implemented (Cobham Resource Consultants, 1988). The secretary of state also accepted the second innovative element envisaged in the CCS's park system, the regional parks, and in the 1981 Countryside (Scotland) Act, legislation was put in place to establish regional parks. In contrast to NSAs, regional parks are not identified by the CCS. The Act was an enabling one and the onus for the identification of regional parks (and indeed to a large extent their administration, planning and management) was left to local authorities. There is little doubt that the Countryside Commission for Scotland has been an important influence on the form taken by landscape conservation in Scotland, although of course not all of their proposals have been implemented. Most notably, despite the support they have given to national parks in 1974 and 1990, the CCS were unsuccessful in seeing them established in Scotland.

The role of local authorities in landscape designations in Scotland

Of course, the Scottish Office and its agencies do not just form their views and determine policy on landscape conservation in isolation. Such views and policy are the products of influences emanating from a diverse range of individuals and organizations operating inside and outside central government. Particularly important here and representing the final factor in shaping the distinctive approach to the planning and management of Scotland's valued scenic areas has been the political influence exerted by Scottish rural local authorities who have had a bearing on the failure of the various attempts to introduce national parks in Scotland.

In the 1940s, despite the upsurge of opinion favouring national parks in England and the support given them in some quarters in Scotland, there was also considerable opposition to national parks, particularly from local authorities. The reasons behind this local authority opposition were complex but can be related to the political and power relationships and the socio-economic structure prevailing at that time in rural Scotland and especially in the Highlands. Firstly, local authorities were concerned that the non-local representation on the proposed national park administration would lead to a loss of local autonomy and a reduction in their power (Cherry, 1975; Sheail, 1975). Secondly, the large landowners – a powerful influence in Scottish countryside planning (Shucksmith and Lloyd, 1983) and also dominant in the tenure structure and land management of the Highlands (especially before the 1950s and the break-up of some of the large estates) – were opposed to national parks because of Ramsay's proposal that land in national parks should be in public ownership (Ferguson, 1988). It is difficult to show that local authorities were directly influenced by landowners but it would be surprising if they did not reflect the views of such an important power group within their constituencies. Thirdly, the issue of securing recreational access, so significant in the argument supporting English national parks, was of less significance in Scotland. Because of the inaccessibility of much of the upland area from centres of population, the lower numbers seeking access to the hills and the less restrictive trespass laws, access to the Scottish hills did not generate the conflicts which emerged in England during the 1930s. Fourthly, protection of the landscape from development, again central to the case for the English national parks, was also less important in Scotland. It has to be remembered that Scotland's remote rural areas, and in particular the Highlands, had experienced decades of out-migration and depopulation which had left an imbalanced population structure and a fragile social and community fabric. By the 1940s, therefore, economic rehabilitation was a priority. The issue facing Scottish rural local authorities was not how to protect the countryside from development but how to promote development in the countryside. The prospect of establishing national parks raised fears amongst local authorities and other representatives of remote rural communities that development opportunities would be stifled and efforts to attract jobs into the Scottish countryside would be overwhelmed. Finally, the long-term demographic decline suffered by the Highlands meant that local authorities had a very limited population base from which to generate finance for service provision. Inevitably, they were concerned about the financial burdens likely to be imposed by national parks (Cherry, 1975; Sheail, 1975). Given the different context within which the debate on Scottish national parks was taking place, it is hardly surprising that what Cherry (1975) refers to simply as the 'strong vested interests' against national parks was enough to steer the secretary of state away from implementing Ramsay's proposals.

Again in the 1970s, Highland Regional Council indicated it was against the creation of Special Parks because it was felt they would centralize decision-making; diminish the role of local authorities and, by adding another tier of government, would increase bureaucracy and delays in decision-making (Highland Regional Council, 1975, 1976). The strength of its opposition led the regional council to include policies opposing the administration and powers associated with the Special Parks within its first structure plan (Highland Regional Council, 1979, 1985). Even when the CCS moved away from the idea of Special Parks, the introduction of NSAs did not go unchallenged by local authorities in the north of Scotland. Indeed development control procedures associated with NSAs were not applicable to the Highland Regional and Western Isles Councils until a year after the rest of Scotland (SDD, 1980) because of the continued challenge to them by these two councils.

Highland Regional Council once again opposed the CCS proposals for national parks in 1990 (Highland Regional Council, 1990). But the regional council was not the only opponent to these proposals. As in the 1940s, support for national parks in Scotland was by no means universal. From the public consultation undertaken on the CCS's recommendations for Scotland's mountain areas, the vast majority of the 230 responses received focused on the national park proposals (CCS, 1991a and b). One hundred and twelve respondents favoured 'special arrangements in designated areas' (which the CCS interpreted as indicating support for national parks). Not unexpectedly, these supporters included the International Union for the Conservation of Nature and Natural Resources, the Countryside Commission for England and Wales, the Loch Lomond Park Authority, the Council for National Parks, the Commission on National Parks and Protected Areas, the Ramblers Association, the British Mountaineering Council and the Mountaineering Council for Scotland. Support however also came from the SDA, NFU (Scotland), the Scottish Landowners' Federation, the Scottish Society of Directors of Planning, COSLA and some local authorities (Stirling and Dumbarton District Councils, Borders, Central, Fife, Strathclyde, Dumfries and Galloway Regional Councils). Despite this, seventy-five respondents were not in favour of the 'special arrangements in designated areas'. These included several Highland authorities (Highland and Tayside Regional Councils; Ross and Cromarty, Badenoch and Strathspey, Kincardine and Deeside and Gordon District Councils) as well as organizations with land-use and development interests in the Highlands, for example, the HIDB, the Scottish Tourist Board, the Scottish Crofters Union, the Red Deer Commission and the John Muir Trust.

The Commission accepted that the responses to its national park proposals were 'mixed' (CCS, 1991b). However, they interpreted the absence of a widespread acceptance of its proposals to its own failure '. . . to communicate sufficiently well the benefits that would accrue for the whole community . . .' (CCS, 1991a, p.38). The secretary of state's interpretation was different. He felt that the public consultation exercise revealed a lack of commitment to national parks in Scotland. Indeed there was 'little interest' in a Ben Nevis/Glen Coe National Park and 'strong opposition' from Wester Ross (Secretary of State for Scotland, 1991). As a consequence, this somewhat patchy support for national parks was used by the secretary of state to justify his decision not to proceed with the CCS's proposals. This position was reinforced more recently with his rejection of a proposal from a minority in the Cairngorms Working Party for a separate Cairngorms Park Authority in favour of a partnership board. The reasons given for rejecting such an authority were that it would be ineffective in tackling land-use issues beyond those able to be dealt with by planning legislation, and that furthermore it did not command widespread local support. Therefore, whilst the Scottish Office, as mentioned in an earlier paragraph, was hardly unequivocal in its support for the CCS's national parks proposals, their demise is probably as much to do with the lack of support from outwith the Scottish Office as within it.

This recurring concern expressed by local authorities (and indeed a variety of other interest groups) about national parks in Scotland, provides an interesting insight into the differing strength of opinion on the importance of landscape protection north and south of the Border. Policy outcomes in rural planning represent a balance or compromise between development and protection – a balance which can vary in time and space (Blowers, 1987). In parts of the United Kingdom, particularly over much of the Midlands, south and east of England, protectionist principles assume great importance, even dominance (Anon., 1995; ARUP Economics and Planning, 1993; Newby, 1980; Newby et al., 1978) and in the run-up to the publication of the 1995 rural white paper for England, a distinct polarization of views clearly emerged (Kirkby, 1995; Traill-Thompson, 1995). However, in Scotland the juxtaposition of some of the most severe of rural Britain's socio-economic problems alongside some of its most spectacular scenery has meant that the balance to be achieved between developmental and protectionist objectives and consequently the nature and direction of landscape conservation policy is not the same as it is in southern Britain.

There is, of course, a danger in taking this view on the relative importance of landscape protection too far. After some of the controversies associated with development proposals in the upland areas of Scotland during the 1980s, it is not suggested that development pressures are not seen as a threat to Scotland's landscapes. Nevertheless, concerns about the consequences of national park designations have meant that they have not commanded the widespread support, particularly at the local level, required to translate the idea into reality.

Scotland's approach to the designation of valued landscapes: an assessment

Despite the different direction chosen in Scotland towards the protection of its most valued landscapes, it is difficult to say whether or not this has produced better results than the approach adopted in England. The evaluation of its landscape designations has been limited. The CCS undertook a review of NSAs and AGLVs in the 1980s (Cobham Resource Consultants, 1988) but this focused on the viewpoints of planning authorities, government agencies and a sample of private-sector companies and other organizations. This review must therefore be seen as a partial assessment only. Moreover a large number of respondents felt it was difficult or inappropriate to make a judgement on the effectiveness of the designations. SNH are currently undertaking a review of all conservation designations in Scotland (Scottish Office, 1994; SNH, 1993, 1994) but the results are not yet available. Hence a full assessment cannot be presented. Nevertheless, some pointers to the strengths and weaknesses of the landscape designations can be highlighted.

The strengths of Scotland's approach to landscape designation

The significance of central government and its agencies in landscape conservation and protection has led to a number of benefits. Through NSAs, additional planning controls have been applied over an extensive area of rural Scotland. In Highland Region in particular, with much of Scotland's best landscapes, 22 per cent of land surface is designated as NSA and is therefore afforded extra protection. However, protection from and control of development is not the only possible outcome of such designation. NSAs as well as the recent partnership initiatives in the Cairngorms and Loch Lomond/Trossachs and the proposed NHAs offer the potential for positive landscape management and recreational provision in parallel with controls and constraints on development. Again the interventionist role taken by central government has meant that, through the CCS (and now SNH), a strategic view can be taken of landscape conservation. Hence, despite the failure to fully implement its proposals, the vestiges of CCS's park system and a hierarchy of landscape designations are in place. Finally, the designation of NSAs (and its predecessor NPDAs) ensured that the 'national interest' was represented when development was proposed in Scotland's most valued landscapes. Moreover, rather than the variability, even inconsistency, in the decision-making of different local authorities, the role and influence of the Scottish Office, the CCS and the SNH means that there has been the potential at least for consistency in decisions on development proposals throughout Scotland.

Nevertheless, despite these advantages, there are also significant weaknesses in the approaches in Scotland to the designation of its valued landscapes. Perhaps the most obvious criticism is that Scotland has too many designations. If all local and national heritage conservation designations are mapped, the picture which emerges is one of proliferation and overlap. It is little wonder that some designations are unclear and confusing to the layperson, developers and professionals alike (Cobham Resource Consultants, 1988; Scottish Office Environment Department, 1991) or that SNH has been asked to undertake a review of conservation designations (Secretary of State for Scotland, 1991; Scottish Office, 1994).

Although it was intended to prepare conservation strategies for NSAs and tourism development proposals of AGLVs, these have never really emerged. Development control powers available for both NSA and AGLVs have tended to predominate in practice. Therefore these designations have become negative restraints on development. Moreover, the available controls are in themselves limited. The designation of an area as an NSA or AGLV can do little to influence agricultural land-use change; moorland reclamation or intensification; poor land management and, until the emergence of integrated forestry strategies and the increased emphasis placed on improved landscape design practices, forestry development. It is hardly surprising that both NSAs and AGLVs are seen by conservationists as too limited and weak to prevent a decline in upland landscape quality.

Yet even if NSAs and AGLVs had been effective in protecting the landscape, criticisms would still be levelled at them because they are too narrow in what they seek to achieve. Many, including CCS and SNH (and the Countryside Commission, the NCC and English Nature) believe that it is more appropriate to pursue a broader-based environmental heritage conservation in which there is a unified approach to the conservation of the landscape, wildlife and the cultural heritage. Social and economic development may even be promoted where appropriate. Indeed there are clear signs in recent years that this broader-based approach is emerging in Scotland. Borders Regional Council intend to designate 'Heritage Areas' in which landscape, wildlife, recreational and educational objectives would be pursued. NHAs are another example of this more comprehensive and integrated approach to heritage conservation. Regional parks too are planned and managed to achieve multi-purpose objectives with landscape protection pursued alongside recreational, agricultural and forestry development.

One of the strengths of the recently established initiatives in the Cairngorms and Loch Lomond/Trossachs is that they are willing to use the controls available through NSA, SSSI, nature reserves and SACs but only as part of a partnership approach guided by an integrated management strategy. However, despite the potential benefits offered by the broader perspective on heritage conservation there are concerns that ultimately the Cairngorms and Loch Lomond/Trossachs initiatives will not effectively resolve the problems faced in these vulnerable but valued landscapes. Both initiatives place considerable reliance on voluntary arrangements and co-operative action. Therefore much depends on 'key players' coming to agreement on the management strategy and specific conservation projects and programmes. But where there is no agreement on or a lack of commitment to a conservation measure, the Cairngorms Partnership or the Loch Lomond Joint Committee will have difficulty in implementing the measure. It is interesting that some members of the Cairngorms Working Party felt that the voluntary approach would be inadequate. A minority report recommended that there should be a statutory park authority able to draw upon legislative powers to fulfil its objectives.

The strength of initiatives is also likely to be tested by the attempts to reconcile their seemingly conflicting dual guiding principles of environmental sustainability and the promotion of economic and social well-being. The experience of the English and Welsh national parks is relevant here. Both the Sandford and Edwards committees (National Parks Review Committee, 1974; National Parks Review Panel, 1991) reached the conclusion that problems had arisen trying to satisfy landscape conservation and economic development objectives but that where a choice had to be made in a national park, the former should be the overriding objective. Ultimately in the Cairngorms and Loch Lomond/Trossachs, the search for compromise may have to give way to a similar conclusion.

Conclusion

The considerable attention given over the years to landscape protection in England and Wales has led to good understanding of the successes and problems associated with the approaches adopted in these two countries. Scotland, however, has not been treated in any great detail in reviews of landscape protection and conservation in Britain. Yet it has developed its own distinctive, even innovative approach to the designation of its most valued scenic areas. But whilst the approach provides interesting and valuable lessons in landscape conservation it is not without its limitations. Too great an emphasis has been placed on protection through the use of development control and not enough has been placed on positive management and integrating the conservation of landscape, wildlife and cultural heritage. Moreover, the variety of landscape designations which now exists have been introduced at different times by different organizations to pursue different objectives. They often overlap with one another and other protective designations. The pattern of landscape designations which exists today is a complex one but it is also disjointed and it is not difficult to understand why the designations are misunderstood and do not command widespread support within Scotland. Although the Scottish approach to the designation of its most valued landscapes is quite distinct from that in England and Wales, it cannot be said that it is better.

References

Anderson, M. 1990. 'Areas of outstanding natural beauty and the 1949 National Parks Act', *Town Planning Review*, Vol.61, No.3, pp.311–39.

Anon. 1995. 'Ruralists call for economic regeneration', *Planning Week*, Vol.3, No.5, 2 February, p.6.

ARUP Economics and Planning 1993. *Rural Development and Statutory Planning* (Salisbury, Rural Development Commission).

Blowers, A. 1987. 'Minerals and planning: the social basis of physical outcomes', in P. Cloke (ed.), *Rural Planning – Policy into Action* (London, Harper & Row).

Blunden, J. and N. Curry 1990. *A People's Charter? Forty Years of the National Parks and Access to the Countryside Act 1949* (London, HMSO).

Borders Regional Council 1991. *The Scottish Borders 2001: The Way Forward Draft Structure Plan* (Peebles, Borders Regional Council).

Brown, R. 1995. 'Scotland's regional landscape designations: are they fit for the future?', unpublished research project submitted for B.Sc. (Hons) in Town and Regional Planning, University of Dundee.

Cairngorms Working Party 1992a. *Cairngorms Working Party Public Consultation Paper* (Edinburgh, Cairngorms Working Party).

Cairngorms Working Party 1992b. *Common Sense and Sustainability – A Partnership for the Cairngorms: Report of the Cairngorms Working Party* (Edinburgh, Scottish Office).

Carter, C. J. 1981. 'The evolution of planning at the regional level in Scotland', *Duncan of Jordanstone College of Art/University of Dundee Occasional Paper No.7* (Dundee, University of Dundee).

Central Regional Council 1991. *Central 2000: The Structure Plan for Central Region Written Statement* (Stirling, Central Regional Council).

Cherry, G. 1975. 'National Parks and recreation in the countryside', *Environmental Planning, 1939–68, Vol.2* (London, HMSO).

Cobham Resource Consultants 1988. *The Effectiveness of Landscape Designations in Scotland: A Review Study* (Perth, Countryside Commission for Scotland/Scottish Development Department).

Countryside Commission for Scotland 1974. *A Park System for Scotland* (Perth, Countryside Commission for Scotland).

Countryside Commission for Scotland 1978. *Scotland's Scenic Heritage* (Perth, Countryside Commission for Scotland).

Countryside Commission for Scotland 1985. *Loch Rannoch and Glen Lyon NSA: Policies for Landscape Conservation and Management* (Perth, Countryside Commission for Scotland).

Countryside Commission for Scotland 1990. *The Mountain Areas of Scotland: Conservation and Management* (Perth, Countryside Commission for Scotland).

Countryside Commission for Scotland 1991a. *The Mountain Areas of Scotland: Conservation and Management – A Report on Public Consultation* (Perth, Countryside Commission for Scotland).

Countryside Commission for Scotland 1991b. *The Mountain Areas of Scotland: Conservation and Management – Results of Public Consultation, News Release* (Perth, Countryside Commission for Scotland).

Crofters Commission 1991. *Crofting in the 1990s* (Inverness, Crofters Commission).

Crofters Commission 1994. *Annual Report 1994* (Inverness, Crofters Commission).

Cullingworth, B. and V. Nadin 1994. *Town and Country Planning in Britain*, 11th edition (London, Routledge).

Curry, N. 1994. *Countryside Recreation, Access and Land-Use Planning* (London, E. & F. N. Spon).

Department of the Environment 1992. *The UK Environment* (London, HMSO).
Department of Health for Scotland 1949. *Technical Broadsheet 16*, DHS Circular 90/1949 (Edinburgh, Scottish Office).
Department of Health for Scotland 1961. *Review of Development Plans*, DHS Circular 86/1961 (Edinburgh, Scottish Office).
Evans, D. 1992. *A History of Nature Conservation in Britain* (London, Routledge).
Ferguson, M. P. 1988. 'National Parks for Scotland?', *Scottish Geographical Magazine*, Vol.104, No.1, pp.36–40.
Ferguson, W. 1968. *Scotland: 1689 to the Present* (Edinburgh, Oliver & Boyd).
Fife Regional Council 1989. *Fife Structure Plan Consultation Written Statement* (Glenrothes, Fife Regional Council).
Gilg, A. 1978. *Countryside Planning: The First Three Decades* (London, Methuen).
Gilg, A. 1985. *Rural Geography: An Introduction* (London, Edward Arnold).
Gilg, A. 1991. *Countryside Planning: Policies for the 1990s* (London, CAB International).
Grampian Regional Council 1990. *The Management of the Eastern Cairngorms* (Aberdeen, Grampian Regional Council).
Grampian Regional Council 1992. *Grampian Region Structure Plan, Draft Written Statement* (Aberdeen, Grampian Regional Council).
Green, B. 1985. *Countryside Conservation – The Protection and Management of Amenity Ecosystems*, 2nd edition (London, Allen & Unwin).
Hall, P., R. Thomas, H. Gracey and R. Drewett 1973. *The Containment of Urban England* (London, George Allen & Unwin).
Highland Regional Council 1975. *Highland Regional Council Structure Plan, Report of Survey* (Inverness, Highland Regional Council).
Highland Regional Council 1976. *Regional Report* (Inverness, Highland Regional Council).
Highland Regional Council 1979. *Highland Regional Council Structure Plan, Report of Survey (update): Written Statement: Changes Likely to Occur 1978–88; Statement of Publicity and Consultations* (Inverness, Highland Regional Council).
Highland Regional Council 1985. *Structure Plan Review – Issues Paper* (Inverness, Highland Regional Council).
Highland Regional Council 1990. *Highland Regional Council Structure Plan 1990 Written Statement* (Inverness, Highland Regional Council).
Hodge, T. and M. Whitby 1983. *Rural Employment – Trends, Options and Choices* (London, Methuen).
Hood, N. 1991. 'The Scottish Development Agency in perspective', *Royal Bank of Scotland Review*, 171, September, pp.3–21.
Hoskins, W. G. 1970. *The Making of the English Landscape* (London, Pelican).
Hunter, H. 1976. *The Making of the Crofting Community* (Edinburgh, John Donald Publishers).
Hunter, J. 1991. *The Claim of Crofting 1930–1990* (Edinburgh, Mainstream Publishing).
Ilbery, B. 1992. *Agriculture Change in Great Britain* (Oxford, Oxford University Press).
Keating, M. and R. Boyle 1986. *The Re-Making of Urban Scotland, Strategies for Local Economic Development* (Edinburgh, Edinburgh University Press).
Kirby, M. J. 1995. 'The future of the English countryside in England', *Proceedings of the Town and Country Planning Summer School*, University of Exeter, 2–13 September, pp.43–5.

Linton, D. L. 1959. 'Morphological contrasts between eastern and western Scotland', in R. Millar and J. Watson (eds.), *Geographical Essays in Memory of Alan G. Ogilvie* (Edinburgh, Oliver & Boyd).

Lloyd, M. G. 1994. 'Innovative strategic land-use planning: National Planning guidelines in Scotland', *Scottish Affairs*, Vol.6, Winter, pp.84–100.

Loch Lomond Planning Group 1986. *The Loch Lomond Subject Plan for Tourism, Recreation and Conservation* (Loch Lomond Planning Group).

Loch Lomond Technical Group 1973. *Loch Lomond Management Plan* (Loch Lomond Technical Group).

Loch Lomond and Trossachs Working Party 1993. *The Management of Loch Lomond and The Trossachs – The Report of the Loch Lomond and Trossachs Working Party to the Secretary of State for Scotland* (Edinburgh, Scottish Office).

Lowe, P., G. Cox, M. MacEwan, T. O'Riordan and M. Winter 1986. *Countryside Conflicts: The Politics of Farming, Forestry and Conservation* (Aldershot, Gower).

Mather, A. S. 1986. *Land-Use* (London, Longman).

Millman, R. 1975. *The Making of the Scottish Landscape* (London, Batsford).

Mingay, G. E. 1986. 'The transformation of Britain', in A. Wheatcroft (ed.), *The Making of Britain* (London, Paladin Grafton).

Moir, J. 1991. 'National Parks-North of the Border', *Planning Outlook*, Vol.34, No.2, pp.61–7.

Moir, J., D. Rice and A. Watt 1995. *Housing in the Countryside: The Locational and Design Policies of Scottish Local Authorities*, Research Paper No.1, Centre for Planning Research, School of Town and Regional Planning (Dundee, University of Dundee).

National Parks Review Panel 1974. *Report of the Committee – The Sandford Report* (London, HMSO).

National Parks Review Panel 1991. *Fit for the Future – Report of the National Parks Review Panel*, CCP 334 (Cheltenham, Countryside Commission).

Newby, H. 1980. *Green and Pleasant Land?* (Harmondsworth, Pelican).

Newby, H., C. Bell, D. Rose and P. Saunders 1978. *Property, Paternalism and Power: Class and Control in Rural England* (London, Hutchinson).

Parry, M. L. and M. L. Slater (eds.) 1980. *The Making of the Scottish Countryside* (London, Croom Helm).

Poore, D. and J. Poore 1987. *Protected Landscapes: The UK Experience* (Countryside Commission, Countryside Commission for Scotland, DoE (N. Ireland), International Union for the Conservation of Nature and Natural Resources).

Prebble, J. 1969. *The Highland Clearances* (Harmondsworth, Penguin).

Reed, M. 1984. 'The Georgian triumph 1700–1830', in A. Wheatcroft (ed.), *The Making of Britain* (London, Paladin Grafton).

Reed, M. 1987. 'The age of exuberance 1500–1700', in A. Wheatcroft (ed.), *The Making of Britain* (London, Paladin Grafton).

Rowan-Robinson, J., M. G. Lloyd and R. E. Eliot 1987. 'National planning guidelines and strategic planning: matching context and methodology', *Town Planning Review*, Vol.58, No.4, pp.369–81.

Rowan-Robinson, J. and M. G. Lloyd 1991. 'National planning guidelines: a strategic opportunity wasting away', *Planning Practice and Research*, Vol.6, No.3, Winter, pp.16–19.

Scottish Development Department 1962. *Development Plans: A Areas of Great Landscape Value; B Tourism Development Proposals*, SDD Circular 4/62 (Edinburgh, Scottish Office).

Scottish Development Department 1969. *The Cairngorms Area: Report of the Technical Group on the Cairngorms Area of The Eastern Highlands of Scotland* (Edinburgh, HMSO).

Scottish Development Department 1974. *North Sea Oil and Gas: Coastal Planning Guidelines* (Edinburgh, Scottish Office).

Scottish Development Department 1975. *The Development of Agricultural Land*, SDD Circular 77/1975 (Edinburgh, Scottish Office).

Scottish Development Department 1977. *National Planning Guidelines for Large Industrial Sites and Rural Conservation* (Edinburgh, Scottish Office).

Scottish Development Department 1980. *Development Control in National Scenic Areas*, SDD Circular 20/1980 (Edinburgh, Scottish Office).

Scottish Development Department 1981. *National Planning Guidelines 1981, Priorities for Development Planning* (Edinburgh, Scottish Office).

Scottish Development Department 1987a. *Development Control in National Scenic Areas*, SDD Circular 9/1987 (Edinburgh, Scottish Office).

Scottish Development Department 1987b. *Development Involving Agricultural Land*, SDD Circular 22/1987 (Edinburgh, Scottish Office).

Scottish Development Department 1987c. *National Planning Guidelines 1987: Agricultural Land* (Edinburgh, Scottish Office).

Scottish Development Department 1990. *Scottish Natural Heritage: The Way Ahead* (Edinburgh, Scottish Office).

Scottish Natural Heritage 1993. *Second Operational Plan: Review of 1992/93 and Working Programme 1993-4* (Edinburgh, Scottish Natural Heritage).

Scottish Natural Heritage 1994. *Annual Report 1993-94* (Edinburgh, Scottish Natural Heritage).

Scottish Natural Heritage 1995. *Boglands–Scotland's Living Landscapes* (Edinburgh, Scottish Natural Heritage).

Scottish Office 1992. *Rural Framework* (Edinburgh, Scottish Office).

Scottish Office 1994. *Cairngorms Partnership: A Statement of Intent by the Secretary of State for Scotland following the advice of the Cairngorms Working Party* (Edinburgh, Scottish Office).

Scottish Office 1995a. *Loch Lomond and The Trossachs: The Response by the Secretary of State for Scotland to the Report of the Loch Lomond and the Trossachs Working Party* (Edinburgh, Scottish Office).

Scottish Office 1995b. *Rural Framework* (Edinburgh, Scottish Office).

Scottish Office Environment Department 1991. *Natural Heritage Areas, Consultation Paper EMP00726.021* (Edinburgh, Scottish Office).

Scottish Office Environment Department 1992. *The Implementation of Natural Heritage Areas: Statement of Government Position Following Consultation, MMF00722,032* (Edinburgh, Scottish Office).

Secretary of State for Scotland 1991. *The Mountain Areas of Scotland: Conservation and Management: Government Response to The Countryside Commission Report*, SML00129.081 (Edinburgh, Scottish Office).

Selman, P. H. (ed.) 1988. *Countryside Planning in Practice: The Scottish Experience* (Stirling, Stirling University Press).

Sharp, T. 1946. *The Anatomy of the Village* (Harmondsworth, Penguin Books).

Sheail, J. 1975. 'The concept of National Parks in Great Britain 1900–1950', *Transactions of the Institute of British Geographers*, Vol.66, pp.41–56.

Shoard, M. 1980. *The Theft of the Countryside* (London, Temple Smith).

Shoard, M. 1987. *This Land is our Land* (London, Paladin Grafton).

Shucksmith, M. and M. G. Lloyd 1983. 'Rural planning in Scotland: a critique', in A. Gilg (ed.), *Countryside Planning Yearbook*, Vol.4 (Norwich, Geo Books).

Sissons, J. B. 1967. *The Evolution of Scotland's Scenery* (Edinburgh, Oliver & Boyd).

Smart, G. and M. Anderson 1990. *The Planning and Management of AONBs, CCP 295* (Perth, Countryside Commission).

Smout, T. C. 1969. *The History of the Scottish People: 1560–1830* (London, Collins).

Taylor, C. 1983. *Village and Farmstead: A History of Rural Settlement in England* (London, George Philip).

Tayside Regional Council 1988. *Tayside Structure Plan 1988 Written Statement* (Dundee, Tayside Regional Council).

Traill-Thompson, J. 1995. *Rural Futures Discussion Paper 243* (Exeter, Agricultural Economics Unit, Exeter University).

Tudor, G. J., E. C. Mackay and F. M. Underwood 1994. *The National Countryside Monitoring Scheme – The Changing Face of Scotland 1940–1970s Main Report* (Edinburgh, Scottish Natural Heritage).

12

The Challenge of Convergence: Countryside Conservation and Enjoyment in Scotland and Wales

KEVIN BISHOP

Introduction

A new chapter in the history of countryside conservation and enjoyment commenced on 1 April 1991 with the formation of the Countryside Council for Wales (CCW). The CCW officially replaced the Nature Conservancy Council (NCC) and Countryside Commission in Wales. For the first time in Britain one agency had responsibility for combining policies for nature conservation with enjoyment and protection of landscapes. The Environmental Protection Act 1990 (which provided for the establishment of the CCW; subsequent reorganizations of the NCC and Countryside Commission; and establishment of a new Joint Nature Conservation Committee), together with the Natural Heritage (Scotland) Act 1991 (which provided for the creation of an integrated agency in Scotland – Scottish Natural Heritage (SNH)) mark the most significant changes in institutional responsibility for countryside conservation and enjoyment since the passage of the National Parks and Access to the Countryside Act 1949. Taken together, this legislation signalled not only the convergence of two hitherto separate strands of countryside conservation but also the devolution of some elements of conservation policy with independent bodies for Wales and Scotland.

For some, these reforms are essentially 'cosmetic', with little restructuring of the aims, roles and methods of the different countryside agencies (Hodge *et al.*, 1994). Others see them as part of a wider political consensus regarding the need to reform institutions and structures to ensure effective and efficient environmental protection (Carter and Lowe, 1994) and others have argued that the process of institutional reform and integration will lead to marginalization of countryside recreation because of the imbalance between powers and duties relating to nature conservation and those relating to general countryside duties (Grove-White, 1994). The purpose of this chapter is to examine the background to and nature of the reforms in Wales and Scotland and provide a preliminary assessment of their impact according to the following questions:

- Has the creation of new unified agencies facilitated the integration of different disciplinary perspectives and working methods?
- How effective are the new agencies in the delivery of their respective remits?
- What are the wider ramifications of institutional reform?

The 'great divide'

Countryside conservation in Britain was characterized, until 1991, by what many have termed the 'great divide' (MacEwen and MacEwen, 1982, 1987). The National Parks and Access to the Countryside Act 1949 (Part 3) established two separate conservation regimes. The Nature Conservancy was given responsibility for 'nature conservation' and 'nature' was defined in the Conservancy's Royal Charter as 'the flora and fauna of Great Britain'. The 1949 Act made the National Parks Commission responsible for the preservation and enhancement of 'natural beauty' which was also defined to include 'flora, fauna and geological and physiographical features'. The Nature Conservancy was given a remit for the whole of Great Britain; the National Parks Commission was responsible only for England and Wales. Over time, the National Parks Commission and the term 'natural beauty' was equated with the appearance of the landscape and the Nature Conservancy concentrated on the conservation of nature. This distinction between aesthetic and scientific conservation is peculiarly British; it is uncommon for nature conservation and landscape to be divided up into entirely separate subjects, dealt with by different authorities, in other European countries (Baldock et al., 1996).

Most authors attribute this division to the differences between the various interest groups lobbying for countryside conservation (Blunden and Curry, 1991). During the nineteenth and early twentieth centuries, separate groups were formed to lobby for the protection of the landscape, wildlife and for better public access to the countryside. Thus the British Vegetation Committee, the Society for the Promotion of Nature Reserves and others lobbied for wildlife conservation; the Council for the Preservation of Rural England, the Council for the Preservation of Rural Wales and others argued for the conservation of scenery; and the Ramblers Association pressed for greater access to the countryside to enjoy both the scenery and nature. Whilst a common denominator between the various groups was their lobbying for national parks they continued to act in an autonomous way, launching campaigns and pressing their own particular demands (Sheail, 1988). Despite these differences John Dower (1945) in his seminal report on *National Parks in England and Wales* argued for the establishment of one agency in England and Wales with responsibility for national parks and national nature reserves. In so doing, he rejected the calls of the Nature Reserves Investigation Committee (1943) for a separate agency to be established to promote nature conservation and establish nature reserves. Dower saw wildlife protection as part of national parks policy, and believed that a proper fusion between nature conservation, landscape protection and promotion of access and recreation would only be achieved if the National Parks Commission was responsible for nature reserves within the parks. On practical grounds he advocated that the Commission should also be responsible for nature reserves outside of the national parks. Dower's vision of a unified agency responsible for all forms of conservation was not to be realized for one primary reason – his underestimate of the importance of the scientific arguments upon which the nature conservation case was built (Phillips, 1995). The Second World War graphically demonstrated the 'power' of science, and ecology was to benefit from this new influence on society; yet Dower's 1945 report gave only cursory coverage to wildlife and nature conservation – nine paragraphs on wildlife and nature conservation compared with more than twenty on access-related issues.

After the war, the nature conservation movement was faced with a choice. One option lay within the national parks world, with nature conservation to be achieved through the new town and country planning system. Another option lay with the establishment of nature reserves for both conservation and scientific research, with their management closely linked to the work of research stations (Phillips, 1995). The choice is clearly illustrated in the reports of the Hobhouse and Huxley Committees of 1947 on national parks and nature conservation respectively. In the words of Phillips (1995):

> When Hobhouse argues aesthetics, Huxley argues science; where Hobhouse has access and public benefit in mind, Huxley has study and learning; where Hobhouse sees local authorities working through the town and country planning system, as the chief deliverers of countryside protection and enjoyment, Huxley wants hands-on ownership and management of nature reserves by scientists. Where Hobhouse opts for a small National Parks Commission, Huxley argues for a large National Biological Service. And, while Hobhouse's attentions had to be focused on England and Wales, Huxley looked at Britain as a whole and indeed set his scheme of things in a broader world vision. Sir Arthur Hobhouse was a respected County Councillor – and Julian Huxley went on to be the first Director General of UNESCO. (p.5)

By the end of 1949, the great divide that was to last for over forty years was in place, with landscape conservation (in the form of national parks and areas of outstanding natural beauty) and countryside enjoyment separated institutionally from nature conservation. There was also a spatial separation: whilst Wales was always seen in partnership with England, Scotland was considered as a separate entity. For example, the Addison Committee (1931) produced a separate report on national parks in Scotland and during the 1940s whilst Dower and Hobhouse were considering the conservation of the English and Welsh countryside as one, there were separate, but parallel studies considering the needs of Scotland (Ramsay, 1947). This spatial division was also enshrined in the 1949 Act which established a Great Britain system of nature conservation but provided for a system of landscape conservation and countryside enjoyment only in England and Wales. With no national parks and no agency to represent any aspect of landscape conservation and countryside enjoyment, there was a policy vacuum in Scotland rather than an institutional division. This apparent anomaly was rectified by the passage of the Countryside (Scotland) Act 1967, which provided for the establishment of a Countryside Commission for Scotland.

The reforms of the late 1960s and early 1970s did nothing to alter the split between nature conservation and landscape – if anything the reforms served to further emphasize the division. Following the Countryside Act 1968, the National Parks Commission was replaced by the Countryside Commission for England and Wales and, as the change of title suggests, this reform extended the division beyond separate systems of protected area into the wider countryside. The Nature Conservancy Council Act 1973 provided for the establishment of the Institute of Terrestrial Ecology, which was to consist of the old Conservancy's research staff and stations, whilst the staff concerned with conservation management and advisory work were to form the new Nature Conservancy Council (NCC) for Great Britain.

With hindsight, the Wildlife and Countryside Act 1981 was to prove significant in securing the fates of the NCC and Countryside Commission. The 1981 Act ensured that the NCC was kept largely occupied with the process of notifying and defending Sites of Special Scientific Interest (SSSI) – a process that proved time- and resource-consuming and often confrontational. In contrast, the Countryside Commission became an independent agency under the same act and was able to use its new freedom to develop innovative partnerships, through the use of its grant-awarding and experimental powers. The new status helped the Commission to become an authoritative voice on countryside issues at the very time that the general public was becoming increasingly interested in the subject (Phillips, 1993). Not only was the Commission able to publish policy statements that offered the government a road to reform but it was able to test some of its ideas by using its experimental powers (the Broads Grazing Marshes Conservation Scheme and Demonstration Farms are two examples where the commission used such powers to good effect).

The end of the 'great divide'

On 11 July 1989, Nicholas Ridley, then secretary of state for the Environment, announced that he intended to reform the conservation agencies in Great Britain. His proposals were to divide the NCC into three separate bodies (one each for England, Scotland and Wales) and partition the Countryside Commission for England and Wales into two. At the same time, the Countryside Commission in Wales and the NCC Wales would be merged into a new 'Countryside Council for Wales' and subsequent legislation was promised to merge the previously separate Countryside Commission for Scotland and NCC Scotland to form a new Natural Heritage Agency for Scotland. The new NCC England and Countryside Commission for England were to remain separate because of the greater density of population and consequent pressure on the land. The stated reason behind the proposals was to devolve the functions of the NCC so that nature conservation could be delivered closer to the ground.

Given that many commentators had criticized the 'great divide' for being artificial and harmful to the interests of conservation (MacEwen and MacEwen, 1982, 1987; Lowe *et al.*, 1986) it might have been expected that these reforms would be welcomed. The reverse was true at a national level where the changes provoked considerable controversy from voluntary and statutory conservation agencies alike. Nicholas Ridley was criticized for presenting his proposals as a *fait accompli* – there was no prior consultation and the reforms were announced in a written answer to a parliamentary question at the end of session. Opponents to the reforms also argued that the proposals themselves would weaken the national and international standing of UK conservation, disperse vital expertise, duplicate effort and subordinate conservation objectives to developmental interests (Lowe, 1990).

A prime motivation for the reforms was the unpopularity of the NCC in Scotland. During the 1980s, tension had grown between the NCC and Scottish landowners over conservation and, in particular, the process of notifying and designating SSSIs that the 1981 Act had required the council to engage in. This tension reached a climax over the well-publicized afforestation of the Flow Country. It seems that Nicholas Ridley and Malcolm Rifkind (then secretary of state for Scotland) were persuaded that an independent Scottish agency was more likely to be responsive to Scottish interests and less antagonistic than a distant English bureaucracy, and that it therefore would be more effective in discharging their functions.

Informed comment suggests that the proposals were actually initiated by the secretary of state for Scotland, who had a feeling of disenfranchisement and lack of ownership as well as lack of control over the work on nature conservation; that Peter Walker, the secretary of state for Wales, saw advantages in an independent conservation body for Wales and so followed the Scottish lead; and that Nicholas Ridley did not oppose (Phillips, 1995). A simple break-up of the NCC would have been strongly opposed and so the proposals had to incorporate integration of countryside and nature conservation interests which had been artificially separated in the 1949 Act. Integration in Wales was also a practical necessity – a Welsh Countryside Commission with a staff of approximately twelve officers was not a viable proposition. Thus it seems that devolution was the driving force for institutional reform and merger of conservation functions a logical consequence of this.

The advantages and disadvantages of merger were never fully debated. The initial response of the conservation bodies (voluntary and statutory) focused on the apparent independence of the four new agencies and lack of reference to any national/international dimension to their work. There was concern that each country would be able to adopt different criteria for the designation of National Nature Reserves and SSSIs. The government addressed this weakness by including in the Environmental Protection Bill provision for the establishment of a joint co-ordinating committee by the new conservation bodies. Even during the passage of the Bill through Parliament, debate still focused on the devolution issue and the role and status of the Joint Nature Conservation Committee. Although many voluntary bodies tabled amendments to the Bill aimed at making conservation more effective, the government steadfastly stuck to its proposals and within eighteen months of first publishing the proposals they were implemented in Part VII of the Environmental Protection Act 1990.

The 1990 Act left Wales with a single organization, and Scotland and England with two each. However, it had already been announced in 1989 that there would be a merger of the Countryside Commission for Scotland and Nature Conservancy Council Scotland. This merger was provided for by the Natural Heritage (Scotland) Act 1991 which set up Scottish Natural Heritage (SNH).[1]

Has the creation of new unified agencies facilitated the integration of different disciplinary perspectives and working methods?

From their inception, both CCW and SNH have had to explore the meaning and significance of their integrated remit and develop styles of working which not only reflected this integration but are sympathetic to and build upon the different cultures of the two countries – the so-called Scottish and Welsh dimensions to countryside conservation and enjoyment.

An important factor in shaping the two bodies was their inheritance. It can be argued that the CCW was handicapped from birth and SNH empowered by their respective inheritance. Despite the proclamations of the secretary of state for Wales that the new Council would not be formed merely by bolting together the Welsh sections of the old agencies, the government resisted attempts by the Countryside Commission to establish a new mandate for the CCW and the Environmental Protection Act 1990 merely combines the statutory duties of the two previously separate bodies. Thus, although a new agency, the council's duties and statutory powers essentially date back to the National Parks and Access to the Countryside Act 1949. For example, the CCW is required to encourage the provision or improvement of recreation opportunities for those 'resorting to the countryside in Wales'; it has to uphold a designation system that still promotes a distinction between nature conservation (SSSIs and National Nature Reserves) and landscape conservation (National Parks and AONBs); but has no new powers. The Council itself, in its consultation document *Threshold 21* (CCW, 1993a), has identified this inheritance as a constraint and its officers have, on more than one occasion, spoken of the need for a new Act of Parliament to update the organization's remit and powers: 'I still firmly believe that the merging of the two 45 year old organisations also demands the means to merge the statutory processes by which the 45 year old systems have worked so far' (Mercer, 1995, p.27).

Whilst the Environmental Protection Act 1990 merely bound together two organizations and their remits, the Natural Heritage (Scotland) Act 1991 provided new duties and powers for SNH. In framing this act, the Scottish Office deliberately sought to consolidate and broaden the remit for the new organization and adapt it to fit Scottish circumstances: 'The Government could have sought Parliamentary approval for their proposals in the Environmental Protection Bill now before Parliament. However, they believe there should be the fullest opportunity for comment and debate' (Scottish Office, 1990, p.1).

The first section of the Natural Heritage (Scotland) Act 1991 is tantamount to a mission statement for SNH. This act was the first piece of legislation in the UK to include a specific reference to the term 'sustainable development'. Under section 1 of the act, SNH is required 'to have regard to the desirability of securing that anything done, whether by Scottish Natural Heritage or any other person, in relation to the natural heritage of Scotland is undertaken in a manner which is sustainable'. Although some have questioned whether the inclusion of the word 'sustainable' has any meaningful effect, it represents an important attempt to shape a remit for SNH that utilizes the vocabulary of the 1990s rather than the 1940s. The idiom of sustainability is very different to the language of preservation that helped shape the National Parks and Access to the Countryside Act 1949 and is still to be found in the Environmental Protection Act 1990. Whilst preservation implies safeguarding a particular resource by setting it aside and preventing change, sustainability has a more dynamic meaning implying management to keep things going and an element of appropriate resource use. It is particularly significant that the word 'sustainable' is not defined, and this has provided SNH with an opportunity to develop its own practical application of the meaning of the phrase (SNH, 1993). The significance of this legislative difference is illustrated by the fact that the CCW has felt it necessary to recouch its objectives in terms of sustainability (CCW, 1993a, b). The phrase 'natural heritage' is used to describe 'the flora and fauna of Scotland, its geological and physiographical features, its natural beauty and amenity' and is, again, an attempt to update the legislative language of the 1940s. The reference to 'Scotland' also places SNH in a clearer position than the CCW as it ensures that the 'natural heritage' includes urban as well as rural areas; in Wales, CCW's general remit for the 'countryside' is confused by the fact that its remit for nature conservation extends into urban areas.

As well as updating the duties of SNH, the Natural Heritage (Scotland) Act 1991 also provided the agency with new powers. Section 4 of the 1991 Act enables SNH to enter into agreements with the occupiers/owners of land in pursuance of any of its purposes. In contrast, CCW can only enter into management agreements to further nature conservation. CCW itself has identified this as a weakness and its consultation document *Threshold 21* contained a proposal to 'seek a landscape management agreement power to parallel the nature conservation one' (CCW, 1993a, p.4). Although SNH lacks the powers that CCW has to develop experimental schemes to further any of its duties it can, under section 5 of the 1991 Act, develop projects and schemes to further its duties and, unlike CCW, has the ability to form companies and partnerships. The power to form companies and partnerships would have undoubtedly been of value to CCW in its pursuit of proposals for an independent Council for Environmental Education in Wales. The 1991 Act also introduced a new category of protected area north of the border – Natural Heritage Areas – which offer SNH the opportunity to demonstrate integrated management of the natural heritage in practice.

These differences have been significant in the way in which the agencies have approached particular issues and cases. It is instructive to note that the CCW has highlighted the imbalances in its powers and duties relating to nature conservation and those relating to general countryside matters and the problems this poses in terms of unevenness of policies and priorities (CCW, 1993a; Mercer, 1995).

Management-based research into the impact of mergers (see Buono and Bowditch, 1989, for example) highlights the importance of organizational culture in affecting the ability of an organization to deliver a new remit and suggests that even if staff are in favour of merger they will still encounter problems in adapting to change. The establishment of the CCW and SNH brought together two very different cultures: the science-based, site-specific, nature conservation interests represented by the NCC, with a reliance on statutory powers and a large complement of staff; and the wider countryside interests represented by the Countryside Commissions, with their tradition of advice and enabling through grant-aid and experimentation. The problems of combining these two cultures was compounded by the imbalance in the numbers of staff transferring to the new bodies. In Wales, at the time of its establishment, NCC staff outnumbered those from the Countryside Commission by 105 to 13 (8:1). In Scotland, the comparable figures were 385 to 63 (6:1). This imbalance created the feeling amongst many outsiders, and some insiders, of an NCC take-over. The inheritance of an organizational frame borne out of the NCC's model of a long thin line of specialists and the choice of their offices in Bangor as the location for CCW's HQ did not help to dissipate fears of an NCC take-over. In practice, the internal integration of the two cultures was considerably assisted by the appointment of additional staff. The massive influx of new staff (the CCW grew from 110 to 200 in its first year and to 300 in its second year, and SNH grew from 450 on its inception to 605 in just twelve months) helped mask the origins of the inaugural staff and provided an opportunity to address imbalances in the skill profile of the inherited staff. The appointment of external staff to senior management posts was particularly significant in moulding a new culture. For example, Ian Mercer – a long-time vocal advocate of institutional integration – was appointed as the first chief executive of the CCW. However, the genuine melding of staff has not been easy, especially as both organizations have sought to implement their integrated remit at the level of the individual. SNH, for example, established a unified staff structure with generic job titles as a deliberate measure to break down professional and occupational barriers. Whilst it is unclear whether the creation of integrated organizations is leading to the development of a new breed of professional who combines in one body the skill mix represented by the staff of the old NCC and Countryside Commission, the impact of integration is clearer when looking at the policies and practices of the agencies (see below).

Both SNH and CCW have sought to build upon the legacy of the two Countryside Commissions by developing a consensus-seeking, consultative style of operation rather than the more authoritative approach often associated with the NCC. Thus the two agencies have attempted to work through others by offering financial incentives rather than imposing restraints. Such a *modus operandi* is also a reflection of the government's ideological stance on countryside conservation issues and its adherence to the voluntary principle. In SNH's case, it was also in part a legal requirement – amendments to the 1991 Act established an Advisory Committee on SSSIs. The concern to establish 'good consumer relations' has extended beyond non-governmental organizations – the traditional allies of such agencies – to local communities and key economic sectors. CCW have attempted to develop partnerships with the Welsh Office Agricultural Department, the Development Board for Rural Wales, the Agricultural Development and Advisory Service and the Welsh Development Agency in the 'socio-economic and agri-environmental area that is critical to sustainable conservation' (Mercer, 1995, p.24) and SNH has 'made a radical shift in our approach to key economic sectors . . . to influence the policies and the financial assistance schemes attached to them, and the resultant effects on the natural heritage' (Crofts, 1995, p.33). Such developments are not necessarily a function of the new integrated remit as English Nature (the Nature Conservancy Council for England) and the Countryside Commission have also broadened their concerns in similar ways (Hodge *et al.*, 1994).

A key theme emerging from the policy and practice advocated and adopted by the CCW is its commitment to community action. The Council believes that its vision of

> a beautiful land washed by clean seas and streams under a clear sky; supporting its full diversity of life, including our own, each species in its proper abundance; for the enjoyment of everybody and providing for the contented work of its rural and sea-faring people (CCW, 1993b)

will only be achieved if it becomes a part of the way all people live and think, 'part of contemporary culture' (CCW, 1993b, p.2). Its commitment to community action can be seen as part of the council's attempt to create a clear working style that separates it from the Countryside Commission and English Nature but is also, to a large extent, a measure of common sense. Wales is a small country and this intimate scale encourages contact even at the national level but it also means that new bodies and outsiders have to win respect, poorly-developed or ill-conceived ideas will be easily spotted (Caldwell, 1993). It therefore makes sense to enlist the support and views of that community, through schemes like Jigso, and attempt to empower them to care for their own environments as with the Council's Community Paths Campaign and its attempt to involve local people in the management of its estate. This engagement with local people is also a theme of SNH's work. Whilst having headquarter offices in Edinburgh and Battleby much of the decision-making, as well as policy delivery, is devolved to its four regions, which all have regional boards comprising locally-based individuals, and thirteen area teams. This structure was requested by the secretary of state for Scotland who, in the second reading of the Natural Heritage (Scotland) Bill, stated 'I fully expect that the great majority of staff in SNH will be based in regional and local offices'.

How effective are the new agencies in the delivery of their respective remits?

The two agencies seem to have found it easier to demonstrate their integrated remit when working in a proactive manner. For example, when developing new policies or schemes. In Wales, the CCW's experimental farm stewardship scheme – Tir Cymen – is a clear demonstration of the Council's integrated remit being applied in practice. Tir Cymen was launched in the summer of 1992 and fulfils a commitment by the secretary of state for Wales to implement such a scheme as part of the government's environmental strategy (HM Government, 1991). Tir Cymen has been introduced by the CCW as a market-based approach to the management of farmland in Wales (Bishop and Phillips, 1993). It is operated under the Council's experimental powers and the scheme is being piloted in three areas: the districts of Meirionnydd, Swansea and Dinefwr. There are a number of important differences between Tir Cymen and the English equivalent, Countryside Stewardship: differences which reflect the council's integrated remit. Countryside Stewardship is based on target landscapes and habitats and only farmers with such land can apply to enter the scheme. In contrast, applicants within the three pilot areas for Tir Cymen must enter the whole farm. Thus Tir Cymen attempts to foster a holistic view of the environment. Such an approach has practical advantages as it avoids the potential problem of intensification of farming on land not covered by an environmental agreement. Providing incentives for the conservation of heather moorland, for example, may encourage the farmer to improve semi-natural grassland elsewhere on the farm to accommodate the sheep he has had to remove from the moor – thus quite possibly resulting in a net environmental loss. Such problems have been encountered in some Environmentally Sensitive Areas, and might apply to Countryside Stewardship – with its emphasis on target landscapes. The 'whole-farm' approach also seems more successful in terms of negotiating new permissive access to the countryside, since the provision of new access will not be tied to particular landscapes and access to unenclosed land is secured through cross compliance under the terms of Tir Cymen agreements.

The evolution of new working methods and different disciplinary perspectives is clearly witnessed in the approaches the new conservation cum countryside agencies in Scotland and Wales have adopted towards protected areas. Already the publication of *Threshold 21* (CCW, 1993a), *Cynnal Cynefin* (CCW, 1993b) and *Sustainable Development and the Natural Heritage: The SNH Approach* (SNH, 1993) illustrates how an integrated agency can promote a more holistic view of environmental problems and environmental solutions within the context of countryside and nature conservation. For example, *Threshold 21* identifies a number of questions about the effectiveness and future role of protected areas, outlining the weaknesses inherent in protected areas and the council's wish to move towards comprehensive environmental management. SNH has also been engaged in a review of designations (see Chapter 11 above) and developing proposals for the operation of Natural Heritage Areas which offer the potential for integrated management of the natural heritage within a broadly defined area (Crofts, 1995).

It has been harder to demonstrate the effects of integration when the agencies have been responding to particular development pressures. For example, the proposals for a barrage across Cardiff Bay and quarrying in Carmel Woods had until 1991 attracted the attention of the NCC because of the effect upon SSSIs. While SSSI designation continued to be the prime motivation for CCW involvement, as the two sagas unfolded, landscape and enjoyment had also to be considered (Mercer, 1995). Even more problematic are proposals for by-laws to control recreational use of Llangorse Lake in the Brecon Beacons National Park, where the access versus conservation debate looms large, and the development of wind farms, which has pitted one environmental group against another. In Wales, the government's energy policy has resulted in more of a rush for wind rather than a dash for gas: in less than three years, Wales has gone from having no commercial wind farms to six such developments, with 213 turbines generating over 70,000 kW. Despite being a clean 'green' form of electricity generation, this rush for wind has become a matter of considerable controversy within and beyond Wales, a controversy that has embroiled the CCW. For example, the Welsh Affairs Committee report into wind energy begins its conclusions not with a recommendation about the use of wind energy, but rather with a criticism of CCW advice: 'We found the casual approach of CCW witnesses to inaccuracies in their evidence to the Committee quite unacceptable from a publicly funded organisation with a statutory responsibility to provide advice on rural issues' (Welsh Affairs Committee, 1994). Some of these difficulties reflect a tension between regional and HQ staff as much as a problem of providing integrated and consistent advice.

It is easy to confuse issues of effectiveness with concern for efficiency.

The term 'efficient' implies competent use of resources (labour and capital, for example), whilst 'effectiveness' is a measure of the consequence of policies and practices. Both organizations have been subject to politically-instigated reviews of their performance that have been concerned with issues of efficiency (financial performance and management) as opposed to questions of effectiveness and these reviews, especially in the case of CCW, have had a wider impact on the work of the agencies.

At the time of the announcement of reforms to the conservation organizations there was concern that the new country bodies for Scotland and Wales would be subservient to the pro-development inclination of the Scottish and Welsh Offices and their respective development agencies. Ministers can exercise control over bodies such as the CCW and SNH through the appointments they make; through the legislation they promote; through the resources they make available; and through the policies they advocate. So, although in technical terms the CCW and SNH enjoy independent status, this status is fragile and the effectiveness of their role as advisors, protectors of the natural heritage and facilitators of countryside enjoyment is largely dependent on political support and goodwill. This dependency and the problems that it can create was clearly illustrated during Mr Redwood's period as secretary of state for Wales.

The Rt. Hon. John Redwood replaced David Hunt as secretary of state for Wales in the summer of 1993, and following his appointment the political climate within which the CCW had to operate changed dramatically. Mr Redwood's occupancy of the Welsh Office marked a turbulent period in Welsh environmental politics. It appeared to many that Mr Redwood was intent on unilateral action to reduce the importance of environmental issues in the Principality. He is quoted as bracketing environmentalists with 'European neo-Nazis' and 'totalitarians in China' and was apparently described by some sources at the Department of the Environment as having declared UDI and being aggressively anti-environment (Lean, 1995). Whilst questioning the efficiency of the CCW, his actions had a severe impact on the effectiveness of the Council to deliver its integrated remit. Within months of replacing David Hunt, Mr Redwood had questioned the effectiveness of designations (with various comments about what constituted a 'nice' number of SSSIs) and, more seriously, brought forward the normal five-year Financial Management and Performance Review (FMPR) of the Council. The FMPR effectively placed the Council in limbo: all recruitment was frozen, work on the five-year strategic plan was held in abeyance, an internal reorganization to improve the efficiency of service delivery was halted and the Council delayed the publication of important policy documents after the secretary of state told them that they should not be formulating policy. The FMPR was submitted to the secretary of state in August 1994 but apparently shelved. A signal of what was to come was provided by a parliamentary question tabled by Sir

Wyn Roberts (formerly a Welsh Office minister with responsibility for countryside issues) which asked the secretary of state for Wales whether he intended to review the functions of the CCW with a view to those functions being transferred to national and local government, and what plans he had to reduce the overhead costs of the CCW. The nature of the question, along with the fact that it was posed by a former minister, suggest that it was pre-arranged. Mr Redwood signalled in his reply that he was personally examining the functions of the Council, and in a subsequent press briefing he stated that his work would supersede the FMPR and result in an 'Action Plan' for the CCW. The results of the secretary of state's review were a £3.37m cut in the grant-in-aid for the Council and a draft action plan which proposed that the CCW should: transfer management of National Nature Reserves to others; withdraw from public-rights-of-way-related work and leave it to local councils; withdraw from education and interpretation, which were regarded as an unnecessary form of PR; and that universities should carry out most research.

The draft action plan generated much controversy. When leaked to the press it led to the headline 'Batty Redwood wants to privatise Snowdon' (Lean, 1995); the subsequent resignation of a member of the CCW's council; and letters to the Prime Minister from leaders of environmental non-government organizations complaining that the cut in grant-in-aid would 'jeopardise the UK's prospects of meeting its international commitments to environmental protection'. The secretary of state pressed ahead with his agenda despite the public outcry and protestations from the CCW that the reduced level of funding was not adequate to allow it to fulfil its statutory duties and functions. The final action plan was published on the Saturday morning of the VE weekend, immediately after local election results – timing that guaranteed minimal press and public attention. The plan, together with cuts in budget, meant that the Council faced a cut of one third in its staff complement between 1994/5 and 1996/7. It emphasized the desire of the secretary of state to see elected local authorities undertake more of the council's work in relation to access to the countryside, country parks and day-to-day management of NNRs and some SSSIs. It also reduced the CCW's ability to: comment on proposed development schemes, finance experimental schemes and implement the Habitats Directive.

The concept of an 'arms-length' agency giving impartial advice to central government, local authorities, individuals and groups on the basis of the research that it undertakes and sponsors was apparently an anathema to John Redwood. So why did this particular secretary of state embark on a process of reform that was aimed at the emasculation of the CCW? A number of factors can be discerned. First, Mr Redwood's ideological stance on environmental issues meant that he saw conservation as an impediment to progress rather than a necessary element of an advanced society. This is illustrated in various quotes about what constitutes a 'nice number of SSSIs', his article in the *Guardian* newspaper on 10 January 1994 and his 'Environmental Agenda for Wales' (Redwood, 1995). Secondly, circumstances led to a feeling of mistrust between the secretary of state and the CCW. For example, in December 1993 HRH the Prince of Wales gave the inaugural CCW environment lecture, which was well received by the public and professional conservationists but regarded as an attack on the government by the secretary of state who assumed that the CCW had written it – Redwood subsequently asked the Council to document its input into the Prince of Wales' lecture. Development proposals for Mostyn Docks, part of a Special Protection Area, also led to friction between the Council and the secretary of state. The secretary of state had declared that the application was only of local importance and the CCW had to remind him that development in such areas should only be allowed where there are 'imperative reasons of overriding public interest'. The fact that Special Protection Areas are designated under European legislation only added insult to injury for a minister whose opposition to Europe has been very clear. Thirdly, this whole episode took place during a period of sustained criticism of the 'quango culture' of government in Wales, which allowed the secretary of state to dress up his proposals as an attempt to empower locally-elected authorities by restraining the authority of an unelected body.

The Redwood agenda not only questioned the very role of the CCW; it also raised the fundamental issue of whether the conservation and enjoyment of our natural heritage is a 'public good' and therefore a legitimate area for public expenditure. The cuts in budget and staff meant that the CCW was unable to pursue its integrated remit and the vision of moving away from protection based on designations to a management system that involves local communities as its statutory duties (the protection of designated sites) had to have first call on the severely limited resources. This, in turn, raised the spectre of a two-tier countryside in Wales consisting of protected sites where 'conservation' could be practised and the rest of the countryside where development could proceed unhindered. The Redwood saga also raised questions of the role of council members – were they political appointees effectively silenced by their allowances (a suggestion that came from the one member who spoke out in public against the cuts) and to whom were they accountable?

What are the wider ramifications of institutional reform?

Probably the most obvious impact of agency reform in Scotland and Wales has been a real increase in the resources available for conservation and facilitation of countryside enjoyment in the two countries. There are more staff in the field and the grant-in-aid given to the CCW and SNH was designed to fund enhanced programmes of work and ensure that both countries were self-sufficient in terms of scientific support (a reservation voiced by the House of Lords Select Committee on Science and Technology, 1990). The establishment of SNH brought a 250 per cent increase in the resources for natural heritage work in Scotland (Crofts, 1995) and in Wales, the establishment of CCW brought a threefold increase in labour resources and a doubling of cash resources (prior to the Redwood era) (Mercer, 1995).

The establishment of the CCW and SNH created a new policy network for countryside conservation and a different set of institutional relations. For example, the sponsoring department for the CCW is the Welsh Office, whereas for its predecessors it was the Department of the Environment. This has had important ramifications for the CCW. The Welsh Office was established in the 1960s and has become a multi-functional department, covering areas such as agriculture, education, health, transport and housing. This could be seen as an advantage because it provides the CCW with access to one department with responsibility for all policy issues in the Principality. However, in reality the Welsh Office remains relatively weak and often functions as little more than a regional arm of the larger sectoral departments in Whitehall. The Welsh Office had no history of involvement in countryside conservation until the establishment of the CCW and it has traditionally been the case that policy in Wales follows that in England. This meant that in practice the Council has had to service the Welsh Office, but also maintain a link with the more powerful departments in England (notably the Agriculture, Environment, Transport and Trade and Industry departments). Whilst there is increasingly a willingness to address particular issues within a Welsh framework – the preparation of a white paper on Rural Wales for example – in practice, this can mean little more than devolution without control. In contrast, the Scottish Office is a larger and more influential voice within the machinery of UK governance. It had a history of involvement in countryside conservation prior to the establishment of SNH, through its sponsorship of the Countryside Commission for Scotland, and was responsible for the development of a Scotland only system for landscape conservation. The particular division of the government department to which an agency communicates is also an important factor in shaping the influence of that agency on government policy and practice.

The impact on policy networks has extended beyond the statutory institutional framework. For example, an important by-product of CCW's establishment was the empowerment of the Welsh voluntary sector. Prior to the Environmental Protection Act 1990, Wales had essentially been treated as another English region, especially in terms of nature conservation. When the proposals for a new Welsh body were announced, the voluntary environmental sector in Wales was poorly developed in comparison to the organizations in England and Scotland: small-scale and constrained by the lack of a Welsh body to fashion policies and practices to protect the Welsh environment. Bodies like the Campaign for the Protection of Rural Wales, whilst concerned about the motives that lay behind the proposals, were enthusiastic about the idea of an authoritative Welsh body with a strong strategic role. The CCW provides the Welsh environmental movement with a new and more accessible outlet for its views and grievances and one that is concerned with fashioning policies suitable for the Welsh context. An immediate impact of the establishment of CCW was the formation of a Wales Wildlife and Countryside Link to bring together the hitherto disparate voices of Welsh environmentalism. Individual groups have also benefited from greater grant-aid, for example the eight Welsh Wildlife Trusts. The Welsh trusts tended to work in isolation prior to the establishment of CCW but now that the body to influence is based in Bangor rather than Peterborough there is a greater degree of collective action – as witnessed by the formation of Welsh Wildlife Trusts Ltd. in 1995. This empowerment and involvement of the voluntary sector is also witnessed in terms of countryside recreation with the formation of a Welsh Access Forum which provides a vehicle for all organizations responsible for either managing land or promoting its recreational use to discuss access issues. It was also recognized by John Redwood, when he was secretary of state for Wales, in his description of Welsh environmental groups as 'CCW pensioners'.

The impact of establishing integrated conservation cum countryside agencies in Scotland and Wales extends beyond the boundaries of those countries. The establishment of the CCW and SNH has helped generate new ideas and a diversity of approaches to countryside conservation and enjoyment. The new agencies have the ability, through their integrated remit, to examine the protected area system as a whole, whilst the Countryside Commission and English Nature are restricted to examining the provisions for landscape protection and nature conservation in isolation, so it is not surprising that both agencies are placing a new emphasis on holistic environmental management. Moves towards such a system, however realistic, have ramifications for England as there is currently a Great Britain system of nature conservation and Wales also shares the legislative base for landscape protection with England.

The continued institutional enshrinement of the 'great divide' in England has, since the merger proposals for Scotland and Wales were first announced, seemed an anomaly. The justification of separate bodies for England because of the 'much greater density of population and consequent pressure on the land' has always seemed weak and served only to emphasize the lack of any rational thinking about the implications of merger in Scotland and Wales. When proposals for a merger of the Countryside Commission and English Nature were announced in 1994, they were treated with suspicion because the government did not advance any case for merger and, in the absence of such a case, it was widely assumed that it was a Treasury-instigated cost-cutting exercise. Nevertheless, the existence of integrated countryside bodies in Northern Ireland, Scotland and Wales continues to point towards the logic of ultimate merger in England.

Debates during the passage of the Environmental Protection Bill about the need for a body to co-ordinate the work of the new agencies and the recommendations contained in the House of Lords Select Committee on Science and Technology (1990) report on the *Nature Conservancy Council* led to the creation of the Joint Nature Conservation Committee (JNCC). The JNCC has been plagued with anomalies from birth (Reynolds and Sheate, 1992). It was argued that if the JNCC was given real powers, this would be contrary to the devolution motives behind the establishment of the CCW and SNH so the committee became, in reality, a servant of the country agencies but without a clear role. Its remit is also illogical as it deals only with nature conservation yet the need for integration of landscape protection and countryside enjoyment matters is arguably just as great. The JNCC's problems have continued in operation with the CCW and, to a lesser extent, SNH seeing it as an important body in its own right but English Nature often viewing it as an impediment to its own actions.

Conclusions

The central philosophy behind rural policy has changed very little since the early years of this century. The leaders of Parliament's three biggest parties wrote to *The Times* on 9 February 1996 pledging their unity in the need to protect 'our countryside in its rich personality and character'; a pledge that repeats almost verbatim the hopes outlined by their predecessors in 1929. However, to argue that 'there has been remarkably little restructuring of the aims, roles and methods of the different countryside agencies' (Hodge *et al.*, 1994) underestimates the importance of the institutional reforms instigated by Nicholas Ridley in 1989. The establishment of the CCW and SNH has resulted in important and significant changes to the institutional framework for countryside conservation. Whilst their creation had more to do with the changing politics of nationalist Britain it broke the framework for countryside conservation established in the period of post-war reconstruction.

The creation of unified agencies for Scotland and Wales has stimulated new thinking about the aims, roles and methods of such bodies. The merging of nature conservation with the protection and enjoyment of landscapes has enabled both agencies to advocate a more holistic approach to countryside management and to question the effectiveness of a countryside protection system that dates back to the 1940s. This process of exploring the meaning of their new remit, coupled with the desire to adopt and promote a style of operation that is respectful of the different cultures of the two countries, is leading to a diversity of working methods. The process of integration has not been easy and is not complete. For example, the holistic approach advocated in *Threshold 21* (CCW, 1993a) was seen by other non-departmental public bodies (quangos) and local authorities in Wales as an attempt by CCW to take-over their functions: highway authorities thought it signalled CCW's intention to take-over their responsibilities for public rights of way and the Welsh Office Agricultural Department (WOAD) was concerned about the statements relating to agriculture.

The question concerning the effectiveness of the new agencies in the delivery of their remits is a difficult one and deserving of further research. In a narrow sense, effectiveness could be gauged by assessing the impact of, for example: policy development; planning advice; grant-aid; and research, but in a wider sense such a question needs to consider whether the model of non-departmental bodies, established by statute, with appointed chairmen and boards is the appropriate one for the delivery of countryside conservation. In practice, the effectiveness question has been confused with political concern for efficiency.

The establishment of the CCW and SNH has created a new policy network for countryside conservation both within, and beyond, their respective countries. Within Wales, the establishment of the CCW has forced the Welsh Office to take a greater interest in countryside issues and is helping to foster a situation where such issues are considered on a Principality-only basis and not as part of an exercise led by the Department of the Environment. The fact that the Welsh Office published a rural white paper (1996) is, in part, a testimony to these changes. In Scotland, the establishment of SNH has further strengthened the interest of the Scottish Office in countryside issues – adding nature conservation to an existing concern for landscape protection. The impact extends beyond official policy networks and includes the empowerment of environmental non-governmental organizations in Scotland and Wales. It also raises the spectre of devolution without control. Whilst the CCW and SNH are officially responsible for the conservation of natural heritage and promotion of its enjoyment in their respective countries they often lack the powers to materially alter the provisions for countryside conservation and enjoyment.

Note

[1] This explanation of the reforms as politically motivated and poorly thought out, whilst accepted by most commentators, is contested by Crofts (1995) who argues that there 'was a long deliberative process in Scotland, albeit only within Government, to determine the style and focus which a Scottish-based, environmental organisation dealing the whole natural heritage should have' (p.28).

References

Addison, C. 1931. *Report of the National Parks Committee*, Cmnd. 3851 (London, HMSO).

Baldock, D., C. Coffey and K. D. Bishop, forthcoming. *The Organisation of Nature Conservation in Selected European Countries*, Papers in Environmental Research, Department of City and Regional Planning (Cardiff, University of Wales Cardiff).

Bishop, K. D. and A. A. C. Phillips 1993. 'Seven steps to market – the development of the market-led approach to countryside conservation and recreation', *Journal of Rural Studies*, Vol.9, No.4, pp.315–38.

Blunden, J. and N. Curry 1991. *A People's Charter?* (London, HMSO).

Buono, A. and J. Bowditch 1989. *The Human Side of Mergers and Acquisitions* (San Francisco, Jossey-Bass).

Caldwell, N. 1993. 'Cyngor Cefn Gwlad Cymru: Trying to break the mould', *ECOS*, Vol.14, Nos.3/4, pp.42–7.

Carter, N. and P. Lowe 1995. 'The establishment of a cross-sector environment agency', in T. S. Gray (ed.), *UK Environmental Policy in the 1990s* (London, Macmillan).

Countryside Council for Wales 1993a. *Threshold 21: A Paper for Discussion* (Bangor, Countryside Council for Wales).

Countryside Council for Wales 1993b. *Cynnal Cynefin: A Commitment by the Countryside Council for Wales* (Bangor, Countryside Council for Wales).

Crofts, R. 1995. 'The merits of merger: the Scottish experience', in K. D. Bishop (ed.), *The Merits of Merger*, Environmental and Countryside Planning Unit (Cardiff, University of Wales Cardiff), pp.28–37.

Dower, J. 1945. *National Parks in England and Wales*, Cmnd. 6628 (London, HMSO).

Grove-White, R. 1994. *England's Green Horizon: A Conservation and Countryside Access Agency for the post-Rio World* (Newbury, British Association of Nature Conservationists).

HM Government 1991. *This Common Inheritance: The First Year Report*, Cmnd. 1655 (London, HMSO).

Hodge, I., W. M. Adams and A. D. Bourn 1994. 'Conservation policy in the wider countryside: agency competition and innovation', *Journal of Environmental Planning and Management*, Vol.37, No.2, pp.199–213.

House of Lords Select Committee on Science and Technology 1990. *Nature Conservancy Council*, House of Lords Paper 33-I, Session 1989–90 (London, HMSO).

Lean, G. 1995. 'Batty Redwood wants to privatise Snowdon', *Independent on Sunday*, 22 January.

Lowe, P. 1990. 'Reforming UK conservation', *Built Environment*, Vol.16, No.3, pp.171–8.

Lowe, P., G. Cox, M. MacEwen, T. O'Riordan and M. Winter 1986. *Countryside Conflicts: The Politics of Farming, Forestry and Conservation* (Aldershot, Gower/Maurice Temple Smith).

MacEwen, A. and M. MacEwen 1982. *National Parks: Conservation or Cosmetics?* (London, George Allen & Unwin).

MacEwen, A. and M. MacEwen 1987. *Greenprints for the Countryside?* (London, Allen & Unwin).

Mercer, I. 1995. 'The merits of merger: the Welsh experience', in K. D. Bishop (ed.), *The Merits of Merger*, Environmental and Countryside Planning Unit (Cardiff, University of Wales Cardiff), pp.20–8.

Phillips, A. A. C. 1993. 'The Countryside Commission and the Thatcher years', in A. Gilg (ed.), *Progress in Rural Policy and Planning*, Vol.3 (London, Belhaven), pp.63–90.

Phillips, A. A. C. 1995. 'The merits of merger: a history and the issues', in K. D. Bishop (ed.), *The Merits of Merger*, Environmental and Countryside Planning Unit (Cardiff, University of Wales Cardiff), pp.3–12.

Ramsay, D. 1947. Scottish National Parks Committee and Scottish Wildlife Conservation Committee, *National Parks and the Conservation of Nature in Scotland* (London, HMSO).

Redwood, J. 1995. 'The environmental agenda for Wales: a statement by the Secretary of State for Wales' (Cardiff, Welsh Office).

Reynolds, F. and W. Sheate 1992. 'Reorganisation of conservation authorities', in W. Howarth and C. P. Rodgers (eds.), *Agriculture, Conservation and Land Use* (Cardiff, University of Wales Press), pp.73–90.

Scottish Natural Heritage 1993. *Sustainable Development and the Natural Heritage: The SNH Approach* (Edinburgh, Scottish Natural Heritage).

Scottish Office 1990. *Scotland's Natural Heritage: The Way Ahead* (Edinburgh, Scottish Office).

Sheail, J. 1988. 'The great divide: an historical perspective', *Landscape Research*, Vol.13, No.1, pp.2–5.

Welsh Affairs Committee 1994. *Wind Energy: Volume 1*, House of Commons Paper 336-I, Session 1993–4 (London, HMSO).

Welsh Office 1996. *A Working Countryside for Wales* (London, HMSO).

13

Language and Planning in Scotland and Wales

CLIVE JAMES and COLIN H. WILLIAMS

Language and the nation

Linguistic minorities in Europe have been facing a crisis since at least the Versailles and Trianon settlements which established the modern European state system. At one level, the recognition of linguistic rights within constituent states is a unique local issue. Collectively, however, the assertion of the rights of minorities to flourish poses a major challenge to the dominant European order, involving issues of individual versus group rights, indigenous versus international forms of cultural expression, the degree of state involvement in the regulation and political channelling of activities in peripheral regions, the institutionalization of minority cultures and the amount of autonomy granted to local authorities to deal with questions of social diversity, local economic development and sustainable growth.

We will be examining several of these issues with reference to the responsiveness of the Scottish and Welsh planning systems to sociolinguistic diversity, for planning can make a significant contribution to the containment and satisfaction of minority demands. Conversely, of course, if the planning system, as an active arm of the state, is operating to maintain the hegemonic position of the majority then it becomes a crucial variable which shapes the environment within which the minority language struggle takes place.

Faced with the inexorable standardization of modern values, ideas, modes of behaviour and economic pressures, Gaelic and Welsh speakers recognize that their range of action is severely limited by their political dependence and marginal economic position. Marginalization takes the form of cultural attrition, demographic replacement and regional structural decline where social dislocation and economic dependency are acute. In an earlier phase of capitalist development, the peripheral regions of Western Europe were characterized by an unbalanced and non-diversified economic base operating through a cultural division of labour. As the global economy expanded and capital investment was transferred from older industrial regions to new locations, decline was accelerated by the inability of local entrepreneurs to redress the balance. Local claims for greater inter-regional equality went unsatisfied as the framers of regional development and social welfare policy were increasingly unable to direct growth into the periphery, thus intensifying local crises (Williams, 1983).

Central to the overcoming of this local crisis is the indigenous culture of the marginal population, since it is culture which serves as the medium for legitimization and institutionalization of power and inequality. In the postwar period, attempts to institutionalize Gaelic and Welsh within education, public administration and the media have met with varying degrees of success. In part this reflects the re-definition of the relationship between the individual, the indigenous language community and society. It also reflects the expanding nature of state involvement in all aspects of social and economic life. Consequently, the relative autonomy enjoyed by Gaelic and Welsh culture is increasingly dependent upon state legitimization and financing. A critical change in the linguistic arguments of late has been a switch in emphasis from urgent promotional work within individual domains, such as education, to a realization that only holistic solutions will establish the conditions whereby cultural reproduction can be sustained. In consequence, the context of language planning and policy has almost become as influential as the content.

It is significant that both conventional land-use planning and language planning are increasingly seen as inter-related for it is our conviction that only a close working relationship between practitioners from different disciplinary backgrounds can effect purposive change which will allow Welsh and Gaelic to flourish once again.

Conventionally, questions of language and culture were inadmissible as determinants of land-use planning in Britain, no matter how significant they may have been at the local level. Recently a concern for 'unity within diversity' has permeated the profession leading to a reformulation of the relationship between the central state and the local/regional periphery. Linguistic considerations within planning documents are currently justified on the grounds that they conserve the local character of distinctive regions. This justification reflects both cultural self-defence arguments and principles of eco-philosophy drawn from the wider society (Williams, 1991b).

Scale and locality: the planning context

Many factors conduce to the creation of an appropriate context for sociolinguistic vitality. The most significant, and hitherto least mobilized, has been the pivotal role of planning in either enabling or in disallowing certain determining influences which have a bearing on language and cultural survival. Planning for language reproduction is, of course, normally associated with corpus and status language planning and does not necessarily take any account of the statutory land-use planning system. This is a great pity for ethno-linguistic vitality is often heavily influenced by the statutory planning process (Nelde *et al.*, 1992).

Clearly language planning is not a precise instrument of social intervention and it is as capable of manipulation as any other aspect of state policy. Neither does it demonstrate an *a priori* commitment to legitimizing threatened indigenous languages. For many struggling linguistic minorities, the overriding difficulty has been their failure to convince state decision-makers to establish a set of statutory agencies for the promotion of the threatened language. For the indigenous community, the problem may be a lack of institutionalized power to transform their situation. For the central state, it may be that regional ethnic differences are perceived as an impediment to the functioning of state-wide programmes of economic development and social integration.

Conscious of this ideological struggle, some language planners and academic interpreters have recognized the contextual effects on language maintenance and language loss and have sought to incorporate environmental and political economy factors directly into their analyses. In this chapter, we hope to extend the debate by systematically examining the relationship between language and the planning context in Scotland and Wales. We are convinced that this domain will become increasingly significant in the years to come and urge professional town and country planners to take a broader interest in the constituent characteristics of the national communities they are serving.

Scotland and Wales: demo-linguistic comparisons

Any comparison of the status of Gaelic and Welsh within the statutory land-use based town and country planning legislation in Scotland and Wales must begin with an appreciation of the role and status each language possesses within their respective countries.

In Scotland, only two local authority areas have a Gaelic-speaking population in excess of 40 per cent of the total population. (All numbers and percentages of speakers quoted for either language refer to the population aged 3 and over who speak that language only or both that language and English as published in the decennial census of population.) These are the Western Isles (a unitary authority where 19,546 spoke Gaelic – 68 per cent of the population) and Skye and Lochalsh District where 4,715 spoke Gaelic – 41 per cent of the population. Although the latter is a

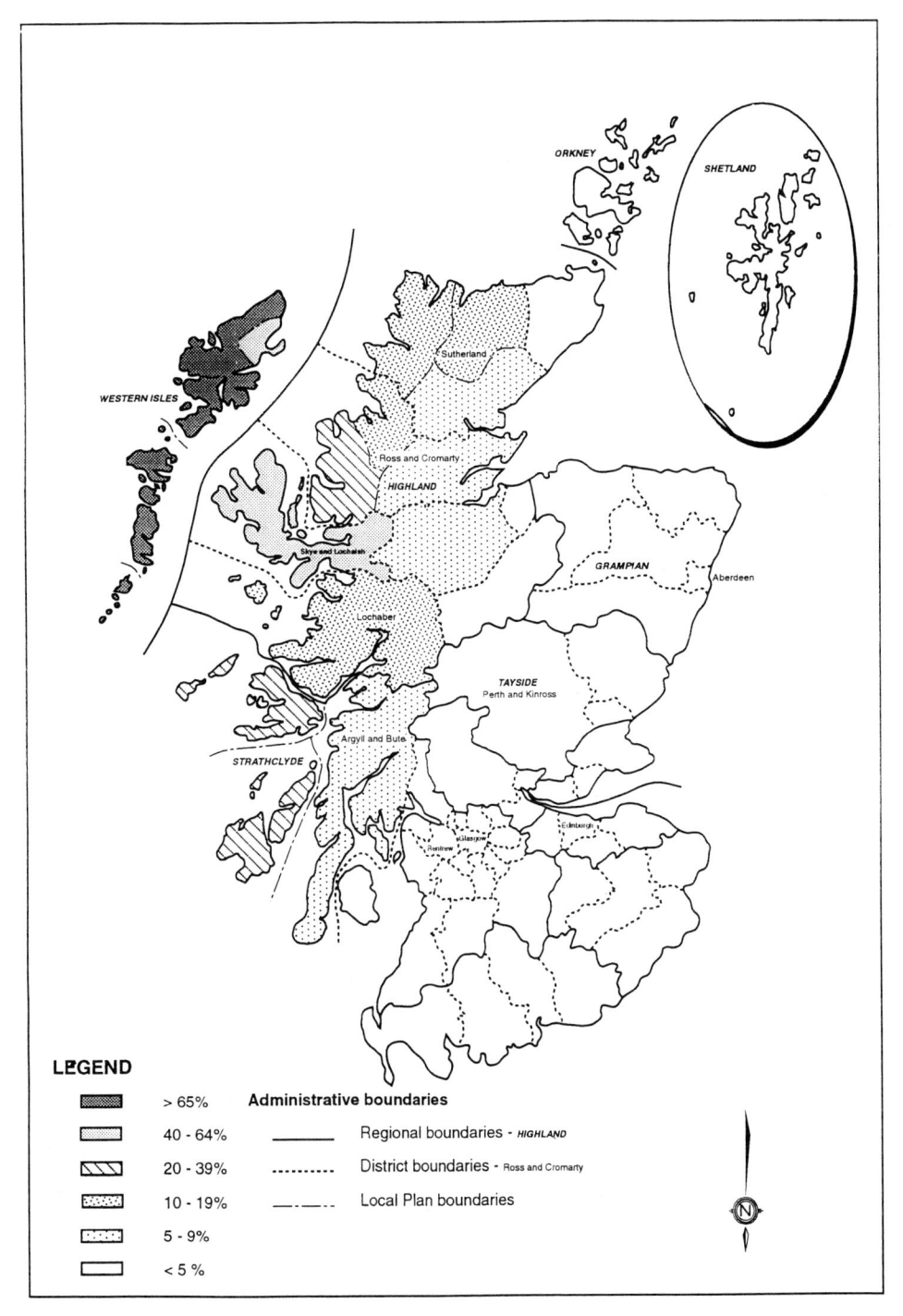

Figure 13.1 Local planning areas and language strength before 1996: Scotland (data derived from local planning authorities and from the 1991 Census)

district council it does not possess land-use planning powers – like all district councils in Highland Region. Together, these two authorities have a combined population of 39,865 (0.8 per cent of the population of Scotland), and a combined Gaelic-speaking population of 24,261 (37 per cent of the Gaelic-speaking population of Scotland). The next most Gaelic-speaking local authorities are as shown in Table 13.1.

Table 13.1 Gaelic-Speaking Local Authorities (over 5 per cent) in 1991

Region	District	Population over 3 years of age	Gaelic speakers	Percentage
Highland	Lochaber	18,582	1,988	10.7
Highland	Sutherland	12,750	954	7.5
Strathclyde	Argyll and Bute	62,736	4,583	7.3
Highland	Ross and Cromarty	47,290	2,812	5.9
Highland	Inverness	59,773	3,476	5.8

Source: Census of Scotland, Registrar-General for Scotland (Scottish Office, 1991).

None of the other forty-nine districts or island council areas has a Gaelic-speaking population in excess of 5 per cent. Only five other districts have in excess of 1,000 Gaelic speakers – the major centres of Aberdeen, Edinburgh, Glasgow and Renfrew, together with the residual Gaelic area of Perth and Kinross. Whereas the historic Gaelic-speaking area of Scotland (broadly Highland Region minus Caithness district, together with the Western Isles, and Argyll and Bute) comprise 43 per cent of the Scottish land area and 5 per cent of the Scottish population, 59.2 per cent of the Gaelic speakers live in this area.

The marginalization of Gaelic reflects its limited geographical strength and relative national insignificance – not surprising perhaps when one considers that the 65,978 Gaelic speakers represent only 1.4 per cent of the Scottish population. Within the structures of the nation, the language is virtually ignored, despite the maintenance of a separate, virulent institutional system based upon distinctive educational, legal and religious domains.

The situation in Wales, by contrast, is significantly different. Of the thirty-seven district councils (that is, the local planning authority areas), eight have Welsh-speaking populations in excess of 40 per cent compared with only two in Scotland (Table 13.2).

The fifteen authorities in Table 13.2 have a combined population of over 763,000 (29 per cent of the total Welsh population) and a combined Welsh-speaking population of 353,000 (70 per cent of all Welsh speakers in Wales).

There are, in addition, a number of local authorities in industrial south

Table 13.2 Welsh-speaking Local Authorities in excess of 20 per cent, 1991

County	Districts	Population over three years of age	Welsh-speaking	Percentage
Gwynedd	Ynys Môn	66,525	41,240	62.0
	Arfon	51,092	38,119	74.6
	Dwyfor	26,246	19,798	75.4
	Meirionydd	31,815	20,816	65.4
	Aberconwy	51,184	18,440	36.0
Dyfed	Ceredigion	60,980	36,026	59.0
	Carmarthen	53,318	30,919	58.0
	Dinefwr	37,297	24,811	66.5
	Llanelli	72,048	33,483	46.5
Clwyd	Colwyn	53,220	13,572	25.5
	Glyndŵr	40,338	16,076	39.8
Powys	Montgomery	50,676	11,796	23.3
	Brecknock	39,836	9,175	23.0
Dyfed	Preseli	67,571	16,454	24.3
W. Glam	Lliw Valley	60,588	22,369	36.9

Source: Census of Population, 1991 (OPCS).

and north-east Wales which have a substantial Welsh-speaking population (between 4,200 and 17,500), comprising some 6 per cent to 18 per cent of the population. All but five of the thirty-seven local planning authorities have in excess of 5 per cent of their population able to speak Welsh. These figures include every planning authority in Gwent. Even the most Anglicized authority in Gwent has 1,450 Welsh speakers.

The language question is so intricately bound up with the life of the nation that no district council would consider itself to be devoid of a Welsh-speaking interest. Whereas the proportionate strength of Welsh varies considerably, it is nowhere so marginalized as is Gaelic in most of Scotland. Only in districts in Gwent, Radnor, South Pembrokeshire and on Deeside does one experience a situation comparable to that which obtains in most of Scotland (outside Highlands and Western Islands). Indeed, only in the border district of Monmouth does the proportionate population fall to 2 per cent – and that figure is in excess of the average for Scotland.

The mere fact that at least 18.9 per cent (508,098) of the population are Welsh speaking gives the language issue a significance which is absent in Scotland. Also the iconography of the landscape reflects an increasingly bilingual society with far greater use of Welsh in public signs, advertisements, place names, the media and general conversation. For example, the

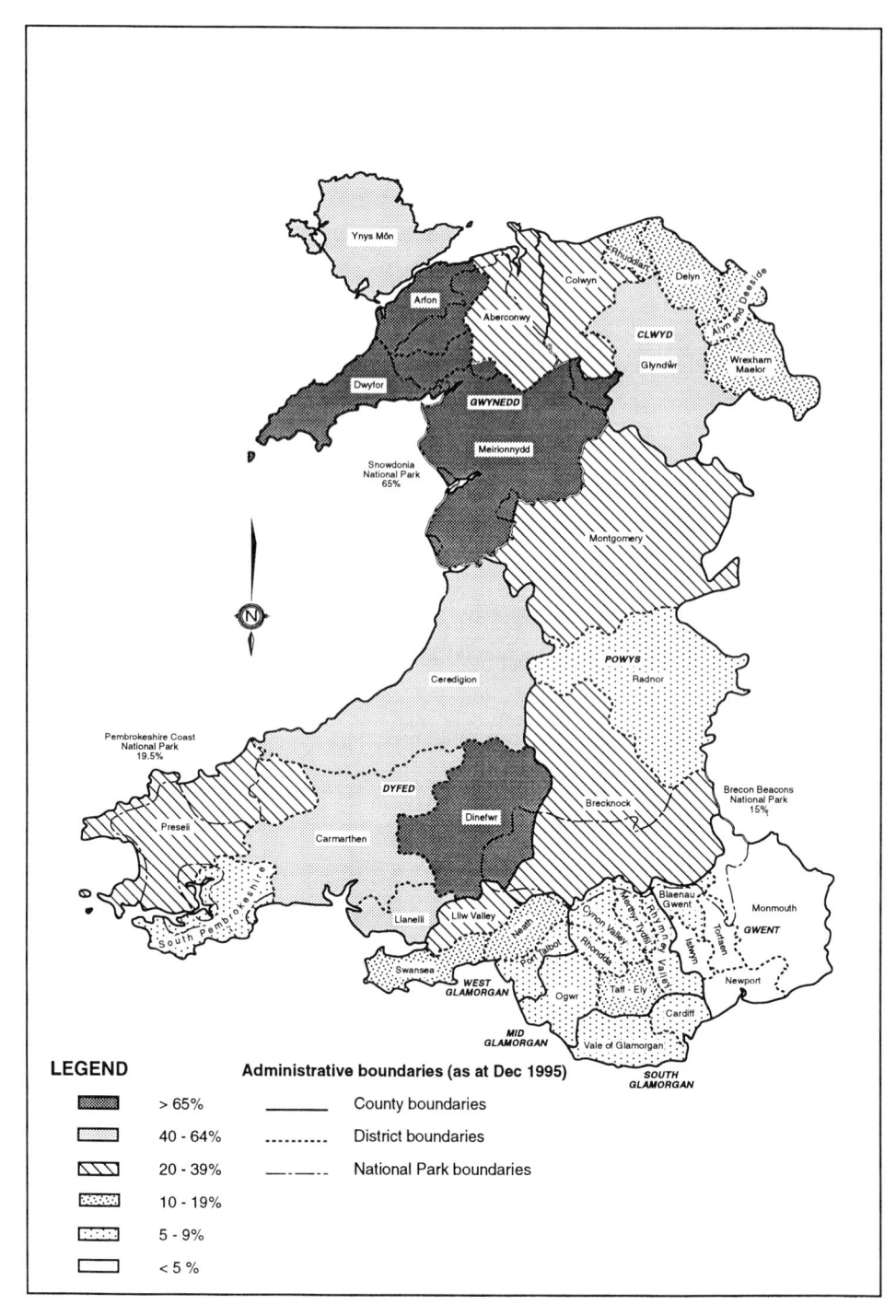

Figure 13.2 Local planning areas and language strength before 1996: Wales (data derived from local planning authorities and from the 1991 Census)

number of Welsh speakers in South Glamorgan, which includes Cardiff, the capital, and its southern suburbs totals 24,500 – which would represent 37 per cent of all Gaelic speakers in Scotland.

Territorial considerations

The dominant theme in the geo-linguistics of Welsh and Gaelic has been the collapse of the territorial strength of the north and west which raises the question as to whether a virulent Welsh or Gaelic culture can survive without their own autochthonous core areas as a resource-base (Williams, 1980a, b, 1995). A critical concern of sensitive planning is how to establish an infrastructure whereby the rights and obligations of Welsh/English and Gaelic/English speakers can be realized in tandem within a changing geographical context.

The ethnic intelligentsia in many of the lesser-used language regions of Europe have stressed the organic authenticity of language. Their focus on the inviolability of the ethnic homeland has given a literal interpretation to the search for roots in the soil, community and landscape of one's *own* people. In Wales, concepts derived from 'cydymdreiddiad tir ac iaith' ('the interpenetration of land and language') have very recently been given practical shape in planning policies which aim to bolster Welsh-speaking communities through environmental improvement and rural-economic diversification (J. R. Jones, 1966). The language movement has rediscovered its 'ecological' heritage, and has re-packaged what were deemed to be rural community issues in the 1920s and 1930s as issues of 'cultural species' survival and as a local response to globalization (Williams, 1994a).

Many individuals are more autonomous, exercising language community without geographical contiguity. Processes such as the in-migration of non-Welsh speakers, mixed marriages, language shift, the revolution in telecommunications and journey to work patterns have all contributed to the fragmentation of the traditional strongholds. Is fragmentation and collapse the inevitable future for these areas? And if so, should we be far less concerned with notions of domination, of territorial control and of resistance to externally-induced change?

If we acknowledge the declining significance of territorial strongholds we are led to depend on factors, such as the mass media to integrate Welsh speakers within a communication network. Yet no matter how comprehensive may be the new social communication system, Welsh speakers will still need a region or a set of spaces wherein their language is dominant, or at the very least, co-equal with English. This is because the routinization of culture and economy can best be accomplished within familiar spaces. However, so many contemporary social processes are non-contiguous that experts are talking of the death of geography, because mass technology has overcome the barrier of space which distance conventionally represents. From this perspective, heartlands are *passé*. Attempts to introduce conventional territorial language planning measures based upon a set of shrinking cultural regions are doomed.

We thus need to identify new ways of adopting a spatial planning perspective to serve an ever-changing reality. One of the determining factors influencing this choice will be the infrastructure currently being developed to support bilingual services. Absolute population increases and percentage and absolute increases of Welsh speakers in Cardiff, Llandrindod, Mold, Caernarfon, Llangefni, Aberystwyth and Carmarthen all point to a relocation of linguistic strength from villages in traditional heartland areas to new urban centres. These changes pose fresh planning challenges.

National institutionalization and bilingualism

Scotland has retained many of its national institutions since the Act of Union and has been successful in further differentiating itself from the rest of the UK in domains such as education, public administration and the law. In contrast national institutions in Wales were repressed following the Act of Union in 1536 until the last quarter of the nineteenth century (see I. G. Jones, 1992). However, Welsh self-confidence was boosted during the period of Victorian nation-building and had regained much of the status it had lost following the Union. Liberal Nonconformity was the spur to the establishment of a set of national institutions which reflected the bilingual character of the modernizing society.

By the time the Town and Country Planning Act of 1947 was enacted a rudimentary infrastructure supporting bilingual services already existed, based largely upon education and public administration. A promising development since then has been the renewed institutionalization of Welsh in public life, and a novel focus on language considerations within the private sector. If a strong institutional base can be constructed nationwide, then this will create new opportunities and domains wherein Welsh may be used as a matter of course. Conventionally, such usage is guaranteed either by reference to territorial language rights or to the personality principle of language rights (Nelde *et al.*, 1992).

The socialization of the next generation of Welsh speakers depends largely upon within-family language reproduction and education. Analysis of the OPCS 1991 data on Welsh households confirms that 26.4 per cent of all households contained Welsh speakers, 56.6 per cent were 'fully Welsh-speaking', of whom only 10.9 per cent contained children (Aitchison, 1995). This is a worrying characteristic of the Welsh-speaking network and does not augur well for the domestic vitality of the language as fully 43 per cent of all Welsh-speaking households contain no children. Many individuals, both old and young, simply cannot communicate in Welsh with any other resident in their home. The general pattern is one of fragmentation and isolation, despite the more encouraging extra-familial trends in education. Today Welsh is a core subject in the National Curriculum in all state schools from five to sixteen years. There are hundreds of natural Welsh-medium primary schools. Every district council area has designated Welsh-medium primary schools (or units) which feed into Welsh-medium secondary schools (or streams).

Institutionalization refers not only to the process of new domain construction, but also to the introduction of formal language planning in specific sectors via the creation of new agencies. A good illustration is 'Pwyllgor Datblygu Addysg Gymraeg' ('The Committee for the Development of Welsh Education') – which performed a significant planning role in the field of education in the period 1986–94. A better, permanent example is the statutory Welsh Language Board (established in 1994) which promises to become the most critical government agency yet in the social history of Welsh. Such status language planning allows for a measure of purposive rather than reactive thought and policy formulation. It also presages a new era of fresh initiatives and holistic interpretation of language in society which, though small-scale, represent grounded local involvement in socio-linguistic issues. The emphasis on planning requires integrated action by a number of agencies and represents a more holistic approach than hitherto has been the norm. Also it is recognized that the concerns and involvement of second-language learners and non-Welsh speakers has to be addressed in a more systematic fashion, thereby extending the bicultural nature of society from both ends of the spectrum.

In consequence, Welsh has entered a new phase of legitimacy, following the passage of the Welsh Language Act in 1993. Support for Welsh can no longer be interpreted as essentially a symbol of resistance to Anglicization, for the language is itself deeply imbued in the process of state socialization. Welsh has become a contested instrument both of reform and of governance, of opposition and of authority. Welsh is increasingly incorporated into the machinery of government, of justice, of public administration and of civic control.

Much central government rhetoric becomes watered down by the time that pragmatic county or local considerations of bilingual service provision are considered. Current concerns about the phasing out of county councils and powerful local education authorities cast doubts on the maintenance of a strong infrastructure which will enable the full implementation of language choice to be realized. The implication for civic rights under this new dependency is clear (Williams, 1993b). With the strengthened Welsh Language Board determining priorities and policies from above, and an increasingly mobilized and expectant public demanding the extension of language rights from below, there could be a vacuum at the level of some local authorities who will be charged with implementing many of these new reforms. Rather than anticipate a stronger uniform pattern of bilingual service provision throughout Wales, it is probable that we shall witness a new round of localized language-related tension because neighbouring local authorities will react differently to the new bilingual regime. Unless bilingual services become a comprehensive statutory requirement underwritten by state financing, then the bilingual programme will always be subject to competition from other sectors of local authority responsibility. Yet to approach language in such a fashion is misguided. It should not be seen as a separate entity competing against road maintenance or social service provision for scarce funding. It is not ancillary to other services in a bi- or multilingual society, but rather the democratic means by which such services are mediated to the constituent citizens. Unless and until that message is accepted in Welsh public life then the legitimacy of providing bilingual (Welsh–English) services will always be subject to fierce debate about a contested social reality.

The battle for planning status in Wales

Two important aspects to consider are the struggle to gain recognition and the current position of Gaelic and Welsh in relation to government advice.

Following local government reorganization in Wales in 1974, the present authors founded Cymdeithas Cynllunio Cymru which aimed to bring together Welsh-speaking planners and other interested professionals. The group highlighted the shortage of Welsh-speaking planning officers in Wales and lobbied the only planning school in Wales, at the then University of Wales Institute of Science and Technology, to provide Welsh-medium training while certain planning authorities started graduate training schemes to encourage Welsh speakers to undertake postgraduate courses leading to professional recognition.

Cymdeithas Cynllunio Cymru's main achievement was the Caernarfon conference in March 1977 when it pressed for full planning status for the Welsh language so that the effect of any planning proposals on the long-term well-being of Welsh would be a material consideration. Among the proponents was the young member of Parliament for Meirionnydd, Dafydd Elis Thomas, who is the current chairman of the Welsh Language Board. That summer the Society hosted a plenary lecture at the National Eisteddfod in Wrexham, in which Colin Williams outlined a strategy for national language planning in Wales calling for a specific body charged with government responsibility for the Welsh language. This was eventually realized in the establishment of the Welsh Language Board (see Williams, 1977, 1989).

Increased concern within the discipline gave rise to a professional view which concurred with the recommendations of the Council for the Welsh Language's report *A Future for the Welsh Language* (1978). This stated:

> It follows from what we have said that the Welsh language should henceforth be built into considerations of health and social work, economic planning, industrial development, housing policies and education and all the other aspects of central and local government which control and affect our lives. The language of a small community can be changed by a few newcomers where, for example, the movement of monolingual English-speaking key-workers accompanying the setting up of a factory, or where there is an inflow of non-Welsh-speakers to fill a council housing estate. We share the view that has been put to us several times that the Welsh language and the culture associated with it should be given special consideration in planning in Wales.

At their *Ysgol Basg* (Easter School) at Llanelwy (St Asaph) in 1981, Cymdeithas yr Iaith Gymraeg presented studies on the decline of Welsh in Clwyd – in the market and retirement town of Abergele, the industrial village of Ffynnongroew and the upland village of Llanefydd – and argued that this was due to deficiencies in the statutory town and country planning system through not assessing the full impact of proposed development upon the community, including the language. A subsequent conference at Llangernyw in 1982 involving language activists, officers and elected members of county, district and community councils called for:

- policy decisions to give planning status to the Welsh language
- an assessment of the impact upon the community and the Welsh language as one of the factors in determining applications for planning permission.
- reports by planning departments on the condition of the Welsh language in all of their territory with recommendations as to improving the situation.
- a section in each development plan on the Welsh language.

In March 1984, Cymdeithas yr Iaith Gymraeg met the secretary of state for Wales. His written reply stated that

> in preparing proposals for the change or replacement of a structure plan and to put others in their place, it is open for County Planning Authorities therefore to produce 'topic reports' on any subject they wish, including the Welsh language. In the same way a district planning authority can do this in relation to local plans.

Then, in October 1986 Dafydd Elis Thomas, MP, asked the secretary of state what his policy was on the effects of planning decisions on the Welsh language. On behalf of the secretary of state, Wyn Roberts replied that

> it is a requirement of local planning authorities in considering planning applications and on the Secretary of State and his Inspectors in considering planning appeals that they may have regard to all material considerations. Policies which reflect the needs and interests of the Welsh language may properly be among these considerations.

In November 1987, Dafydd Wigley (MP, Caernarfon) asked questions connected with the Welsh language and planning. These were answered by Ian Grist. The exchange can be summarized as follows:

- No guidance on the local language and planning had been offered to local planning authorities.
- On appeals, it was a requirement to consider all material considerations, including the character and way of life of a community and the needs and interests of the Welsh language.
- The needs and interests of the Welsh language in development plans can already be included, as language is a constituent part of the aim of protecting the character and way of life of communities.
(Parliamentary Questions nos. 495, 496 and 498 of 1987/88)

The first sign of this occurring was in December 1987. A Cheshire-based building company had been refused planning permission by Glyndŵr DC to add eighteen homes to the existing twenty-eight in the tiny Welsh-speaking village of Llanrhaeadr in Dyffryn Clwyd, near Denbigh. The Inspector, Mr Rhys Davies stated,

> Bearing in mind the Secretary of State's view, as regards the Welsh language, that the needs and interests of the Welsh language are important considerations, it seems to me that they should carry considerable weight in considering the impact of development.

The appeal was dismissed.

A year later (December 1988), the Welsh Office issued Circular 53/88 *The Welsh Language: Development Plans and Planning Control* which summarized the previous four years' advice. It read

- where the Welsh language is a component of the social fabric of a community, it should be considered in formulating land use policies in development plans.
- the explanatory memorandum on local plans should in appropriate

circumstances set out the regard taken to the Welsh language in formulating their proposals.
- policies in a development plan relating to the Welsh language are a material consideration in dealing with a planning application and an appeal.
- decisions must be based on planning grounds and must be reasonable, that is related to the development and use of land.'

While the circular was a significant step forward, it had its limitations. The language issue is not the supreme consideration. Planning authorities will decide if it is appropriate for them to include policies relating to the needs and interests of the language in their development plans. There are no indications as to how local authorities or inspectors are to implement the provisions of the circular.

Several more planning aspects had significant linguistic inputs in their cases, some succeeding and others failing. The government set up the non-statutory Welsh Language Board in 1988, whose purpose was to advise the secretary of state on the desired form of new Welsh language legislation. Both Dafydd Wigley, MP, and Lord Prys Davies had proposed amendments to the Town and Country Planning Act 1971 to place a 'duty for planning authorities to consider the Welsh language'. Their proposals, put forward in 1985 and 1986 respectively, were similar and sought to:

add the state of the Welsh language in those districts in Wales to the matters to be included in the surveys of planning areas in Section 6 (3).
- make it obligatory in local plans for 'those local planning authorities in Wales to contain remarks for the development of the Welsh language in their area' in Section 11 (3).
- insert a new section (58A)
'The Welsh Language in Wales.
The effects of proposed developments on the linguistic character of a community may be a material consideration for the determination of planning applications by planning authorities in Wales'. (Williams, 1989)

The intent was to make it obligatory for planning authorities to use their powers, later clarified in Circular 53/88, by modifying primary legislation and so removing the question of inspector's interpretation of the circular. In their report to the secretary of state, the Welsh Language Board decided not to recommend amendments to the planning legislation in their proposals for a new Welsh Language Act, but they were of the opinion that immigration and development required the urgent attention of the secretary of state. However, when the Welsh Language Bill was published there was no reference to planning matters and no amendments were made before the Welsh Language Act, 1993, received Royal Assent.

Planning guidance in Wales is published by the Welsh Office. Traditionally this has followed a few months behind the Marsham Street equivalent with a few minor changes. However, under John Redwood's influence as secretary of state a much condensed revised planning guidance for all subjects was published as a consultation draft – *Planning Policy Guidance (Wales)*. The draft guidance was issued simultaneously in English and Welsh versions. In paragraph 44, the philosophy of Circular 54/88 and previous Parliamentary Answers is summarized. It is clearly stated that the Welsh language is a component of social fabric and appropriate in forming land-use policies. As in all policy matters, the reasoned justification must be stated.

1995 also saw the publication of a consultation draft of *Planning Guidance (Wales): Unitary Development Plans in Wales*. In paragraph 13, the planning authorities are reminded of the requirement of the Welsh Language Act 1993 that English and Welsh must be treated on the basis of equality in the conduct of public business. Thus all documents, notices, advertisements and other materials in consultation and local inquiry must be in both Welsh and English. In local inquiries simultaneous translation must be provided unless it is most unlikely not to be used and authorities are obliged to ensure that anyone wishing to use Welsh has the opportunity to do so.

Structure planning in Wales

The relative strength of the Welsh language within the eight county councils in Wales (the structure plan authorities) is as follows:

Table 13.3 Welsh speakers by county, 1991

County	Total population over three years of age	Welsh speakers	Percentage
Gwynedd	226,862	138,413	61.0
Dyfed	331,528	144,998	43.7
Clwyd	392,812	71,405	18.2
Powys	113,333	22,871	20.2
W. Glam	347,779	53,268	15.0
M. Glam	511,656	43,263	8.4
S. Glam	375,857	24,541	6.5
Gwent	423,794	10,339	2.4

All exceed the Scottish average for Gaelic speakers of 1.8 per cent.

The first structure plans in Wales, sometimes based upon the pre-1974 'historic' counties, were approved by the secretary of state for Wales in the

1970s. In the late 1980s and early 1990s, these were replaced by new plans based on the 'new' post-1974 counties and reflected the planning philosophies of the eight county council planning authorities. It is the plans for the four rural counties of Gwynedd, Dyfed, Clwyd and Powys which have been examined in this chapter in relation to the status given to the language. Structure plans for the other counties contain no significant reference to the language.

When evaluating the status of Welsh (or Gaelic) in a development plan, one should consider three elements:
1. Does the plan examine the role of the language within the fabric of society and community in the plan area?
2. Are there specific policies relating to the language?
3. Do the combined package of policies assist the survival and continuation of distinct language communities?

The Gwynedd and Dyfed documents are entirely bilingual, Clwyd and Powys have a bilingual written statement and an English explanatory memorandum whilst the three Glamorgans and Gwent plans are in English only.

Significantly, the Gwynedd Structure Plan (adopted 1993) includes as the fifth of its six strategic policies:

> to recognise that the Welsh language is a material consideration in assessing the implications of development in Gwynedd. This will be implemented in a manner which ensures that the aim of safeguarding and nurturing the use of the Welsh language in Gwynedd is achieved.

By contrast the very last of the forty-nine strategic aims of the Powys Structure Plan (adopted 1992) is: 'to support and encourage the development of the Welsh language in communities'.

In the Clwyd Structure Plan (adopted 1989) the fourth, and last, objective is: 'to have specific regard to the aspirations of local communities and local needs' and continues under 'social considerations' when discussing 'the scale of housing development' that 'at the local level also, many small, often predominantly Welsh-speaking communities do not want to see an influx of outsiders.'

The Review (1986) of the Dyfed Structure Plan, which included a section entitled 'The Welsh language as a Structure Plan issue', acknowledged the reduction in the numbers of Welsh speakers as one factor in 'planning for uncertainty'. It is under the section on urban and rural conservation that an alteration is proposed to encourage 'developments beneficial to safeguarding Welsh speaking communities'. However, the statutory planning system is seen as having only limited impact on the future of the language.

In the Gwynedd Structure Plan, there is no further policy relating specifically to Welsh. Its continued wellbeing is an integral part of the plan, especially of the housing policies. The plan, as submitted to the secretary of state, was to restrict new housing provision to proven local need and employment related movement. In modifying the plan before approving it, the secretary of state rewrote the housing policies and removed all reference to differentiation in the housing market and so supported the lobby of the Land Authority for Wales and House Builders Federation and overruled the support of the Campaign for the Protection of Rural Wales, the Welsh Language Society, the Countryside Council for Wales and the Welsh Language Board. A concession was the policy on affordable housing for local need. However, the 'needs and interests of the Welsh language' remains the third of ten factors to be considered when assessing the scale and phrasing of new housing development. What is evident from comparing the submitted plan and modifications is the different interpretation as to how the plan can best 'take the needs and interests of the language into account' (Circular 53/88).

The Powys Structure Plan includes Policy CS10 – on the Welsh Language – which states that:

> The needs and interests of the Welsh language will be a material consideration when development proposals are being determined in areas which are significantly Welsh speaking. Developments that safeguard and facilitate the use of the Welsh language will be permitted providing that there are no unacceptable planning, access, service and amenities problems.

The main policy considerations are:

- the relevance of the Welsh language as a material consideration;
- the very strong connection between land use/development and community/language issues;
- the Welsh language was not a major issue during plan preparation;
- all physical development takes place within a policy framework that has social implications;
- social factors include community, cultural and traditional issues and language is implicit in all of these, whether it be English, Welsh, or a particular dialect of either;
- to facilitate the continued use and growth of usage of Welsh;
- the connection between housing for local needs and the emphasis on community need and local circumstances and the interaction between social communication and land use planning;
- the need to encourage the right type of economic, residential and social developments that would bring benefits.

Following the adoption of the first Clwyd Structure Plan, under pressure from the Welsh Language Society, the county council added a statistical appendix entitled 'The Welsh Language in Clwyd' to the Report of Survey. The current Clwyd Structure Plan, when submitted to the secretary of state, did not contain any policy reference specifically to the Welsh language. However, in his modifications to the plan he amended Policy B5 relating to allocating land or giving planning permission for housing development as a tenth factor to be regarded, namely 'the needs and interests of the Welsh language'.

Similarly, Dyfed included a supplementary assessment, 'The Welsh Language as a Structure Plan Issue', to its revised Structure Plan in 1983. Curiously, this was phrased in conservation terms and likened language conservation to landscape conservation. The current Dyfed Structure Plan states, in relation to housing development (Policy H9) that:

> It is the policy of the County Council that all residential and related development should take full account of the character of the urban or rural setting in terms of scale, site, design, landscaping and the use of materials as well as the effect on the social and cultural characteristics of the area.

Under 'Urban and Rural Conservation' between policies on afforestation and new coal powered power stations are two policies. The first, EN13, is identical to H9 except that the words 'residential and related' are omitted. Policy EN14 states that, 'It is the policy of the County Council that subject to other relevant structure plan policies there will be a presumption in favour of developments beneficial to the safeguarding of the Welsh speaking communities in Dyfed.'

Policies in Clwyd, Dyfed and Powys emphasize employment, housing, transport, tourism, recreation, conservation and community development in Welsh-speaking areas. They advocate positive measures on the maintenance and enhancement of balanced communities which are as, if not more, important than a simplistic policy 'to save the Welsh language'.

We see, here, a consistent interest in the Welsh language as a planning issue, a response to local popular pressure, but no evidence of a sophisticated development in professional thinking on this topic.

Structure planning in Scotland

In Scotland, the regional and island area councils are the structure planning authorities. Their linguistic composition is as follows:

Table 13.4 The Linguistic Character of Regional and Island Authorities, 1991

Region	Population over three years of age	Gaelic-speaking	Percentage
Border	100,292	460	0.5
Central	257,776	1,612	0.6
Dumfries and Galloway	142,531	515	0.4
Fife	328,180	1,477	0.5
Grampian	484,514	2,491	0.5
Highland	196,303	14,713	7.5
Lothian	698,590	4,205	0.6
Strathclyde	2,162,418	18,283	0.8
Island Areas			
Orkney	18,834	92	0.5
Shetland	21,572	105	0.5
Western Isles	28,569	19,546	68.4

Only two exceed the national proportion of Gaelic speakers (1.8 per cent) and only one exceeds the Welsh average of 18.9 per cent. Consequently, only the development plan policies in Highland and Strathclyde regions and the Western Isles will be examined in this chapter.

The linguistic preference of the three structure plans is revealing. They all have English explanatory memoranda or survey reports, Strathclyde has a unilingual English written statement as does Highland save for its Gaelic Heritage chapter while the Western Isles alone has a bilingual written statement.

In the 'Report of Survey' (1983) for the Western Isles Structure Plan direct reference to Gaelic is limited to education policy. The approved Western Isles Structure Plan (adopted 1986/7) is based upon a strategic settlement network and four geographic policy area groups. No reference is made to the Gaelic language. This is surprising at first reading, when one considers that, outside Stornoway, the islands' capital, and the military centre of Balivanich, Gaelic was spoken by 90 per cent of the total population in 1981. But the basic philosophy of the plan is community development. Housing, employment and community service policies are all directed towards reducing out-migration and retaining the population in the areas outside the two heavily anglicized nodes.

When Highland Regional Council was reviewing its initial structure plan in 1985 *Comunn na Gaidhlig* (CnaG) submitted comments in the form of an issue paper. Its core feature was the neglected value of the cultural and linguistic heritage as a valuable human resource. The Gaelic presence in the region was categorized as:

1. areas where the language remains a community-wide medium of communication (e.g. parts of Skye),
2. areas with large concentrations of native speakers in a mainly English milieu (e.g. Inverness and Fort William),
3. west coast areas where there is a residual native Gaelic pressure and significant numbers of learners,
4. an east coast strip with only immigrant Gaelic speakers.

It states 'in the past linguistic and cultural factors have tended not to be given due consideration in the process of development planning in the Highlands'. It was believed that only when a community's language and culture was valued by the powers that be was it likely to have self-confidence to become involved in the process of development. In planning for social and economic development regard should be given to the implications of strategies upon the cultural environment and should seek to identify opportunities to strengthen the cultural and linguistic fabric of the community. For example, new housing – council and private – should be located in crofting townships rather than growth centres such as Portree or Bradford. The correct approach to tourism development should be both sensitive to the effects of tourism on the Gaelic language and culture and the potential that exists to market the area's Gaelic identity to the benefit of the indigenous population in both cultural and economic terms. There was concern that nature conservation issues might prejudice much needed economic development. Lack of training to enable local Gaelic speakers to avail themselves of newly generated employment opportunities was also cited as an issue to be faced.

The approved Highland Structure Plan (1990) lays great emphasis on community development with its commitment to 'sustain and enhance the Region's distinctive cultural identity'. When planning sub-regions are examined it is stated that

> Skye is the main Gaelic speaking area in the Region. The Gaelic heritage of the area is expressed in the culture and attitudes of the people as well as in the pattern of development. It is important that development proposals reflect this cultural heritage, notably in relation to tourism development.

In the tourism section of the plan it is envisaged that the Tourism Action Area for Skye and Lochalsh will consider 'natural and Gaelic heritage and outdoor pursuits'.

In the bilingual section on 'Gaelic Heritage', the important relationship between Gaelic and the development of local economies is stressed. However, the possible danger of overwhelming fragile cultures is noted and the need to assess the implication of development for the cultural environment, especially in relation to tourism. Policy P115 states that the Council will pursue a range of initiatives to sustain and enhance the economy of Gaelic areas. In particular in assessing development perspectives and in the allocation of land through Local Plans, the Council will pay special regard to traditional and historical influences on the pattern of development.

The Strathclyde Structure Plan (1991) covers the Argyll and Bute District Council area which includes the southern islands of the Gaelic-speaking Inner Hebrides. Naturally the plan concentrates upon the problems of the Clydeside conurbation. However, it aims to sustain 'Remote Rural Areas', which include all of Argyll and Bute. Yet no specific mention is made of Gaelic. There is an emphasis on the vitality of settlements such as Oban, Tobermory, Port Ellen and Bowmore, and on rural service centres including the islands of Coll, Tiree, Colonsay and Mull in order to maintain the viability of the communities. Housing provision in remote rural settlements was to be made in accordance with local housing needs.

Local planning in Wales

There has been a plethora of local plans in Wales since 1991 which have given greater attention to the factors which influence the maintenance of Welsh-speaking communities.

Gwynedd

Consideration of the Welsh language in Gwynedd has occurred in two phases – before and after the issuing of Circular 53/58. In the earlier period the key issue was how to limit ownership of new homes by predominantly English-speaking non-local people – as second homes, holiday lettings or for retirement. The debate in the Welsh Office over acceptable policies paralleled similar discussions in Cumbria and the Lake District, and the outcome was to adopt policies based upon the model agreed by the Department of the Environment and the English planning authorities. It should be noted that none of the Gwynedd plan's policies contained explicit references to the Welsh language. It was accepted that in the plan areas 'local' was equivalent to 'Welsh speaking' (excepting certain historic situations). Adequate housing and employment were essential prerequisites so as to retain Welsh-speaking populations in their localities. Development of housing in excess of local need would lead to their purchase by outsiders for either second home, retirement or holiday letting and hence enable seasonal or in-migration of non-local, and non-Welsh-speaking, persons.

A new, more confident era in local plan preparation was initiated following the publication of Welsh Office bilingual Circular 53/88 on *The Welsh Language Development Plans and Planning Control* and the movement towards producing local plans covering the whole area of a local planning authority. Following the circular, local plans in Gwynedd contained explicit references to fostering, or sustaining, the language. For example, in the Dwyfor Local Plan the status of Welsh remains the paramount policy whereby 'the Council will ensure, through the policies of the local plan, that new developments recognise, support and strengthen the social, cultural and linguistic identity of the plan area', where 75 per cent of the resident population speaks Welsh.

The concern with housing remained, however; for example, Arfon BC produced their Rural Arfon Local Plan for the area of the former slate-mining villages between the coastal plain and the Snowdonia National Park. This is another intensely Welsh-speaking area (82 per cent in 1981). In the plan area, Welsh speakers tend to chose new housing in the less remote villages while immigrants are drawn to the remote settlements by relatively cheap housing and an attractive environment. These trends were intensified by the availability of substantial improvement grants in the late 1970s and early 1980s. Again this illustrates the effect which housing and planning policies designed to combat specific problems (the distribution of the growth in population and the improvement of older housing) have on Welsh. Where the language is vulnerable, this demonstrates the importance of not initiating dramatic changes in housing and population policies, unless such policies are designed to have a beneficial linguistic effect. Other policies state that new tourism developments should not 'undermine the area's cultural and linguistic character'.

Dyfed and Powys

In these areas, too, the key issue is the relationship between meeting housing need, new housing development and the future of Welsh-speaking communities. In Dyfed and Powys, policies similar to those of Gwynedd are used in the latest plans, though it could be argued that the North Wales plans try to weave consideration of the language into every aspect of their policies whereas the Dyfed and Powys plans tend to isolate concern for the language in specific policies, some of which are couched in general terms. An extreme example of the latter is the Brecon Beacons National Plan whose area is split into a largely Anglicized north (with residual Welsh-speaking communities) and the top end of Cwm Tawe 'where the Welsh language and culture still plays a prominent role in social and business activities'. One of the plan's eight objectives recognizes the intrinsic importance of protecting the language. However, it is only in the tourism section that the linguistic objective is elaborated. where it is determined that the impact of tourism development 'shall not place the social, cultural or linguistic vitality of any settlement under threat'.

More comprehensive considerations characterize southern Dyfed's planning. Following a Cymdeithas yr Iaith Gymraeg conference on planning responsibilities in the district, Carmarthen District Council adopted on 7 November 1983 quite radical policies on Welsh in conjunction with local economic policies. In the 1993 district-wide local plan for Carmarthen District Council, Welsh is discussed in relation to housing policies. 'The effect of new housing on the Welsh language is a matter of concern in formulating Local Plans and determining planning applications'. The housing policies develop provision for 'local needs' and 'affordable housing'. Under 'Community Services', Policy CS1 states that

> in considering development proposals in areas and communities where the use of the language is a component of their social fabric, the Council will have regard to the impact on Welsh speaking communities. Development proposals likely to be prejudicial to the needs and interests of the language will not be permitted.

Unfortunately, such communities are not specified.

Dinefwr BC raced into the district-wide plan era in 1995. With its industrial core in Dyffryn Aman, the area is also linguistically strategic, representing a transition between the rural Welsh-speaking heartland and the largely Anglicized valley communities further east. As Table 13.2 shows, it is the most Welsh-speaking of all the south and west Wales district council areas. The Plan's first goal is 'to protect and improve the social, cultural, linguistic identity and quality of life of all residents within the Borough', through ensuring 'that housing development is appropriately related to community facilities and does not prejudice the cultural and linguistic characteristics of existing communities' and striving to improve the economic situation locally.

The Plan's housing policies take up all of Dyfed SP's allocation for the district. The impact of residential development proposals upon the viability of language and culture is an important material consideration. Considerable attention is given to defining the 'local' and 'need' aspects of the 'local need' housing bias. Tourism policies favour developments which positively promote Welsh culture and heritage. Welsh is to be strengthened generally by encouraging bilingual signage in business, translation facilities and Welsh learning centres.

In contrast to these plans, the 1996 Local Plan for Llanelli is stubbornly unilingual English, despite attempting to plan for the future of important Welsh-speaking areas such as Cwm Gwendraeth where the Welsh

Language Board is funding a major community language initiative. The policy towards the Welsh language is hidden in the middle of the section on infrastructure and mirrors the weakness of Circular 53/88 (Llanelli BC, 1996).

In a similar vein, the Pembrokeshire Coast National Park has consistently virtually ignored its Welsh heritage. However, the consultation draft of its local plan does concede that an overall decline is taking place in the number of Welsh speakers. It acknowledges that development can adversely affect the future interest of Welsh-speaking communities and that it will be a material consideration in development controls of residential development (Pembrokeshire Coast NPA 1995).

In central Wales, local plans for both Montgomery and Cardigan identify settlements where Welsh speaking is being eroded. Montgomeryshire DC published its bilingual consultation draft of its district wide local plan in 1993. The Council is actively seeking to promote Welsh culture and maintains that in terms of Circular 53/88 'the Welsh language is a component of the social fabric of a community' in the Llanfair Caereinion, Llanfyllin and Machynlleth planning areas. Sixteen community council areas, where 40 per cent or more of the population speak Welsh, are identified as they 'need special planning policy attention if the Welsh language and culture are to be safeguarded in Montgomeryshire'. 'In these extensive rural areas the Welsh language does have land use planning consequences'. Their strategy aims for a careful balance in planning policies between avoiding the swamping effect of large-scale in-migration and excessively restrictive policies which would lead to community decline. Their housing policy develops these norms further:

> The Council regards the protection and promotion of the Welsh language and culture as a proper planning consideration throughout Montgomeryshire. The Welsh language and culture will form a particularly important material consideration when determining planning applications in the following settlements where the language is widely used.

Thirty-three localities are then listed where 'housing development proposals in these settlements shall cater strongly for local needs. Where housing developments are proposed in the settlement listed above, the Council will seek planning obligations to ensure that at least half of the dwellings remain in the local need housing market indefinitely, for use by Welsh speakers and meeting the criteria' for affordable housing in settlements. This policy is the first to refer specifically to 'Welsh speakers'. Housing policies are supplemented by policies for economic development throughout the district. When monitoring of the local plan is discussed it is proposed to use the decennial census, analysis of planning permissions for the preparation of local need housing, local 'jigsaw' studies and housing need surveys.

A more radical approach emerged in CD Ceredigion's draft Local Plan. The decline of Welsh there is attributed to rural depopulation, in-migration and the lack of local employment opportunities. The linguistic objectives of the plan are:

> to seek the conservation of the Welsh language in areas of Ceredigion, particularly where a high proportion of the population is Welsh speaking;

> to seek and ensure the co-existence of the linguistic communities throughout Ceredigion and to recognise their contribution to its culture and every day social life.

In late 1993, the planning committee intended to achieve this by:

- supporting proposals for development which can be demonstrated to be beneficial to the needs and interests of the language;
- to limit occupation of new and converted dwellings in five community council areas where 70 per cent or more of the population spoke Welsh, to persons whose origins are or who have previously lived for 5 years in the district or within 25 miles of it;
- to allocate land for employment generating purposes in these same five communities.

In early 1994, the council lowered the threshold to 50 per cent, making the policy applicable to the whole district excepting six communities – Aberystwyth and three neighbouring communities, New Quay and Aberporth – and the university college town of Lampeter. At this lower level it may prove impossible to defend the policy for planning, political and possibly legal reasons. However, Ceredigion can propose planning policies related to cultural factors such as language and local residency if the following conditions are met:

- that the social fabric of the community is significantly dependent upon the survival of these cultural factors;
- those factors have a relationship with the manner in which land in the area is developed and put to use;
- other relevant planning considerations relating to the potentially negative aspects of such social engineering are taken into account.

Meanwhile the Commission for Racial Equality threatened CD Ceredigion with legal action and there was predictable opposition from the local building industry. The Welsh Office response listed five areas of concern.

Foremost is 'the lack of detailed background and justification for the high level of housing allocations'. In interpreting the generous housing allocation in the Dyfed SP (which was based on the period of large-scale housebuilding in rural areas, mainly for retirement in-migration), the local planning authority doubled an already generous allocation and added another half to acknowledge existing planning consents. Thus while the council acknowledged the ill-effects of large and rapid population increases in the past, it provides generous allocations to its own local plan to stimulate this same problem in the future. In fact the Welsh Office, in drawing the council's attention to eighteen communities where the proposed levels of expansion 'appears out of scale with the current size of the village' and making the general observation that 'a reappraisal of the development boundaries of smaller settlements is desirable', may, in this instance, be more supportive of the Welsh language than the local planning authority. However, Ceredigion DC has not been afraid of ignoring reports from the Welsh Office, Audit Commission or Ombudsman into their decisions in housing and planning matters.

Local planning in Scotland

It would be difficult to argue that local planning has been a significant vehicle for promoting, or protecting, the use of Gaelic. In areas where there is a significant Gaelic-speaking population, local plans have referred to data on language use, but no implication for planning policies are drawn. Oblique references fall into two categories: first, a recognition that the distinctive Gaelic culture of small areas can bolster tourism, for example, the Mull, Coll and Tiree Local Plan, adopted 1985, advocates bilingual road signs as a tourist attraction; secondly, there is concern in a number of plans about the corrosive effects on local cultures and communities of incomers and second homes, concerns which are shared with Wales. Thus the Islay, Jura and Colonsay Local Plan notes that 'Gaelic is still widely spoken, but mainly among the older generation. In 1981, 43 per cent of Islay's people spoke it, 43 per cent in Colonsay and 21 per cent in Jura'. On Jura native 'Diurach' people are being displaced by incomers and 26 per cent of the island's houses are holiday or second homes as are some 21 per cent of Colonsay's houses.

Community action in Scotland

Due to the different linguistic situation, both nationally and in the Gaelic-speaking areas, there has been a closer relationship between community development and planning for the survival of Gaelic. A Gaelic-medium college of further education has existed at Sabhal Mor Ostaig on Skye since 1973 which focuses on business, media, social and Highlands and Islands studies to equip practitioners to work in Gaelic communities.

Its first students graduated when the Highlands and Islands Development Board (HIDB) financed community co-operatives (*co-chomun*) modelled on Irish Gaeltacht developments. Full-time Gaelic-speaking field officers, one Catholic and one Protestant, began work in November 1977. Subsequently, co-operative enterprises were established throughout the Western Isles and to a lesser extent in north-west Sutherland, Skye, Lochalsh, Moidart and Islay. Although all of the *co-chomun* revitalized their localities, very few have actually been administered or worked through Gaelic.

Crofting, which is a unique type of landholding, comparable to the historical Welsh *tyddyn*, is central to Highlands and Islands society. The main crofting areas are along the north and west mainland from Caithness/Sutherland to Lochalsh, together with the Outer Hebrides, Skye and Tiree. Areas with the highest proportion of registered crofters (17.5 per cent or more), excepting north and west Sutherland, are also areas where Gaelic is strongest – the Outer Hebrides, Skye, Applecross and Tiree. Other crofting concentrations are along the west coast to Ardnamurchan, south-west Mull and Canna where the language remains in a residual state. Naturally, attempts at revitalizing crofting have important consequences for Gaelic communities. The Western Isles Integrated Development Programme (1982–7, partly EC funded), the North West Development Programme (1983–93) and the Skye Development Programme (both HIDB funded) all helped to revitalize crofting. The Crofters Commission's new entry scheme seeks such revitalization through new local tenancies. Interestingly for a Scottish body, four of the seven commissioners are Gaelic speakers. It is probably not a coincidence that the purchase of the North Lochinver Estate in Assynt, western Sutherland, was followed by a revival of interest in Gaelic. Argyll and Bute District Council policy guidelines on housing in rural areas have a general presumption against new housing in rural areas. However, the only exception is new housing on subdivisions of croft land as it is considered that the occupants are certainly likely to be in local need and, possibly, Gaelic-speaking.

The HIDB adopted a 'think big' strategy in its growth years from establishment in 1965, fuelled by the 'oil boom', but since 1976 its 'look small' strategy has supported community enterprises, decentralization of its offices and decision-making and greater attention to remote areas. The HIDB commissioned its Gaelic Report group to prepare an analysis of the current situation which appeared, as *Cor Na Gaidhlig* (*Language, Community and Development*) in 1982. *Comunn na Gaidhlig* (CnaG) was established in September 1984 as a result of the *Cor na Gaidhlig* report. It argues that 'the basis of the national policy for Gaelic should be that every Gaelic-speaker in Scotland has the right to use Gaelic in as many situations as possible' (*Towards a National Policy for Gaelic*, 1986). Its role is to formulate and implement national policy and identify community needs and realizable objectives. While land-use planning is not directly mentioned, economic development is seen as being either highly supportive or inimical to linguistic development, a healthy linguistic situation being a considerable source of communal strength, leading to the involvement of the Industry Department for Scotland, the Department of Agriculture and Fisheries for Scotland and the Scottish Development Department.

At the conference 'Forward with Gaelic', held at Aviemore in 1993, Roy Pedersen stated that the Gaelic language and culture could be harnessed as a powerful motor for economic development if it could widen its reach through radio, television and Gaelic arts and optimizing the economic and social benefits of cultural tourism, more and better jobs and increased income for local populations. He defined the whole of the traditional Gaelic-speaking area as a 'priority' area and added Tayside Region, Stirling District, Aberdeen District, Edinburgh District and 'greater' Glasgow.

Sproull (1993) identified a 'Gaelic Economy' and 'Gaelic Industry' which encompassed the consumers and producers of Gaelic services, including all those activities and jobs whose principal purpose is the provision of Gaelic-related goods and services. He estimated that the 'Gaelic industry' supports 1000 full-time equivalent jobs and adds £41 million to Scotland's GDP. Social development could make both an indirect and direct contribution to economic development as in Tiree, Harris, South Uist, Barra and North Skye, though very few entrepreneurs gave consideration to linguistic and cultural factors in tourism.

Following the Aviemore conference, CnaG formulated their *Strategy for Gaelic Development in the 21st Century* (1994). CnaG, in partnership with the HIE network (mainly the LECs), intends to use Gaelic as a motor for economic development by exploiting opportunities for new Gaelic based businesses, including media, leisure and cultural tourism. Gaelic presence in existing businesses will be furthered by area-based development officers. Additional partners will include Scottish Enterprise, the Scottish Tourist Board and SCOTVEC (the Scottish vocational training organization). CnaG has been contracted by HIE to foster and deliver Gaelic-related social and economic development in the business and commercial sectors and to develop job-creating projects relating to Gaelic. Since 1993 under the 'Fionan' ('vine') label, four development officers have been based at Fort William (Lochaber), Kyle of Lochalsh (including Skye), Ullapool (Western Mainland) and Golspie (Eastern Mainland) to stimulate the

Gaelic economy. A parallel programme is to convert the much-publicized advantages of Gaelic tourism into reality with CnaG working with HIE, the LECs, the National Trust for Scotland, Scottish National Heritage and Historic Scotland. Gaelic tourism is seen to comprise:
- an association with a beautiful, dramatic and clean landscape;
- traditional and contemporary Gaelic arts, that are vibrant and distinctive; interest in minority cultures and languages;
- Gaelic culture as an increasingly appreciated part of the pan-European culture.

It is estimated that Gaelic tourism should be capable of generating an identity with an annual turnover of £20 million employing 2,000 people.

We may ask whether this heavy emphasis on the 'Gaelic economy' is a classic example of exceptionalism? Will the 'Chinese laundry syndrome' emerge where Gaelic institution supports Gaelic institution? There appears little concern about the daily existence of the crofter and his ancillary occupations and what language he speaks. This contrasts greatly with the situation in Wales where the aim is to normalize the position of Welsh throughout society.

As its contribution to the new partnership with CnaG, Highlands and Islands Enterprise, as successor to HIDB, has formulated its Gaelic policies in *A Strategy For Gaelic: Development in the Highlands and Islands of Scotland* (1993). One of its three objectives is to 'integrate Gaelic initiatives with economic, social and environmental development'. Among the nine specific priorities for implementation are to:
- assist in the development of a new Gaelic broadcasting industry (especially training and development);
- improve employment opportunities through targeted training programmes (in areas such as the media, teaching Gaelic language, the arts and management);
- provide a versatile delivery service free for Gaelic development including training and business growth (including utilizing new technology);
- initiate a series of pilot and research projects to exploit and demonstrate the possibilities of development through Gaelic (including cultural tourism, Gaelic producers, Gaelic as a development tool, and study of the effects of development potential on out- and in-migration).

Three reasons are given to justify direct involvement in support for Gaelic development:
- improving economic performance through growing self-confidence among individuals and communities;
- developing social and tourism benefits from the culture;
- specific business development and training.

HIE have defined their area into four zones based upon the current status of Gaelic:
areas where Gaelic is used in daily life (Western Isles and, to a lesser extent, Skye);
areas where Gaelic had a strong hold until recently and retains clear emotional commitment (Western Mainland and other island areas);
Inverness, Cromarty Firth/Moray Firth area where there has been a substantial in-migration of Gaelic speakers;
Orkney, Shetland and most of Caithness where Gaelic has little relevance.

HIE sees policies to strengthen economic self-confidence through Gaelic as particularly relevant to the first two zones outlined above where the language has the strongest hold. In and around Inverness where there are diverse engines of economic success there is also considerable scope for development and job creation based on Gaelic. A recent HIE report (1993/4) contains examples of local enterprise in action:
- Argyll and the Islands – capitalizing on the visit of the Mod [the Scottish Eisteddfod] to Dunoon and the Fionan project in Oban and Lorne;
- Lochaber – new cultural heritage interpretation centre at Ballachulish, new cultural centre at Glenuig, Gaelic playgroup at Acharacle;
- Skye and Lochalsh – LEADER (EU) projects for community and business development, develop the benefits of cultural tourism (e.g. 'Blas dan Iar' – 'Taste of the West'), doubling the size of Sabhal Mor Ostaig, development of Canan Ltd (high-quality merchandizing material);
- Western Isles – Harris Tweed redevelopment strategy, pharmaceutical industry growth on Lewis.

Throughout the Highlands and Islands, almost 350 Community Action Grant projects have been assisted at a cost of £1,100,000. Within Argyll, eight local partnerships are being established to promote Gaelic. That on Tiree and Coll has appointed a local heritage officer, while the Lorne Gaelic Partnership aim to develop an action plan for Gaelic in the Oban area.

CnaG has stimulated local working groups in the Western Isles, Skye, Mull and Islay to implement a ten-year plan for their communities. Such groups provide an interface between the community and various agencies seeking to realize the mutually supportive development of economic and linguistic factors in the traditional industries of fishing, farming, whisky, and crofting without sacrificing new opportunities for growth and enrichment.

The 1990s saw more elaborate plans for Lochaber and North and West Sutherland where the 'Gaelic industry' and the 'Gaelic economy' were incorporated into the plans. Business projects were identified such as a Gaelic bookshop, craftshop, tearoom and translation service. Local businesses are encouraged, partly through Fionan, to offer a unique experience by raising the profile of the language, by celebrating the living musical tradition, by promoting local museums and by providing residential courses. All this is reinforced by an increased recognition of the interdependence of human and natural ecology.

A further step has been to bring all the plans in Argyll and Bute together in a Gaelic partnership. Its mission is to 'develop the Gaelic language within the area by increasing its use, improving its status, improving its quality and ensuring its relevance to educational, economic and cultural needs'. Above all it seeks to re-establish the unselfconscious use of Gaelic in the community.

Conclusion

Contemporary language planning recognizes the need for more holistic perspectives on the problems facing lesser-used language speakers. This is reflected in the wider range of issues discussed in recent studies on the role of language planning in economic development, community regeneration, and questions of accessibility (Wessels and Beck, 1994); in accommodating in-migrants (Dafis (ed.), 1992; van Langevelde, 1993) and in relating questions of community leadership, social cohesion and confidence in language-use to the formal framework of bilingual public services, the operation of the voluntary sector and the increased penetration of the private sector. But because planning is an interventionist process, and the language issues are so deeply embedded in the fabric of society, the question of measuring the effectiveness of planning on language vitality in a regional context has become a critical issue.

It is also recognized that the old bastions of Gaelic and Welsh no longer serve as either a necessary or sufficient basis for language reproduction. Newer forms of interaction and social communication networks are being established. Thus while Glasgow, like Liverpool and London for the Welsh, is no longer the *de facto* capital of Gaeldom, new centres have emerged. Inverness is the undisputed capital of the Highlands and Islands and, together with Easter Ross, contains the headquarters of most Gaelic institutions. With primary and secondary education in Gaelic, it is mimicking the experience of Mold in Clwyd as a cultural anchor. In the Western Isles, Stornoway, under Comhairle Nan Eilean, has developed as the capital of the outer isles with administrative, health and cultural centres. Portree – which experienced a 28 per cent increase in population over the period 1981–91 – will be the focus of the decentralized administration of the new Highland Council and is now linked to the Western Mainland by the controversial Skye bridge. Even Oban shows signs of remembering its Gaelic past. Will these core regional centres be sufficient to guide Gaeldom into the twenty-first century?

In Wales, it is in the industrial south-east and north-east that the most promising signs of language growth are recorded. We may anticipate that unitary authorities like Cardiff, Caerphilly and Wrexham will pay greater attention to the role of the Welsh language within their areas. In such places, Welsh speakers constitute a different form of communication network from the more conventional communities we have been discussing. Community without propinquity is a better characterization of such networks in Anglicized towns. However, given the trends described above and elsewhere (Aitchison and Carter, 1993; Williams, 1989, 1995) it is likely that conventional Welsh language communities will become more and more fragmented and be re-constituted as nodes within a more fluid and plural socio-linguistic context. Thus the question of the role of planning in influencing the socio-linguistic character of Welsh settlements will remain, though it is in planning authorities which serve the heartland areas that it will be most acutely analysed.

Throughout Europe we are only beginning to chart the relationship between the planning profession and indigenous and exogenous cultures. Though the planning policy review process was initially slow to incorporate linguistic and socio-cultural community characteristics, it is inconceivable that future regional and local plans will not take full account of the statutory obligations laid upon local authorities by, for example, the provisions of the Welsh Language Act and their implementation through the Welsh Language Board. In both Wales and Scotland, the planning system will continue to reflect a society in which the exact implications of exercising language rights in specific domains are still being realized. In that respect, it remains one of the most critical, if contested, instruments of our democracy.

Acknowledgements

Colin H. Williams wishes to acknowledge the support of the Welsh Language Board, who through a Community Language Planning Development grant, encouraged investigative fieldwork and thinking on these issues.

References

ACE/HI 1994. *The Directory of Community Enterprises in the Highlands and Islands of Scotland* (Inverness, The Association of Community Enterprises in the Highlands and Islands).

Aitchison, J. W. 1995. 'Language, family structure and social class, 1991 census data', presentation to the 'Social History of the Welsh Language' Conference, Aberystwyth, 16 September.

Aitchison, J. W. and H. Carter 1993. 'The Welsh language in 1991 – a broken heart and a new beginning?', *Planet*, Vol. 97, pp. 3–10.

Ambrose, J. A. and C. H. Williams 1981. 'On the spatial definition of minority: scale as an influence on the geolinguistic analysis of Welsh', in E. Haugen, J. D. McClure and D. Thompson (eds.), *Minority Languages Today* (Edinburgh, Edinburgh University Press), pp. 53–71.

Anglesey Borough Council 1980. *Anglesey Population Survey, 1977* (Llangefni, Anglesey BC).

Arfon BC and Isle of Anglesey BC 1980. *Menai Strait Local Plan* (Caernarfon and Llangefni, Arfon BC and Isle of Anglesey BC).

Arfon BC 1983. *The Situation of the Welsh Language in Arfon and the Planning Implications*, Report for Planning Committee, December 1983 (Caernarfon, Arfon BC).

Arfon BC 1987. *Rural Arfon Local Plan Written Statement* (Caernarfon, Arfon BC).

Argyll and Bute DC 1988a. *Mull, Coll and Tiree Local Plan 1st Review and Alterations and Monitoring Report* (Lochgilphead, Argyll and Bute DC).

Argyll and Bute DC 1988b. *Islay, Jura and Glensay Local Plan 1st Review and Alterations and Monitoring Report* (Lochgilphead, Argyll and Bute DC).

Argyll and Bute DC 1988c. *Advertisement Policy and Associated Guidelines* (Lochgilphead, Argyll and Bute DC).

Argyll and Bute Gaelic Partnership 1995. *Community Development Plan* (Oban, Comun na Gaidhlig).

Assembly of Welsh Counties 1993a. *Strategic Planning Guidance in Wales, Overview Report* (Cardiff, AWC).

Assembly of Welsh Counties 1993b. *Strategic Planning Guidance in Wales, Topic Report* (Cardiff, AWC).

Beacham, A. 1964. *Depopulation in Mid Wales* (London, HMSO).

Bradford, S. M. 1992. 'Tourism and cultural development', *Community Enterprise*, Issue 3, pp. 4–5.

Breathnach, P. et al. 1984. *Aspects of Rural Development in the Scottish Highlands and Islands*, Occasional Paper No. 4, Geography Department, Maynooth College, Ireland.

Campbell, M. 1987. *Gaelic in Mull. A Ten Year Development Plan* (Inverness, Comunn na Gaidhlig).

Carmarthen DC 1985. *Planning and the Welsh Language* (Carmarthen, Carmarthen DC).

Carmarthen DC 1993. *Carmarthen District Local Plan*, 2 vols. (Carmarthen, Carmarthen DC).

Carter, H. and W. K. Davies (eds.) 1975. *Urban Essays: Studies in the Geography of Wales* (London, Longman).

Carter, H. 1976. 'Mawredd le bu mieri?', *Y Traethodydd*, Hydref, tt. 231–40.

CD Dwyfor 1982. *Rural Dwyfor Local Plan Written Statement* (Pwllheli, CD Dwyfor).
CD Dwyfor 1994. *Dwyfor Local Plan. Consultative Draft* (Pwllheli, CD Dwyfor).
Ceredigion DC 1976. *Aberystwyth Area Plan. Interim Appraisal* (Aberaeron, Ceredigion DC).
Ceredigion DC 1978. *Aberaeron and New Quay Area Plan. Issues Report* (Aberaeron, Ceredigion DC).
Ceredigion DC 1995. *Ceredigion Local Plan (consultative draft)* (Aberaeron, Ceredigion DC).
Clwyd CC n.d. *Clwyd Structure Plan: Appendix. The Welsh Language in Clwyd* (Mold, Clwyd CC).
Clwyd CC 1991a. *Clwyd Structure Plan Policies and Memorandum* (Mold, Clwyd CC).
Clwyd CC 1991b. *Clwyd Local Plan Scheme* (Mold, Clwyd CC).
Clwyd CC 1994. *Development Plans in Clwyd* (Mold, Clwyd CC).
Colwyn BC 1985. *Land Use Planning and the Welsh Language. Local Plan Topic Report* (Colwyn Bay, Colwyn BC).
Colwyn BC 1993. *Colwyn Borough Local Plan. Draft Written Statement* (Colwyn Bay, Colwyn BC).
Comhairle nan Eilean 1976. *Regional Report* (Stornoway, The Council).
Comhairle nan Eilean 1983. *Western Isles Structure Plan. Report of Survey* (Stornoway, The Council).
Comhairle nan Eilean 1988. *Western Isles Structure Plan. Written Statement* (Stornoway, The Council).
Comhairle nan Eilean 1989. *Western Isles Tourism Strategy* (Stornoway, The Council).
Comhairle nan Eilean 1994. *Barra and Vatersay Local Plan* (Stornoway, The Council).
Comhairle nan Eilean 1995. *Broadbay Local Plan Consultative Draft* (Stornoway, The Council).
Comunn na Gaidhlig 1985. *Outline Submission to Highland Regional Council. Structure Plan Review. Gaelic Language and Culture* (Inverness, Comunn na Gaidhlig).
Comunn na Gaidhlig 1986. *Towards a National Policy for Gaelic* (Inverness, Comunn na Gaidhlig).
Comunn na Gaidhlig 1989. *Gaelic Progress Report 1982–1989* (Inverness, Comunn na Gaidhlig).
Comunn na Gaidhlig 1994a. *Ag Obair Dhuibhse* (Inverness, Comunn na Gaidhlig).
Comunn na Gaidhlig 1994b. *Gaidhlig 2000. A Strategy for Gaelic Development into the 21st Century* (Inverness, Comunn na Gaidhlig).
Cooke, P. 1978. 'Some problems and contradictions for Welsh language planning', *Cambria*, Vol.5, No.2, pp.167–72.
Cor na Gaidhlig 1982. *Language, Community and Development: The Gaelic Situation* (Inverness, HIDB).
Council for the Welsh Language 1978. *A Future for the Welsh Language* (Cardiff, Welsh Office).
Crofters Commission 1991. *Crofting in the '90's* (Inverness, Crofters Commission).
Currie, R. 1988. *Gaelic in Islay. A Ten Year Development Plan* (Inverness, Comunn na Gaidhlig).
Cymdeithas Cynllunio Cymru 1978. *Statws Cynllunio i'r Iaith* (Caernarfon, CCC), 1-III-1978.

Cymdeithas yr Iaith Gymraeg 1986. *Planning a Future for the Welsh Language on Ynys Môn* (Caernarfon, Pwyllgor Rhanbarthol Gwynedd, Cymdeithas yr Iaith Gymraeg).
Cymdeithas yr Iaith Gymraeg n.d. *Planning and Language* (Aberystwyth, Cymdeithas yr Iaith Gymraeg).
Cymdeithas yr Iaith Gymraeg (n.d.) *Colwyn – Tourism* (Aberystwyth, Cymdeithas yr Iaith Gymraeg).
Cymdeithas yr Iaith Gymraeg 1984a. *Planning a Future for the Welsh Language in Carmarthen District* (Aberystwyth, Cymdeithas yr Iaith Gymraeg).
Cymdeithas yr Iaith Gymraeg 1984b. *Planning a Future for the Welsh Language in Clwyd* (Aberystwyth, Cymdeithas yr Iaith Gymraeg).
Cymdeithas yr Iaith Gymraeg 1985a. *Planning a Future for the Welsh Language in North Preseli* (Aberystwyth, Cymdeithas yr Iaith Gymraeg).
Cymdeithas yr Iaith Gymraeg 1985b. *Planning a Future for the Welsh Language in Ceredigion* (Aberystwyth, Cymdeithas yr Iaith Gymraeg).
Cymdeithas yr Iaith Gymraeg 1986. *Cynllunio Dyfodol i'r Iaith* (Aberystwyth, Cymdeithas yr Iaith Gymraeg).
Dafis, Ll. (ed.) 1992. *Yr Ieithoedd Llai: Cymathu Newydd-Ddyfodiaid* (Caerfyrddin, Cydweithgor Dwyieithrwydd yn Nyfed).
Davies, J. 1993. *The Welsh Language* (Cardiff, University of Wales Press).
Davies, K. 1989. 'Planning for the Welsh language?', *Rural Wales*, pp.18–19.
Dinefwr BC 1994. *Dinefwr Local Plan* (Llandeilo, Dinefwr BC).
Dyfed CC 1986. *Dyfed County Structure Plan Review. Proposals for Alteration. Consultation Report* (Carmarthen, Dyfed CC).
Dyfed CC 1986. *Structure Plan Review. The Welsh Language as a Structure Plan Issue* (Carmarthen, Dyfed CC).
Dyfed CC 1990. *Dyfed Structure Plan (including Alterations No.1)* (Carmarthen, Dyfed CC).
Economic Associates Ltd. 1966. *A New Town in Mid Wales* (Cardiff, HMSO).
Fforwm Ddwyeithrwydd Gwynedd 1995. *Tuag at Strategaeth Iaith i Ogledd-Orllewin Cymru* (Caernarfon, Fforwm Ddwyieithrwydd Gwynedd).
Fforwm Iaith Genedlaethol 1991. *Strategaeth Iaith, 1991–2001* (Aberystwyth, Fforwm yr Iaith Gymraeg).
Fionan 1994. *Living Gaelic – Gaelic at Work* (Inverness, Comunn na Gaidhlig).
Glyndŵr DC 1990. *Glyndwr District Local Plan. Written Statement and Proposals and Map* (Rhuthun, Glyndŵr DC).
Grist, Ian 1987. 'Parliamentary Questions for Answer, 24 November 1987, Nos.495, 496, 497 and 498', 87/88 (London, Hansard).
Gruffydd, P. 1995. 'Remaking Wales: nation-building and the geographical imagination, 1925–50', *Political Geography*, Vol.14, No.3, pp.219–39.
Gwynedd CC 1977a. *Anglesey Structure Plan. Written Statement* (Caernarfon, Gwynedd CC).
Gwynedd CC 1977b. *Caernarvonshire Structure Plan. Written Statement* (Caernarfon, Gwynedd CC).
Gwynedd CC 1977c. *Meirionnydd and Dyffryn Conwy Structure Plan. Written Statement* (Caernarfon, Gwynedd CC).
Gwynedd CC 1979. *Ardudwy L.P. Issue Report No. 19. Local Plans and the Welsh Language* (Caernarfon, Gwynedd CC).
Gwynedd CC 1981. *Ardudwy Local Plan. Written Statement* (Caernarfon, Gwynedd CC).

Gwynedd CC 1982. *Llanelltyd Local Plan. Written Statement* (Caernarfon, Gwynedd CC).
Gwynedd CC 1993. *Gwynedd Structure Plan. Written Statement* (Caernarfon, Gwynedd CC).
Harris, N. and M. Tewdwr-Jones 1995. 'The implications of local government reorganisation in Wales: purpose, process and practice', *Environment and Planning C Government and Policy,* Vol.13, pp.47–66.
Hatfield Polytechnic 1982. *Housing Survey in Dwyfor District* (Hatfield, School of Natural Sciences).
Hetherington, P. 1981. 'Uncovering the roots of co-operation', *North,* Vol.7, March/April, pp.4–7.
Highland RC 1976. *Highland Regional Report* (Inverness, Highland RC).
Highland RC 1982. *Skye and Lochalsh LP. Written Statement* (Inverness, Highland RC).
Highland RC 1990. *Highland Region SP. Written Statement* (Inverness, Highland RC).
Houston, G. 1987. *An Interim Assessment of the IDP for Agriculture and Fish-farming in the Western Isles* (Inverness, HIDB).
Iomairt na Gaidhlig 1994. *A Strategy for Gaelic Development in the Highlands and Islands of Scotland* (Inverness, Highland and Islands Enterprise).
James, Clive n.d. 'Planning for the future of the Irish and Welsh languages – some comparisons', mimeo.
James, Clive 1974. 'The language in Gwynedd. State of the heartland', *Planet,* No.23, Summer.
James, Clive 1975. 'The language in Clwyd', *Planet,* No.28, August.
James, Clive 1978. 'The language in Dyfed', *Planet,* No.43. June.
James, Clive 1986. 'Planning for the language', *Planet,* No.55, Feb/March, pp.63–7.
James, Clive 1991. 'What future for Scotland's Gaelic-speaking communities?', in C. H. Williams (ed.), *Linguistic Minorities, Society and Territory* (Clevedon, Multilingual Matters), pp.173–218.
James, Clive 1993. 'Cynlluniau datblygu a'r iaith Gymraeg', *Cymru Wledig,* Hydref, tt.14–15.
Jones, I. G. 1992. *Mid-Victorian Wales: The Observers and the Observed* (Cardiff, University of Wales Press).
Jones, J. E. 1993. Llythyr dyddiedig 1 Mawrth 1993 o Gadeirydd Bwrdd yr Iaith Gymraeg at yr Ysgrifenydd Gwladol dros Cymru [letter, 1 March 1993].
Jones, J. R. 1966. *Prydeindod* (Llandybie, Llyfrau'r Dryw).
Jones, J.W. 1989. 'Bwrdd yr Iaith Gymraeg a chynllunio', *Cymru Wledig,* Haf, t.14.
van Langevelde, A. P. 1993. 'Migration and language in Friesland', *Journal of Multilingual and Multicultural Development,* Vol.14, No.5, pp.393–411.
Lewis, G. J. 1975. 'Suburbanisation of rural Wales', in H. Carter and W. K. Davies (eds.), *Urban Essays: Studies in the Geography of Wales* (London, Longman).
Llanelli BC 1996. *Borough of Llanelli Local Plan* (Llanelli, Llanelli BC).
Lloyd, Alun 1987. 'Y meistr estron a'r Gymraeg', *Y Faner,* 6, III, 87.
Lochaber Gaelic Development Group 1994. *10 Year Development Plan 1994–2004* (Fort William, Lochaber Gaelic Development Group).
Manchester Polytechnic 1982. *A Study of the Housing Market in Parts of Dwyfor, Gwynedd* (Manchester, Department of Governmental and Geographical Studies, Manchester Polytechnic).

MacAoidh, I. A. 1986. *Gaelic in Skye. A Ten Year Development Plan* (Inverness, Comunn na Gaidhlig).
MacAoidh, I. A. 1986. *Gaelic in the Western Isles. A Ten Year Development Plan* (Inverness, Comunn na Gaidhlig).
MacKinnon, K. 1991. 'Language-retreat and regeneration in the present-day Scottish Gaidhealtachd', in C. H. Williams (ed.), *Linguistic Minorities, Society and Territory* (Clevedon, Multilingual Matters), pp.121–49.
MacKinnon, K. 1992. *An Aghaidh Nan Greag: Despite Adversity – Gaeldom's Twentieth Century Survival and Potential* (Inverness, Comunn na Gàidhlig).
MacKinnon, K. 1994. *Gaelic in 1994: Report to EU Euromosaic Project* (Black Isle, SGRUD).
Menter a Busnes 1994. *A Quiet Revolution: The Framework of the Academic Report* (Aberystwyth, Menter a Busnes).
Mid Glamorgan CC n.d. *Draft Replacement Structure Plan* (Cardiff, Mid Glamorgan CC).
Montgomeryshire DC 1993. *Montgomeryshire Local Plan. Written Statement (consultation draft)* (Welshpool, Montgomeryshire DC).
Mudiad Adfer 1984. *Cynllunio Dyfodol i'r Fro Gymraeg* (Bangor, Adfer).
Nelde, P. H., N. Labrie and C. H. Williams 1992. 'The principles of territoriality and personality in the solution of linguistic conflicts', *Journal of Multilingual and Multicultural Development*, Vol.13, No.5, pp.387–406.
North West Sutherland Gaelic Working Group 1992. *A Ten Year Gaelic Development Plan for North and West Sutherland* (Inverness, Comunn na Gaidhlig).
Parker, R. 1985. *Cynllunio Dyfodol i'r Iaith yng Ngheredigion* (Caerfyrddin, CS Dyfed).
Pedersen, R. N. 1989. 'Social redevelopment and community enterprise in the Highlands and Islands', Irish NW Community Development Institute Conference on Problems of Peripheral Areas of Europe, May.
Pedersen, R. N. 1993. *The Dynamics of Gaelic Development* (Inverness, Iomairt na Gaidhealtachd).
Pembrokeshire Coast National Park Authority 1995. *Pembrokeshire Coast National Park Local Plan* (Haverfordwest, Pembrokeshire Coast NPA).
Planning Aid 1984. 'Information and comment on planning aid in practice. Planning and culture in the world experience', *Network*, Vol.1, No.3, November.
Powys CC 1994. *Powys County Structure Plan (draft replacement). Deposit Version. Written Statement, Explanatory Memorandum and Consultation Statement* (Llandrindod Wells, Powys CC).
Prattis, J. I. 1987. *Celtic and Bilingualism Policy: The 'Feis'*, Centre for Research on Ethnic Minorities, Department of Sociology and Anthropology (Ottawa, Carleton University).
Preseli DC 1979. *Rural Areas Planning Study. Findings and Policies* (Haverfordwest, Preseli DC).
Rennie, F. W. 1994. *The Harris Integrated Development Programme* (Stornoway, Research and Rural Development Consultancy).
Roberts, Wyn 1986. 'Parliamentary Question for Answer, 27 October 1986, No.1495, 85/86' (London, Hansard).
Robertson, J. H. G. 1986. *The Western Isles IDP: Further Lessons in Human Ecology* (Portree, Habitat Scotland).
Schiavone, T. 1985. 'Language: the territorial imperative', *Radical Wales*, No.2, Spring.

Schiavone, T. 1988a. 'Statws cynllunio i'r iaith Gymraeg', *Cymru Wledig*, Hydref, t.286.
Schiavone, T. 1988b. 'Buddugoliaeth Llanrhaeadr. Rhan I', *Tafod y Ddraig*, Chwefror, tt.8–9.
Schiavone, T. 1988c. 'Buddugoliaeth Llanrhaeadr. Rhan 2', *Tafod y Ddraig*, Mawrth, tt.8–9.
Scottish Homes 1990a. *Local Market Analysis Studies of Rural Areas: Lewis and Harris*, Research Report 8 (Edinburgh, Scottish Homes).
Scottish Homes 1990b. *Northwest Sutherland*, Research Report 9 (Edinburgh, Scottish Homes).
Scottish Homes 1990c. *Ardnamurchan and South-West Lochaber*, Research Report 11 (Edinburgh, Scottish Homes).
Shankland Cox and Associates 1970. *Deeside/Dyfyrdwy. A Report* (London, Shankland Cox and Associates).
Snowdonia National Park Authority 1995. *Eryri: Local Plan – Consultative Draft. Written Statement* (Penrhyndeudraeth, Snowdonia NPA).
Sproull, A. 1993. *The Economics of Gaelic Language Development* (Glasgow, Glasgow Caledonian University).
Sproull, A. 1996. 'Regional economic development and minority language use: the case of Gaelic Scotland', *International Journal of the Sociology of Language*, forthcoming.
Starmore, G. 1984. 'The ups and downs of a crofters' co-op', *Voluntary Action*, July, pp.11–12.
Strathclyde Regional Council 1976. *Strathclyde Regional Report* (Glasgow, Strathclyde RC).
Strathclyde RC 1991. *Strathclyde Structure Plan Written Statement (The Consolidated Structure Plan)* (Glasgow, Strathclyde RC).
Thomas, C. 1992. *A Planning Strategy to Support the Welsh Language*, M.C.D. dissertation, University of Liverpool.
Thomas, John 1985. *Cynllunio a'r Iaith Gymraeg* (Caerfyrddin, CD Caerfyrddin).
Watson, A. and R. D. Watson 1982. *Tourism, Land Use and Rural Communities in Mountain Areas. The Swiss Approach and its Relevance for Scotland* (Aberdeen, Grampian Regional Council).
Welsh Council 1971a. *A Strategy for Rural Wales* (Cardiff, Welsh Office).
Welsh Council 1971b. *An Economic Strategy for North West Wales* (Cardiff, Welsh Office).
Welsh Council 1973. *Mid Wales – Growth Town Programme* (Cardiff, Welsh Office).
Welsh Office 1981. *The Welsh Language in Wales* (Cardiff, HMSO).
Welsh Office 1988. *The Welsh Language: Development Plans and Planning Control*, Circular 53/88 (Cardiff, Welsh Office).
Welsh Office 1991. *Planning and Housing*, Circular 31/91 (Cardiff, Welsh Office).
Welsh Office 1992. *County Monitors of the 1991 Census* (Cardiff, Welsh Office).
Welsh Office 1993. *Welsh Social Survey* (Cardiff, Welsh Office Statistical Section).
Welsh Office 1993. *Rural Housing*. Cm 2375 (London, HMSO).
Welsh Office 1995a. *Planning Policy Guidance (Wales): Consultation Draft* (Cardiff, Welsh Office).
Welsh Office 1995b. *Planning Guidance (Wales): Unitary Development Plans in Wales* (Cardiff, Welsh Office).
Wessels, C. and C. M. Beck 1994. 'Accessibility and language characteristics in

Catalonia', *Tijdschrift voor Economische en Sociale Geografie*, Vol.85, No.2, pp.130–40.

Williams, C. H. 1977. 'Cynllunio iaith yng Nghymru, Rhan 1', *Barn*, 179 (Rhagfyr), tt. 392–3.

Williams, C. H. 1980a. 'Cynllunio iaith yng Nghymru, Rhan 2', *Barn*, 179 (Ionawr), tt.2–5.

Williams, C. H. 1980b. 'Language contact and language change in Wales,1901–1971: a study in historical geolinguistics', *The Welsh History Review*, Vol.10, No.2, pp.207–38.

Williams, C. H. 1983. 'Wisdom, survival and the turning screw: Welsh culture in the eighties', *The Journal of General Education*, Vol.34, No.4, pp.319–29.

Williams, C. H. 1985. 'Public gain and private grief: the ambiguous nature of contemporary Welsh', *The Transactions of the Honourable Society of Cymmrodorion*, pp.27–48.

Williams, C. H. 1989. 'New domains of the Welsh language: education, planning and the law', *Contemporary Wales*, Vol.3, pp.41–76.

Williams, C. H. (ed.) 1991a. *Linguistic Minorities, Society and Territory* (Clevedon, Multilingual Matters).

Williams, C. H. 1991b. 'Language planning and social change: ecological speculations', in D. F. Marshall (ed.), *Language Planning. Focusschrift in Honour of Joshua A. Fishman* (Amsterdam, John Benjamins), pp.53–74.

Williams, C. H. (ed.) 1993. *The Political Geography of the New World Order* (London, Wiley).

Williams, C. H. 1994a. *Called Unto Liberty: On Language and Nationalism* (Clevedon, Multilingual Matters).

Williams, C. H. 1994b. 'Development, dependency and the democratic deficit', *Journal of Multilingual and Multicultural Development*, Vol.15, Nos.2 & 3, pp.101–27.

Williams, C. H. 1995. 'Questions concerning the development of bilingual Wales', in R. Morris Jones and P. A. Singh Ghuman (eds.), *Bilingualism, Education and Identity* (Cardiff, University of Wales Press), pp. 47–78.

Williams, C. H. 1996. 'Ethnic identity and language issues in development', in D. Dwyer and D. Drakakis-Smith (eds.), *Ethnicity and Development: Geographical Perspectives* (London, Wiley), pp.45–85.

Williams, G. 1979. 'Sociological bases of a language planning programme for Wales', *Cambria*, Vol.6, pp.70–6.

Index

Note: Page references in *italics* refer to Figures; those in **bold** refer to Tables

Abercrombie, Sir Patrick 138, 139, 140
Aberdeen Green Belt 161
Aberffraw 148
Aberystwyth 148, 192
Access to the Mountains Bill 204
Act of Union
   (1536) 272
   (1707) 114
Agricultural Revolution 226–7
agricultural subsidies 183, 190
agriculture 187
Agriculture Development and Advisory Service 252
Alloa Green Belt 161
Alternative Economic Strategy (AES) 27
Angus District Council 217
Area Initiatives 26
areas of employment deficit 126
Areas of Great Landscape Value (AGLV) 216, 217, 230, 234, 236
Areas of Outstanding Natural Beauty (AONB) 49, 203, 216
Areas of Regional Landscape Significance 216
Argyll and Bute District Council 290
Assembly of Welsh Counties 68, 69
Assisted Area 11
Atlantic Arc 18
Ayr Green Belt 161

bad neighbour development 45
Bevan, Aneurin 3
Bird Protection Areas 204
Borders Regional Council 236
branch-plant syndrome 82
Brecon Beacons National Park 254

Brecon Beacons National Plan 285
British Airports Authority v. *Secretary of State for Scotland* 45
British Mountaineering Council 233
British Vegetation Committee 244
Broads Grazing Marshes Conservation Scheme 247
Bryce 204
Buchanan, Colin 139, 150, 151
Buffer Zones 170
Business Connect network 88
Bute, Marquess of 149

Caernarfon 149
Cairngorms 206, 210–16, *212*
Cairngorms and Loch Lomond/Trossachs Partnership 211–16, *214*, *215*, 224, 229–30
Caithness 126
Campaign for the Protection of Rural Wales (CPRW) 170, 259, 280
Capital City Partnership of Scottish Homes 147
Cardiff 71, 101, 133–4, 147–56, 170
   Butetown 154
   city centre 151–4
   development 147–8
   docks 149
   nationalism and post-war regionalist consensus 149–51
   rise to dominance 148–9
Cardiff Bay 151–4
Cardiff Bay barrage 254
Cardiff Bay Development Corporation 152, 153, 156
Cardiff City Council 150

Cardiff Tourism Study 148
Carmarthen 70
Carmel Woods, quarrying in 254
Central Scotland: a Programme for Development and Growth 33
Ceredigion 70
Ceredigion District Council 62
Ceredigion Local Plan 288–9
Chamber of Commerce 141, 143
Circular 14/1960 161
Circular 16/912 *Planning Obligation* 48
Circular 24/1985 (*Development in the Countryside and Green Belts*) 161, 162, 167, 169
Circular 30/86 *Housing for Senior Management* 61
Circular 42/55 170
Circular 53/88 *The Welsh Language - Development Plans and Planning Control* 61, 69, 276, 280, 285
Circular 61/81 *Historic Buildings and Conservation Areas* 61
Citizen's Charter 72
Civic Trust Regeneration Unit 197
clientelist countryside 184
Clwyd Structure Plan 174–5, 281
Clyde Valley Regional Plan 33, 162
Clydeside 19, 139, 140
coal industry 19, 63, 104
  strike (1984–5) 104
Colonsay, island of 126
Commission for Racial Equality 288
Commission on National Parks and Protected Areas 233
Community Paths Campaign 252
commuting 24
Companies Act (1985) 124
Compaq 165
Comunn na Gaidhlig (CnaG) 282, 290–1, 292, 293
contested countryside 184
Countryside Commission 249
Cor Na Gaidhlig 290, 291
COSLA 233
Council for Environmental Education in Wales 250
Council for National Parks 233
Council for the Preservation of Rural England 244
Council for the Preservation of Rural Wales 244

Council for the Welsh Language 275
council house rents 139
council housing 140
Country Landowners' Association 171
Country Parks 203
Countryside (Scotland) Act
  (1967) 205, 246
  (1981) 217, 218, 231
Countryside Act (1968) 246
Countryside Commission 171, 186, 216, 236, 252, 259, 260
Countryside Commission for England 247
Countryside Commission for England and Wales 233, 246, 247
Countryside Commission for Scotland (CCS) 50, 205, 228, 230–2, 234, 236, 247, 248, 258
Countryside Commission in Wales 247–61
  Financial Management and Performance Review (FMPR) 255–6
countryside conservation 243–61
  see also valued landscape designation
Countryside Council for Wales 173, 176, 216, 243, 247, 280
Countryside Employment Programme 185
Countryside Stewardship 187, 253
Craig, James 136
Craig Meagaidh 206
Crofters Commission 224, 290
crofting 194, 227–8, 290
Cwmbran 59
Cwmdeithas yr Iaith Gymraeg 275, 286
Cymdeithas Cynllunio Cymru 274
Cynnal Cynefin 254

Darling, Sir William 137
Davies, Lord Prys 277
deforestation 225
Demonstration Farms 247
development agencies in Scotland 115–20
Development Board for Rural Wales (DBRW) 25, 58, 92, 188, 189, 190, 192, 252
Development Commission 224
Development Control - A Guide to Good Practice 72

devolution, Scottish 183
district and island councils 130
Dower report 205, 245, 246
Dunblane Green Belt 161
Dundee Project 119
Dundee, removal of Green Belt 159, 161
Dwyfor Local Plan 285
Dyfed Structure Plan 279, 281

East Kilbride 139
Easter Ross 126
Edinburgh 133–47, 154–5
　business park development 144–5
　as capital of Scotland 136–8
　City By-pass 146–7
　Civic Survey and Plan 138
　'Count Me In' 142–4
　development 136–40
　as European capital city 144–7
　Holyrood Park 165
　International Festival 139
　New Town 136, 137
　Old Town 137
　research park 145
　Green Belt Agreement 165
Edinburgh City Centre Local Plan 168
Edinburgh Green Belt 165–8, *166*
Edinburgh Green Belt Trust 168
Edinburgh International Conference Centre 144
Edinburgh South-East Wedge Joint Study Area 167–8
Edinburgh Summit 16
Edinburgh University Research Centre 167
Edinburgh Vision 143
Edinburgh's Capital 141–2, 143, 146
Edwards, Nicholas 61, 150, 152
Effectiveness of Green Belts, The 159, 169
electronics/electrical industries 20, 22–3, 83
emigration 19
Employment Training (ET) 107
employment, decline in 21
enclosure 226–7
Enforcement of Planning Control in Scotland, The 49
English Nature 186, 236, 252, 259, 260
Enterprise Zones 26
Environmental Protection Act (1990) 243, 248, 249, 250, 258

environmental sustainability 211
Environmentally Sensitive Areas (ESAs) 213, 253
Erskine 165
ERVET 89
European Agricultural Guidance and Guarantee Fund 16
European Commission 17, 18, 95
　see also European Union
European Community 186
European Community Support Frameworks 16, 25, 26, 28
European Economic Community 15, 27
European Monetary Union 27
European Partnerships 26
European Regional Development Fund (ERDF) 16, 18
European Social Fund (ESF) 16, 18
European Union 2, 15–18, 51, 77, 109
　Committee of the Regions 14
　Directive 85/337 51
　Directive 90/313 51
　Environmental Policy 204
　Integrated Development Project 185
　STRIDE programme 86
　Structural Funds 14, 16, 21, 27, 190–1
exports 23–4

Farrell, Terry 144
Faulds Park, Inverclyde 165
Firths Initiative 129
fish farming 194
fish stock conservation 183
fishing industry 193–4
Flow Country 206, 210
food and drink sectors 20
foreign direct investment 23
　mode of, 1984–91 **84**
　regional performance index **83**
forest resources 183
Fort William 126
fragile remote areas 125–6
Further Education colleges 85, 88
Future for the Welsh Language, A 275
Future of Development Plans, The 41, 60, 68

Gaelic language 195
　community action and 289–94
　demography 266–8, *267*, **268**

local planning and 289
in regional and island authorities **282**
structure planning and 281–4
territorial considerations 271–4
Gaskin Report 121
GDP 21, 23, 26
Geddes, Patrick 33, 136
Glasgow 19, 134, 137, 139
   International Garden Festival (1988) 142
   'Miles Better' Campaign 142
Glasgow Eastern Area Renewal (GEAR) project 1, 139
Glasgow Green Belt 162–5, *163*, 177
Glyndŵr 70
grant-in-aid (GIA) 80, 189, 258
Greater London Council (GLC) 27
Green Barriers 170, 171, 174–5, 176
Green Belts, Scotland 159–70, *160*, **161**, 176–8
Green Belts for Wales – A Positive Role for Sport and Recreation 159
Green Spaces 173
Green Wedges 170, 171, 176
Greening the Conurbation 165
Grist, Ian 276
Gumley, Sir Louis 136
Gwent Structure Plan (1991) 173–4
Gwent urban growth management 173–4
Gwynedd Structure Plan 70, 279, 280

Hague, William 66
Harris super-quarry 183
Heriot-Watt University 167, 168
Heritage Areas 216, 236
Heritage Coasts 203, 216
Highland Council 295
Highland Regional Council 232–3, 282
Highland Structure Plan 283
Highlands and Islands Development Board (HIDB) 115–17, 185, 188, 192, 193, 194, 195, 196, 224, 233
Highlands and Islands Enterprise 25, 115, 123–7, 188, 190, 194, 200, 224, 290, 292, 293
Historic Scotland 292
Hobhouse, Sir Arthur 245, 246
Hobhouse Committee and Report 205, 245
Hodge, Margaret 143

House Builders Federation 171, 280
Housing (Scotland) Act (1988) 129
housing 150, 151
Housing Act (1974) 47
Housing Corporation in Scotland 129
Hunt, David 89, 92, 104, 170, 255
Huxley, Julian 245
Huxley Committee 245

immediate areas 126
immigration 19
Improvement Act (1753) 135, 136
Industrial Pollution Inspectorate 130
Industry Department for Scotland 119
information technology 25, 88, 182
Inner Urban Areas Act (1978) 58
Insch 197
Institute of Terrestrial Ecology 246
International Union for the Conservation of Nature and Natural Resources 233
Islay, Jura and Colonsay Local Plan 289
Islwyn 71

Jacobite Rebellion 135
Jigso 252
John Muir Trust 233
Joint Nature Conservation Committee 243, 260
Jones, Dr Gwyn 90

Kelly, Michael 142
Kerevan, Councillor George 143, 144
Kernow (Cornish language) 73
Kinnock, Neil 3
Knighton 197

Labour Party 3
Lake District National Park 206
Land Authority for Wales 58, 64, 69, 280
Land Register for Scotland 46
Land Use Summary Sheet 36, 38
land-use planning in Wales 54–74
   controlling development 72–4
   developing an agenda 60–7
   development plan coverage 70–4
   emergence of territorial and nationalistic planning 57–60
   legislative and administrative structure 54–7

strategic planning delivery 67–70
Lands Tribunal 48
Lands Tribunal for Scotland 48
Landscape Areas of Regional Importance 216
language 6, 264–95
　national institutionalization and bilingualism 272–4
　scale and locality 265–6
　Scotland and Wales: demo-linguistic comparisons 266–71
　territorial considerations 271–4
　see also Gaelic language; Welsh language
Laurencekirk 197
Law Society of Scotland 45
Lazarowicz, Mark 143
LEADER projects 293
Less Favoured Area status 223
Linwood 139
Llandrindod Wells 149
Llanelli Local Plan 286
Llangorse Lake 254
Llantrisant, proposed new town 59
Llŷn 197
local enterprise companies (LECs) 25, 124–5, 126–7, 129, 188, 189, 194, 200, 292
　job creation and retention **195**
Local Government Commission 56
Local Government etc. (Scotland) Act (1994) 35, 40, 127
Local Government (Miscellaneous Provisions) Act (1982) 47
Local Government (Scotland) Act (1973) 33, 34, 35, 38, 40, 41, 42, 123
Local Government (Wales) Act (1994) 56
Local Government in Wales: A Charter for the Future 56
local government, Wales 54–7
local plan scheme 42
Locate in Scotland 118
Loch Lomond Park Authority 216, 233
Lothian and Edinburgh Enterprise Limited (LEEL) 143, 144, 146, 147
Lothian Regional Council 167
Lothian Structure Plan 167

Maastricht Treaty 14, 16, 28, 29
Major, John 127
Martin, J. S. B. 39
McDaid v. Clydebank District Council 45
Meier, Richard 145
Merthyr 149
metal manufacturing industries 20
migration 24
Miller, Keith 145
Miller Group 144
Ministry of Defence land 218
Montgomeryshire 70
Morton v. HM Advocate [1938] 49
Mostyn Docks 257
Motherwell District 165
motor component industry 83
motor industry 88, 139
Mountaineering Council for Scotland 233
Mull, Coll and Tiree Local Plan 289

national identity 3–7
National Library of Wales 148
National Museum of Wales 149
National Nature Reserves 248, 249, 256
National Park Direction Areas (NPDAs) 207, 228
National Park Directions 49, 50
national parks 49, 203, 204, 237
National Parks and Access to the Countryside Act (1949) 204, 205, 243, 244, 246, 249, 250
National Parks Commission 244, 245, 246
National Parks in England and Wales 245
National Planning Guidelines (NPGs) 36, 38, 60, 121, 122
National Planning Policy Guidelines (NPPGs) 37, 38, 121, 161, 162, 178
National Scenic Areas (NSAs) 50, 207–9, *208*, **209**, 228, 230, 232, 234, 235, 236
National Trust for Scotland 292
nationalization 20
Natural Heritage (Scotland) Act (1991) 50, 129, 243, 248, 249, 250, 252
Natural Heritage Agency Scotland 247
Natural Heritage Areas (NHA) 50, 209–16, 229, 250, 254

Nature Conservancy Council (NCC) 236, 243, 244, 246, 251–2, 254
Nature Conservancy Council Act (1973) 246
Nature Conservancy Council for England 247, 252
Nature Conservancy Council for Scotland 247, 248
Nature Conservancy Council for Wales 247
Nature Reserves 203, 204
New Edinburgh Ltd 144
new towns 59, 135, 139
Newcastle-upon-Tyne Green Belt 177
Newcastle-upon-Tyne Unitary Development Plan 177
Newport 170
Newtown-Caersŵs, proposed new town 59
NFU (Scotland) 233
North Cornwall District Council 73
North East of Scotland Joint Planning Advisory Committee 121
North Sea oil 194
North West Development Programme 290
North West Fife Rural Initiative 198
Nuffield Inquiry 60
Nuffield Report (*Town and Country Planning*) (1986) 35

oil and gas industries 22, 122, 194
opencast mining 63
Operation Wizard 90
opposition planning 58
Outdoor Recreation Resources Review Commission (US) 230

Partnership Initiatives 209–16
paternalistic countryside 184
Patterson report 39
Peak District National Park 206
Peat Marwick McLintock 145
Pedersen, Roy 291
Pembrokeshire Coast National Park 287
Penrhys 98
Plaid Cymru 57, 58
Planning Agreements: Consultation Paper and Draft Guidance 47
Planning and Compensation Act (1991) 47, 48, 49, 55, 61, 65, 71, 72
Planning Guidance (Wales): Unitary Development Plans 175, 278
Planning Policy Guidance (PPGs) 58, 60, 61, 62, 63, 64, 65, 70, 122
Planning Policy Guidance (Wales) 66, 175, 176, 278
poverty 19
Powys Structure Plan 279, 280
Preseli-Pembrokeshire 70
preserved countryside 184
Prestwick Green Belt 161
privatization 20, 183
Programme for the Valleys (PFV) 98–111
  new investment and reduction of unemployment 105–7
  regional initiative and national policies 107–8
  second phase 109–11
Pwyllgor Datblygu Addysg Gymraeg 273

R v. Greenwich London Borough Council, ex parte Patel 45
R. v. Secretary of State for the Environment, ex parte Kent [1988] 46
Ramblers Association 233, 244
Ratepayers' Action Group of Edinburgh (RAGE) 140
rates 139, 140
Ravenscraig Steelworks 165
Redwood, John 7, 64, 65, 66, 67, 80, 89, 92, 104
regional councils (Scotland) 34, 50
regional development agencies 25, 84
regional development aid 19
Regional Development Grant (RDG) scheme 105, 106, 107
regional planning authorities, abolition of 43
Regional Planning Guidance Notes 62
regional planning in Scotland 113–30
Regional Selective Assistance (RSA) 105, 106, 107
regionalism 2
Register of Sasines 46
Replacement Structure Plan (South Glamorgan) 172

Review of the Town and Country Planning System in Scotland: The Way Ahead 170
Review of the Management of Planning 46
Rhondda 70
Rhondda Fach 98
Rhondda Valley 98
Ridley, Nicolas 41
recreation 218
Red Deer Commission 233
Redwood, John 255, 256, 257, 259, 278
regional parks 217–18, 228
Renfrew County Council 217
Ridley, Nicholas 247, 248, 260
Rifkind, Malcolm 41, 247
Rights of Way Society 204
river purification boards 130
Roberts, Sir Wyn 255–6, 276
Royal Commission on Local Government in England 34
Royal Commission on Local Government in Scotland 34
Royal Town Planning Institute (RTPI) 69, 70
Rural Arfon Local Plan 285
rural community councils 185
rural development 181–201
 context in Scotland and Wales 182–4
 definitions 184–8
 institutions of 188–91
 local policy and practice 195–8
 policies and practice: agencies 191–5
 small community revival projects **196**
Rural Development Area 185, 189
Rural Development Commission (RDC) 185–6, 188, 189, 191
Rural Framework 186
Rural Housing 62

Scott, Sir Walter 136
Scott Report 205
Scottish Affairs Committee 116, 126, 128
Scottish Assembly 3
Scottish Committee of the Council on Tribunals 45
Scottish Crofters Union 233
Scottish Development Agency (SDA) 115, 118–20, 143, 145, 146, 188, 233

Scottish Development Department (SDD) 33, 41, 230
SDD Circular 20/1980 50
SDD Circular 4/1975 39
Scottish Economy 1965–1970: a Plan for Expansion, The 33
Scottish Enterprise 25, 29, 115, 123–7, 169, 188, 291
Scottish Environmental Protection Agency 129–30
Scottish Financial Services Centre 144
Scottish Homes 129
Scottish Landowners' Federation 233
Scottish Law Commission 45
Scottish Metropolitan Properties 144
Scottish Natural Heritage (SNH) 50, 129, 168, 228, 236, 243, 248, 249, 251–3, 255, 258–60, 292
Scottish National Orchestra 142
Scottish National Party (SNP) 3
Scottish Office 7, 28, 32, 42, 120–1, 155, 186, 255
 Co-ordinating Group 39
 Environment Department 33, 37
Scottish Office Development Department (SODevD) 33, 37
 SODevD Circular 12/1996 47
Scottish Opera 142
Scottish planning system
 administrative structure 32–5
 development control 43–50
  development in the countryside 49–50
  enforcement 48–9
  planning agreements 46–8
  publicity for planning applications 45–6
  role of the courts 44–5
 development plans 40–3
 national policy 35–8
 regional reports 38–40
Scottish Rights of Way Society 204
Scottish Society of Directors of Planning 233
Scottish Special Housing Association 129
Scottish Tourist Board 145, 233, 291
SCOTVEC 291
Select Committee on Land Resource Use in Scotland 34, 36, 121
Select Committee on Scottish Affairs 45

self-determination 3
self-employment 28
Shaw, Professor Jack 143
shipyards 139
SICRAS 224
Single European Act 14, 17
Single European Market (1992) 14, 16, 27, 144
Sites of Special Scientific Interest (SSSIs) 203, 204, 210, 229, 246–9, 252, 254, 256, 257
Skye Development Programme 290
small and medium enterprises (SMEs) 27, 28, 85, 86, 88
Social Chapter 28, 29
Society for the Promotion of Nature Reserves 244
Sony 84
South Glamorgan County Council 153 Structure Plan 172
South Glamorgan urban growth management 172–3
South Pembrokeshire 70
south Wales
 post-war development strategy 101–3
Special Areas of Conservation 204
Special Landscape Areas 170
Special Parks 205, 206, 232
Special Protection Area 257
sport and recreation 171
Sports Council for Wales 159, 171
SPRI 89
Stirling Green Belt 161
Stoppard, Tom 147
Strategic Planning Guidance in Wales - Process and Procedures 68
strategic planning guidance (SPG) 68, 69
Strategy For Gaelic: Development in the Highlands and Islands of Scotland, A 292
Strategy for the 1990s 192
Strathclyde 128
Strathclyde Integrated Development Operation 28
Strathclyde Regional Council 42
Strathclyde Structure Plan 62–4, 284
sunrise industries 104
Supplier Association 86
Sustainable Development and the Natural Heritage: The SNH Approach 254
sustainability 183

Swansea 70, 149, 170

Tayside 128
Tayside Regional Council 217
Technical Advice Notes for Wales (TANS(W)) 67
technology club 86
technology transfer 25
telecommunications 25, 182, 199
territorial nationalism 65
Thatcher, Mrs 90, 127, 140, 144
This Common Inheritance 170
Thomas, Dafydd Elis 274, 276
Threshold 21 249, 250, 254, 261
Tibbalds Colbourne Partnership 148
'Tiger Economies' 15
Tir Cymen 253
Topic Report on Rural Wales 187
tourism 23, 145–6, 193, 194, 197, 199, 217
Town and Country Planning Act
 (1947) 216, 272
 (1971) 55, 277
 (1990) 55
Town and Country Planning (General Development) (Scotland)
 Order (1948) 229
 Order (1975) 45
 Order (1981) 45
 Order (1992) 45, 46
Town and Country Planning (Scotland) Act
 (1969) 40
 (1972) 40, 43, 46, 50
Training Agency in Scotland 188
Training and Enterprise Councils (TECs) 25, 84, 88, 107, 185, 188, 189
Training for Work 107–8
Traverse Theatre 144
Trawsfynydd nuclear power station 192
Troon Green Belt 161
Tulk v. *Moxhay* 47

unemployment 19, 20, 21–2, 89, 90
Union of the Scottish and English Parliaments (1707) 135
unitary development plan (UDP) 71
Unitary Development Plans in Wales 66
University College of Wales, Aberystwyth 148

urban development grants 151
urban growth management
  in Scotland 159–70
  in Wales 170–6

Vale of Glamorgan 172
Vale of Glamorgan Unitary Authority 172
Valleys Programme (1988) 58
valued landscape designation 203–37
  assessment of Scottish approach 234–7
  strengths 235–7
  differences between England and Scotland 204–6
  factors influencing Scottish 218–34
    climatic influences 223–8
    historical and cultural 225–8
    influence of geology on scenery 219–23
    role of local authorities 231–4
    role of Scottish Office and its agencies 228–31
  National Parks and mountain areas of Scotland 206
  Ramsay Reports 205
  of regional and local significance 216–18
  regional parks 217–18
  Scottish landscape protection 206–16
  similarities between Scotland and England 204
  special parks 205–6
village envelopes 188
vocational education and training (VET) 107

Wales Wildlife and Countryside Link 259
Wales: The Way Ahead 57, 58, 59, 68, 101, 102, 150
Walker, Peter 63, 89, 92, 104, 150, 248
Welsh Access Forum 259
Welsh Affairs Committee 187–8
Welsh Development Agency (WDA) 25, 29, 58, 64, 69, 77–96, 102, 103, 171, 188, 190, 193, 252
  business services strategy 85–8
  failure of self-regulation 90–1
  fallibility 91–3
  future of 93–6

inward investment strategy 82–5
regulation of 89–91
relations with Welsh Office 93
scandals 90–1, 92
skills development 88
Source Wales programme 86
structure and resources 78–82, *79, 81*
technology support programme 86
Welsh Development Agency Act (1975) 78
Welsh District Planning Officers Society 171
Welsh language 59, 61–2, 69, 73, 187, 192, 294
  demography 268–71, **269**, *270*
  local planning 284–9
    Dyfed and Powys 285–9
    Gwynedd 284–5
  national institutionalization and bilingualism 272–4
  planning status and 274–8
  structure planning and 278–81
  territorial considerations 271–4
  Welsh speakers by county **278**
Welsh Language Act (1993) 273, 277, 295
Welsh Language Board 273, 275, 277, 280, 287, 295
Welsh Language Society 280, 281
Welsh Medical Technology Forum *87*, 88
Welsh Office 7, 54–74, 102, 103, 151, 155, 186, 255, 258
Welsh Office Agricultural Department (WOAD) 252, 261
Welsh Wildlife Trusts 259
Wester Ross National Park, proposed 206
Western Isles 125
Western Isles Integrated Development Programme 290
Western Isles Structure Plan 282
whisky industry 20, 22, 23
Whitland 148
Wigley, Dafydd 276, 277
Wildlife and Countryside Acts 204, 246
Williams, Colin 274
windfarms 63, 254
women, employment of 21
World War I 19
Wrexham Maelor 70, 71

'Y Fro Gymraeg' 4
Younger, George 38

Youth Training 108